UNVEILED!

The Ancient Secrets of Daniel & The Revelation of Jesus Christ

JOAN H. RICHARDSON

Copyright © 2017, 2020 by Joan H. Richardson

Unveiled!
The Ancient Secrets of Daniel & The Revelation of Jesus Christ
by Joan H. Richardson

Printed in the United States of America.

ISBN 9781545602058

All rights reserved solely by the author. The author guarantees all contents are original and do not infringe upon the legal rights of any other person or work. No part of this book may be reproduced in any form without the permission of the author. The views expressed in this book are not necessarily those of the publisher.

Unless otherwise indicated, Scripture quotations taken from the King James Version (KJV)–*public domain.*

Scripture quotations taken from the Holy Bible, New International Version (NIV). Copyright © 1973, 1978, 1984, 2011 by Biblica, Inc.™. Used by permission. All rights reserved.

Scripture quotations taken from the New American Standard Bible (NASB). Copyright © 1960, 1962, 1963, 1968, 1971, 1972, 1973, 1975, 1977, 1995 by The Lockman Foundation. Used by permission. All rights reserved.

Scripture quotations taken from the New King James Version (NKJV). Copyright © 1982 by Thomas Nelson, Inc. Used by permission. All rights reserved.

Scripture quotations taken from the Young's Literal Translation (YLT)–*public domain.*

Scripture quotations taken from the Holman Christian Standard Bible (HCSB). Copyright © 1999, 2000, 2002, 2003, 2009 by Holman Bible Publishers, Nashville Tennessee. All rights reserved.

Tree of Life (TLV) Translation of the Bible. Copyright © 2015 by The Messianic Jewish Family Bible Society.

Scripture quotations taken from the English Standard Version (ESV). Copyright © 2001 by Crossway, a publishing ministry of Good News Publishers. Used by permission. All rights reserved.

Underscores in the biblical text are added for emphasis.
Brackets are added outside the text for clarification.

www.xulonpress.com

UNVEILED!

Contents

In Remembrance vi
Dedication vii
About Jigsaw Puzzles ix

Part 1 The Ancient Secrets of Daniel 17

Introduction .... From Revelation 17.......................... 19

CHAPTER 1 Wild Beasts! .... Daniel 7 21

> The Sea ... The Lion ... The Bear ... The Terrible Beast
> The Little Dictator ... The Altar of Pergamon
> Quick like a Leopard! ... What's a Head?
> Approaching the Throne ... A Deceiver's Diversity
> Divisions, Divisions! ... The Last kingdom

CHAPTER 2 What about Dreams? .... Daniel 2 43

> Just One Stone ... The Image
> Where Have All the Vandals Gone?
> The Hunnic Effect ... Ten Horns or Ten Toes?
> Thy kingdom Come!

Part 2 The Revelation of Jesus Christ 53

Prologue to the Revelation .... The Mystery of Babylon 55

Chapter 1 .... Introducing the Son of Man 63

Chapter 2 .... Exhortations to 4 Churches 69

Chapter 3 .... Exhortations to 3 Churches 79

Chapter 4 .... 4 Creatures before the Throne 83

iii

UNVEILED!

Chapter 5 ……….. The Lamb Takes the Scroll …..…............... **85**

Chapter 6 ………....... The 1st Six Seals ..……................. **89**
   The 4 Horsemen … The Martyrs … The Judgments

Chapter 7 …..……... 144,000 Virgins of Israel …...…..…..… **93**
       The Victors in Heaven

Chapter 8 ……..….. The 7th Seal & 4 Trumpets ……….......… **103**

Chapter 9 ……..…... The 5th & 6th Trumpets …....……….… **105**
  1st Woe, Apollyon Rises … 2nd Woe, Army of 200 Million

Chapter 10 …...…….... John's Little Scroll ……....……… **111**

Chapter 11 ……… Last of 6th & the 7th Trumpets ……....… **113**
   2 Witnesses in 2nd Woe … Last Judgment at 3rd Woe

Chapter 12 …..……. A Woman & A Dragon ……....……… **127**
       The Signs in Heaven

Chapter 13 …...…… A Beast & A Two-horned Lamb ……..… **135**
    The Mark or Martyrdom … The Tribulation

Chapter 14 …..……. Virgins at the Throne ….....…..……... **155**
     The 3 Messengers … The 2 Harvests

Chapter 15 …..……. Song of Moses & the Lamb ….....……. **173**
    A Tabernacle in Heaven … Preparing for Wrath

Chapter 16 …..…...…. 7 Bowls of Wrath …….....………. **181**

Chapter 17 …..…… The Woman on a Scarlet Beast ….....…… **187**
   7 Heads Are 7 Mountains … 10 Horns with No kingdom Yet
     The Beast that Was … The 8th King

Chapter 18 …..… The Judgment of Mystery Babylon …..…… **203**

Chapter 19 ….…...... A Celebration & The Return ….…....… **215**
      The Battle of Armageddon
    Destruction of the Beast & False Prophet

UNVEILED!

Chapter 20 .... Chaining Satan ... 1st Resurrection **229**
    kingdom Age ... Satan Is Released ... Gog & Magog
        Satan Is Destroyed ... The Great White Throne

Chapter 21 .... New Heavens & A New Earth **243**
    New Jerusalem ...The Marriage of the Lamb

Chapter 22 .... An Everlasting Kingdom **255**
    The River of Life ... Alpha & Omega ... The Light of the City

The Child 263
Isaiah 18 267
Order of Events 271
Epilogue 281
Appendix to Chapter 13 293
Scriptural Order 299

The Writer 303
Contact Information 309
Endnotes 311
References 328
Bibliography... 329
Recommended Videos 331

In Remembrance

Jesus told His disciples He was *going away* and said, *If ye loved me, ye would rejoice, because I said, I go unto the Father: for my Father is greater than I. (from Jn. 14:28)*

I wondered what love was, but now I know love never fails. God planned our marriage before time began. I loved Mike deeply, but I always thought he loved me more. After so many years, now I realize my love shined most brightly the day I rejoiced for him.

If I could live life over, I'd choose Mike again because we were made for each other.

Dedication

^{2} And I saw a mighty angel proclaiming with a loud voice, "Who is worthy to open the scroll and break its seals?" ^{3} And no one in heaven or on earth or under the earth was able to open the scroll or to look into it, ^{4} and I began to weep loudly because no one was found worthy to open the scroll or to look into it. ^{5} And one of the elders said to me, "Weep no more; behold, the Lion of the tribe of Judah, the Root of David, has conquered, so that he can open the scroll and its seven seals."
(Rev. 5:2-5 ESV)

Unveiled! is dedicated to its Revelator,
... for the testimony of Jesus is the spirit of prophecy.

(Revelation 19:10c; cf. 1:2, 9; 12:17; 19:10a)

... "It is written. 'Man shall not live by bread alone, but by every word that proceeds from the mouth of God."
(From Mat. 4:4 NKJV; cf. Deut. 8:3)

UNVEILED!

About Jigsaw Puzzles

Several months ago I visited a local discount bookstore and purchased a jigsaw puzzle of a map of the world. I encouraged myself, "Five hundred pieces won't take a genius."

As I began organizing the shapes and colors and separating their piles, I was certain I was short-changed. There didn't seem to be enough pieces to frame the thing. It perturbed me that I'd expected a complete puzzle from a discount store. I scolded myself, "Well, you get what you pay for!" Nevertheless, I decided to put the pieces together as well as I could without all the parts and with many pieces that didn't look like they belonged at all.

Persevering to finish my project, I thought of the puzzle our family spent weeks putting together. It was at least a thousand pieces, all the same shape, and nearly the same color—blue and gray dinosaurs in a swamp. Five of us worked in our spare time till completing it. We learned something about life: **Don't throw out the puzzle before putting all of its pieces together.**

Finally, after testing my patience, the 500 pieces found their places, and the map of the world made sense. It was a satisfying and a sobering moment. As I looked back on it, I saw how wrong I was about the shapes not fitting. At times I didn't understand where the parts went, but when I tried them, if they fit they stayed. At last they all worked perfectly, and its border neatly framed the entire puzzle. Not one single piece was missing and no extras remained. Its proper parts were there all along.

Writing this book was a lot like putting that puzzle together. Some pieces were hard to understand. How could they be what they were? I called out, "How can that be?" And He replied with a vision. I said, "This is hard to believe!" But when I believed, it made perfect sense. The more I believed, the more He revealed until all of its pieces fit, and I saw the whole world in a new way.

I was able to write these books because I didn't write them alone. I asked the questions; the Spirit of God had the answers. It took a team. I believed the Lord as I wrote, and He responded faithfully. After all, this work was His idea, not mine.

Unveiled! was written by faith and for faith because without faith, it's impossible to please God. Study the words and believe God only. Be objective. Think outside the box. In Revelation the elders sing the Lamb alone is worthy to take and unseal its scroll. As we exercise our faith to believe, we hear His voice.

UNVEILED!

I never wanted to be a writer but began after the morning in late 2003 when He quietly shouted me awake, "Write a book!" I published *A Thorn in My Flesh* in late 2009. Next He silently spoke in January 2010: "The church is divided by deceptions," leading me to discover the truth of His words. I did the research and found the apostasy was systematized in the 4th century but had begun long before. He urged me to write the truth, and I wrote as His Holy Spirit revealed it to me.

I found strongholds that had prevented my faith in the Word and tore down the deceptions to believe with the Spirit as my Teacher in writing *The Union*. My quest for the truth led me into mysteries, which I extracted from the first book. They developed as *Mysteries of the Ancient Word*. Then prophecies popped out of the mysteries. Each book gave birth to another. I had no plan.

I wasn't a writer and didn't know what to expect. The Spirit led me along the way. Soon the internet opened up to me. I was inundated with the information I needed. As I wrote I learned.

I saw the Revelation in Daniel 7 and studied both together to better understand Daniel. To avoid confusion I prayed for a key in Revelation to clarify Daniel 7. My prayer was answered when I extracted Revelation from *Mysteries* to simplify its text.

As I read its words, suddenly the opposite happened when I realized the order of Revelation. How did we miss it? Then I knew He was doing the impossible—unveiling the *Apocalypse!* I separated the prophecies from the book of mysteries as another book was born through the Revelation and Daniel 7. He's been my Teacher since January 2010; that's how I write.

I searched the Bible to confirm my findings and leaned on the Spirit in prayer. He took me through the details, correcting names and dates, which are important. Metaphors opened before their evidence confirmed them. History took my breath away!

I learn in quietness, yielded but confident, dependent on my Rabbi who'd anointed me and given me His mantle. He did not open His Revelation to a scholar, because God doesn't share His glory with anyone. It didn't take a genius to believe Him. By my insistence on knowing the truth, His Holy Spirit unveiled it.

I dared to believe their words, and He opened scriptures I'd never understood. The scattered pieces of the puzzle neatly fit in their places as I searched history till I saw it all together. My far greater difficulty lay in turning its picture into words.

About Jigsaw Puzzles

His apostles were men in humble circumstances, not scholars with computers and high tech at their fingertips, but He opened their minds to see the world like never before. We understand His parables and prophecies as He opens our eyes to them.

Scholars rarely understand what the prophets wrote. As a result, we've believed the prophets didn't mention the greatest war in history, which returned His people to their land. But He doesn't do a thing without revealing it to the prophets. (Amos 3:7) He authorizes our faith to believe in Him by His grace and opens our minds if we turn to Him as our Schoolmaster, our Rabbi.

Paul urges us to demolish strongholds, words we've received that are honored above the Word of God. He had been taught the deceptions but went to Arabia to discover the truth, not from any man but with the Holy Spirit as his Teacher. (Gal. 1:14-17)

The arguments are in our flesh and in the traditions and teachings we've received. If we believe men, they often affirm us regardless of truth, but if we believe God, He rewards us:

> [4] For the weapons of our warfare are not fleshly but powerful through God for the tearing down of strongholds. We are tearing down false arguments [5] and every high-minded thing that exalts itself against the knowledge of God. We are taking every thought captive to the obedience of Messiah— (2 Cor. 10:4-5 TLV)

> [27] But the anointing which ye have received of him abideth in you, and ye need not that any man teach you: but as the same anointing teacheth you of all things, and is truth, and is no lie, and even as it hath taught you, ye shall abide in him. (1 Jn. 2:27)

Unveiled! has two goals: to clarify the prophecies and to prepare us for the future. By believing His words, we accept God as He is without distorting His nature. Our beliefs should change when what we think we know contradicts the Bible.

> [9] He said, "Go *your* way, Daniel, for the words *are* shut up and sealed until the time of the end. (Dan. 12:9 ESV)

As I wrote, words triggered words. When Daniel's details fit Revelation, I saw a fuller picture. I was "getting" it. Poring over documentaries I saw the prophecies clarify their evidence. In my weakness, He provided His strength.

UNVEILED!

The two parts of *Unveiled!* interact, covering several epochs of history, especially as it relates to Israel. Each part shines its light on the other part's prophecies. After reading *Unveiled!* start to finish, turn back and forth for greater understanding. Draw pictures, take notes, read slowly.

The Scriptural Order is on pp. 300-01. Don't worry about the complexity; it's a jigsaw puzzle. The material is not easy, so I repeat things periodically as reminders to show where its words fit history. If our ideas are challenged, we compare the words of God to history and ignore opinions, even our own.

You'll find the Bible is proven true by the testimony of its prophecies. If we read the Bible without believing its words, we may question whether we want to know the truth. Maybe we've been *ever learning, and never able to come to the knowledge of the truth. (2 Tim. 3:7)* It takes tenacity, but if the Spirit lives in us, we ought to search for the truth till we find it. (Acts 17:10-12)

Like the Bereans, I believe God literally unless He speaks symbolically, as He often does in prophecy. Then I "press in" to "see" the visions, praying and meditating till my spirit and mind understand.

The Holy Spirit prodded me to search out literal meanings of words I thought I knew but hadn't understood. The Bible confirmed history as He unveiled His words to me. Many years ago He'd led me out of far more confusing things because I refused to quit. Maybe it's why He taught me His Logic, using me for His glory, not despite my past, but because of it.

If we neglect meditating on its words, we miss the meanings. Biblical words can be enigmatic, especially prophecies, but the title *Apocalypse* is from the Greek, *apŏkalupsis*, "to uncover or reveal." *Unveiled!* sheds light on the connections of history to words meant to be revealed for us to *see* at the end of the age.

Believing the Word is like eating the whole lamb at the first Passover in Egypt—guts, brains, and all! (Ex. 12:8-9) Now it's time for us to chew the parts that are hard to swallow; to take them in, and to digest them.

[26] "But the Helper, the Holy Spirit, whom the Father will send in My name, He will teach you all things, and bring to your remembrance all things that I said to you.
(Jn. 14:26 NKJV) – Hundreds of verses came to mind.

About Jigsaw Puzzles

The main body of *Unveiled!* reveals the Revelation, step-by-step, validating everything by history, scriptures, and revelations that put the pieces together. The Order of Events begins on page 271 and clarifies its progression.

The Revelation of Jesus Christ was concealed until the end of this age because the future had to pass for history to reveal its mysterious words. Understanding prophecies requires revelations by His Holy Spirit. No scholar could have figured this out; in fact it wasn't meant to be figured out; it had to be unveiled—but not to a scholar. As most people would agree, this writer is the least likely choice for the honor, but only God is glorified in this.

Please put a bookmark at page 19; another at chapter 13, page 135; and a third at chapter 17, page 187. When you come to a reference to those chapters, you can flip to your bookmark to find it. That saves you time and clarifies the scriptures as you compare them with others. It also condenses a book that would otherwise be a cumbersome tome. (These chapters interweave.)

In Part 1, Revelation 17 introduces Daniel 7. Some of 17 occurred long before John was in exile on the Isle of Patmos. Other parts lead to Daniel's prophecy. As time goes on, Daniel 7:23-38 returns us to Revelation (on pp. 38-42).

The Revelation is for believers, Jews or gentiles. The history of its faith dates to the ancient Jewish faith. We're about to enter that history to learn about the future and the thousand-year reign of the Messiah, our Lord and Savior Jesus Christ. It continues to the last judgment and from then to eternity. There's plenty to know, and it's all condensed into the Revelation, the true tale of two cities and their kingdoms, Babylon and Jerusalem.

Our part is to properly divide its words by the Spirit of its Author and to search out its times and seasons by history, current events, and scriptures. Finally, it's up to us to receive it, taking up its cross to follow Jesus, apart from which we're not worthy to be His disciples. (Mat. 10:37-39) Revelation tests our faith.

Its prophetic details are astonishing, affirming the testimony of Jesus Christ. That's why *Unveiled!* is an important book for all of us.

> "And behold, I am coming soon. Blessed is the one who keeps the words of the prophecy of this book."
> (Rev. 22:7 ESV) – Yeshua, of His Revelation from the Father

UNVEILED!

Prayer and meditation are essential because we can't understand spiritual words by figuring them out. *The just shall live by his faith. (Hab. 2:4 b)* The brain, like our flesh, is given life by our spirits. (Jas. 2:26) The mind of Christ is in the life of His Spirit:

> [10] ... For the Spirit searches everything, even the depths of God. [11] For who knows a person's thoughts except the spirit of that person, which is in him? So also no one comprehends the thoughts of God except the Spirit of God. [12] Now we have received not the spirit of the world, but the Spirit who is from God, that we might understand the things freely given us by God. [13] And we impart this in words not taught by human wisdom but taught by the Spirit, interpreting spiritual truths to those who are spiritual. (1 Cor. 2:10b-13 ESV) – the spiritual mind

As God said, our prayers go up as incense, pure offerings to Him. Like incense, apart from the fire, their words are impotent:

> [11] For from the rising of the sun even unto the going down of the same my name shall be great among the Gentiles; and in every place incense shall be offered unto my name, and a pure offering: for my name shall be great among the heathen, saith the LORD of hosts.
> (Mal. 1:11) [This prophecy is fulfilled.]

> [8] ... having every one of them harps, and golden vials full of odours, which are the prayers of saints. (Rev. 5:8b)

Significant Details

A Bible at your side helps for the parenthesized references. Concordances aid as the Spirit brings words to mind. For phrases like *the Great Sea*, Biblegateway.com is a tool to find frequency or usage. Literal translations validate exact words though manuscripts vary. Aramaic, Hebrew, and Greek lexicons are essential.

'Church' refers to institutional churches or to multitudes who profess to believe, so the word is not capitalized. The Greek *ekklesia,* like *sunagōgē,* is a congregation, a gathering, an assembly. Wherever we are in the *ekklesia,* or *sunagōgē,* holiness is the requirement of everyone who confesses Jesus'/Yeshua's name.

His full name in Hebrew is *Yehoshua,* "YHVH is Salvation," or "YHVH saves," shortened as *Yeshua, meaning* "salvation."

About Jigsaw Puzzles

It's transliterated "Joshua."[a] *Iesous* is its Greek equivalent. Since the language of the Roman Empire was Greek,[b] His disciples spoke Greek as well as Aramaic and perhaps Hebrew.[c]

The first King James Version of 1611 called Him *Iesus;* much later, it was "Jesus."[d] Both *Yeshua* and "Jesus" are used in this text. A growing number of Jews are finding Him as their Savior, using His Hebrew name, Yeshua. Had it been used it in 1611, there would be no different understanding today, but in the past, Hebrew was not commonly spoken—not even by the Jews. Their language was revived just before the nation was, but who knew? (Zeph. 3:9)

Occasional underlining highlights words relative to the text. Verses are indented in sans serif, distinguishing them from my own words. Occasional verses are in *italics.* The Scriptures have few *italicized* words, added for clarity by translators. Concerning upper or lower case: "Scriptures" refers to the Holy Bible; lower case "scripture(s)" points to a particular passage or verse(s).

The words *man* or *men* most often refer to mankind or to person(s) as a generic word. This is common in the Bible and is acceptable since God formed woman out of man, calling both *Adam*, "man(kind)" (in Gen. 2:22). We are thus all mankind and should not be offended. In Jesus Christ there's *neither male nor female (from Gal. 3:28),* since God is Spirit and cares more about the contents of our hearts than our natural differences.

The unspoken Hebrew name of God [YHVH], in Biblical texts is "Lord." In the TLV, it is *ADONAI.* Both have two sizes of font to indicate His holy name. The substitute for *Adonai* is "Lord" in most Biblical texts. *Elohim* [the plural One], "God." *Adonai YHVH* is "Lord God." Some have "G-d", respecting Jewish tradition. Here it is "God" since He made His holy name *famous among the gentiles*—of all people!

Titles, e.g., "king, president, tsar, or emperor" are lower case unless used with names, e.g., King Cyrus. Exceptions to this rule are the titles of the Lord and His Kingdom.

BC meant "Before Christ" for fifteen hundred years till its recent change to "Before the Common Era," BCE. *Anno Domini,* "In the year of our Lord," was once abbreviated AD but recently was made CE. The former abbreviations are in this text to honor the Creator of this magnificent universe.

UNVEILED!

UNVEILED!

Part 1

The Ancient Secrets of Daniel

But thou, O Daniel, shut up the words, and seal the book, *even* to the time of the end: many shall run to and fro, and knowledge shall be increased. (Dan. 12:4)

UNVEILED!

Introduction from Revelation 17

Revelation 17 introduces Daniel 7 to affirm its time. Put on your thinking cap; it's a jigsaw puzzle. Here's the picture: Seven supernatural kings rule seven kingdoms. Each ostensibly has its own king, but the scarlet beast is the most cunning king of all.

Imagine living in the days of Rome. Let's see his vision as John did when the angel told him the scarlet beast *was* [on earth] and [now] *is not, and yet is* [because it still exists]. Furthermore, it's *about to come up out of the abyss.* Not only that, but the scarlet beast John sees, <u>the beast that was, and is not, even he is the eighth, and is of the seven,</u> *and goeth into perdition. (17:11)*

Now we know that after all seven fall, one of the seven, the scarlet beast, returns to rule an eighth kingdom. *Even he is the eighth, and is of the seven.*

> ⁸ 'The beast that thou didst see: it was, and it is not; and it is about to come up out of the abyss, and to go away to destruction, and wonder shall those dwelling upon the earth, whose names have not been written upon the scroll of the life from the foundation of the world, beholding the beast that was, and is not, although it is. ⁹ 'Here [is] the mind that is having wisdom; the seven heads are seven mountains, upon which the woman doth sit, ¹⁰ and there are seven kings, the five did fall, and the one is, the other did not yet come, and when he may come, it behoveth him to remain a little time; ¹¹ and the beast that was, and is not, he also is eighth, and out of the seven he is, and to destruction he doth go away. ¹² 'And the ten horns that thou sawest, <u>are ten kings</u>, who a kingdom did not yet receive, but authority as kings the same hour do receive with the beast, ¹³ these have one mind, and their own power and authority to the beast they shall give over; (Rev. 17:8-13 YLT)

After Jesus ascended Michael and his angels fought Satan and his, but the dragon lost and was banished to earth. (Rev. 12:9) Cast out in John's time, the scarlet beast was *about to come up out of the abyss. (17:8)* At that time five kings had fallen: *and there are seven kings: five are fallen <u>and one is</u>. (17:10a)* This means **the king of Rome *is* sixth**, <u>but the scarlet beast is absent</u>. After losing the war in heaven, he'd soon rise from the abyss to force the fall of Rome and snatch it as an illegitimate king of the sixth capital city a few centuries after her destruction in 476.ᵉ

Introduction

After the fall of the Roman Empire, in 752 another Roman Empire was in the making but by fraud. The dragon had risen to rule hundreds of fiefs and duchies with popes. "The Donation of Constantine" supposedly bequeathed the former empire to the church.[f] But the dragon used a hoax when he led the fearful and deceived church to gain an empire for himself, which he kept for over a thousand years till it finally fell to the seventh king.

In 800 her pope crowned the king of France Charlemagne as its first "Holy" Roman emperor.[g] In 962 the king of Germania Otto the Great was its co-ruler. Afterward German kings commonly ruled with its popes, and it became the "Holy" Roman Empire of the German Nation, a title that faded as time passed.[h]

The seventh king would conquer Rome: *and the other is not yet come; and when he cometh, he must continue a short space. (Rev. 17:10b, p. 19)* In 1806 Napoleon vanquished the (H)REGN but others twice defeated and twice exiled him by 1816.[i]

In Revelation five preconditions describe the next beast, the scarlet one John saw: he's *the eighth ... of the seven* [kings]; he returns with ten *kings which have received no kingdom as yet* [in John's time]; but they *receive power as kings one hour with the beast. These have one mind, and shall give their power and strength unto the beast ...* and he *goeth into perdition (in 17:11-13).* The ten are with the dragon for a short time, just *one hour.*

Rome's hundreds were eventually reduced to two European empires. After WW1 twelve nations came out of them, but two were politically neutral.[j] In twelve years Hitler rose after the ten *received* their crowns by a treaty *the same hour with the beast.* The eighth king rose as Adolf Hitler to take the ten and conquer more while leaving the neutral ones undisturbed.[k] With Berlin in ruins, he lost the war, and *the beast was slain (in Dan. 7:11).*

Of seven kings (in 17:10), the dragon was the king who ruled Rome by popes and kings like pawns on a chessboard. Bismarck built a German Federation for Prussia, making Berlin its capital in 1871. It was known as the Second Reich of the (H)REGN.[l]

In 1934 Hitler became the führer over the Third Reich after Bismarck essentially regained the empire.[m] The dragon ruled the German Empire out of the Roman Empire of the German Nation as the beast *of the seven, ...* who *also is eighth.* In the hour when the ten *received* their kingdoms, the beast entered the man. Now let's see him lose the greatest war of all in Daniel 7:

Wild Beasts!

CHAPTER 1

7 In the first year of Belshazzar king of Babylon, Daniel saw a dream and visions of his head as he lay in his bed. Then he wrote down the dream and told the sum of the matter. ²Daniel declared, "I saw in my vision by night, and behold, the four winds of heaven were stirring up the great sea. ³And four great beasts came up out of the sea, different from one another. ⁴The first was like a lion and had eagles' wings. Then as I looked its wings were plucked off, and it was lifted up from the ground and made to stand on two feet like a man, and the mind of a man was given to it. ⁵And behold, another beast, a second one, like a bear. It was raised up on one side. It had three ribs in its mouth between its teeth; and it was told, 'Arise, devour much flesh.' ⁶After this I looked, and behold, another, like a leopard, with four wings of a bird on its back. And the beast had four heads, and dominion was given to it. ⁷After this I saw in the night visions, and behold, a fourth beast, terrifying and dreadful and exceedingly strong. It had great iron teeth; it devoured and broke in pieces and stamped what was left with its feet. It was different from all the beasts that were before it, and it had ten horns. ⁸I considered the horns, and behold, there came up among them another horn, a little one, before which three of the first horns were plucked up by the roots. And behold, in this horn were eyes like the eyes of a man, and a mouth speaking great things.

⁹ "As I looked,

>thrones were placed,
>   and the Ancient of Days took his seat;
>his clothing was white as snow,
>   and the hair of his head like pure wool;
>his throne was fiery flames;
>   its wheels were burning fire.

¹⁰ A stream of fire issued
>   and came out from before him;
>a thousand thousands served him,
>   and ten thousand times ten thousand stood before him;
>the court sat in judgment,
>   and the books were opened.

The Ancient Secrets

[11] "I looked then because of the sound of the great words that the horn was speaking. And as I looked, the beast was killed, and its body destroyed and given over to be burned with fire. [12] As for the rest of the beasts, their dominion was taken away, but their lives were prolonged for a season and a time.

[13] "I saw in the night visions,
and behold, with the clouds of heaven
there came one like a son of man,
and he came to the Ancient of Days
and was presented before him.
[14] And to him was given dominion
and glory and a kingdom,
that all peoples, nations, and languages
should serve him;
his dominion is an everlasting dominion,
which shall not pass away,
and his kingdom one
that shall not be destroyed.

[15] "As for me, Daniel, my spirit within me was anxious, and the visions of my head alarmed me. [16] I approached one of those who stood there and asked him the truth concerning all this. So he told me and made known to me the interpretation of the things. [17] 'These four great beasts are four kings who shall arise out of the earth. [18] But the saints of the Most High shall receive the kingdom and possess the kingdom forever, forever and ever.'

[19] "Then I desired to know the truth about the fourth beast, which was different from all the rest, exceedingly terrifying, with its teeth of iron and claws of bronze, and which devoured and broke in pieces and stamped what was left with its feet, [20] and about the ten horns that were on its head, and the other horn that came up and before which three of them fell, the horn that had eyes and a mouth that spoke great things, and that seemed greater than its companions. [21] As I looked, this horn made war with the saints and prevailed over them, [22] until the Ancient of Days came, and judgment was given for the saints of the Most High, and the time came when the saints possessed the kingdom. (Dan. 7:1-22 ESV) Cont'd.

Wild Beasts!

²³ Thus he said, The fourth beast shall be the fourth kingdom upon earth, which shall be diverse from all kingdoms, and shall devour the whole earth, and shall tread it down, and break it in pieces.
²⁴ And the ten horns out of this kingdom are ten kings that shall arise: and another shall rise after them; and he shall be diverse from the first, and he shall subdue three kings.
²⁵ And he shall speak great words against the most High, and shall wear out the saints of the most High, and think to change times and laws: and they shall be given into his hand until a time and times and the dividing of time.
²⁶ But the judgment shall sit, and they shall take away his dominion, to consume and to destroy it unto the end.
²⁷ And the kingdom and dominion, and the greatness of the kingdom under the whole heaven, shall be given to the people of the saints of the most High, whose kingdom is an everlasting kingdom, and all dominions shall serve and obey him.
²⁸ Hitherto is the end of the matter. As for me Daniel, my cogitations much troubled me, and my countenance changed in me: but I kept the matter in my heart.
(Daniel 7:23-28)

The Sea

The Great Sea appears fourteen times in the Word, clearly the waters of the Mediterranean, the western border of Israel.[1] A vision carries Daniel far from Babylon to the Mediterranean Sea, agitated by four winds. In perilous days four beasts rise, not just from *a sea* or *many waters,* but out of the earth (in 7:17), the floor of the Great Sea. Out of hell they rise to their place in time.

As he lay in bed dreaming, Daniel envisioned its tumultuous waves, *and four great beasts came up from the sea, <u>diverse one from another</u>*—supernatural kings working by men. The most formidable among them had ten horns on his head, the same ten horns John saw over six centuries later, but look—a little horn rose up after them (in 7:8)!

The Lion

⁴ The first was like a lion with eagle's wings. As I watched, <u>its wings were pulled off</u> and it was lifted off the ground. It was made to stand upon two feet like a man, and the heart of a human was given to it. (Dan. 7:4 TLV)

The Ancient Secrets

The rampant lion standing on two feet was England's in the 17th century. Others had lions as beasts, but earlier her lion was standing on all fours. The first to adopt the lion on the Great Seal was Richard the Lion Heart in the 12th century.[2] King James I set its lion upright on two feet in 1603.[3] In 1611 he commissioned an official translation of the Holy Bible into the English language.

In the 18th century, her colonies in America were freed from their motherland just as the eagle's wings were pulled from the lion's back. The Revolutionary War was the price of freedom.

Sixty years later in 1837, Queen Victoria was on the throne. The Christian Queen chose Benjamin Disraeli as prime minister, the first Jew with an important role in the British government.[4] PM for two terms, he was her closest confidante till the Queen's reclusion after her husband, Albert, died.

When she gained international sovereignty in the Near East, Disraeli named her, "Empress of India."[5] In 1900 her empire was the largest in history, with one-fourth the land mass on earth and one-fifth of its population.[6] English became the world's second language, and the gospel circled the earth.

England's Secretary of State Balfour proposed the British-ruled Palestine for the Jews in 1917 in a note to Lord Rothschild. April 25, 1920: the "Balfour Declaration of Intent to Establish a Zionist State for the Jews" was made international law by the "Palestine Mandate" at the San Remo Conference in Italy.[7] Its borders were defined by the Allies until April 1921 when oil-rich Arabs pressed Great Britain for more land.[8]

Arabs populated 90% of it all, so Churchill partitioned 77% as Trans-Jordan, east of the river.[9] The League of Nations finally provided 23% of the original land grant for the Jews, but the league lacked the military power to enforce its decisions.

In 1938 Hitler entered German-speaking European lands. To avoid conflict with the Nazis, in a peace proposal, PM Neville Chamberlain annexed the land surrounding Czechoslovakia and its natural resources to Hitler in the infamous "Munich Pact."[10] But the dictator proved land for peace wasn't what he wanted at all when he attacked Poland on September 1, 1939. Britain and France declared war but too late.[11] If they'd foreseen what would happen, they would have challenged Germany from the start.

Out of Parliament, Winston Churchill, who loved the Jews, could only watch as Britain's "White Paper" suppressed Jewish

Wild Beasts!

immigration and limited their land holdings in what had become British Palestine.[12] He was incensed; however, by May 1940 politics changed. Appeasement had failed and the prime minister resigned. As a result, the king chose Winston Churchill as his replacement to lead Great Britain for the remainder of the war.[13]

Churchill proved his gifts of oratory and diplomacy, winning Roosevelt's favor. One hundred sixty-five years of distrust was healed. Congress passed the Lend-Lease Act on March 11, 1941, adding destroyers to the British, Chinese, and Russian forces.[14]

When Germany bombed London, newsreels caught Winston walking her streets and lifting people from the rubble. Above the chaos his courage inspired the nation. He bolstered the Brits, and they were thrilled by the king's choice; yet after the war, he lost reelection to a socialist with no sympathy for the Jews.

The Bear

Following the fall of the Russian Tsar Nicholas II during the February 1917 Revolution, various parties vied for power.[15] A provisional government stepped in.[16] The fallen bear rose up on one side by responding to three fascist leaders who would incite a socialist revolution; the bear had taken them in. Their voices established the Union of Soviet Socialist Republics in 1922.[17]

> [5] "And suddenly another beast, a second, like a bear. It was raised up on one side, and *had* three ribs in its mouth between its teeth. And they said thus to it: 'Arise, devour much flesh!' (Dan. 7:5 NKJV)

Karl Marx and Friedrich Engels were Germans who lived in England when they wrote and published "The Communist Manifesto" in 1848.[18] After their deaths, its theory grew popular. In twenty-five years Vladimir Lenin, Josef Stalin, and Leon Trotsky founded the USSR by its revolutionary ideas. Lenin spearheaded the Bolshevik October Revolution of 1917, overthrowing the provisional government and then making the state its god.[19] The philosophy soon proved itself fascist, authoritarian, and brutal.

After executing the tsar and his family, Lenin's leadership was undisputed. Trotsky led its Red Army.[20] Stalin was general secretary of the central committee of the communist party until Lenin's death in 1924 when he took his place. Impoverishing its people, despite its promises, Marxism failed to fulfill them.[21]

The Ancient Secrets

The new premier ordered the execution of the intelligentsia; then sentenced to death ten million political opponents with Jews and Christians. Trotsky, a Jew himself, was exiled but absconded to Mexico where his comrade ordered his assassination in 1940.

The Terrible Beast

Rome was pillaged by the Visigoths in 410 and finally fell to the Vandals in 476. The Huns, the fiercest tribe of all, were paid to stay out but drove the others into the city. Not long after Attila's death in 453, his tribes disbanded, settling in Germania and Austria where they intermarried and raised families.[22]

Stephen II, an 8th century pope, gained the Papal States by Pippin the Short of France who warred against the Lombards to win Italia's central cities for Rome.[23] In 800 Leo III crowned Charlemagne, Pippin's first son, as the first allegedly Christian emperor who had ruled France and the Lombards.[24] [Lords of fiefs and kinglets were also named "Holy Roman Emperors"—at times with kingless years between them.[25]]

The pope in 962, John XII, sought protection from jihadists, relying on the more brutal king of Germania Otto the Great to shield the church.[26] Otto had no capital or established form of government, often true of the church's emperors." German kings shielded the (Holy) Roman Empire of the German Nation, or (H)REGN, at intervals for eight hundred forty-four years.

> [7] After this I saw in the night visions, and behold, a fourth beast, terrifying and dreadful and exceedingly strong. It had great iron teeth; it devoured and broke in pieces and stamped what was left with its feet. It was different from all the beasts that were before it, and it had ten horns. (Dan. 7:7) [Its lands were in hundreds of pieces.]

As a rule the only capital of the (H)REGN was Rome, just a façade of a capital whose government was non-existent. Unlike other beasts, the church empire was an amalgamation, hundreds of tiny lands: fiefs, territories, hamlets, duchies—people without nations, too weak to defend themselves.[27] She hired mercenaries to enforce her dogma, indoctrinating and oppressing millions.

Prior to 1059 emperors chose or deposed popes by disputes, power grabs, corruption, and scandals. For hundreds of years, the popes controlled kings, threatening them with excommunication,

Wild Beasts!

which they feared would send them to hell. Meanwhile, believers in Jesus Christ were imprisoned, tortured, and burned at the stake for having a Bible, preaching the gospel, praying in their native tongue, or objecting to the church *orthodoxy,* its "right opinion." In the case of others, simply for being born Jewish. [28]

Napoleon's victory of 1806 ended the era of the imperialist church. His French Confederation, a watershed in history, was independent of the Vatican. He revolutionized education, revived the arts, and reformed the government. He quickly consolidated its lands, reducing hundreds to one hundred. The dissolution of the (H)REGN was his greatest contribution to history.[29] After his defeat at Waterloo by England, Holland, and Prussia, the Council of Vienna further merged his lands to thirty-nine states in 1816.[30]

In 1871 following the Franco-Prussian War, Berlin became the first capital of the German Empire by its founder, Otto von Bismarck. The "Iron Chancellor" subjected the thirty-nine states under Prussian authority as the German Federation.[31]

The Little Dictator

Five years to the day that a political assassination incited WW1 (1914–18), on June 28, 1919, the Treaty of Versailles was signed to go into effect in January 1920. It split the empires into twelve European nations.[32] Two were politically neutral; the rest filled the footprint of the REGN. Ten kings would <u>receive</u> their crowns (in Rev. 17:12), not by the war, but by its treaty. On cue, in just twelve years, a seditionist rose in Germany (in 7:8).

Gabriel foretold these events centuries before. The kingdom the angel described to Daniel would be Roman, out of which the ten horns rose in central Europe about a century after her church empire fell. A little horn rose after them, a chancellor from a corporal! How could a little horn be greater than the others? The small horn held Hitler, speaking as a mouth for the terrible beast from a hundred thirty years before him. (7:7) And lo, *eyes as the eyes of man are in this horn, and a mouth speaking great things. (Dan. 7:8 YLT)* After the seventh king, ten kings rose, and after them, the dragon spoke as a man in a little horn. (Dan. 7:8, p. 21)

They said the Great War would end all war, but hard times were in the air. For twelve years Germany lived in the ashes and memories of ruined hopes when the Great Depression overcame

The Ancient Secrets

her. After having lost her sons in the war, poverty deepened her despair. Disheartened, she called out for hope and a future.

Convicted of treason as a political revolutionist, Adolf Hitler was released from prison, serving just eight months of an already lenient five-year sentence.[33] He applied for citizenship and then membership in the National Socialist German Worker's Party, or Nazis. Thirty years after Bismarck, he mesmerized the Germans, captivating their population with his passionate speeches, full of promises, flatteries, and convictions.

In 1930 construction was finished, and Berlin's Pergamon Museum housed the Altar of Zeus, aka the Altar of Satan.[34] In 1932 Hitler ran for president. With just one-third the vote, he lost; but Hindenburg, the incumbent, returned to office in failing health and chose the former corporal as his chancellor, making him commander-in-chief, the second highest office in the land.

Hitler supervised the nation's emergency powers and used them to subvert his competitors. When the Parliament building burst into flames, it provided the crisis by which he suddenly put its laws, civil rights, education, and culture under Nazi control.[35]

It didn't take long, just six months later, near the time of Hindenburg's last breath, Hitler merged the roles of president and chancellor[36] and created the Third Reich. He put his actions to the vote and won by an overwhelming margin as *der führer,* "the leader." After pinning runaway inflation on the Jews, he vowed, "Change!" and seemed like a hero to them, commanding their confidence.[37] What was it about the man that gave him such power and authority over millions who clung to his every word?

After crafting a pledge of personal allegiance, he ordered his army to honor its words as each soldier dedicated his life. The people followed suit en masse as he dismissed the constitutional democracy of a republic to form the Nazi socialist government.[38]

Bismarck conquered the lands the dragon had shattered into hundreds of pieces by ten kings centuries before. The kings were given their nations by a treaty in 1920, and the dragon regained them in 1938. Thus he won his wars until at last he lost. (7:7-11)

The ten kings empowered him for more (in Rev. 17:13), but *three of the first horns were plucked up by the roots (in 7:8).*[39] Hitler uprooted the first three, like pulling up a plant, roots and all. His large, impassioned crowds idolized him and silenced the opposition. The prophecy's ten kingdoms were the following:

Wild Beasts!

1.) **Germany**'s republic fell after President Hindenburg died. From corporal to chancellor to *führer,* Hitler put the issue to a vote. 95% of registered voters allegedly cast votes; 88% of the plebiscite approved a dictatorship.[40] A soft coup gave a seditionist control over the former Democratic Republic of Germany.

2.) **Austria**'s military conflicts and power transfers made her government weak and vulnerable. Her instability encouraged the malcontents to riot for their native son. Weighing his options, their king conceded without a shot as thousands went to the streets to welcome the arrival of a dictator.[41]

3.) **Czechoslovakia** was a gift to Hitler from the Munich Pact, signed September 30, 1938, by Italy, Germany, France, and Britain. The agreement infamously gave the Sudetenland, i.e., the German-speaking areas around the nation, to Hitler as "land for peace." With rights to electrical power, coal, and steel, added to the nation's grief, he owned Czechoslovakia in a day.[42]

> [8] "I was considering the horns, and there was another horn, <u>a little one</u>, coming up among them, before whom <u>three of the first horns were plucked out by the roots</u>. And there, in this horn, *were* eyes like the eyes of a man, and a mouth speaking pompous words. (Dan. 7:8 NKJV)

Who has *eyes like the eyes of man, and a mouth?* The man spoke by a dragon whose kings ruled ten nations. To the west the Germans loved him, but Belgium resisted.[43] Hungary reluctantly joined him and later declared war on him. Italy resisted but lost. Three fell without a shot, yet all ten *on its head* agreed: *These have one mind, and shall give their power and strength unto the beast. (Rev. 17:13)* Whoever tried to put an end to it failed.

> [20] "and <u>the ten horns that were on its head</u>, and the other horn which came up, <u>before which three fell</u>, namely, that horn which had eyes and a mouth which spoke pompous words, whose appearance *was* greater than his fellows. (Dan. 7:20 NKJV)

He easily plucked up Germany, Austria, and Czechoslovakia to defeat Poland, Luxembourg, Netherlands, Belgium, Slovenia, France, and Italy, strategizing to conquer more.

The beast prevailed against the saints, but God would give them the Kingdom and send him to perdition. (7:21-22; Rev. 17:8)

The Ancient Secrets

Daniel's saints were Jews—set apart, sanctified, like the saints in 165 BC (in Dan. 8:24).

The Altar of Pergamon

In 1889 the Altar of Zeus went to Berlin from Pergamon. (See Rev. 2:13) Long ago Romans joined the Greeks to worship there.[44] Those were the days when Greeks gave human sacrifices on that altar. Rome visited its site when killing Christians was a sport. In 1941 Nazis were murdering the Jews in Europe.

Neither the kaiser [i.e., "caesar"] of Prussia nor Bismarck his chancellor was the little horn. The prophecy waited for the man who would fulfill all of its words. After his horns received their nations, the terrible beast spoke by Hitler who boasted of a super race while targeting the Jews. A staunch Darwinist, the fascist touted ethnic cleansing as the blasphemous beast he'd received.[45]

On May 22, 1939, Mussolini and Hitler signed an agreement for international defense. The "Pact of Friendship and Alliance" was called the "Pact of Steel."[46] On September 1, 1939, Nazis invaded Poland, violating the Munich Pact by their act of war.

Hirohito of Japan joined the "Friendship Alliance," and the triad formed the "Tripartite Pact," September 27, 1940.[47] It was allegedly to "... establish and maintain a new order of things calculated to promote the mutual prosperity and welfare of the peoples concerned. ... to extend cooperation to such nations in other spheres of the world as may be inclined to put forth endeavors along lines similar to their own, in order that their ultimate aspirations for world peace may be realized."[48] Though multitudes believed them, they were all liars.

A truculent strategist groomed an army of terrorists, and the ten kings whose nations he'd gain agreed. "Change!" appealed to the masses, no matter what it meant. By his leadership, men committed unspeakable crimes against humanity while Catholic and Protestant clergy ignored the genocide. They overlooked the apostle's warning not to boast against the Jews. (Rom. 11:18) The Vatican agreed to it by "compromise and conciliation" (like the 4th century bishops); thus the dragon led a nation into the Jewish holocaust and another world war, hoping to conquer the world.[49]

Germany was one of the largest nations in Europe, yet Hitler convinced the nation to shed blood for more land as in the Far East Hirohito did the same. The founder of radical Islam also

Wild Beasts!

colluded with Hitler.[50] Mussolini and Hirohito added to the war dead—sixty million souls; one in ten were Jews.

Martin Luther discovered the scripture for everlasting life by grace through faith and turned men's blindness into sight, but in later writings, he was blinded by his animus for the Jews. Yet they were blinded for the nations to be saved till the day the Jews regained Jerusalem. Even so, he ignored the letter to the Roman church that Jews can be grafted in again.[51] As unnatural branches we can be cut off from their olive tree—the witness of our faith's Jewish roots. (Romans 11) For generations professing believers had read his scornful words that abetted their murders in WW2.

In 1942 Hitler led his army against his allies in Leningrad, Moscow, and Stalingrad, killing perhaps a million Jews on the way.[52] The icy Russian winter was more than the returning Nazis could endure; many froze to death in the fields. God reigns over nature and kings, judging men in days of war or peace. (Ecc. 3:8)

On November 9, 1938, *Kristallnacht,* the "Night of Broken Glass," authorized Germans to pillage Jewish shops, smash their windows, ruin merchandise, and vandalize their homes, making the Jews pay for the damages. Nazis banned their meetings and burned their synagogues and books, even Holy Bibles![53] Bigotry intensified from name-calling, rock-throwing, and gang beatings to public murders.

Quick like a Leopard!

President Woodrow Wilson made the former senator from New York Franklin D. Roosevelt his secretary of the navy from 1912–20. F.D.R. contracted infantile paralysis while visiting an orphanage in 1921. He was thirty-nine. Determined to persevere though polio had paralyzed half his body, he met the challenge to win the 1932 election.[54] Across the world, von Hindenburg chose Hitler as his chancellor, the role his hero Bismarck had enjoyed.

Eleven years after WW1, the sobering reality of the 1929 Stock Market Crash stifled the Roaring Twenties and yielded to the Great Depression.[55] The freefall of the economy preceded her Great Drought that lasted nearly ten years.[56] By God's grace, America became undefeatable, strengthened in her catastrophes.

She had known the grief of WW1, having lost her sons in its battles. In early 1941 Americans resisted the idea of engaging in another foreign war though the government supported the British

The Ancient Secrets

Royal Navy, supplying ships in the Atlantic where the conflict was close to home, and Congress passed the Lend-Lease Act.

December 7, 1941, Japan attacked the U.S. naval base where most of her ships were anchored, Pearl Harbor, Hawaii. Out of the blue, bombers demolished her fleet in the Pacific and forced the end of America's isolation.[57] Two thousand four hundred and three died in the harbor attack.[58]

The next day Roosevelt addressed the houses of Congress. The "Declaration of Intent to Declare War" [59] was made official December 8. The Senate voted 82–0 and the House, 388–1.[60] On December 11 Hitler and Mussolini declared war on the U.S.[61]

After the calamities that preceded the Second World War, the president foresaw the way to victory over our adversaries who he thought might have otherwise consumed the world. Inner strength was required, and his positive attitude was contagious.

WW1 politics had weakened her armed forces. She'd begun rebuilding her air force, but America still needed trained troops, artillery, tanks, submarines, ships, machine guns, rifles, bombers, canons, and munitions, as well as uniforms, backpacks, canteens, and k-rations, and all the essentials of warfare.

Draft notices flooded post offices, calling men to duty, and long lines formed around recruiting stations. Furniture, clothing, and automobile factories were redesigned to make war products. Nylon wasn't for stockings anymore—it was for parachutes.

In 1942 in his "State of the Union" message, Roosevelt spoke to Congress and the national radio audience: "<u>Speed</u> will count. Lost ground can always be regained—but time, never. Speed will save lives; speed will save this Nation which is in peril; speed will save our freedom and our civilization, and slowness has never been an American characteristic!" [62]

F.D.R. emphasized "speed" four times, the main asset of the four-winged beast that had already shot through this writer like a high-speed documentary on America at war! God alone knew an eagle became a leopard with four wings of a bird. [Aram.: *owph* is correctly, "bird" {71x}. KJV and YLT see "fowls," flying in the air {42x}, an archaic translation of the word.]

"In 1940, the U.S. army was smaller than that of Rumania: only 174,000 men in uniform, wearing tin hats and leggings issued during WW1, and carrying rifles designed in 1903." [63] Entering the conflict two years and three months late, "American

Wild Beasts!

industry provided nearly two-thirds of all the Allied military equipment produced during the war." [64]

Americans sacrificed what had seemed essential but paled in comparison to helping their boys fight for freedom. Hollywood inspired audiences to invest in war bonds and to use their ration cards. Unemployed people of color, homemakers, retirees, and the physically and mentally challenged composed the war effort. "The War was won at home" was an adage in every household.

Joash the king sought Elisha for advice to defeat Aram. The prophet told him to strike a bunch of arrows on the ground. He hit dirt three times, angering Elisha. Three times weren't enough. Five or six times would have destroyed the enemy. The triumph relied on its king's passion to win. (2 Kg. 13:14-19)

Roosevelt commanded, "Speed!" He called for the leopard, and his resonant voice led to America's most important victory. The leopard's greatest asset is its speed. A camouflaged beast rose as the eagle became a leopard, rushing to rescue freedom from the jaws and claws of a terrible beast. A leopard propelled America as an opponent of tyranny, redirecting the course of the war when, at its tipping point, her troops were among the heroes who rescued Jews from the death camps of Europe where her battle-hardened generals wept for the gaunt survivors.

Roosevelt incited his Republican critics when the Supreme Court agreed to pass his "Executive Order for the Internment of Japanese Citizens." [65] He argued it would avert a national crisis, but the country would never forget its national offense.

At the time of Daniel's vision, none of these nations existed, but twenty-five hundred years later, God used a world war to end His vengeance and favor His chosen people by returning them to their land and establishing the nation for His kingdom to come. (See Is. 40:1-5; Jer. 16:16-18) Each attempt to divide Israel ends in greater divisions of our own lands.

Leaders publically prayed for the wisdom and strength to win with the help of God. The nation rushed to the war half a world away that conscripted her sons into the greatest conflict in history, but the God of Israel would be with them. As the Lamb is a Lion, and the serpent is a dragon, the eagle became a leopard though by peril. Invisible kings and their kingdoms are beasts, [metaphors of their attributes], made visible by mortal leaders and nations. [Jesus is the Lamb as a Savior, the Lion as King.]

The Ancient Secrets

Though we see them as flesh and blood, the kings in these battles are the spiritual kind. The scarlet beast *devoured and broke in pieces* the lands it gained by savage kings long before they received kingdoms. Divided nations are an easy catch.

Three beasts, *each different from the other (in 7:3)*, won the war when Jews were the saints set apart for the glory of God. At the end, *the beast was slain, and his body destroyed and given to the burning flame (in 7:11)*. Decades later Hitler's bodyguard said he'd ordered it burned and buried to prevent its discovery.[66]

Having promised the land to their forefathers, God favored His Jews. ... *and judgment was given to the saints of the Most High*, and *the time came that the saints possessed the kingdom. (7:22)* The Kingdom of David would be established forever by restoring the Jews to the promised land, fulfilling the promises to Abraham, Isaac, and Jacob as well as the oracles of the prophets.

Following Roosevelt's death, Japan killed over half as many of the Allies in the Pacific as since its war began. His advisors assured President Truman a land invasion would cost a million lives. Weighing the alternatives, on August 6 he dropped the H-bomb on Hiroshima.[67] Without a truce in sight, three days later, he targeted Nagasaki, and it was suddenly clear: *the leopard was given dominion (in Dan. 7:6)*. Now watch the dates:

Germany invaded Poland on September 1, 1939. On the 3rd, Britain and France declared war on Hitler. The Pacific conflict officially ended in a treaty September 2, 1945, on Tokyo Bay. It was September 1 in Washington, D.C.[68]

God sent messages to the nations by events on Gregorian calendar dates: biblically, "one" is unity or singularity, "three" is of God; "four" is earthly; "six" is of man; "seven," of completion or perfection; "eight," of beginnings; "ten," of judgment or law; "fifty," of liberty, and "five" concerns grace or provision.

David had more than enough stones to fell the giant when he took five; with five loaves, Jesus fed five thousand men besides women and children; five talents went to a servant who doubled them. Each time the provision had plenty left over. God showed the Jews grace and provision by granting them the Kingdom, not by their own merit, or else grace is no longer grace. (Rom. 11:6)

Hitler's "Final Solution" sent its first shipment of Jews from German ghettos to concentration camps in late 1941. Europe's first death camp was in Chelmno, Poland, operational December

Wild Beasts!

8, 1941, the day the U.S. declared war on Japan.[69] The war ended in Europe on May 8, 1945, three years and five months later.

Exactly six years and six months after Kristallnacht, the last death camp, Stutthof, was closed by the Allies on May 9, 1945, after an estimated six million Jews were murdered in Europe.[70]

Israel proves God judges sin. If we sin, we too must repent or be judged as He did Israel. Historically, God sent His enemies to judge His people, and the judgments were horrible. Their sin was odious to God when He scattered them:

> [19] And I scattered them among the heathen, and they were dispersed through the countries: according to their way and according to their doings I judged them. ...
> [23] And I will sanctify my great name which was profaned among the heathen, which ye have profaned in the midst of them; And the heathen shall know that I am the LORD, saith the Lord GOD, when I shall be sanctified in you before their eyes. [24] For I will take you from among the heathen, and gather you out of all countries, and will bring you into your own land. (Ezk. 36:19, 23-24)

> [24] Who gave up Jacob to the looter,
>   and Israel to the plunderers?
> Was it not the LORD against whom we have sinned?
>   in whose ways they would not walk,
> and whose law they would not obey? (Is. 42:24 ESV)

What's a Head?

The heads on the leopard are its leaders. Most often *rosh* described Israel's tribal leaders {349x}. [Aram.: *rë'sh* is "head," and is *rö'sh*, meaning "top, foremost, first" in Hebrew.] The leopard is a beast with four *heads*, unlike the other's ten *horns*, or kings.

> [6] "After this I looked, and there was another, like a leopard, which had on its back four wings of a bird. The beast <u>also had four heads</u>, and dominion was given to it. (Dan. 7:6 NKJV) – It was the camouflaged beast of prophecy.

The Constitution names four offices that serve our national interests: a president, a speaker of the house of representatives, a president of the senate, and a chief justice of the supreme court[71] serve within the system's checks and balances as its four heads, leading the executive, legislative, and judicial branches.

The Ancient Secrets

The leaders' duties are in three Articles of the Constitution. In Article 1, the speaker of the house and the president of the senate lead their legislators, ensuring both the populace and their various states are well served. The senate and house create and vote on legislative bills, taxation, and declarations of war.

The house can impeach a president for bribery, treason, or high crimes and misdemeanors. The senate holds impeachment trials. Their services are listed in the ten sections of Article 1.

In Article 2 the president preserves, protects, and defends the Constitution of the United States and is commander-in-chief of the armed forces and national militia. As head of the executive branch, he/she commissions officers and, by advice and consent of the senate, makes treaties and appoints ambassadors, judges, justices of the supreme court, and other public ministers.

The president also grants pardons and reprieves; ensures laws are rightly executed; may issue executive orders, and at times, may convene or adjourn one or both houses of congress. He/she ratifies or objects to congressional bills, but congress can overturn a veto by a two-thirds vote in both houses: Article 1, section 7. The president makes foreign policy and trade pacts to be ratified by congress. The particulars are in four sections.

In Article 3 the chief justice of the supreme court is head of nine appointed judges. He/she discerns the constitutionality of laws and treaties; tries cases of public ministers, consuls, and ambassadors, and cases between states or in which the nation has a part. Read the three sections of Article 3.

Approaching the Throne

[12] 'And the ten horns that thou sawest, are ten kings, who a kingdom did not yet receive, but authority as kings the same hour do receive with the beast, [13] these have one mind, and their own power and authority to the beast they shall give over; [14] these with the Lamb shall make war, and the Lamb shall overcome them, because Lord of lords he is, and King of kings, and those with him are called, and choice, and stedfast.' (Rev. 17:12-14)

In the distant future, the apostles would watch Him ascend to a cloud, but in the mystery of eternity, Daniel saw the Son of man rising to heaven out of the clouds after the victory of WW2:

Wild Beasts!

> ¹³ "I was watching in the night visions,
> And behold, <u>*One* like the Son of Man</u>,
> <u>Coming with the clouds of heaven</u>!
> <u>He came to the Ancient of Days</u>,
> <u>And they brought Him near before Him</u>.
> ¹⁴ Then to Him was given dominion and glory and a kingdom.
> That all peoples, nations, and languages should serve Him.
> His dominion is an everlasting dominion which shall not pass away,
> And His kingdom *the one*
> Which shall never be destroyed. (Dan. 7:13-14 NKJV)

As a result, Israel returned to the land, and the Jews gained Jerusalem. According to Jesus, the gentiles' days are fulfilled (in Lk. 21:24). Now Jews are receiving Jesus, and we're wondering if it's the end of the age![72]

> ¹⁷ 'These four great beasts are four kings who shall arise out of the earth. ¹⁸ But the saints of the Most High shall receive the kingdom and possess the kingdom forever, forever and ever.' (Dan. 7:17-18 ESV)

February 4–11, 1945: Churchill, Stalin, and Roosevelt met in Yalta, Ukraine, to partition Germany and plan the UN. Seven weeks after the war, the Allies signed the UN Charter on June 26 in a skating rink in Flushing Meadows, NY. Article 80 on page 15 affirms the Balfour Declaration as international law.[73]

Not long afterward, the UN agreed to change their own international law by granting the Golan Heights to Syria for her oil, despite her alliance with Hitler that cost them their sons. Then on November 29, 1947, UN Resolution 181 gave the Jews a meager portion of the original land grant.[74] The general secretary of the United Nations announced its tally as Jews listened to their RCA Victors at home: "33 yes; 13 against; 10 abstentions."[75]

African and European borders were decided in Italy twenty-five years earlier. In 1947 they increased, but the Jewish borders were reduced.[76] May 14, 1948, the Jews acquiesced, and Israel was reborn with just 12% of her legal boundaries from 1920.[77]

Hours after her rebirth, Israel faced her first threat when Egyptian planes roared over the celebration at midnight, and her War of Independence began. Like Gideon's, a relatively small, poorly equipped army battled against the sophisticated troops of Egypt, Lebanon, Trans-Jordan, Syria, Saudi Arabia, and Iraq till the war ended in March 1949 with Israel holding her ground.[78] With Jacob in their genes and God on their side, they'd reentered the Promised Land to face the giants once again.

The prophecies of their return were proven. Faced with Arab nations that built up their arms and announced their war strategy to the world, in June 1967 the Six Day War began with a pre-emptive strike by the Jews. Israel regained Samaria ["the West Bank"]; Mt. Hermon ["the Golan Heights"], and Jerusalem; then, restored the oil-rich Sinai to Egypt for peace.[79] (See Lk. 21:24)

In 1947 Great Britain reduced the Jews' land and then lost an empire. One of a commonwealth of fifty-four nations, the Queen is now a figurehead, but the UK includes just England, Scotland, Northern Ireland, and Wales.[80] Great Britain no longer exists.

In 1991 Russia lost her empire when socialism bankrupted it. Marxism prohibited the human rights America has enjoyed: freedom of religion, speech, press, assembly, and self-defense, taken for granted in the U.S., but Marxism collapsed.[81] When we no longer hold the ideals of our founding fathers, we too will fall.

And _the rest of the beasts have caused their dominion to pass away:_ (7:12a YLT) Their dominion was over Germany after the war, but they dissolved that alliance after returning Europe to its previous nations and leaving Germany as its people's republic. The three main allies planned the UN, which would usurp their dominion though they continued as nations whose sovereignties divided them. (Lk. 11:17)

A Deceiver's Diversity

He recalls the vision, but Daniel wants to hear more about the last beast. The heavenly man sounds redundant, but is he? (7:23-27) The fourth beast would return: [23] _The fourth beast shall be the fourth kingdom ... diverse from all kingdoms ... and shall devour the whole earth._ [24] _And the ten horns out of this kingdom are ten kings that shall arise: and another shall rise after them; and he shall be diverse from the first._ (7:23-24) The next empire (in Rev. 13:1) has the power and throne of the dragon. The ten horns out of this kingdom shall arise again, _and another [beast] shall rise after them ... diverse from the first._ The _first_ to rise after the ten was also _the first_ to rule an illegitimate empire.

Wild Beasts!

Babylon was his first capital; then Rome; then Berlin, but the next beast would be his fourth kingdom: At Berlin's fall, the dragon gave *his power, his throne, and great authority* to the leopard, the bear, and the lion. (Rev. 13:2) The Allies signed the UN charter created by Alger Hiss in June 1945.[82] By receiving his power, unlike all other kingdoms, its beast *devours the whole earth (7:23) ... and power was given him over all kindreds, and tongues and nations. And all who dwell upon the earth shall worship him, whose names are not written in the book of life of the Lamb slain from the foundation of the world. (Rev. 13:7b-8)*

Out of this kingdom, the ten horns shall arise in the alliance of the next beast (in 13:2); *and another shall rise after them* who is *diverse from the first (in Dan. 7:11)*. Its mystery is **its key**: This ruler is <u>another beast</u> that rises after the ten but is unlike the little horn who also spoke as a dragon, the terrible beast that gave his throne to the next beast, formed by the three.

After the beast with ten horns rises in Revelation 13, <u>another rises</u>—but not as *the first*. Not as the little horn that rose after the ten for WW2, nor as the beast that rises with his throne. He has neither seven heads nor ten horns and neither iron teeth nor brass claws, but *speaks as a dragon* with *horns like a lamb (in 13:11)*.

And he shall subdue three kings (in 7:24)—namely, the three that got his throne! He rises out of perdition (in Rev. 17:11) with horns like a lamb (in Rev. 13:11). Then how can he *subdue* the three? By his own authority, which he never gave the beast.

To differentiate the times of the beasts, the writing turns to poetry and future tense, alluding to the elusive dragon. He's hard to spot, winding his way as a serpent, hiding but being unveiled by the history that hounds him. Like catching an eel, he slips from our grip only to reappear.

The dragon would rise after the ten kings again, but *diverse from the first* that rose after them *(in Dan. 7:24)* <u>though he'd been the first beast</u>, *whose deadly wound was healed (in Rev. 13:12)*. A little bit like a lamb, he's *another beast coming up out of the earth* that speaks like a dragon (in Rev. 13:11).

With another religious empire *diverse from the first* he once had, he deceives the world for its worship in Revelation. He may deceive the saints with his false prophet who does fake miracles by his devils. The dragon with horns like a lamb is the father of lies. The spirit of the beast identifies him in yet another repeated prophecy: in Daniel 11, he was *the abomination of desolation*. Jesus spoke of his return (in Mat. 24:15-22; cf. Dan. 11:31; 12:11).

The enemy enters a temple as an *abomination of desolation* again, and Jerusalem receives him before he ravages her. Yeshua said people would be saying Jesus had returned when He hadn't. He corrected the thought, saying He'd return to earth like lightning across the skies—not on a cloud. He comes on a cloud right after the tribulation to rescue the elect only (in Mat. 24:23-31).

At last the ten kings return to the beast whose mortal wound was made well by his assumed enemies. With one mind the ten kings give him their power (in Rev. 17:15-18). Not <u>plucking up three</u> by the roots like the first, he abases three kings:

> [24] And the ten horns out of this kingdom are ten kings that shall arise: and <u>another</u> shall rise after them; and he shall be <u>diverse from the first</u>, and he shall subdue three kings. (Dan. 7:24)

The ten horns' crowns were restored after WW2. *The fourth beast shall be the fourth kingdom (in 7:23)* means the fourth beast that rose after them in Daniel gives *his power, his throne, and great authority* to the dragon's fourth kingdom that devours the world. The allies have his ten horns and seven heads, the devil's power and dominion. Then *diverse from the first, another* rises, speaking as a dragon and subduing the three (in Rev. 13:2-3).

The ancient insurrectionist that was slain, the devil, *the first beast, whose deadly wound was healed, subdues* the three before him *(in Rev. 13:12)*. One of its seven heads is healed; the capital city is the throne the dragon gave the beast. After his capital is healed, the dragon rises out of the earth to rule its throne.

Centuries ago he'd stomped the land to pieces, but the fourth kingdom devours *the whole earth, and shall tread it down, and break it in pieces* too. His Third Reich was Germany; his fourth kingdom devours the world but is destroyed forever (in 7:26).

The one with the dragon's throne has the microphone till the dragon with two horns like a lamb rises with all his authority and takes the mike to subdue the three beneath him. He's an eighth king like Antiochus IV.

Divisions, Divisions!

Bestial forms can be altered. [Aram.: $sh^en\hat{a}^{\circ}$, "diverse" {5x}, often it's "change/alter." {16x}] The beast is *diverse,* changed:

Wild Beasts!

he *was slain and his body destroyed (in Dan. 7:11)*. Satan is the serpent, the dragon, a scarlet beast, a terrible beast, the destroyer and the deceiver but has two horns like a lamb in Revelation 13.

A few mistranslated words are in the best Bible versions. One is *ciphrah,* or *"book." It is rolled together as a <u>scroll</u> (in Is. 34:4)*. Unknown in the days of King James I, Psalm 139 should also have *ciphrah* as "scroll": *[15]My substance was not hid from thee, when I was made in secret, curiously wrought in the lowest parts of the earth. [16]Thine eyes did see my substance, yet being unperfect; and in thy [scroll] all my members were written, <u>which in continuance were fashioned</u>, when as yet there was none of them.(from Ps. 139)* Its script is figuratively the double-helix of DNA, the scroll only its Author could have written.

> [25] And he shall speak great words against the most High, and shall wear out the saints of the most High, and think <u>to change times and laws</u>: and they shall be given into his hand until a time and times and the dividing of time. (Dan. 7:25) [This is about the beast in Rev. 13:1-2, 5-10.]

Time, times, and half a time [in many versions] is literally, *time, times, and <u>a division of a time</u>. (Dan. 7:25 YLT)* [Aram.: $p^e lag$, "split"] In KJV and Geneva Bible of 1599, it reads, *the dividing of time* {1x} as it is in the Authorized KJV {1x} and in the Complete Word Study OT {1x}. It is otherwise used for the dividing of the earth and its watercourses {4x}. Unequally split, not halved. Here, the *times* are years, not decades or centuries. *Time, times, and a division of a time* pass while the beast rules the earth even after its tribulation ends when immediately, the sun is dark, the moon is red, and the earth quakes. (Rev. 6:12-17)

Biblical Hebrew months are thirty days long. The number of *times* is more than three, but *1,260 days* or *forty-two months* are not the *times* here. Unlike *time, times and half a time* as *forty-two* [30-day] *months,* or *1,260 days;* it is *time, times, and the dividing of a time,* making an unequal division to shorten its time—split short: *And except those days be shortened, there should no flesh be saved: but <u>for the elect's sake</u>, those days shall be shortened. (Mat. 24:22, 29)* Thus the elect are in the hands of the beast for fewer than the forty-two months he is allotted (in Rev. 13:5).

At the end of Daniel 7, the Kingdom is *given to the people of the saints*—the inheritance of Messiah promised to Abraham—

believers of all nations, not just their own (in 7:18). *The gifts and the calling of God are without repentance (in Rom. 11:28-29).* New covenant believers are *the people of the saints* (Gen. 18:18-19; 22:18; 26:4-5; Eph. 2:19) At the end Jews and gentiles of all nations are grafted into the olive tree by faith in Jacob's Savior. Once joined to God, as one we pray, "Thy Kingdom come," for Yeshua to return and supplant wickedness with righteousness.

> [27] And the kingdom and dominion, and the greatness of the kingdom under the whole heaven, shall be given to <u>the people of the saints of the most High</u>, whose kingdom is an everlasting kingdom, <u>and all dominions shall serve and obey him</u>. (Dan. 7:27) [Literally accurate]

Jerusalem has been associated with Melchizedek since the day He met Abram near her walls. (Gen. 14:18-20) Four thousand years later, the Jews regained the city and made her their capital once again. The trouble over Jerusalem is the reason His return is near; what seems to be their curse is a hidden blessing. He said,

> [24] They will fall by the edge of the sword and be led captive among all nations, and Jerusalem will be trampled underfoot by the Gentiles, until the times of the Gentiles are fulfilled. (Lk. 21:24 ESV)

God gathers all nations that divide His land to Armageddon. Whether nations are blessed or cursed depends on how they treat Israel because God chose the land and the people as His own (in Is. 51:4, 14:25; Jer. 2:7, 16:18; Ezk. 36:1-11, 38:16; Jl. 1:6, 3:2).

"Gainsaying" is a word in the KJV and YLT. [Grk.: *antilĕgō*, is "to speak against in order to gain advantage for one's self."] If we only receive what we want to believe, we refuse the cross but expect its benefits. (Lk. 21:15; Ti. 1:9; Acts 10:29) In gainsaying, we will not be spared; therefore we must repent:

> [19] You will say then, "Branches were broken off so that I could be grafted in." [20] Granted. But they were broken off because of unbelief, and you stand by faith. Do not be arrogant, but be afraid. [21] For if God did not spare the natural branches, he will not spare you either.
>
> [22] Consider therefore the kindness and the severity of God: sternness to those who fell, but kindness to you, provided that you continue in his kindness. Otherwise, you also will be cut off. (Heb. 11:19-22 NIV)

What about Dreams?

CHAPTER 2

During the Babylonian captivity, four Judeans were chosen above all the wise men in Nebuchadnezzar's court. In discerning dreams and visions, the Jew Daniel was outstanding.

One night, the king had disturbing dreams. He called for his wise men to both reveal and interpret his dreams or be slain. But that was impossible, they said. Furious, he sent a decree to kill them all. The guards went out and found Daniel who learned of it and was granted the time he requested to pray. Then God gave the answer to Daniel. Saving the rest from the sword he said,

> [31] "You, O king, were watching; and behold, a great image! This great image, whose splendor *was* excellent, stood before you; and its form *was* awesome. [32] This image's head was of fine gold, its chest and arms of silver, its belly and thighs of bronze, [33] its legs of iron, its feet partly of iron and partly of clay. [34] You watched while a stone was cut out without hands, which struck the image on its feet of iron and clay, and broke them in pieces. [35] Then the iron, the clay, the bronze, the silver, and the gold were crushed together, and became like chaff from the summer threshing floors; the wind carried them away so that no trace of them was found. And the stone that struck the image became a great mountain and filled the whole earth.
>
> [36] "This is the dream. Now we will tell the interpretation of it before the king. [37] You, O king, *are* a king of kings. For the God of heaven has given you a kingdom, power, strength, and glory; [38] and wherever the children of men dwell, or the beasts of the field and the birds of the heaven, He has given *them* into your hand, and has made you ruler over them all—you *are* this head of gold. [39] But after you shall arise another kingdom inferior to yours; then another, a third kingdom of bronze, which shall rule over all the earth. [40] And the fourth kingdom shall be as strong as iron, inasmuch as iron breaks in pieces and shatters everything; and like iron that crushes, *that kingdom* will break in pieces and crush all the others. [41] Whereas you saw the feet and toes, partly of potter's clay and partly of iron, the kingdom shall be divided; yet the strength of the iron shall be in it, just as

The Ancient Secrets

you saw the iron mixed with ceramic clay. ⁴² And *as* the toes of the feet were partly of iron and partly of clay, so the kingdom shall be partly strong and partly fragile. ⁴³As you saw iron mixed with ceramic clay, they will mingle with the seed of men; but they will not adhere to one another, just as iron does not mix with clay. ⁴⁴ And in the days of these kings the God of heaven shall set up a kingdom which shall never be destroyed; and the kingdom shall not be left to other people; it shall break in pieces and consume all these kingdoms, and it shall stand forever. ⁴⁵ Inasmuch as you saw that the stone was cut out of the mountain without hands, and that it broke in pieces the iron, the bronze, the clay, the silver, and the gold—the great God has made known to the king what will come to pass after this. The dream is certain, and its interpretation is sure." (Daniel 2:31-45 NKJV)

Just One Stone

Throughout the analogy the metals represent empires. Like its metal each of them was inferior in splendor to the one it overtook, but each was stronger than its predecessor until its feet. Its bronze thighs and iron legs were divided kingdoms, but even more divided were its feet and toes, which were partly strong and partly fragile, divided within themselves.

David slew Goliath with just one stone, a perfect fit for the young man's sling. (1 Sam. 17:50) But another Stone will fell a giant far greater than Goliath. ... *it shall break in pieces and consume all these kingdoms, and it shall stand forever. (2:44c)*

When all nations unite against her, Israel's Cornerstone will destroy their armies, and Babylon the Great will turn to ashes: *And whosoever shall fall on this stone shall be broken: but on whomsoever it shall fall, it will grind him to powder. (Mat. 21:44; cf. Is. 8:14-15)* Israel's King will crush them all together.

Two events were foretold in the king's dream: In the days of the ten kings, a stone strikes its feet and breaks them in pieces (in 2:34) when God sets up a kingdom that will never be defeated or left to others (in 2:44). God established Israel after ending His vengeance in World War Two.

A Stone will crush her enemies when Jerusalem rises like a mountain over the earth (in 2:35, 44c). God gave His Son the Kingdom; as Immanuel, He redeemed the whole world. (Is. 7:14)

What about Dreams?

The Image

King Nebuchadnezzar dreamed of an idol. Its gold head was the illustrious king himself. (Dan. 2:38) Daniel said God created the king to rule Babylon. (2:37) Isaiah had already condemned the worship of gold idols (in Is. 46); yet as kings before him had done, Nebuchadnezzar demanded worship from the city that had risen out of Babel itself. (See pp. 55-58)

Two other empires preceded Babylon—Egypt and Assyria, but go unmentioned in the king's dream. Why?

> [23] In that day there will be a highway from Egypt to Assyria, and the Assyrians will come into Egypt and the Egyptians into Assyria, and the Egyptians will worship with the Assyrians. [24] In that day Israel will be the third *party* with Egypt and Assyria, a blessing in the midst of the earth, [25] whom the LORD of hosts has blessed, saying, "Blessed is Egypt My people, and Assyria the work of My hands, and Israel My inheritance.
> (Is. 19:23-25 NASB)

The dream Daniel revealed to him exalted Nebuchadnezzar, its gold head. His mind was inflated with pride. In the third chapter, he ordered his sculptors and goldsmiths to build a great gold statue and commanded its worship by the entire kingdom.

The Jewish prophets refused to bow to the idol and were cast into a blazing furnace. When its fiery flames had no effect on them—nor on a fourth [man] in the furnace, the king of Babylon passed a decree: No one may speak against the Hebrews' God, yet the king himself was unchanged.

In Daniel 4 the king gave the testimony of his salvation. He said he had a dream about a tree, which Daniel interpreted as a prophetic warning before the king lost mind by exalting himself. His pride drove him mad so that he ate grass in the wild like a beast till he confessed, "God alone is Sovereign." Sent into the wilderness for months, the king was enlightened by humility and returned to reality. He learned God is greater than all kings and can humble the proud. Then he ordered Babylon to worship the God of Israel. He had come to the faith. The people obeyed his law but, unchanged by God, returned to idolatry at his death.

In Daniel 5 his son became king and held a banquet. The rich kingdom made gods out of its possessions. Drinking out of gold goblets from the temple, he praised the gods of gold, stone, and wood. Within the hour, the new king saw the fingers of a man writing on the plaster wall. Visibly shaken he asked Daniel to interpret its meaning. Its prophetic words came to pass that night when King Belshezzar was slain and the kingdom went to Darius the Mede, raised up by God. Thus Medo-Persia gained Babylon as the silver chest and arms.

In Daniel 6 King Darius admired Daniel and planned to make him head of the kingdom. This incited Daniel's enemies who devised a law for the king to sign, commanding that no one may petition any god but must ask the king for all their needs for the next month; transgressors were thrown to the lions.

Darius was dismayed when they nabbed Daniel in prayer, but Persian laws signed by its king were permanent. He fasted the night Daniel was thrown to the lions, and no—not a scratch!

No idol is in the story, just the requirement of the people's dependency on the king for their needs. That makes us pause to think. Daniel escaped the lions' den unharmed, but his enemies and their families were thrown to the lions and eaten. At the end Darius sent a decree to his kingdom to fear Daniel's God.

When Greece overcame Persia, she accepted the Babylonian gods of Persia. Babylon's late dynasties were Persian and Greek; their kings proudly reckoned themselves Babylonian.

The idol's bronze belly, Greece, was metaphorically a goat whose great horn was broken (in Dan. 8:21). When Alexander the Great died, four horns divided his empire when four generals divvied up the lands. The greatest dynasties were the Seleucid and Ptolemaic, the idol's bronze thighs. Each of them overcame Israel, but as iron hammers bronze, Rome conquered all that was Greek, receiving all that was Babylonian by 30 BC.[83]

Its peculiar geography made its empire untenable for Rome. Diocletian divided it with Byzantium and Rome as its capitals. The Byzantine Empire continued a thousand years after Rome fell in 476.[84] Its city became Constantinople but fell to Turkish jihadists as the second foot from its iron legs.

Because thou hast seen iron mixed with miry clay, <u>they are mixing themselves with the seed of men</u>: and they are not adhering one with another, even as iron is not mixed with clay (in Dan. 2:43 YLT).

What about Dreams?

Her scarlet beast (in Rev. 17:3) had been Babylon's dragon, passing <u>Greek and Roman</u> power to a terrible beast as the <u>bronze claws</u> and <u>iron teeth</u> of the (H)REGN (in Dan. 7:7). Afterward he ruled with his altar behind the walls of Babylon in Berlin.

Where Have All the Vandals Gone?

Daniel interpreted the king's dream, describing an unusual event: the iron kingdom was the strongest and most brutish but would be divided within itself (in 2:41). Its empire was split in two, and its iron mixed with humankind, the clay feet and toes.

What could have literally *mingled with the seed of men?* The iron kings are not men but fallen angels, leading devils to affect nations. Men who worship false gods are open to receive devils.

Savages out of the east and north invaded Rome, trashed the city, and forced marriages, mixing their seed with mortals. The bishops built an empire on a lie from their fear of the invasions.

The apostate church hired European kings to protect her as a false religio-political empire rose, divided by popes and kings, already partly weak and partly strong by the mixture. After its fall, the ten kings received their kingdoms out of its empire. At Hitler's rise, the people were divided and unable to oppose him.

In the days of these kings (from 2:44a) the dream's ten toes were kings in collusion with the dragon. These remain till Israel pulverizes them by the King of kings, a far-reaching prophecy in Revelation 13–16 and 17:15 through chapter 19.

Rome fell to the Visigoths and Vandals, savage tribes that migrated to central Europe. Fleeing from the Huns, they invaded Rome, raped their women, and married them for their offspring.

Both sides of the Roman Empire had professed Christianity for centuries. The city to the east was renamed Constantinople after its emperor died, but in 1453, jihadists broke through its walls and called it Istanbul.[85] They changed most of its churches into mosques and made it the head of the Ottoman Empire. Eyewitnesses described gory brutalities, "showing no mercy from the weakest to the greatest." Rape victims were forced to intermarry, mingling the seed of men with the iron savages.[86]

Mixing iron with the seed of men affected human nature: Lombards, Celts, Turks, Vandals, Goths, Visigoths, Vikings, jihadists, and Huns—nomadic tribes—were fathers of nations who'd become barbarians. When iron kings mixed with the seed of men, the civilizations fell.[87] How could they possibly stand while divided?

The Hunnic Effect

In the 8th century, out of weakness and fear, church leaders called on Europa's rulers; in the 9th they established a church empire with military power. In the 10th popes turned to the brutal Germanic kings whose forefathers were Huns. In 962 Otto the Great was the first German "Holy Roman Emperor." [88]

The church empire conquered its people by wars and oppression. From 962 till 1806, the REGN was most often ruled by Roman popes and German kings. When men worshiped idols and false gods, they physically received devils until their nations were divided by the unnatural composition of their seed.

The Hunnic effect and Hitler's interest in the occult incited the people to heinous crimes against Jews [the chosen people], and churches were ambivalent or complicit by the deceiver. The antichrist spirit rises when men receive evil ideas and are roused to hatred and slander. Their fascism silences its opposition till the day the LORD changes everything.

Other Huns left the Asian steppes to settle in Russia. Was it why Russian Marxists killed sixty-two million opponents, often for being Jews or Christians? [89] Marxism incites genocide.

In *The Communist Manifesto,* Marx imagined socialism as a return to the Middle Ages' feudalism with its government as the landlord.[90] Marxism is a repressive political theory that deceives its minions. It appears generous until faith and freedom are outlawed. Marxism sheds blood worldwide; its beast is the deceiver; the truth is his enemy.

Thy Kingdom Come!

After losing the war in heaven, Satan and his angels were cast down to the earth. Out of its abyss, foreign spirits entered mankind. (Rev. 12:9) *Woe unto the inhabiters of the earth and of the sea! for the devil is come down unto you, having great wrath, because he knoweth that he hath but a short time (in Rev. 12:12).*

Each kingdom was known by its capital city, the throne of its empire. The sixth kingdom was Rome, crushing all that opposed her. Unlike the other parts of the idol, its feet came out of Rome

What about Dreams?

when the iron mingled with the seed of men and broke its lands into pieces to destroy their strength. At last its ten toes were also weakened by the mixture. When the iron kingdom mingled with the seed of men, it weakened the iron and divided the clay, proving its power was not of clay, but of iron.

Huns terrorized Europa with no objectives but to murder, rape, and pillage. Ancient historians said Huns were "evil beasts who emerged from the wilderness to wreak havoc on civilization."[91] Even secular writers called them "devils."

Odoacer was a Hunnic general in Rome's army who deposed the last emperor, Romulus Augustus in 476.[92] Unable to manage the sprawling Hunnic Empire after Attila died, his tribes had disbanded years before. Most tribes had spread through Europa, but the Huns had gone to Germania and Austria, intermarried and raised families, creating divisions among the people.[93]

After World War One, ten kings received their nations, which they would give to the red dragon.[94] At the end of World War Two, he gave his throne to the beast that was like a leopard with a mouth like a lion and feet like a bear. It wasn't his idea to lose the greatest war of all on account of the Jews. It was God's plan. Today Israel's war and ours is with invisible forces. We see flesh and blood, but our war is not with what we see, but against the powers of darkness:

> [10] Finally, my brethren, be strong in the Lord, and in the power of his might. [11] Put on the whole armor of God, that ye may be able to stand against the wiles of the devil. [12] For we wrestle not against flesh and blood, but against principalities, against powers, against the rulers of the darkness of this world, against spiritual wickedness in high *places*. (Eph. 6:10-12)

The dragon has taken most of Eurasia with his kings. He'll unite the East and West to gain their worship. He's losing time and is frantic to achieve his goal. As the terrible beast, he nearly wiped out the Jews but lost his throne and faced the Judge who sent him to perdition and gave the Jews the Kingdom (in Dan. 7:18). The victims received their victories by the Name they'd profaned (in Rev.17:14)—what abundant grace!

An evil world serves Satan, hating the name and the nature of God, but that doesn't change the goodness of God. Slanderers and liars continue to the end, but we look up to the Lord who helps and strengthens us. We cast our cares on Him by faith, for without faith, we can't please God. (Heb. 11:6)

The nations are coming together as the whole statue for a common cause—to annihilate Israel and destroy the Christian faith, trying to turn the faithfulness of God into a lie. The statue of Babylon the Great stands tall till the end of this age when the Stone that strikes its feet and toes becomes a great mountain that reigns over all the earth. Though men pursue the depths of hell, the light of God's words prevail for eternity.

Mystery Babylon is the statue's gold head, its capital city, its great international throne. Imagine kings joining a plot with their enemies to destroy the only nation God calls His own. They say they are wise but are fools, giving in to depraved lusts, unnatural affections, and reprobate minds. (Rom. 1:18-32)

The European Union is divided. They are only united by the ten kings who agree to give their kingdom to the dragon (in Rev. 17:16-17). Jihadists and others are altering Europe. Each influx of violent extremists means more divisions, but the dragon's kings will force their union by conforming them to do their will with their most effective weapons of warfare: fear and deception.

In the days of the seven heads, or mountains, in Revelation 17, men were empowered by far greater forces than the ten horns that received their kingdoms after WW1, but the power of the later kings is in their weaponry, not in their authority. Now the end of all flesh on earth is possible. The ten lesser kings are far more destructive than those who reigned before them; yet this was prophesied many centuries before it was comprehensible.

All nations have entered Babylon. Its image symbolizes all kingdoms—from the east to the west—till the seed of men has mingled with the iron at the end of the age so that all of them fall together, crushed by the Stone of Israel.

> [43] As you saw iron mixed with ceramic clay, they will mingle with the seed of men; but they will not adhere to one another, just as iron does not mix with clay. [44] And <u>in the days of these kings</u> the God of heaven shall set up a kingdom which shall never be destroyed; and the kingdom shall <u>not be left to other people</u>; it shall break in pieces and consume all these kingdoms, and it shall stand forever. (Dan. 2:43-44 NKJV)

What about Dreams?

After 1920 the ten nations were unable to unite against Hitler since their kings were in union with the dragon (in Rev. 17:12-13). Their iron mixed with the seed of men to weaken and divide them till the dragon ruled them. It's been replicated in America.

A false politico-religious empire rises for the dragon's fourth kingdom, Mystery Babylon (in Rev. 13–18), looking like a savior to religious people, but its nations are united against God's Lamb.

> [11] And I saw heaven opened, and behold a white horse; and he that sat upon him was called Faithful and True, and in righteousness he doth judge and make war. [12] His eyes were as a flame of fire, and on his head were many crowns; and he had a name written, that no man knew, but he himself. [13] And he was clothed with a vesture dipped in blood: and his name is called The Word of God. [14] And the armies which were in heaven followed him upon white horses, clothed in fine linen, white and clean. [15] And out of his mouth goeth a sharp sword, that with it he should smite the nations: and he shall rule them with a rod of iron: and he treadeth the winepress of the fierceness and wrath of Almighty God. [16] And he hath on his vesture and on his thigh a name written, KING OF KINGS, AND LORD OF LORDS. (Rev. 19:11-16)

The Stone that bruised the dragon's head will win again. The once rejected Cornerstone crushes the clay, iron, bronze, silver, and gold <u>together as one</u>, turning them to dust, strewn to the wind, and forgotten: *Then was the iron, the clay, the brass, the silver, and the gold, <u>broken to pieces together</u>, and became like the chaff of the summer threshing floors; and the wind carried them away, that no place was found for them: and the stone that smote the image became a great mountain, and filled the whole earth. (Dan. 2:35)* The gold head of Babylon the Great falls at last, and Jerusalem rises above all the mountains on earth.

The seven heads are seven mountains. Jerusalem is destined to be the highest mountain of all. (Is. 2:1-3, p. 188) In His eternal love for her, it's how Yeshua sees His Bride. Though deserted for nearly two thousand years, her people have returned to her, fulfilling the prophecies. The Word of God causes things to exist before they appear because *the testimony of Jesus is the Spirit of prophecy (in Rev. 19:10).*

The Revelation

UNVEILED!

Part 2

The Revelation of Jesus Christ

And he said to me, "Do not seal the words of the prophecy of this book, for the time is at hand.
(Rev. 22:10 NKJV)

The Revelation

Prologue

The Mystery of Babylon

After the flood, Noah set up an altar for thank offerings, but three generations later, his great-grandson became a founder of cities and promoted the sculpting of idols. Nimrod, the eighth in the line of Cush the son of Ham, built an infamous tower. Defiantly, the king was rebuilding the culture that was destroyed, provoking God who remembered the grace He'd promised Noah: He'd never again destroy the whole world with a flood.

By wisdom the LORD had a plan. Dividing their speech into many languages, He confused the city and scattered its people across the earth. They resettled, founding cities that grew into nations. *He hath shown strength with his arm; he hath scattered the proud in the imagination of their hearts. (Lk. 1:51)*

Under Nimrod, the "Babel–onians" built a tower to reach to the heavens as Lucifer had done by coveting the throne of God. Though they left Babel, she never left them.

And they said, Go to, let us build us a city and a tower whose top may reach unto heaven ... (Gen 11:4a) God spoke to Lucifer: *For thou hast said in thine heart, I will ascend into heaven, I will exalt my throne above the stars of God... I will ascend above the heights of the clouds; I will be like the most High. (Is. 14:13a, 14)*

The historian Josephus wrote that Nimrod built the tower to be higher than the floodwaters to thwart any plans of God for another deluge. He noted they'd "used tar for mortar" to waterproof its walls.[95] (See Gen 11:3) Nimrod knew that Noah and his sons coated the ark *with pitch to float.* He did not doubt the historicity of the flood. Its story was repeated by many ancient cultures as a result of their ancestors' migration from Babel.[96]

Babel's civilization scattered across the earth, influencing the world. After Babylon's Baal and Nebo, Greeks worshiped Satan as Zeus. (Rev. 2:13) Enthroned in Babylon Nebo was their "god of science and learning, writer of destiny." But Isaiah prophesied that Nebo [Satan] himself was destined for captivity (in Is. 46:1-2; Rev. 20:1-3).

Nebuchadnezzar is translated, *"Nebo protect the servant," or "Nebo protect the border."* Until his madness the king trusted in Nebo, the false god of his ancestors. In Daniel 2, the head of the idol was its king's, but till that time, Nebo [Lucifer] was his king.[97] Nevertheless, when he called out to God He answered.

The Revelation

11 Now the whole earth had one language and one speech. ² And it came to pass, as they journeyed from the east, that they found a plain in the land of Shinar, and they dwelt there. ³ Then they said to one another, "Come, let us make bricks and bake *them* thoroughly." They had brick for stone, and they had asphalt for mortar. ⁴ And they said, "Come, let us build ourselves a city, and a tower whose top *is* in the heavens; let us make a name for ourselves, lest we be scattered abroad over the face of the whole earth."
⁵ But the LORD came down to see the city and the tower which the sons of men had built. ⁶ And the LORD said, "Indeed the people *are* one and they all have one language, and this is what they begin to do; now nothing that they propose to do will be withheld from them. ⁷ Come, let Us go down and there confuse their language, that they may not understand one another's speech." ⁸So the LORD scattered them abroad from there over the face of all the earth, and they ceased building the city. ⁹Therefore its name is called Babel, because there the LORD confused the language of all the earth; and from there the LORD scattered them abroad over the face of all the earth. (Gen. 11:1-9 NKJV)

Josephus wrote, "The place wherein they built the tower is now called *Babylon* because of the confusion of that language which they readily understood before; for this reason it was that the city was called *Babylon*; for the Hebrews mean by the word *Babel*, 'Confusion.'" [98]

⁸ Cush begot Nimrod; he began to be a mighty one on the earth. ⁹ He was a mighty hunter before the LORD; therefore it is said, "Like Nimrod the mighty hunter before the LORD." ¹⁰ And the beginning of his kingdom was Babel, Erech, Accad, and Calneh, in the land of Shinar. (Gen. 10:8-10 NKJV)

The Biblical evidence of Babel's original location is seen in the Hebrew name *Zerubbabel*, or *zerub Babel*, translated, "shoot of Babylon."[99] Conceived in Babylon during the captivity of the Jews, his name reveals the original site of the city. Archeologists dispute its location today, yet from its tower, men had defied God and fled in confusion.

Prologue

Here's a scholarly explanation: In 1906 Theophilus Pinches, Assyriology* professor at UC of London, wrote an essay about Nimrod and his worship as king of the gods. According to Pinches, idolatry was practiced in Babel. [Page numbers are from the essay.] Pinches refers to the most ancient epic poetry, *Gilgamesh:* "The tenth chapter of Genesis tells us of the story of Nimrod, who cannot be any other than the Merodach of the Assyro-Babylonian inscriptions [of Gilgamesh] ... but the god of Merodach, if he be, as seems certain, a deified Babylonian king, must have been identified with the stars that bear his name after his worshippers began to pay him the divine honor as the supreme deity. (pp. 12-13) "The Greeks called the Babylonian Merodach by the name of Zeus ... concerning the importance of Babylon, Merodach's city, later on, there is no doubt whatever. (p. 16) ... "The great cities and the temple towers were pervaded by the god whose abode they were. (p. 17) "With the Babylonians, the gods were represented as stone at an early date, and it's possible that wood was also used. (p. 21) "All the great cities of Babylonia were sacred places, the chief in renown and importance in later days being the great city of Babylon, where Esagila, 'the temple of the foundation of heaven and earth' held first place. This building is called by Nebuchadnezzar, 'the temple tower of Babylon,' and may be better regarded as the site of the ... 'Tower of Babel.'" (p. 23) [100] [*Assyriology is the study of the history, language, and antiquities of Assyria and Babylon.]

Babel's king, Nimrod, had a role in *Gilgamesh* as *Baal,* or "lord."[101] *Beelzebub* means "lord of flies" or "lord of dung." [102] In its poetry, Satan ruled Babel as Nimrod, the eighth listed in the lineage of Cush, son of Ham, son of Noah (in Gen. 10:7-8).

The third expert witness of Babylon as Babel shows a mortal king who was worshiped and idolized. Throughout history, kings have demanded worship. Some made idols and built towers "to heaven" as Nimrod, their forerunner, had done. People are awed by skyscrapers, but exalting these things is idolatry.

"Babylon" is the Greek transliteration of the Hebrew, *Babel.* In Jewish tradition, the Tower of Babel was destroyed, but when Jews were captives in Babylon, they "recognized it in the famous temple of Belus, the present *Birs Nimrud,* a huge mound, about two hundred fifty feet high and twenty-three hundred feet in circumference, situated west of Hillah on the Euphrates." [103]

The Revelation

Straddling both sides of its river, Babylon contained the temple of Belus [Bel/Baal] and its city Hillah. Approximately two hundred square miles, Babylon's perimeter is fifty-six miles, larger than NYC—a fourth witness, revealing Babylon as Babel.

It's a Conspiracy!

Unseen kings, powers, and principalities have been striving for millennia. Our warfare is with the evil ones, not with mortals. The interventions of God affect events by prayers of saints who agree with His Word; but its prophecies must be fulfilled for the great tribulation of the martyrs and saints who were chosen for the first harvest of believers at Christ's appearing.

We must believe God rather than men. We can only expose the darkness by knowing the truth. The words of God enlighten us who receive them because His words are like the light of day.

Lucifer is translated, "brightness." He was the light carrier in heaven and even now disguises himself as an angel of light, pleasure, and truth, but the envious one reigns in the darkness by deception and fear.[104] (2 Cor. 11:13-15)

As king of Babel, he'd influenced Egypt, Assyria, Babylon, Persia, Greece, Rome—Israel, and the church! False prophets rose by him. England, France, Germany, Europe, all of Asia, America—now all the world is affected by his deceit. Babylon has persuaded the world against God by her spirit. The dragon's throne is the mystery the scarlet beast carries in chapter 17.

When the Medes and Persians defeated her empire, Babylon influenced their people, which was natural since they'd begun in her. The Greeks adopted their culture in the Seleucid Dynasty. Their empire "was basically a Babylonian one with a Greek veneer—but Babylonian to the core."[105] After Alexander the Great, the Seleucids were known as "Babylonian kings," reigning over the land of Nimrod, calling themselves by Lucifer's title, "king of Babylon." (Is. 14:3-20)

Babylon's effect on the Persian, Greek, and Roman worlds was tangible. Their kings gained a motherland from those before them, but Babylon birthed them all. Romans and Greeks bowed to Baal, the Babylonian "god of gods," aka Zeus by the Greeks and Jupiter by the Romans.[106] Worshiping idols, men received devils and became savages.

Prologue

From the Mediterranean Sea to Persia, they adored Baal. The Seleucids embraced the worship of false gods and constructed the Temple of Zeus. (Rev. 2:13) Their gods fascinated Romans who visited its altar. Greek and Roman artisans made their living from sculpting images for their wealthy clients and depended on the popularity of idols for an income. Israel fell by worshiping such false gods, just as the institutional church did, but idols are nothing to us if our hearts are true to Jesus Christ.

Soon after their journey through the wilderness, the Hebrews turned to the nations and became rebellious and immoral, even sacrificing their children to Baal. How Israelites suffered when they turned from God! They were nearly destroyed but were saved because God keeps His promises to the forefathers.

Antiochus IV in Jerusalem

The Hellenized Jews received Antiochus the Great (III) into Jerusalem and refreshed his beasts. He spoke favorably of them for this in letters to his colleagues.[107]

Forced out of Egypt by the Roman army, in 167 BC his son Antiochus IV [called *Epiphanes* or, "God Manifest"] entered the temple in Jerusalem to set up an idol of Zeus, commanding his own worship as God. He burned Hebrew scrolls, outlawed the Mosaic covenant, and ravaged Judea with a great slaughter.[108]

Exalted as the "god of gods," the eighth Seleucid king spoke like a dragon. Yeshua said it returns before He does: *When ye therefore shall see the abomination of desolation, spoken of by Daniel the prophet, stand in the holy place, (whoso readeth, let him understand:) (Mat. 24:15)* A king like Antiochus rises as *the abomination of the desolation* once more.

Mystery Babylon has the attributes of the ancient city God cursed. Although Babylon can't rise again, the spirit of her evil culture still dominates nations and seduces leaders. In 1945 she seduced Germany and fell, crushed with Berlin, but was healed.

[19] And Babylon, the glory of kingdoms, the beauty of the Chaldees' excellency, shall be as when God overthrew Sodom and Gomorrah. [20] It shall never be inhabited, neither shall it be dwelt in from generation to generation: neither shall the Arabian pitch tent there; neither shall the shepherds make their fold there. (Is. 13:19-20)

The Revelation

Knowing the end is at hand, devils stalk the world to kill, steal, and destroy. God is testing hearts; who will agree with the deceivers and destroyers? They know a kingdom cannot stand when it's divided against itself and are determined to destroy the saints and the nations. They achieve their goals by deceiving and dividing us or else by deceiving and uniting us to deceive others.

The truth is the only weapon we have to defeat the powers of darkness. If we think we can't know the truth, we'll believe lies, and if we think we know it by what we've been taught, we are already deceived. The Word and the Holy Spirit, its Author, are the true light. And these two are One.

The prophecies must take place, but believers must also gain victories to receive their crowns. After recognizing our enemy, we should expose his darkness by the truth. When we understand the Word and speak by its faith, we shine like a light on a hill.

Beware of habitual or addictive sins, the personal deceivers, and of teachings that contradict the Word and indoctrinate the churches. We must believe God and please Him rather than those who appeal to our natural desires. We will be tempted to unite irrespective of the truth, but *this is the condemnation, that light is come into the world, and men loved darkness rather than light because their deeds were evil. (Jn. 3:19)* If we love the truth, we will be saved. Jesus is *the way, the truth, and the life (in Jn. 14:6).* Shunning none of it, discerning and believing the truth is crucial to knowing the Word of God.

Teachers who don't guard their hearts can turn the ears of men to myths. Deceiving spirits repeat their lies to instill them in their listeners till they indoctrinate us. When the Bible challenges our faith, it warns us of our false beliefs. It's difficult to see from inside the box, but the Scriptures are not limited by its walls. <u>The light of the words that confuse us exposes the strongholds that prevent us from believing them</u>. If we tear down the strongholds to believe God alone, we'll understand His words.

> 4 I solemnly charge *you* in the presence of God and of Christ Jesus, who is to judge the living and the dead, and by His appearing and His kingdom: [2] preach the word; be ready in season *and* out of season; reprove, rebuke, exhort, with great patience and instruction. [3] For the time will come when they will not endure sound doctrine; but *wanting* to have their ears tickled, they will

Prologue

accumulate for themselves teachers in accordance to <u>their own desires</u>, ⁴ and will turn away their ears from the truth and will turn aside to myths. (2 Tim. 4:1-4 NASB)

Midnight is here. We must expose the darkness by the truth. At this hour, the enemy is wild with rage. Devils frenetically rush in furious confusion. It's happening all around us. It was foreseen by the prophets. When deceit is rampant, God sends a great delusion to all who refuse to believe the truth. (2 Thes. 2:11)

It's the end of the gentile age. We're facing great tribulation, and afterward the sun turns black and the moon turns red and the stars fall from the sky and the powers of the heavens are shaken. Then Jesus Christ appears with the great trumpet's sound. When we see the signs of His coming, He tells us, "Look up." We're pregnant with hope until He descends on a cloud and we shake off the dust to meet Him in the air! (See 1Thes. 4:16-17)

Now let's study the differences in the beasts—their crowns, their heads, and their horns, indicating their times, their places, and their positions throughout history. We'll review some things about *the beast which was, is not, and yet is*, and *the beast that is the eighth of the seven.* Throughout Revelation we'll learn even more: we'll discover the eras of the trumpets and the bowls and know what to expect in advance of their arrivals.

History's events have taken millennia to transpire, yet not many words fill the timelines; they took no time from eternity. Since prophecy is the knowledge of events before their time, it's helpful to have a sense of time's elasticity as we look into them.

Imagine how centuries seem from heaven's view. Prophecies foretell their eras that way. When history fulfills them, the reality of their words should wake us up to believe them. We must read *The Revelation of Jesus Christ* by faith in its Author. There's no other way to understand its words.

This particular prophetic book was unsealed millennia ago. As Jesus our Lord said, He gives the hidden manna to him who overcomes. It's not a free lunch, and we shouldn't expect to eat its manna by struggling for years to figure it out. It belongs to him who overcomes.

Yeshua won the war over Death the day He rose from the depths of hell to the Father's right side in heaven. From that holy place, He opened the seals of the scroll for its *Apocalypse*.

The Revelation

The Revelation of Jesus Christ

CHAPTER 1

1 The revelation from Jesus Christ, which God gave him to show his servants what must soon take place. He made it known by sending his angel to his servant John, **2** who testifies to everything he saw—that is, the word of God and the testimony of Jesus Christ. **3** Blessed is the one who reads aloud the words of this prophecy, and blessed are those who hear it and take to heart what is written in it, because the time is near.

4 John,
To the seven churches in the province of Asia:

Grace and peace to you from him who is, and who was, and who is to come, and from the seven spirits before his throne, **5** and from Jesus Christ, who is the faithful witness, the firstborn from the dead, and the ruler of the kings of the earth.

To him who loves us and has freed us from our sins by his blood, **6** and has made us to be a kingdom and priests to serve his God and Father—to him be glory and power for ever and ever! Amen.

7 "Look, he is coming with the clouds,"
  and "every eye will see him,
  even those who pierced him";
  and all peoples on earth "will mourn because of him."
  So shall it be! Amen.

8 "I am the Alpha and the Omega," says the Lord God, "who is, and who was, and who is to come, the Almighty."

9 I, John, your brother and companion in the suffering and kingdom and patient endurance that are ours in Jesus, was on the island of Patmos because of the word of God and the testimony of Jesus. **10** On the Lord's Day I was in the Spirit, and I heard behind me a loud voice like a trumpet, **11** which said: "Write on a scroll what you see and send it to the seven churches: to Ephesus, Smyrna, Pergamum, Thyatira, Sardis, Philadelphia, and Laodicea."

12 I turned around to see the voice that was speaking to me. And when I turned I saw seven golden lampstands, **13** and among the lampstands was someone like a son of

The Revelation

man, dressed in a robe reaching down to his feet and with a golden sash around his chest. ¹⁴ The hair on his head was white like wool, as white as snow, and his eyes were like blazing fire. ¹⁵ His feet were like bronze glowing in a furnace, and his voice was like the sound of rushing waters. ¹⁶ In his right hand he held seven stars, and coming out of his mouth was a sharp, double-edged sword. His face was like the sun shining in all its brilliance.

¹⁷ When I saw him, I fell at his feet as though dead. Then he placed his right hand on me and said: "Do not be afraid. I am the First and the Last. ¹⁸ I am the Living One; I was dead, and now look, I am alive for ever and ever! And I hold the keys of death and Hades. ¹⁹ "Write, therefore, what you have seen, what is now and what will take place later. ²⁰ The mystery of the seven stars that you saw in my right hand and of the seven golden lampstands is this: The seven stars are the angels of the seven churches, and the seven lampstands are the seven churches. (Revelation 1:1-20 NIV)

Insights

The Father gave the revelation to Jesus Christ to impart it to His faithful servant John who would pass it on to the messengers of the churches in Asia, now SW Turkey.[109] Writing the words of Messiah, the apostle takes no credit, but glorifies the One who freed us from our sins by His blood to serve His God and Father.

Jesus Christ is the Man uniquely fathered when the Word of God was born in the flesh as His Son. The prophet Nathan spoke as the oracle of God, foretelling the descendant of David who'd be born the Son of God: *I will be to him a father, and he shall be to me a son. (in 2 Sam. 7:12-14)* By faith the virgin received the Word of God in her seed, forming the unique Son from David's lineage. (Is. 7:14; Lk. 3:23-38; Lk. 1:35; John 1) He is the eternal Word from God's heart to mankind. (Jn. 14: 9-11; 16:13-15, 28)

His Word is the Reason for all that exists; thus within all that exists is His reason. With words as thoughts, He speaks to us. As the Word, He brings purpose and reality into existence. He is the Life; apart from Him, nothing has life. He made everything out of nothing by His Wisdom *so that things which are seen were not made out of things which do appear.* **(Heb. 11:3b)** And His

Insights: Chapter 1

power holds it all together. He gives nature its order, symmetry, and design throughout the expanding universe. Everything that exists came from nothing but the Word of God. Atoms were formed by the power, brilliance, and energy of His Word. He is nature's Lawmaker and life's Breath. (Rom. 1:18-25; Col. 1:16-17)

His Word brings clarity to the obscure and wisdom to the fool. In Yeshua men see the Word of God by the Light that pierces spiritual darkness. He invades, disrupts, and overcomes whatever rebels against its Maker. (2 Pet. 3:10-13)

He overcame Death and Hell and is therefore worthy to open the Revelation (in 5:5). As a man His God is our God. The Son of God and of man is our Mediator, our "go-between," reconciling us to God by His blood in the new covenant. (Jer. 31:31-33) No other mediator exists between God and man (in 1 Tim. 2:5).

Conceived by the virgin's seed, the Son of David was born, but His biological Father was the Spirit of God. (Gal. 3:19-20; 1 Tim. 2:5; Heb. 8:6, 9:15; Is. 7:14; 2 Sam. 7:12-16) Few rabbis could imagine David's seed would be the seed of a woman, but God had made His plan known from the beginning. (Gen. 3:15)

His own people rejected Him and gave Him over to Roman soldiers who beat Him with rods, scourged Him with whips, and crucified the Lamb of God who paid for our sins as though He had done the wrongs:

> [12] When your days are fulfilled and you lie down with your fathers, I will raise up your offspring after you, who shall come from your body, and I will establish his kingdom. [13] He shall build a house for my name, and I will establish the throne of his kingdom forever. [14] <u>I will be to him a father, and he shall be to me a son</u>. When he commits iniquity, I will discipline him with the rod of men, with the stripes of the sons of men, [15] but my steadfast love will not depart from him, as I took it from Saul, whom I put away from before you. [16] And your house and your kingdom shall be made sure forever before me. Your throne shall be established forever.'" (2 Sam. 7:12-16 ESV)

> [7] He was oppressed, and he was afflicted, yet he opened not his mouth: he is brought as a lamb to the slaughter, and as a sheep before her shearers is dumb, so he opened not his mouth. He was taken from prison and from judgment, and who shall declare his generation? for

The Revelation

he was cut off out of the land of the living: for the transgression of my people was he stricken. (Is. 53:7-8)

²¹ For our sake he made him to be sin who knew no sin, so that in him we might become the righteousness of God. (2 Cor. 5:21 ESV)

God suffers long and is kind. He laughs and He mourns. He is pleased or angered. He felt His Son's pain, and He knows our pain. Israel tore His heart, and yet He sees their tears and wipes them dry. God is compassionate but, in judgment and in wrath, is untouched by His adversaries. (Ps. 2:1-5; Ps. 37; Prov. 1:22-33; Mat. 13:41-43; 23; 24:45-51; 25:29-30; Mk. 9:44-49; Rev. 18:1-20)

We who truly believe take His words to the world, living by them and telling the true gospel till Jesus comes. Each one must do his part without envy or selfish ambition.

⁹ And be found in him, not having mine own righteousness, which is of the law, but that which is through the faith of Christ, the righteousness which is of God by faith: (Phl. 3:9)

The One amid the Lamps

... Christ the power of God, and the wisdom of God. Because the foolishness of God is wiser than men; and the weakness of God is stronger than men." (1 Cor. 1:24b-25) The Holy Spirit came upon Yeshua in the Jordan to empower Him in our weakness for He came in the *likeness of sinful flesh. (Rom. 8:3-4)* He rose from the dead for us and is exalted above all others.

The apostle John knew the Son of God as the eternal Word in mortal flesh, born as the perfect Sacrifice. At Pentecost Peter spoke to Jews in Jerusalem, saying, *Repent and be baptized ... in the name of Jesus Christ for the remission of sins, and ye shall receive the gift of the Holy Ghost. (from Acts 2:38) ... For verily he took not on him the nature of angels: but he took on him the seed of Abraham. (Heb. 2:16; cf. 2 Sam. 7:12-16)* He indwells us by the same Spirit for believers to know Him.

In the fear of God, we turn from evil, but if we spurn the fear of God, we'll die in our sins. He Himself feared God, and His cry was heard from Gethsemane. (Heb. 5:7) We can't love Him and remain in sin, but shunning sin, we overcome it by the power and authority of Jesus Christ. He lives in us to give life to our

Insights: Chapter 1

bodies by victory over our sinful nature. As we live by faith, we yield to the nature of His Spirit, and the nature of our flesh dies.

He expressed the Father by His Word in our mortal flesh as the Son of man with the fullness of the Spirit and the Word in Him. He said, ... *If I go not away, the Comforter will not come unto you; but if I depart, I will send him unto you. (from Jn. 16:7)* Had He remained, He could not have come to us. Yeshua relied on His Father for wisdom, power, and authority, yet is One with the Father as His Word; God is Spirit. He was the Word in the Spirit in the beginning, hovering over the face of the waters. (Gen. 1:2) And He's the Word of God today, the eternal Truth in the unchanging nature of God, which enters us by His Word.

The voice John heard behind him stunned the apostle *like the sound of a trumpet* alerting him. Suddenly, he was *in the Spirit*—what does that mean? There's another dimension to life, which is not of this world. John was instantly there!

Jesus is the Revelator who showed His glory to the prophet who wrote down visions for generations to search out. His truth convicts our hearts and transforms our lives, so we trust in these words though John wrote them two thousand years ago as an eyewitness of the Son of God. The prophets before him had written about Jesus. Then John saw their words fulfilled in part.

Every word of God is life to us, but hypocrites profess the faith without acting on His words by faith. Each time we receive His words and allow them to change our hearts, we turn from the darkness of our hypocrisies to the light of His truth.

Yeshua holds *the keys of death and hell (in Rev. 1:18)* since He is the Word of God: *⁴And I say unto you my friends, Be not afraid of them that kill the body, and after that have no more that they can do. ⁵But I will forewarn you whom ye shall fear: Fear him, which after he hath killed, hath power to cast into hell. (Lk. 12:4-5)* The Almighty said, *I kill, and I make alive. (Dt. 32:39)*

When meteorologists describe tornadoes, earthquakes, wildfires, floods, hurricanes, lightning strikes, radical temperatures, droughts, volcanoes, tsunamis, and infestations, they remind us, though not far off, God is in control and judges nations:

¹⁹ Behold, <u>a whirlwind of the LORD is gone forth in fury, even a grievous whirlwind: it shall fall grievously upon the head of the wicked.</u> ²⁰ The anger of the LORD shall

The Revelation

not return, until he have executed, and till he have performed the thoughts of his heart: <u>in the latter days ye shall consider it perfectly</u>. ²¹ I have not sent these prophets, yet they ran: I have not spoken to them, yet they prophesied. ²² But if they had stood in my counsel, and had caused my people to hear my words, then they should have turned them from their evil way, and from the evil of their doings. ²³ <u>Am I a God at hand, saith the LORD, and not a God afar off</u>? (Jer. 23:19-23)

We teach God cares about each of us but often believe He neglects the nations and doesn't control the weather very well either. Maybe we haven't believed in His greatness at all.

The first to read and hear this book, the seven churches, were far from perfect congregations but were made examples for us, wherever their practices exist—even in the most sinful places as the church in Pergamon was. The churches were in a perilous moral condition by the influence of an ungodly culture, tempting them to compromise their godly values.

What would we be like if we were to believe we're eternally secure no matter what we do? Yet most of us have believed that and have no fear of God, wondering why we must repent. We've taken in the world and have become like it, participating with its ways by our acceptance of them. That is not true Christianity, but hypocrisy that comes by the apostasy.

The last verses of its first chapter prepare us for more of the mysteries in Revelation: past, present, and future events to John, many of which are history to us while some are daily news and others are yet to come. (See 1:19) Many of us are bored by the Word, but to be bored is to be blind to its contents. It's an irony.

Speaking to the congregations, Jesus addresses each of us in a personal way. His instructions are for everyone with an ear to hear, receive, repent, and obey the warnings of His words since that's what it means to believe. *He that hath an ear, let him hear what the Spirit saith unto the churches. (Rev. 2:29)* It's personal. He speaks to you and me. Although the Lord often hides the treasures of His Kingdom, He unsealed His *Apocalypse* for the one who overcomes to read, hear, and believe.

The Revelation of Jesus Christ

CHAPTER 2

2 "To the angel of the church of Ephesus write,

'These things says He who holds the seven stars in His right hand, who walks in the midst of the seven golden lampstands: ² "I know your works, your labor, your patience, and that you cannot bear those who are evil. And you have tested those who say they are apostles and are not, and have found them liars; ³ and you have persevered and have patience, and have labored for My name's sake and have not become weary. ⁴ Nevertheless I have *this* against you, that you have left your first love. ⁵ Remember therefore from where you have fallen; repent and do the first works, or else I will come to you quickly and remove your lampstand from its place—unless you repent. ⁶ But this you have, that you hate the deeds of the Nicolaitans, which I also hate.

⁷ "He who has an ear, let him hear what the Spirit says to the churches. To him who overcomes I will give to eat from the tree of life, which is in the midst of the Paradise of God."'

⁸ "And to the angel of the church in Smyrna write,

'These things says the First and the Last, who was dead, and came to life: ⁹ "I know your works, tribulation, and poverty (but you are rich); and *I know* the blasphemy of those who say they are Jews and are not, but *are* a synagogue of Satan. ¹⁰ Do not fear any of those things which you are about to suffer. Indeed, the devil is about to throw *some* of you into prison, that you may be tested, and you will have tribulation ten days. Be faithful until death, and I will give you the crown of life.

¹¹ "He who has an ear, let him hear what the Spirit says to the churches. He who overcomes shall not be hurt by the second death."'

¹² "And to the angel of the church in Pergamos write,

'These things says He who has the sharp two-edged sword: ¹³ "I know your works, and where you dwell, where Satan's throne *is*. And you hold fast to My name, and did not deny My faith even in the days in which Antipas *was* My faithful martyr, who was killed among

The Revelation

you, where Satan dwells. ¹⁴ But I have a few things against you, because you have there those who hold the doctrine of Balaam, who taught Balak to put a stumbling block before the children of Israel, to eat things sacrificed to idols, and to commit sexual immorality. ¹⁵ Thus you also have those who hold the doctrine of the Nicolaitans, which thing I hate. ¹⁶ Repent, or else I will come to you quickly and will fight against them with the sword of My mouth.

¹⁷ "He who has an ear, let him hear what the Spirit says to the churches. To him who overcomes I will give some of the hidden manna to eat. And I will give him a white stone, and on the stone a new name written which no one knows except him who receives *it*.'"

¹⁸ "And to the angel of the church in Thyatira write,

'These things says the Son of God, who has eyes like a flame of fire, and His feet like fine brass: ¹⁹ "I know your works, love, service, faith, and your patience; and *as* for your works, the last *are* more than the first. ²⁰ Nevertheless I have a few things against you, because you allow that woman Jezebel, who calls herself a prophetess, to teach and seduce My servants to commit sexual immorality and eat things sacrificed to idols. ²¹ And I gave her time to repent of her sexual immorality, and she did not repent. ²² Indeed I will cast her into a sickbed, and those who commit adultery with her into great tribulation, unless they repent of their deeds. ²³ I will kill her children with death, and all the churches shall know that I am He who searches the minds and hearts. And I will give to each one of you according to your works.

²⁴ "Now to you I say, and to the rest in Thyatira, as many as do not have this doctrine, who have not known the depths of Satan, as they say, I will put on you no other burden. ²⁵ But hold fast what you have till I come. ²⁶ And he who overcomes, and keeps My works until the end, to him I will give power over the nations.

²⁷ *'He shall rule them with a rod of iron;*
  They shall be dashed to pieces like
   the potter's vessels"—

as I also have received from My Father; ²⁸ "and I will give him the morning star. ²⁹ "He who has an ear, let him hear what the Spirit says to the churches." ' (Rev. 2:1-29 NKJV)

Insights: Chapter 2

Insights

Jesus commends the **Ephesian** congregation for recognizing the false apostles who would have led them astray from the true doctrines of salvation. Though they called themselves apostles, they were liars. They are among us today, leading congregations and audiences to believe lies that contradict the Bible. When lies are mixed with the truth, even the truth becomes suspect.

False teachers ignore the Word, rationalizing or embellishing it, leading multitudes into lies they purport are true. Deceptions are common, yet few recognize the apostasy that has increased to this day. The church is called to employ the gifts of the Spirit and to change the world by glorious works and holy speech.

Plenty of professing Christians and even scholars believe no one can know the truth, but in Ephesus they spotted heresies and stood against them. They persevered in the Holy Spirit, serving Yeshua by good works. He found no fault in that.

Though they labored without growing weary of doing good, the Lord was displeased because they'd left their first love, and the attitude of the heart was more important than all their godly works. They might have fallen away from their enthusiasm for the Word of God, which would have drawn them nearer to Him.

Has the fire in our hearts turned to ashes by other things that distract us from Him? Jesus was our first love. If we take time in prayer, serve others, and spread the gospel, do we take the time to search the Word of God and sit at Jesus' feet? Do we have *ears to hear* the Spirit who seeks to teach us?

Yeshua warns us to return to our first love, or He will move our lampstand from its place—a strong admonition! What would our nation be like without the church? *Remember therefore from whence thou art fallen, and repent and do the first works ... (1:5)*

After our new birth, we received His words and revelations of the Spirit but soon turned to men and saw Jesus second-hand through their eyes. This distanced us from the truth that the Spirit teaches in the Word of God. He wants us to believe and share the true gospel, discipling others as He did; but beyond that, to hear the voice we often shun. Like the Ephesians, we must repent.

He hates elitism in the church. Someone led the Ephesians to blend with the immoral culture. By their status in the church,

The Revelation

Nicolaitans persuaded some of them to sin. [Gr.: Niko+ *laos+ton*, means "power over people." [110]] Their attitude remains in churches today, but His Kingdom is unlike that. Jesus served others and lived in holiness as the Son of God, saying, "Follow me." He said He is the only Way that leads to life. Shunning His example is not an option. We can't love Him and exclude others.

His blood removes our shame and guilt, and He fills us with His righteousness. He opens our eyes and ears to see and hear. When we consider His words and receive them, they make their indelible mark in our hearts: *"He that hath an ear, let him hear what the Spirit saith unto the churches. (Rev. 2:29)* The one who overcomes by faith in Him is rewarded from the tree of life. (2:7)

Christ urged the believers in **Smyrna** to live and walk in His Spirit, enduring to the end. He knew the blasphemy of people who said they were Jews but were liars. They persecuted Jewish believers, *"speaking evil of them."* He called them *a synagogue of Satan (in 2:9)*, referring to Jews who sought to destroy them.

At Pentecost, thousands of Jews repented and believed in Yeshua. For some time, the believers were doing mighty works but were opposed by religious leaders while winning many Jews to repentance, baptizing them in the name of the Father, the Son, and the Holy Spirit while teaching them to obey His commands.

The Synagogue of the Freedmen falsely accused Stephen, a godly saint who testified to the Sanhedrin, the tribunal that led him out of the city and stoned him. Before his conversion Paul witnessed it, holding their coats as they killed him. (Acts 6:1-8:3)

Persecution increased in Jerusalem. Of all the believers, only the apostles stayed in the city. On his way to arrest them, Paul was arrested by God, chosen to discover the gospel in the scrolls and write about its new covenant. Thus Paul won the gentiles to Jesus and discipled the churches but never forgot the Jews.

After Paul's conversion the Jerusalem church enjoyed a time of peace. (Acts 9:1-30) The gospel multiplied in Galilee, Judea, and Samaria. (Acts 9:31) Paul went to synagogues every Shabbat. The *synagogue of Satan* disdained Jewish believers, yet Paul won converts in synagogues every Sabbath. (Acts 18:4) Like the church, the synagogue is its people, not just a building.

The Greek word for synagogue is *sunagogé*, an assembly or gathering. In the letter by Jacob [James], believers met together

Insights: Chapter 2

in the *sunagogé*. *(Jas. 2:2)* The earliest NT congregations were full of Jews who met on the Sabbath in synagogues, beginning with the assemblies in Jerusalem. (Acts 13:42; 18:4)

Persecution against the Jerusalem assemblies sent its saints into Judea and Samaria and then to the nations where multitudes of Jews believed. They confirmed the gospel by miracles and even won gentiles for Christ, unaware that Peter too was winning gentiles though his commission was to the Jews (in Gal. 2:7-8). Smyrna's church expected persecution, faithful to death to gain the crown of life. (Acts 11:19-23; also Acts 2:41; 4:4; 5:14; 8:1-3)

> ³ For I could wish that I myself were accursed, *separated* from Christ for the sake of my brethren, my kinsmen according to the flesh, ⁴ who are Israelites, to whom belongs the adoption as sons, and the glory and the covenants and the giving of the law and the *temple* service and the promises, ⁵ whose are the fathers, and from whom is the Christ according to the flesh, who is over all, God blessed forever. Amen. (Rom. 9:3-5 NASB)

Today many Jews hate Yeshua out of ignorance, blindness, and indoctrination as Paul had. Some Jews are raised to hate Jesus; many Arabs are raised to hate Jews; today people hate Christians too; atheists hate God. Men are divided from God and from one another by hatred and lies, but by His Son, God creates one new man as those who trust in Jesus' death and resurrection from all nations, all colors, and all ethnicities.

Some Jews respect Jesus, and many have believed in Him whose families reject them. His holy name is *anathema* to them. It cost Jewish lives for two-thousand years, yet they don't see it as the hand of God. It cost their killers too.

After celebrating Pentecost in the city, Jewish believers left for their homelands. Some began a congregation in Rome, and the gentiles joined them. When the city expelled Jews for dividing her culture, the economy fell, so she quickly took them back.

The Jews rejoined her now gentile church, and Paul taught them their part in the olive tree and corrected their differences.[111] False brothers had taught them doctrines of devils, telling them to return to Moses' laws, but he disdained the idea. What divides Jews from gentiles does not deliver them from sin; only the Holy Spirit can do that. It was why Jesus made all foods clean. (Acts

The Revelation

10:15; 15:22-29; Mat. 15:17-20; Mk. 7:14-23) Christ came to die for the sins of the world to make us all clean as one new man.

> ⁹ And David says,
>
> > "LET THEIR TABLE BECOME A SNARE AND A TRAP,
> > AND A STUMBLING BLOCK AND A RETRIBUTION TO THEM.
> > ¹⁰ "LET THEIR EYES BE DARKENED TO SEE NOT,
> > AND BEND THEIR BACKS FOREVER."
>
> ¹¹ I say then, they did not stumble so as to fall, did they? May it never be! But by their transgression salvation has come to the Gentiles, to make them jealous.
> (Rom. 11:9-11 NASB)

Since Yeshua makes the two one, we must not be divided by a kosher table—it's a trap! We're not under the law anymore; we're free to make choices, but let's walk in the Spirit, not rely on the works of the flesh. *Now we know that what things soever the law saith, <u>it saith to them who are under the law</u> that every mouth may be stopped, and all the world may become guilty before God. Therefore by the deeds of the law there shall no flesh be justified in his sight: for <u>by the law is the knowledge of sin</u>. (Rom. 3:19-20)*

God can easily make them Israel who are sons of Israel and can cut off those who cut off Israel. When Abraham heard God, not by the law or by human nature, but in the fear that perfected his faith, he obeyed, and his faith succeeded by his fear of God. Isn't it in the Word? (See Gen. 22:9-14) Search it out.

> ²⁰ You foolish man, do you want evidence that faith without deeds is useless? ²¹ Was not our ancestor Abraham considered righteous for what he did when he offered his son Isaac on the altar? ²² You see that his faith and his actions were working together, and his faith was made complete by what he did. ²³ And the scripture was fulfilled that says, "Abraham believed God, and it was credited to him as righteousness." ²⁴ <u>You see that a person is justified by what he does and not by faith alone</u>.
> (Jas. 2:20-24 NIV; cf. Gen. 15:6)

His faith *was credited to him as righteousness (in Gen. 15:6).* When that was written, it was known that Abraham had feared God and obeyed Him by offering his son, proving his faith.

Insights: Chapter 2

When Moses descended the mountain, he found the people in reckless sins and added the handwritten laws to return their hearts to God from Egypt. Those laws were nailed to the cross, but not His moral laws, which He writes, not on stone now, but in our hearts forever. There's a lot to learn about righteousness, governance, prophecy, faith, wisdom, morality, and justice in the Hebrew Bible, but none of us are under the Mosaic covenant.

God didn't tell the Jews what they wanted to hear, but spoke the truth. His words counsel us in all our trials, and His Spirit empowers our faith, but we can't be in Him unless the Spirit is in us. The Holy Spirit distinguishes us from the unbelieving world.

Paul addresses Smyrna's poverty and suffering but says they are spiritually rich. He doesn't lecture them on prosperity or on wealth management but encourages them in all their tribulations, trials, and hard times. If we suffer for the faith, enduring to the end, we receive the crown of life. Christ commands us to overcome the trials that test our faith. His Word goads us to *walk by faith* because faith must be active and living to be effective.

Jewish and gentile believers are in this grace together as one body (in Eph. 2:15-16). Smyrna's church experienced persecution, tribulation, and death, but Jesus promised, *He that hath an ear, let him hear what the Spirit saith unto the churches; he that overcometh shall not be hurt of the second death. (Rev.2:11)*

To the assembly in **Pergamos**, He speaks of His Word as sharper than a two-edged sword. It penetrates our hearts by its truth and with conviction. It's a weapon against sin. We should be careful to properly handle a two-edged sword.

The Word of God is in His Spirit, and His Spirit gives the Word its life: *For the word of God is quick and powerful, and sharper than any two-edged sword, piercing even to the dividing asunder of soul and spirit, and of the joints and marrow, and is a discerner of the thoughts and intents of the heart. (Heb. 4:12)*

When His words take root in our hearts, we live by faith in them through the Holy Spirit, not by the law. If we're under the law, we're obligated to it and are condemned because we can't keep it, but are always slaves to guilt. On the other hand, if we walk in the Spirit, we are free and blameless. (Rom. 8; Jn. 15) It could become a habit, walking in His righteousness!

The Revelation

Long before Christ, the king of Moab hired Balaam to curse the Israelites, but God refused to curse and made him bless them instead. (Jos. 13:22) [Soothsayers are for hire; prophets are not.]

The so-called prophet contrived a way for God to curse the Hebrews. He convinced Balak to lure them with idols and sexual immorality, knowing God would destroy all who did such things. (Rev. 2:14; Num. 31) Seduced by her friends, Israel paid a high price, but not all of them were destroyed. They'd been chosen to serve God, delivered from the slavery of the Egyptian culture.

We each are uniquely created, but if we are the focus of our ministries, we are in danger of Balaam's reward. For money the prophet led a king to tempt Israel to sin, hoping God would curse His own people to fill his own purse. Soothing their consciences, we tempt people into lethargy by pleasing them, but God would turn them from sin by alerting those *with ears to hear* His voice.

Pergamon was in the Roman Province, Asia [Turkey], when Greeks called themselves "Babylonian kings." [112] Jesus' servant Antipas was baked to death inside an idol by its worshipers in that city. Traditions tell us he sang praises to God, enduring to the end.[113] Jesus says, *He that hath an ear, let him hear what the Spirit saith unto the churches; To him that overcometh will I give to eat of the hidden manna, and will give him a white stone, and in the stone a new name written, which no man knoweth saving he that receiveth it. (Rev. 2:17)* [*Saving* is archaic for "except."]

To the angel of the assembly in **Thyatira**, He twice names their works, saying the last were greater than the first; however, though they had done good deeds, they'd ignored sexual sins. Does the grace of God ignore sin? Jesus would kill them if they didn't repent. He isn't a pushover.

Men He called "servants" were adulterating by a prophetess and eating foods sacrificed to idols. They were worse than the world. He cursed the woman on her bed and killed her children. No gentle Jesus there! He gave His life as a Lamb but is also a Lion. Can we continue in sin? Not at all. Repent or be lost.

Christ speaks about our thoughts: <u>*I am he which searcheth the minds and hearts*</u> *(in 2:23)*. We must not condemn ourselves, but should judge ourselves. If we sin, He's there at our return. There is great danger in the hardened heart that refuses to repent, continuing to sin until it's reprobate beyond remedy.

Insights: Chapter 2

⁹ No one born of God makes a practice of sinning, for God's seed abides in him; and he cannot keep on sinning, because he has been born of God.
(1 Jn. 3:9 ESV)

The prophetess' teachings were accepted in the congregation by men who relished her immoral ideas, but Jesus said, *I say unto you, That whosoever looketh on a woman to lust after her hath committed adultery with her already in his heart. (Mat. 5:28)*

His Spirit searches us out and judges our thoughts and deeds. We need the Holy Spirit to empower us over our sinful nature, to minister to one another's needs, and to reveal the works of Christ to the world around us.

He is our Righteousness when we repent and believe Jesus is alive and hears our prayers. Faith is trusting that if we confess our sins, He cleanses and empowers us to overcome them.

Some kept themselves holy, rejecting the prophetess' impure teachings. The Lord commanded them to get rid of her and her ideas and to hold onto good works till His return. Yeshua would kill her, but would they be rid of her words? Churches bring people together with similar beliefs, but only the truth can make us holy, not our agreements. These are matters of the mind.

The Word broaches the topic of sexuality by its required moral standards. Like salvation, it has responsibilities. Have we abused the gift by following our lusts and hiding under grace as we sin? How can we live apart from good works? Will He say, *Well done, thou good and faithful servant. ... Enter thou into the joy of thy Lord? (See Mat. 25:21* or, *Depart from me, ye that work iniquity? (from Mat. 7:23)* Don't bet your life on grace without works, and don't trust in works except by the Holy Spirit.

Sexual immorality is not sanctified in heterosexual marriage, including sodomy. If we are possessed by immoral ideas, we'll be lost in <u>our unbelief</u> in the God who sees us but is unseen. But if we consecrate our minds and hearts, we sanctify ourselves.

If our thoughts oppress us, we're not in sin though sin is in our flesh. Even so, we're in bondage, not yet free of the sin in our flesh. It's the carnal mind of Paul's cry for help in Romans 7, resolved by walking in the Spirit, not the flesh. The mind set on the Spirit is life; but the mind set on the flesh is death to us. (Rom. 8:5-17)

The Revelation

We might be teachers, but as long as we're in bondage, we are not free ourselves. Though sin is in the nature of the flesh, we can't live by it; but living by faith, we put it to death by the cross that binds us to Christ's righteousness.

Sexuality and love are gifts that unite a man with his wife physically and emotionally. That was the purpose of its creation. We can't separate love from sexuality and find fulfillment.

The way to purity and peace of mind is like all other spiritual battles: by persevering in faith and in the fear of God, we confess our sin to Him as long as it takes to be free of it. *If we confess our sins, He is faithful and just to forgive us our sins, and to cleanse us from all unrighteousness. (1 Jn. 1:9)* The victory may take time, or it may be instantaneous. Either way perseverance finds its rewards, forgetting the past by faith for the future.

How we receive the gift of salvation reveals our relationship with God in Jesus Christ. Do we live by faith in Him, continuing to walk in the Spirit, or neglect our salvation by turning back to the carnal ways we once lived, insulting His grace and gambling away our covenant with God? Since He set us free, let's walk in the Spirit and live. The wise are armed with His words in our hearts, prepared like watchmen on a wall who see the horsemen riding.

[26] And he who overcomes, and keeps My works until the end, to him I will give power over the nations.

[27] 'He shall rule them with a rod of iron;
They shall be dashed to pieces like
the potter's vessels'—

as I also have received from My Father; [28] "and I will give him the morning star.

[29] "He who has an ear, let him hear what the Spirit says to the churches." ' (Rev. 2:26-29 NKJV) [The morning star is like the Alpha and Omega as the last light of the night and the first light of the morning.]

The Revelation of Jesus Christ

CHAPTER 3

3 "Write to the angel of the church in Sardis:

"The One who has the seven spirits of God and the seven stars says: I know your works; you have a reputation for being alive, but you are dead. ²Be alert and strengthen what remains, which is about to die, for I have not found your works complete before My God. ³Remember, therefore what you have received and heard; keep it, and repent. But if you are not alert, I will come like a thief, and you have no idea at what hour I will come against you. ⁴But you have a few people in Sardis who have not defiled their clothes, and they will walk with Me in white, because they are worthy. ⁵In the same way, the victor will be dressed in white clothes, and I will never erase his name from the book of life but will acknowledge his name before My Father and before His angels.

⁶"Anyone who has an ear should listen to what the Spirit says to the churches.

⁷"Write to the angel of the church in Philadelphia:

"The Holy One, the True One, the One who has the key of David, who opens and no one will close, and closes and no one opens says: ⁸I know your works. Because you have limited strength, have kept My word, and have not denied My name, look, I have placed before you an open door that no one is able to close. ⁹Take note! I will make those from the synagogue of Satan, who claim to be Jews and are not, but are lying—note this—I will make them come and bow down at your feet, and they will know that I have loved you. ¹⁰Because you have kept My command to endure, I will also keep you from the hour of testing that is going to come over the whole world to test those who live on the earth. ¹¹I am coming quickly. Hold on to what you have, so that no one takes your crown. ¹²The victor: I will make him a pillar in the sanctuary of My God, and he will never go out again. I will write on him the name of My God and the name of the city of My God—New Jerusalem, which comes down out of heaven from My God—and My new name. ¹³"Anyone who has an ear should listen to what the Spirit says to the churches.

The Revelation

[14] "Write to the angel of the church in Laodicea:

"The Amen, the faithful and true Witness, the Originator of God's creation says: [15] I know your works, that you are neither cold nor hot. I wish that you were cold or hot. [16] So, because you are lukewarm, and neither hot nor cold, I am going to vomit you out of My mouth. [17] Because you say, 'I'm rich; I have become wealthy and need nothing,' and you don't know that you are wretched, pitiful, poor, blind, and naked, [18] I advise you to buy from Me gold refined in the fire so that you may be rich, white clothes so that you may be dressed and your shameful nakedness not be exposed, and ointment to spread on your eyes so that you may see. [19] As many as I love, I rebuke and discipline. So be committed and repent. [20] Listen! I stand at the door and knock. If anyone hears My voice and opens the door, I will come in to him and have dinner with him, and he with Me. [21] The victor: I will give him the right to sit with Me on My throne, just as I also won the victory and sat down with My Father on His throne.

[22] "Anyone who has an ear should listen to what the Spirit says to the churches." (Revelation 3:1-22 HCSB)

Insights

The Christian community in **Sardis** was comfortable with an appearance of piety but was privately defiled. Outwardly, some of us may look like fine people though we're not really alive and growing, but are dead and dying. God sees our hearts and minds and knows our secrets yet forgives us if we repent.

If we refuse to yield to His words, unless we repent, we'll be lost. If we're breathing, we must be ready to repent. If we live for ourselves and not for God, we won't be prepared for the end. Let's guard our hearts and minds and be holy: living in Christ daily, we are worthy by *works done in faith*, not by empty words.

Some deny Christ by keeping secret, ungodly desires in their hearts and minds; that's unbelief. We can't walk with Him in white by hiding from Him. He knows everything and doesn't need us to tell Him, but having a relationship with God means we turn to Him with confidence for our deliverance. Faithfully, He hears our confession and forgives us, washing us clean.

Insights: Chapter 3

If our hearts are open to the truth, our names **are not** blotted out of the Book of Life. Our Brother Jesus is our Advocate to the Father. It's a relationship. *He that hath an ear, let him hear what the Spirit saith* ... a personal relationship. Living by faith we're rewarded **on the last day** when many call out, "Lord, Lord!" but lived like hypocrites. (Mat. 24:48-51; 2 Pet. 2:9-22)

Jesus addresses the messenger of the **Philadelphia** church, which has not denied His name, but has kept His command to endure. He opens a door, a way of escape from the hour of trial that tests every living soul on earth. (1 Cor. 10:13)

Some stood against them, claiming to be Jews but were liars. They were of *the synagogue of Satan*. All real Jews entrust our hearts and souls to the Savior. All who walk in the Spirit are His. If we don't live by faith, we don't belong to Him. We are not under the law, but by faith, we act by His Spirit who lives in us.

Jews and gentiles might profess faith in Jesus but hold to the laws of Moses. The new covenant is unlike Abraham's covenant where circumcision and tithing are required, but Abraham gave freely, and Yeshua said the sons are free. (Mat. 17:26) Peter and Paul agreed; these men put us under bondage neither they nor their fathers could bear. Laws and rules of other covenants were made obsolete by the new and better one. (Acts 15:10-11; Gal. 5:1)

Faith in Yeshua isn't rigid or impersonal. His Spirit writes His commandments in our hearts. By the new covenant, He leads us, *saying, This is the way, walk ye in it (in Is. 30:21)*. If we keep His words and persevere, the rewards are everlasting. Let's be pillars in the true Sanctuary. The victor is in the Father, in the Holy Spirit, in Messiah, and in New Jerusalem forever.

[13] "Anyone who has an ear should listen to what the Spirit says to the churches. (Rev. 3:13 NKJV)

The last message is to the angel of the church in **Laodicea**: Rich in material wealth but spiritually impoverished, its church is lukewarm, not zealous to serve. We give thanks for our wealth but are unconscious of our poverty. If we love the things of this world, God's love is not in us. Unless we repent, He'll remove the church from our nation. He will literally vomit us out. Our lukewarm attitudes make Him sick to His stomach. Do we have *ears but don't hear* the Spirit speaking? (3:15-22)

The Revelation

By circumventing the truth, we've been lukewarm. We've been idolaters; we've wanted our own way: *They that make a graven image are all of them vanity; and their delectable things shall not profit; and they are their own witnesses; they see not, nor know; that they may be ashamed. ... [18] They have not known nor understood: for he hath shut their eyes, and they cannot see; and their hearts, that they cannot understand. (Is. 44:11, 18)* This is what God does to idolaters.

When the Scriptures seem dull to us, the truth is, we've been dull to them by our idolatries. His words live in us by our faith in them, so when we receive them, we live by them—not as under the law, but we live by faith in His words as His Spirit leads us.

If He showed wrath to the Jews who hardened their hearts, what happens to us who claim their heritage but are in unbelief? The things that refine the saints also define us. Let's remember the day we vowed our lives to Him and repent. *The word is nigh thee, even in thy mouth, and in thy heart: that is, the word of faith, which we preach. (Rom. 10:8; cf. Dt. 30:9-14)*

> [19] As many as I love, I rebuke and discipline. So be committed and repent. ... [21] The victor: I will give him the right to sit with Me on My throne, just as I also won the victory and sat down with My Father on His throne. (Rev. 3:19, 21 HCSB)

Jesus was speaking to all churches, not just to seven. Less is expected of new believers than of teachers, pastors, prophets, or apostles, and of us who have believed for many years. Looking back, we see His work, cleansing us in time. If we haven't been changed or haven't believed the words of God, then we could be the false teachers, false prophets, false apostles, and yes, false believers who must repent. If we want Jesus Christ in control of our lives, by faith in His power, we *press on toward the mark of the high calling of God in Christ Jesus. (Phil. 3:14)*

Most like the Laodicean church, the American church sees herself as strong and spiritual but is weak and carnal, easy prey to false teachings that steal our souls. If we've fallen but repent, Jesus will lift us up again. We must love one another and pray for one another; bless our enemies, and don't gossip. Believe the Word. We *live by faith, not by sight.* If we live like materialists, we will die in our sins. (See Hab. 2:4; Gal. 3:11; Heb. 10:38)

The Revelation of Jesus Christ

CHAPTER 4

4 After this I looked, and there before me was a door standing open in heaven. And the voice I had first heard speaking to me like a trumpet said, "Come up here, and I will show you what must take place after this." [2] At once I was in the Spirit, and there before me was a throne in heaven with someone sitting on it. [3] And the one who sat there had the appearance of jasper and ruby. A rainbow that shone like an emerald encircled the throne. [4] Surrounding the throne were twenty-four other thrones, and seated on them were twenty-four elders. They were dressed in white and had crowns of gold on their heads. [5] From the throne came flashes of lightning, rumblings and peals of thunder. In front of the throne, seven lamps were blazing. These are the seven spirits of God. [6] Also in front of the throne there was what looked like a sea of glass, clear as crystal.

In the center, around the throne, were four living creatures, and they were covered with eyes, in front and in back. [7] The first living creature was like a lion, the second was like an ox, the third had a face like a man, the fourth was like a flying eagle. [8] Each of the four living creatures had six wings and was covered with eyes all around, even under its wings. Day and night they never stop saying:

> "'Holy, holy, holy
> is the Lord God Almighty,'
> who was, and is, and is to come."

[9] Whenever the living creatures give glory, honor and thanks to him who sits on the throne and who lives for ever and ever, [10] the twenty-four elders fall down before him who sits on the throne and worship him who lives for ever and ever. They lay their crowns before the throne and say:

> [11] "You are worthy, our Lord and God,
> to receive glory and honor and power,
> for you created all things,
> and by your will they were created
> and have their being."
> (Revelation 4:1-11 NIV)

The Revelation

Insights

The voice John heard was stunning. It transported him to heaven where he observed mysterious sights. Twenty-four elders sat on thrones, surrounding the God manifested as the Father. Reading it aloud again, we sense the beauty of His glory.

In Revelation 4, 5, 6, 7, 14:3, 15:7, and 19:4, *living creatures* are not the same as the others in chapters 11, 13, 14, 15, 16, 17, 19, and 20. The four in heaven are rightly *living creatures. (NIV)* [Gr.: *zoon, creatures* with resurrection life, or *zoe*] They are unlike the lower beasts that fall to rise from the sea, the bottomless pit, or the earth. [Gr.: *therion*, or wild beasts] The four are heavenly, thriving with life, nearest the throne, worshiping day and night.

Every day supernatural ones observe us, and angels minister to the saints according to the will of God, yet we are unaware of our eyewitnesses and helpers. The LORD Most High is a Refuge. He has given angels charge over us. Knowing the intentions and inclinations of our hearts, He cares about our lives though we often live as though He's unaware of us while heroes of the faith are watching us day and night. (Heb. 12:1)

As Jesus said, *Beware of false prophets, which come to you in sheep's clothing, but inwardly they are ravening wolves. Ye shall know them by their fruits. Do men gather grapes of thorns or figs of thistles? (Mat. 7:15-16)* Some are unaware of their great errors, so we must be *wise as serpents and harmless as doves. (see Mat. 10:16)* Cleaving to His words, we remain cautious.

On the last day, everything will be clear to us. Let's be alert because He comes for each of us when we least expect Him. From the babe to the aged, we wake from our sleep to bow at His feet on that Day when He only receives His chosen ones whom He foreknew before there was a world. We walk in the light of His Word and are transparent with Him.

In both Revelation and Daniel, the wild beasts are fallen but supernatural, while the four living creatures in chapter 4 worship the Father by whose will all things were created. In chapter 5 the same living creatures are giving thanks for the redemption of people from every language, tribe, and nation. They sing a new song about the Kingdom of priests to God who were ransomed by His blood, and they worship the Lamb who is worthy to take the scroll from the right hand of the One on the throne:

The Revelation of Jesus Christ

CHAPTER 5

5 Then I saw in the right hand of him who was seated on the throne a scroll written within and on the back, sealed with seven seals. ²And I saw a mighty angel proclaiming with a loud voice, "Who is worthy to open the scroll and break its seals?" ³And no one in heaven or on earth or under the earth was able to open the scroll or to look into it, ⁴and I began to weep loudly because no one was found worthy to open the scroll or to look into it. ⁵And one of the elders said to me, "Weep no more; behold, the Lion of the tribe of Judah, the Root of David, has conquered, so that he can open the scroll and its seven seals."

⁶And between the throne and the four living creatures and among the elders I saw a Lamb standing, as though it had been slain, with seven horns and with seven eyes, which are the seven spirits of God sent out into all the earth. ⁷And he went and took the scroll from the right hand of him who was seated on the throne. ⁸And when he had taken the scroll, the four living creatures and the twenty-four elders fell down before the Lamb, each holding a harp, and golden bowls full of incense, which are the prayers of the saints. ⁹And they sang a new song, saying,

> "Worthy are you to take the scroll
>   and to open its seals,
> for you were slain, and by your blood you ransomed
>   people for God
>   from every tribe and language and people and
>   nation,
> ¹⁰ and you have made them a kingdom and priests to
>   our God,
>   and they shall reign on the earth."

¹¹Then I looked, and I heard around the throne and the living creatures and the elders the voice of many angels, numbering myriads of myriads and thousands of thousands, ¹²saying with a loud voice,

> "Worthy is the Lamb who was slain,
> to receive power and wealth and wisdom and might
>   and honor and glory and blessing!"

The Revelation

¹³ And I heard every creature in heaven and on earth and under the earth and in the sea, and all that is in them, saying,

> "To him who sits on the throne and to the Lamb
> be blessing and honor and glory and might
> forever and ever!"

¹⁴ And the four living creatures said, "Amen!" and the elders fell down and worshiped. (Revelation 5:1-14 ESV)

Insights

The powerful angel who stands at the throne of God asks the multitudes, *Who is worthy to open the scroll and to loose the seals of it? (from 5:2 YLT)* John weeps aloud. Of the billions, is there not one worthy soul? The scroll reveals world history, the judgments of God, the war between good and evil, the end of the world, and the creation of a new and everlasting universe.

Who is able to open it? In all of heaven, dare anyone break its seals? A Lion is in the Lamb, approaching the throne to open the scroll as the elders and living creatures worship and sing.

Jesus is the Lion of Judah, the Root of David, supporting, anchoring, nourishing, and sustaining life. The Father is on the throne as the Ancient of Days whose Spirit is in His Son, One with Him as His eternal Word, the Seed conceived by the virgin to live in our flesh among us. (See Jn. 1; cf. Gal. 3:19) Yeshua has a name identified with God: *his name is called The Word of God. (from Rev. 19:13b)* He was and is and will always be the Word of God, *the express image of his person (in Heb. 1:3).* The interlinear reads, *the representation of the reality of him (ZGE),* i.e., of God who is Spirit. His Son opens the prophecy as His Word.

Terrible kings and beasts, tribulations and persecutions, wars and famines, earthquakes and twisters, judgments and rewards are in the scroll. The *Apocalypse* is about to be unveiled, but who can read it? and who would dare? Sure, at the end of the Book, we win, but what happens between now and then?

Only His Son is worthy to receive the scroll from the right hand of God. Heaven worships Him because the scroll is the *Revelation of Jesus Christ,* proving His is the Spirit of prophecy by the truth of its words. With its seals undone, everyone and

Insights: Chapter 5

everything alive should worship our holy God as they worship the Lamb who took the scroll and opened its seals. His name is above every other. He took our sins in His body and died, but His blood washed them away. He proved it by rising to life:

> [5] You know that *Yeshua* appeared in order to take away sins, and in Him there is no sin. [6] No one who abides in Him keeps on sinning; no one who sins has seen Him or known Him. [7] Children, let no one mislead you! The one who practices righteousness is righteous, just as Yeshua is righteous. [8] The one who practices sin is of the devil, for the devil has been sinning from the beginning. *Ben-Elohim* appeared for this purpose—to destroy the works of the devil. [9] No one born of God practices sin, because God's seed remains in him. He cannot sin, because he is born of God. (1 Jn. 3:5-9 TLV) [*Ben-Elohim*, "Son of God."]

The living creatures of chapters 4 and 5 may lead redeemed nations. Beasts lead kingdoms on earth, and the living creatures are unusually wise. Twenty-four elders [twelve as apostles] are its judges; His Kingdom's elect are kings and priests to God. (1:6; 5:10; Mat. 19:28)

How to See Jesus

Near the day of Passover, the Greeks were looking for Him, hoping to hear the wisdom of His words. Knowing the gentiles would turn to Him though His own people would reject Him, He must have felt the import of their presence:

> [20] Now there were some Greeks among those who were going up to worship at the feast; [21] these then came to Philip, who was from Bethsaida of Galilee, and *began to* ask him, saying, "Sir, we wish to see Jesus." [22] Philip came and told Andrew; Andrew and Philip came and told Jesus. [23] And Jesus answered them, saying, "The hour has come for the Son of Man to be glorified. [24] Truly, truly, I say to you, unless a grain of wheat falls into the earth and dies, it remains alone; but if it dies, it bears much fruit. [25] He who loves his life loses it, and he who hates his life in this world will keep it to life eternal. [26] If anyone serves Me, he must follow Me; and where I am, there My servant will be also; if anyone serves Me, the Father will honor him. (Jn. 12:20-26 NASB)

The Revelation

If we serve Him, we follow Him; if we love our lives, we lose them; if we hate our lives in this world, we live forever. In dying we bear fruit; emptied of ourselves, we are filled with His Spirit; we don't work but He does, and we rest in Him as we act by faith. More than a philosophy, it's a way of life. Israel set an example: brothers of a common lineage united with one mind:

> ... ²and he went out to meet Asa and said to him, "Hear me, Asa, and all Judah and Benjamin: The LORD is with you while you are with him. <u>If you seek him, he will be found by you, but if you forsake him, he will forsake you.</u> ³For a long time Israel was without the true God, and without a teaching priest and without law, ⁴but when in their distress they turned to the LORD, the God of Israel, and sought him, he was found by them. ⁵In those times there was no peace to him who went out or to him who came in, for great disturbances afflicted all the inhabitants of the lands. ⁶They were broken in pieces. Nation was crushed by nation and city by city, for God troubled them with every sort of distress. ⁷But you, take courage! Do not let your hands be weak, for your work shall be rewarded." ...
>
> ¹⁴They swore an oath to the LORD with a loud voice and with shouting and with trumpets and with horns. ¹⁵And all Judah rejoiced over the oath, for they had sworn with all their heart and had sought him with their whole desire, and he was found by them, and the LORD gave them rest all around. (2 Chr. 15:2-7, 14-15 ESV)

In the days of the prophets of Judah and Israel, information about their future filled the prophecies to overflowing, pregnant with expectation:

> ⁴⁰And I will make an everlasting covenant with them, that I will not turn away from them, to do them good; but I will put my fear in their hearts, that they shall not depart from me. ⁴¹Yea I will rejoice over them to do them good, <u>and I will plant them in this land assuredly with my whole heart and with my whole soul.</u> ⁴²For thus saith the LORD; Like as I have brought all this great evil upon this people, so will I bring upon them all the good that I have promised them. (Jer. 32:40-42) [This is the only scripture where God reveals the will of His whole heart and soul.]

The Revelation of Jesus Christ

CHAPTER 6

6 Then I saw when the Lamb opened one of the seven seals, and I heard one of the four living creatures say with a voice like thunder, "Come!" ² I looked, and behold, there was a white horse. The one riding on it had a bow, and a crown was given to him. He went out as a conqueror so he might conquer.

³ When the Lamb opened the second seal, I heard the second living creature saying, "Come!" ⁴ Then another horse came out, fiery red. The one riding on it was permitted to take peace from the earth, so that people would slaughter one another. He was given a great sword.

⁵ When the Lamb opened the third seal, I heard the third living creature saying, "Come!" And behold, I saw a black horse. The one riding on it held a balance scale in his hand. ⁶ Then I heard something like a voice in the midst of the four living creatures saying, "A quart of wheat for a denarius, and three quarts of barley for a denarius—but do no harm to the oil and wine!"

⁷ When the Lamb opened the fourth seal, I heard the fourth living creature saying, "Come!" ⁸ Behold, I saw a horse, pale greenish gray. The name of the one riding on it was Death, and Sheol was following with him. Authority was given to them over a fourth of the earth, to kill by the sword and by famine and by plague and by the wild beasts of the earth.

⁹ When the Lamb opened the fifth seal, I saw under the altar the souls of those slaughtered for the sake of the word of God and for the witness they had. ¹⁰ And they cried out with a loud voice, saying, "O Sovereign Master, holy and true, how long before You judge those who dwell on the earth and avenge our blood?"

¹¹ Then a white robe was given to each of them, and they were told to rest a little while longer, until the number of their fellow servants was complete—their brothers and sisters who were to be killed as they had been.

¹² I saw when the Lamb opened the sixth seal, and there was a great earthquake. The sun became as black as

The Revelation

sackcloth made of goat's hair, and the full moon became like blood. ¹³ The stars of heaven fell to the earth like a fig tree drops unripe figs when shaken by a great wind. ¹⁴ The heaven ripped apart like a scroll being rolled up, and every mountain and island was moved from their places.

¹⁵ Then the kings of the earth and the great men and the military commanders and the rich and the mighty and everyone—slave and free—hid themselves in the caves and among the rocks of the mountains. ¹⁶ And they tell the mountains and the rocks, "Fall on us, and hide us from the face of the One seated on the throne and from the wrath of the Lamb. ¹⁷ For the great day of their wrath has come, and who is able to stand?"
(Revelation 6:1-17 TLV)

Insights

The Lamb opens each seal, and as He does, each of the four living creatures calls out his horseman to judge the earth. Soon after the inception of the church, the horsemen incite nature and humankind. The great tribulation, the first resurrection, and the ascension immediately precede His wrath (in 6:12-17). Seals are for signs and judgments.

At **the first seal**, its beast is a lion with circumspect vision, calling to a rider on a white horse, focused on conquering. The disciples asked for the signs of His coming at the end of the age,

⁴ And Jesus answered and said unto them Take heed that no man deceive you ⁵ For many shall come in my name saying I am Christ and shall deceive many
(Mat. 24:4-5) [The ancient Greek was not punctuated.]

After the resurrection, the war in heaven ended. The dragon and his angels were hurled to earth in chapter 12. Not long after that, a church empire rose, but its invisible king institutionalized idolatry. When the leaders gave up the good fight of faith, they subjected their followers to the enemy. The result was an entirely different "gospel." The apostasy forced its conversions by the spirit of antichrist. Many bishops claimed the place of Christ yet killed their opponents. Like the rider on the white horse, they appeared righteous but were deceivers, professing equality with Jesus Christ while misleading the church to conquer the world.

Insights: Chapter 6

Yeshua's Kingdom is true, and He is its sole Foundation; no one is comparable to Him. He gives us crowns who overcome deceiving spirits by faith in the Word of God alone:

> ³³ These things I have spoken unto you, that in me you might have peace. In the world ye shall have tribulation: but be of good cheer; I have overcome the world. (Jn. 16:33)
>
> ¹⁰ The thief comes only to steal and kill and destroy. I came that they may have life and have it abundantly. (Jn. 10:10 ESV) – Yeshua

The Lamb breaks the **second seal**. The second beast, an ox with six wings and eyes all around, calls the *fiery red* horse and its rider to *take peace from the earth, and that they should kill one another: and there was given unto him a great sword. (6:4)*:

> ⁹ And when you hear of wars and chaos, do not be terrorized; for these things need to happen first, but the end will not come at once."
> ¹⁰ Then He continued telling them, "Nation will rise up against nation, and kingdom against kingdom. (Lk. 21:9-10 TLV) – Yeshua

At the **third seal**, the living creature with a face like a man calls to the rider on the black horse, rationing, limiting sustenance, regulating prices. The Lord commands the horseman: *A measure of wheat for a penny, and three measures of barley for a penny; and see thou hurt not the oil and wine. (6:6)* The oil and wine are precious and should not be abused.

> ¹¹ And great earthquakes shall be in divers places, and famines, and pestilences; and fearful sights and great signs shall there be from heaven. (Lk. 21:11) – Yeshua

By faith in Jesus, who is alive from the dead, we accomplish the impossible and prove the Word true. He's our Provider:

> ¹⁴ He causeth the grass to grow for the cattle and herb for the service of man: that he may bring forth food out of the earth; ¹⁵ and wine that maketh glad the heart of man, and oil to make his face shine, and bread which strengtheneth man's heart. (Ps. 104:14-15) – Yeshua

The Revelation

The Lamb opens the **fourth seal**. Its living creature, an eagle with six wings and eyes all around, sends a horseman to judge the earth like those before him, but this one rides a greenish-gray horse, the color of Death. Its place follows him as Sheol:

> ²² And except those days be shortened, there should no flesh be saved: but for the elect's sake, those days shall be shortened. (Mat. 24:22) – Yeshua

The horsemen are in the news, reminding us that He stands at the door and knocks for us to open to Him.

As He opens **the fifth seal**, Yeshua hears the prayers of the martyrs under the altar who long for God to judge the killers of His holy ones. They're not vengeful, but long for righteousness to prove justice against those with hands full of blood; He hasn't done that yet. *Then shall they deliver you up to be afflicted, and shall kill you: and ye shall be hated of all nations for my name's sake. (Mat. 24:9)* Chapter 13 fits as the fifth seal till Jesus comes on a cloud for the elect (in Mat. 24:29-31; 1 Thes. 4:16-17; cf. Rev. 6:12-17) Martyrs under the altar are told to rest till the killing of others who'd die as they had is complete.

At **the sixth seal**, after we who resist the beast and his mark are caught up, seven angels take seven bowls from the Sanctuary in heaven to pour out His wrath. (16:2) *Immediately after the tribulation,* at the **sixth seal,** Christ comes on a cloud as men hide from His wrath. (Mk. 13:24-27) The sun is black; the moon is red; the heavens and earth are shaken. Yeshua shouts; martyrs rise to life; the archangel cries out; the great trumpet of God is heard; 144,000 lead His elect who are caught up together to join the Lord in the air while Israel grieves for her Son. It isn't a secret; Jesus described it long ago:

> ²⁹ Immediately after the tribulation of those days shall the sun be darkened, and the moon shall not give her light, and the stars shall fall from heaven, and the powers of the heavens shall be shaken: ³⁰ And then shall all the tribes of the earth mourn, and they shall see the Son of man coming in the clouds of heaven with power and great glory. ³¹ And he shall send his angels with a great sound of a trumpet, and they shall gather together his elect from the four winds, from one end of heaven to the other. (Mat. 24:29-31; cf. Rev. 6:12-17; 14:1; 1 Thes. 4:13-18)

The Revelation of Jesus Christ

CHAPTER 7

7 And after these things I saw four angels standing on the four corners of the earth, holding the four winds of the earth, that the wind should not blow on the earth, nor on the sea, nor on any tree.
² And I saw another angel ascending from the east, having the seal of the living God: and he cried with a loud voice to the four angels, to whom it was given to hurt the earth and the sea,
³ Saying, Hurt not the earth, neither the sea, nor the trees, till we have sealed the servants of our God in their foreheads.
⁴ And I heard the number of them which were sealed: and there were sealed an hundred and forty and four thousand of all the tribes of the children of Israel.
⁵ Of the tribe of Juda were sealed twelve thousand. Of the tribe of Reuben were sealed twelve thousand. Of the tribe of Gad were sealed twelve thousand.
⁶ Of the tribe of Aser were sealed twelve thousand. Of the tribe of Nephthalim were sealed twelve thousand. Of the tribe of Manasses were sealed twelve thousand.
⁷ Of the tribe of Simeon were sealed twelve thousand. Of the tribe of Levi were sealed twelve thousand. Of the tribe of Issachar were sealed twelve thousand.
⁸ Of the tribe of Zabulon were sealed twelve thousand. Of the tribe of Joseph were sealed twelve thousand. Of the tribe of Benjamin were sealed twelve thousand.
⁹ After this I beheld, and, lo, a great multitude, which no man could number, of all nations, and kindreds, and people, and tongues, stood before the throne, and before the Lamb, clothed with white robes, and palms in their hands;
¹⁰ And cried with a loud voice, saying, Salvation to our God which sitteth upon the throne, and unto the Lamb.
¹¹ And all the angels stood round about the throne, and about the elders and the four beasts, and fell before the throne on their faces, and worshipped God,
¹² Saying, Amen: Blessing, and glory, and wisdom, and thanksgiving, and honour, and power, and might, be unto our God for ever and ever. Amen.
¹³ And one of the elders answered, saying unto me, What are these which are arrayed in white robes? and whence

The Revelation

came they?
¹⁴ And I said unto him, Sir, thou knowest. And he said to me, These are they which came out of great tribulation, and have washed their robes, and made them white in the blood of the Lamb.
¹⁵ Therefore are they before the throne of God, and serve him day and night in his temple: and he that sitteth on the throne shall dwell among them.
¹⁶ They shall hunger no more, neither thirst any more; neither shall the sun light on them, nor any heat.
¹⁷ For the Lamb which is in the midst of the throne shall feed them, and shall lead them unto living fountains of waters: and God shall wipe away all tears from their eyes. (Revelation 7:1-17)

Insights

The **fifth seal** opens (in 6:9), and the great tribulation begins in chapter 13. The spirits under the altar call for justice but must wait till others die as they had before they are avenged.

Four angels hold back **the winds of the sixth seal** until one from the East seals Israel's male virgins, the firstfruit to ascend after the dead rise at the first resurrection of the fall harvest (in Rev. 20:4-5). [Its martyrs rise from the dead before its survivors ascend with them.] (See 7:1-8, 9-17; also 14:1-5; 14:14-16; 15:1-5)

Jesus is *the firstfruits from the dead (in 1 Cor. 15:20),* but the tribulation ends when the male virgins are sealed, *redeemed from among men—the firstfruits unto God and to the Lamb (in 14:4):*

> ¹⁵ For if the casting away of them be the reconciling of the world, <u>what shall the receiving of them be but life from the dead</u>? ¹⁶ For if the firstfruit is holy, the lump is also holy; and if the root be holy, so are the branches. ... ²³ And they also, if they abide not still in unbelief, shall be grafted in: for <u>God is able to graft them in again</u>. ... ²⁵ For I would not, brethren, that ye should be ignorant of this mystery, lest ye should be wise in your own conceits, that blindness in part is happened to Israel, until the fullness of the Gentiles be come in. (Rom. 11:15-16, 23, 25)

The passage refers to the virgins' ascension as the firstfruits, subsequent to the first resurrection *after the tribulation (in 14:4; Mat. 24:29-31).* The four winds (in 7:1) are the keys (to 6:13): after

Insights: Chapter 7

the virgins are sealed to ascend, angels let loose the winds. At the **sixth seal**, stars fall *like a fig tree drops untimely figs when shaken by a great wind,(6:13)*. Its winds shake the powers of the heavens after the virgins are sealed. Men tremble at His wrath (in 6:12-17) Every eye sees Jesus as a Lamb on the throne at the right hand of power, coming on a cloud for His elect. He shouts and a great trumpet sounds. (Rev. 6:16; cf. Mat. 24:29-31, p. 146) The dead rise before the firstfruits ascend with the elect following after.

The Jews' foremost desire was their peers' acceptance. They loved the honor that came from men more than honor from God (in Jn. 12:43). They weren't alone in that; its unbelief is in the church today. As a result He further hardened the Jews to resist Him but reconciled gentiles to Himself (in Rom. 9:18, 25, 27).

> —not only to the adherent of the law but also to the one who shares the faith of Abraham, who is the father of us all, ¹⁷ as it is written, "I have made you the father of many nations"—in the presence of the God in whom he believed, who gives life to the dead and calls into existence the things that do not exist. (Rom. 4:16b-17 ESV) [The law [Torah] is like a teacher in Gal. 3:24]

The firstfruits are sanctified—*set apart for God.* By his faith in God's promise, Jacob's sons were holy. In their unbelief, the Jews were cut off, but the nations were brought in to provoke their jealousy. Although Jews were holy, their behavior revealed their disbelief. We are also holy, but whoever boasts against the Jews proves his own disbelief. Since they were cut off, we can be cut off too, contrary to the teachings of men. (Rom. 11:17-21)

The Firstfruits

After the male virgins are sealed, the first harvest begins (in 14:14), not before. Martyrs who died for the testimony of Jesus and for the Word of God, unwilling to worship the beast and its image and refusing its mark in their foreheads or hands, rise to life at **the first resurrection**. They return to reign with Christ for a thousand years. [Gr.: *anistemi* means "stand up."] Survivors are *caught up together with them in the clouds to meet the Lord. (1 Thes. 16-17)* [Gr.: *perileipo*, "left over" (pass.: survive)] *And he shall send his angels with a great sound of a trumpet, and they shall gather together his elect from the four winds, from one end* *of heaven to the other. (Mat. 24:31)* It's the first of two harvests (in Rev. 20:4-5). *Like a fig tree, shaken by a great wind (Rev. 6:13),* stars fall from the sky, and the dance of the virgins begins:

> ¹¹ For the LORD hath redeemed Jacob, and ransomed him from the hand of *him that was* stronger than he. ¹²Therefore they shall come and sing in the height of Zion, and shall flow together to the goodness of the LORD, for wheat, and for wine, and for oil, and for the young of the flock and of the herd: and their soul shall be as a watered garden; and they shall not sorrow any more at all. ¹³ Then shall the virgin rejoice in the dance, both young men and old together: for I will turn their mourning into joy, and will comfort them, and make them rejoice from their sorrow. (Jer. 31:11-13; cf. Is. 51:11; 61:3)

When He woke Lazarus to life out of death, Jesus shouted, "Lazarus, come out!" (John 11) He shouts at His appearing. Paul wrote to a church that thought the living ascend but not the dead. He replied to their fear for the dead: the dead rise, *anistemi,* before the living are *caught up together with them:*

> ¹⁵ According to the Lord's word, we tell you that we who are still alive, who are left until the coming of the Lord, will certainly not precede those who have fallen asleep. ¹⁶ For the Lord himself will come down from heaven, with a loud command, with the voice of the archangel and with the trumpet call of God, and the dead in Christ will rise first. ¹⁷ After that, we who are still alive and are left will be caught up together with them in the clouds to meet the Lord in the air. And so we will be with the Lord forever. ¹⁸ Therefore encourage one another with these words. (1 Thes. 4:15-18 NIV) [Gr.: *Parousia* is "nearness," translated "coming." *Anistemi* is "stand up, arise, or get up."]

Believers who remain alive and are worthy are taken up with those chosen to rise from the dead. Together they meet the Lord in the air led by 144.000 male virgins. (3:15-19) After His wrath is poured out, Jesus returns to Jerusalem with the victorious ones.

> ³ It is God's will that you should be sanctified: that you should avoid sexual immorality; ⁴ that each of you should learn to control your own body in a way that is holy and honorable, ⁵ not in passionate lust like the pagans, who

Insights: Chapter 7

> do not know God; ⁶ and that in this matter no one should wrong or take advantage of a brother or sister. The Lord will punish all those who commit such sins, as we told you and <u>warned you before</u>. ⁷ For God did not call us to be impure, but <u>to live a holy life</u>. (1 Thes. 4:3-7 NIV)

We obey by faith and are neither barren nor unfruitful in the knowledge of Christ. If we surrender our lives to God as living sacrifices, abiding in His words, we may survive the beast and his mark to ascend as the living together with the martyrs to meet the Lord in the air:

> ³⁴ "Be careful, or your hearts will be weighed down with carousing, drunkenness and the anxieties of life, and that day will close on you suddenly like a trap. ³⁵ For it will come on all those who live on the face of the whole earth. ³⁶ <u>Be always on the watch, and pray</u> that you may be able to escape all that is about to happen, and that you may be able to stand before the Son of Man."
> (Lk. 21:34-36 NIV) [Lit: "begging that ye may be able" – ZGE; "praying that ye may be accounted worthy to escape..." – YLT]

> ⁵ This is evidence of the righteous judgment of God, that <u>you may be considered worthy of the kingdom of God</u>, for which you are also suffering— ⁶ since indeed God considers it just to repay with affliction those who afflict you, ⁷ and <u>to grant relief to you</u> who are afflicted as well as to us, when the Lord Jesus is revealed from heaven with his mighty angels ⁸ in flaming fire, inflicting <u>vengeance on those</u> who do not know God and on those who do not obey the gospel of our Lord Jesus. ... ¹¹ To this end we always pray for you, that our God may make you <u>worthy of his calling</u> and may fulfill every resolve for good and every work of faith by his power,
> (2 Thes. 1:5-8, 11 ESV)

Angels catch us up, and His indignation falls in a flash—! Apart from holiness, no one can see the Lord until His coming. (Heb. 12:14) *For the Lord himself shall descend from heaven with a shout, with the voice of the archangel, and with the trump of God: and the dead in Christ shall rise first:* (1 Thes. 4:16)

> **15** Then I saw another great and wonderful sign in heaven: seven angels who have seven plagues—the

The Revelation

last ones, for with them God's wrath is finished. ²And I saw something like a sea of glass mixed with fire, and those who had overcome the beast and his image and the number of his name standing by the sea of glass, holding the harps of God. ³And they are singing the song of Moses the servant of God and the song of the Lamb, ...

⁵After these things I looked, and the Temple of the Tent of Witness in heaven was opened. ⁶Out of the Temple came the seven angels having the seven plagues, dressed in pure bright linen and wearing wide gold sashes around their chests. (Rev. 15:1-3a; 5-6 TLV)

The elect martyrs rise from their graves. We who survive tremble at the sound of the great trumpet of God, but as our legs fail, angels catch us up to meet the Lord. But *the dead in Christ rise [stand up] first.* In other words, no one ascends to meet the Lord in the air before the first resurrection of its martyrs.

The first of Tishrei is the Feast of Trumpets, a sabbath rest—a holy convocation, a large gathering. It's Rosh Hashanah, the season of His coming on a cloud at the first resurrection and the trumpet of God *immediately after the tribulation* (in Mat. 24:29).

Ten Days of Awe are sanctified to repent and be reconciled to God. Tishrei 10th is Yom Kippur, the Day of Atonement, a sabbath for fasting, an offering by fire, and *a solemn assembly.*

Jesus returns to destroy the prophet and the beast, and a great angel locks Satan in hell, sealing him in. Tishrei 15th is a *shabbat* for the Feast of Booths. Jerusalem hails Yeshua to His throne on the Day of Sukkot, under a tent for the marriage of the Lamb.

Prophetically, Sukkot's harvest is figuratively gathered when the earth is *full of the knowledge of the* LORD *as the waters cover the sea (in Is. 11:9; Hab. 2:14).* Its **eighth day** is its last sabbath, a portent of **the Day outside of time** (in Rev. 2o:11-15).

The Ark of God

But Noah found grace in the eyes of the Lord. (Gen 6:8) He built the ark in godly fear. The Lord led the animals into it, male and female, two by two and shut its door when the rain began.

The air is still, and the virgins are sealed. The sun doesn't shine; the moon isn't lit; stars fall from heaven—its powers are

Insights: Chapter 7

shaken. Jesus appears at the trumpet of God on Yom Teruah. His shout raises the dead; the archangel calls the firstfruits; the great trumpet blasts; the mighty tremble, and angels catch up the elect.

> [16] Then it came to pass on the third day, in the morning, that there were thunderings and lightnings, and a thick cloud on the mountain; and <u>the sound of the trumpet was very loud</u>, so that all the people who *were* in the camp trembled. ... [19] And when <u>the blast of the trumpet</u> sounded long and became louder and louder, Moses spoke, and God answered him by voice.
> (Ex. 19:16, 19 NKJV) [Moses spoke and God listened.]

> [18] Now all the people saw the thunderings, and the lightnings, and <u>the noise of the trumpet</u>, and the mountain smoking: and when the people saw *it*, they removed and stood afar off. [19] And they said unto Moses, Speak thou with us, and we will hear: but let not God speak with us, lest we die. [20] And Moses said unto the people, Fear not: for God is come to prove you, and that his fear may be before your faces, that ye sin not. (Ex. 20:18-20)

> [14] Then the LORD will be seen over them,
> And His arrow will go forth like lightning.
> <u>The Lord GOD will blow the trumpet</u>.
> And go with whirlwinds from the south.
> (Zec. 9:14 NKJV)

> [13] And it shall come to pass in that day *that* the great trumpet shall be blown and they shall come which were ready to perish in the land of Assyria, and the outcasts in the land of Egypt, and shall worship the LORD in the holy mountain at Jerusalem. (Is. 27:13)

> [5] <u>God is gone up with a shout, the LORD with the sound of a trumpet</u>. [6] Sing praises to God, sing praises: sing praises unto our King, sing praises. (Ps. 47:5-6)

Tribulations precede our joy. Rosh Hashanah, Yom Teruah, is the Day of Trumpets; on Yom Kippur Israel calls out for the One who atoned for her; at Sukkot He returns for her. The feasts are prophetic figures of actual events, but their times are sealed:

> 5 Now concerning the times and the seasons, brothers, you have no need to have anything written to you.[2] For you yourselves are fully aware that the day of the Lord

The Revelation

> will come <u>like a thief in the night</u>. ³While people are saying, "There is peace and security," <u>then sudden destruction</u> will come upon them as labor pains come upon a pregnant woman, and <u>they will not escape</u>. ⁴But you are not in darkness, brothers, for that day to surprise you like a thief. ⁵For you are all children of light, children of the day. We are not of the night, or of the darkness. ⁶So then let us not sleep, as others do, but let us keep awake and be sober. ⁷For those who sleep, sleep at night, and those who get drunk, are drunk at night. ⁸But since we belong to the day, let us be sober, having put on the breastplate of faith and love, and for a helmet the hope of salvation. ⁹For God has not destined us for wrath, but to obtain salvation through our Lord Jesus Christ, ¹⁰who died for us so that whether we are awake or asleep we might live with him. ¹¹Therefore encourage one another and build one another up, just as you are doing. (1 Thes. 5:1-11 ESV) [Wrath comes like a thief.]

> ²¹ Whoever has my commandments and keeps them, he it is who loves me. And he who loves me will be loved by my Father, and I will love him and manifest myself to him." (Jn. 14:21 ESV) [Obedience is the key.]

Our carnal nature opposes the words of God. Apart from Him we are evil. *Have I now become your enemy by telling you the truth? (Gal. 4:16 NIV)* God *deliver us from evil! (Mat. 6:13)* The tribulation is **not** the indignation of God. A separate event, His wrath is after the persecution that tests our faith:

> ²⁶ "Just as it was in the days of Noah, so also will it be in the days of the Son of Man. ²⁷ People were eating, drinking, marrying and being given in marriage up to the day <u>Noah entered the ark</u>. Then the flood came and destroyed them all. ²⁸ "It was the same in the days of Lot. People were eating and drinking, buying and selling, planting and building. ²⁹ But the day <u>Lot left Sodom</u>, fire and sulfur rained down from heaven and destroyed them all. (Lk. 17:26-29 NIV)

<u>His warnings qualify us to whom His promises apply</u>. Those who want Him want to be like Him. We who believe confess Jesus as our Lord and live by our faith. Believing in the power of God to conform us to His Son, we press into our high calling.

Insights: Chapter 7

> [10] Many shall be purified, and made white, and tried; but the wicked shall do wickedly: and none of the wicked shall understand; but the wise shall understand. [11] And from the time that the daily sacrifice shall be taken away, and the abomination that maketh desolate set up, there shall be a thousand two hundred and ninety days.
> (Dan. 12:10-11) [See "Of Times ..., pp. 294-6]

What was before comes again, but its days are shortened. Yeshua comes when the virgins are asleep. Half are looking up. Our vessels are full; our lamps are lit; our hearts are His:

> 25 "At that time the kingdom of heaven will be like ten virgins who took their lamps and went out to meet the bridegroom. [2] Five of them were foolish and five were wise. [3] The foolish ones took their lamps but did not take any oil with them. [4] The wise ones, however, took oil in jars along with their lamps. [5] The bridegroom was a long time in coming, and they all became drowsy and fell asleep.
> [6] "<u>At midnight</u> the cry rang out: 'Here's the bridegroom! Come out to meet him!'
> [7] "Then all the virgins woke up and trimmed their lamps.
> [8] The foolish ones said to the wise, 'Give us some of your oil; our lamps are going out.'
> [9] "'No,' they replied, 'there may not be enough for both us and you. Instead, go to those who sell oil and buy some for yourselves.'
> [10] "But while they were on their way to buy the oil, the bridegroom arrived. The virgins who were ready went in with him to the wedding banquet. And the door was shut.
> [11] "Later the others also came. 'Lord, Lord,' they said, 'open the door for us!' [12] But he replied, 'Truly I tell you, I don't know you.' [13] Therefore keep watch, because you do not know the day or the hour. (Mat. 25:1-13 NIV)

The darkest hour describes the spiritual condition of the world when the announcement goes out *at midnight*:

> [35] "Therefore, be on the alert—for you do not know when the master of the house is coming, whether in the evening, at midnight, or when the rooster crows, or in the morning—[36] in case he should come suddenly and find you asleep. (Mk. 13:35-36 NASB)

The Revelation

The rest of the dead rise again on the **last day** when we are judged by our deeds, even idle words and unclean thoughts.

Remember, God is loving, kind, and benevolent. Our Creator desires our companionship. He knows us well. We strive to enter in by faith, trusting in His workmanship as we seek His Kingdom and His righteousness. Jesus Christ came in our flesh as a man who understands our weaknesses. He is our Friend, born *the wonderful Counselor, mighty God, everlasting Father, Prince of Peace. (See Is. 9:6)* Have faith in God. He is good.

To his contemporaries, Paul wrote, *we must all stand before the judgment seat of Christ. (Rom 14:10b)* This is at the last trump on the last day when the rest of the dead rise and is normative. Saints from ages past rise **on the last day**. We have all sinned, but by dying to our own desires, we can believe the words of God and gain the mind of Jesus. Resurrections are extraordinary; each has its own purpose:

> [9] Therefore we also have as our ambition, whether at home or absent, to be pleasing to Him. [10] For we must all appear before the judgment seat of Christ, so that each one may be recompensed for his deeds in the body, according to what he has done, whether good or bad. (2 Cor. 5:9-10 NASB) [His throne is high on a *bema*.]

Our bodies turn to dust by death, and no one is amazed. Why not believe that out of dust they'll be transformed by life?

> [15] My substance was not hid from thee, when <u>I was made in secret,</u> *and* <u>curiously wrought in the lowest parts of the earth.</u> [16] In thy book [scroll] all *my members* were written, *which* in continuance were fashioned, when *as yet there was* none of them. [17] How precious also are thy thoughts unto me, O God! how great is the sum of them! [18] *If* I should count them, they are more in number than the sand: when I awake, I am still with thee. (Ps. 139:14-18; cf. 1 Cor. 15; Divisions, p. 40]

The prophecies are often out of order; they're designed that way. The events in chapter 8 do not immediately follow chapter 7; those in 14 do. As chapter 6 ends, the firstfruits are sealed in 7; they are in heaven before the elect who resisted the beast in chapters 14 and 15. The elect are chosen from among us to meet Christ in the air before the angels pour out His wrath.

The Revelation of Jesus Christ

CHAPTER 8

8 When the Lamb opened the seventh seal, there was silence in heaven for about half an hour. ² Then I saw the seven angels who stand before God, and seven trumpets were given to them. ³ And another angel came and stood at the altar with a golden censer, and he was given much incense to offer with the prayers of all the saints on the golden altar before the throne, ⁴ and the smoke of the incense, with the prayers of the saints, rose before God from the hand of the angel. ⁵ Then the angel took the censer and filled it with fire from the altar and threw it on the earth, and there were peals of thunder, rumblings, flashes of lightning, and an earthquake.
⁶ Now the seven angels who had the seven trumpets prepared to blow them.
⁷ The first angel blew his trumpet, and there followed hail and fire, mixed with blood, and these were thrown upon the earth. And a third of the earth was burned up, and a third of the trees were burned up, and all green grass was burned up.
⁸ The second angel blew his trumpet, and something like a great mountain, burning with fire, was thrown into the sea, and a third of the sea became blood. ⁹ A third of the living creatures in the sea died, and a third of the ships were destroyed.
¹⁰ The third angel blew his trumpet, and a great star fell from heaven, blazing like a torch, and it fell on a third of the rivers and on the springs of water. ¹¹ The name of the star is Wormwood. A third of the waters became wormwood, and many people died from the water, because it had been made bitter.
¹² The fourth angel blew his trumpet, and a third of the sun was struck, and a third of the moon, and a third of the stars, so that a third of their light might be darkened, and a third of the day might be kept from shining, and likewise a third of the night.
¹³ Then I looked, and I heard an eagle crying with a loud voice as it flew directly overhead, "Woe, woe, woe to those who dwell on the earth, at the blasts of the other trumpets that the three angels are about to blow!"
(Revelation 8:1-13 ESV)

The Revelation

Insights

At **the seventh seal,** the Messianic Kingdom has continued a thousand years. In chapter 8, Mystery Babylon is ancient history. Armageddon was made a graveyard named Hamon-Gog one thousand years earlier. The beast and false prophet were cast into the lake of fire at the last bowl of wrath after **the sixth seal.**

As the thousand-year reign of Yeshua (in 20:6) is ending on earth, a revolt strives against the King, and heaven is silent for a half an hour when the Lamb opens **the seventh seal** (in 8:1). Its somber moment faces the end of time. A censor contains prayers of the saints. Filled with fire it's cast to the earth as seven angels prepare to sequentially sound their trumpets.

Today the Messianic Kingdom is a mystery. Its details are in the prophecies of the Tenakh (OT). Before chapter 8 we read of the first resurrection and the ascension of the elect, but beginning with 8, we're at the end, not just of this age, but of time itself.

The rebellion exposes evil human nature. Evidence of the revolt is in Rev. 9:20-21; 11:7-10; 11:17-18; 20:7-9; Ps. 2. At that time, the first angel blows a trumpet, prompting the wrath of God on a rebellious world. Each trumpet calls to its synchronous plagues. The first four trumpeters precede the **three great woes** of the last three trumpeters in chapters 9 and 11.

The first ones initiate four plagues: 1. Hail and fire also fell in Egypt when Moses opposed Pharaoh to let the Hebrews go. Massive areas of the earth and its trees are burned, and the green grass is gone. 2. A mountain in flames falls into the sea. A third of the waters turn to blood, and a third of the ships are destroyed, costing multitudes of lives. 3. A toxic substance burns in the sky, embittering a third of the rivers and streams. Many people and animals are killed by its poison. 4. A third of the day and of the night are darkened. Temperatures plummet, signaling death.

Finally, the **three great woes** start off with a terrible event: The red dragon and his angels are loosed out of hell. Chained, locked, and sealed in its pit; after Yeshua reigns for a thousand years (in 20:6-7), Satan is released in chapter 9. (cf. 20:2, 7) Bursting from the bottomless pit at last, with teams of stinging locusts, he is eager to torment and destroy mankind but is assigned only those who lack the seal of God on their foreheads:

The Revelation of Jesus Christ

CHAPTER 9

9 Then the fifth angel sounded: And I saw a star fallen from heaven to the earth. To him was given the key to the bottomless pit. ² And he opened the bottomless pit, and smoke arose out of the pit like the smoke of a great furnace. So the sun and the air were darkened because of the smoke of the pit. ³ Then out of the smoke locusts came upon the earth. And to them was given power, as the scorpions of the earth have power. ⁴ They were commanded not to harm the grass of the earth, or any green thing, or any tree, but only those men who do not have the seal of God on their foreheads. ⁵ And they were not given *authority* to kill them, but to torment them *for* five months. Their torment *was* like the torment of a scorpion when it strikes a man. ⁶ In those days men will seek death and will not find it; they will desire to die, and death will flee from them.

⁷ The shape of the locusts was like horses prepared for battle. On their heads were crowns of something like gold, and their faces *were* like the faces of men. ⁸ They had hair like women's hair, and their teeth were like lions' *teeth*. ⁹ And they had breastplates like breastplates of iron, and the sound of their wings *was* like the sound of chariots with many horses running into battle. ¹⁰ They had tails like scorpions, and there were stings in their tails. Their power *was* to hurt men five months. ¹¹ And they had as king over them the angel of the bottomless pit, whose name in Hebrew *is* Abaddon, but in Greek he has the name Apollyon.

¹² One woe is past. Behold, still two more woes are coming after these things.

¹³ Then the sixth angel sounded: And I heard a voice from the four horns of the golden altar which is before God, ¹⁴ saying to the sixth angel who had the trumpet, "Release the four angels who are bound at the great river Euphrates." ¹⁵ So the four angels, who had been prepared for the hour and day and month and year, were released to kill a third of mankind. ¹⁶ Now the number of the army of the horsemen *was* two hundred million; I heard the number of them. ¹⁷ And thus I saw the horses

The Revelation

in the vision: those who sat on them had breastplates of fiery red, hyacinth blue, and sulfur yellow; and the heads of the horses were like the heads of lions; and out of their mouths came fire, smoke, and brimstone. [18] By these three *plagues* a third of mankind was killed—by the fire and the smoke and the brimstone which came out of their mouths. [19] For their power is in their mouth and in their tails; for their tails *are* like serpents, having heads; and with them they do harm.

20 But the rest of mankind, who were not killed by these plagues, did not repent of the works of their hands, that they should not worship demons, and idols of gold, silver, brass, stone, and wood, which can neither see nor hear nor walk. [21] And they did not repent of their murders or their sorceries or their sexual immorality or their thefts. (Revelation 9:1-21 NKJV)

Insights

A great rebellion triggers the breaking of a **seventh seal** that precedes its seven angels, each with a trumpet, starting in chapter 8 and continuing through 11. After the thousand years of peace under Messiah, even before Satan is released, the lawlessness of sinful humanity has spread. As it turns out, peace on earth is not what people want after all, but insurrection and rebellion against the governance of God. By repentance we grow close to God, but refusing to repent, we are doomed. Realizing the potential of our own flesh in others, we love them because God loves us.

In 20:1-3 an angel comes *down from heaven, having the key to the bottomless pit* to lock up the devil *till after the thousand years.* In 9:1 an angel falls to the earth with a key to the pit at the **fifth trumpet** when the abyss is unlocked.

20 Then I saw an angel coming down from heaven, having the key to the bottomless pit and a great chain in his hand. [2] He laid hold of the dragon, that serpent of old, who is *the* Devil and Satan, and bound him for a thousand years; [3] and he cast him into the bottomless pit, and shut him up, and set a seal on him, so that he should deceive the nations no more till the thousand years were finished. But after these things he must be released for a little while. (Rev. 20:1-3 NKJV)

Insights: Chapter 9

Satan rises as *Apollyon,* "the destroyer" from the abyss, and the preceding passage from Revelation is fulfilled. (20:1-3, p. 106; cf. 9:11) God uses the devil to mete out destruction and to test and purify His saints at the end. (See Is. 54:16-17; Job 1:6-12) **Three woes** are sent by the last three trumpets, starting in 9 and culminating in chapter 11. The era of the trumpets is revealed by the **fifth trumpet** at the **first great woe when the key** of this prophecy is handed to a fallen angel who **unlocks the abyss.**

The angel opens the pit to release Apollyon and his swarms; thus the trumpets begin after Yeshua's thousand-year reign. The first four trumpeters blow their horns; then the lord of the locusts is loosed at the fifth angel's trumpet, the **first great woe.** The dragon, Apollyon, rises out of the pit as its captive. (See 20:7-8)

> ⁴ The appearance of them <u>is as</u> the appearance of horses, and <u>as horsemen</u> so shall they run. ⁵ <u>Like</u> the noise of chariots on the tops of mountains shall they leap, <u>like</u> the noise of a flame of fire that devoureth the stubble, <u>as a strong people</u> set in battle array. ... ⁷ They shall run <u>like mighty men</u>; they shall climb the wall <u>like men of war</u>; and they shall march every one on his ways, and they shall not break their ranks: ⁸ Neither shall one thrust another; they shall walk every one in his path: and *when* they shall fall upon the sword, they shall not be wounded. ⁹ They shall run to and fro in the city; they shall run upon the wall, they shall climb up upon the houses; they shall enter in at the windows <u>like a thief</u>. (Joel 2:4-5, 7-9) [This is full of similes and metaphors.]

Joel saw locusts rise from the smoke with their king, but unlike locusts, they don't eat plants, but torture people without killing them. If they fall on a sword, they aren't wounded. In chapter 9 they harm no one with the seal of God on his forehead:

> ¹³ In Him you also *trusted,* after you heard the word of truth, the gospel of your salvation; in whom also, having believed, <u>you were sealed with the Holy Spirit</u> of promise, ¹⁴ who is the guarantee of our inheritance until the redemption of the purchased possession, to the praise of His glory. (Eph. 1:13-14)

During the millennial reign, saints and sinners live on earth. In 9:1 the angel blows the fifth trumpet, bringing the **first great**

The Revelation

woe. Rising *out of the smoke* with Apollyon, the tormenters have stings like scorpions, making men writhe in agony but without killing them though they long for death. Arriving in swarms they neither look like locusts nor resemble anything natural: if they're men, their hair is like women's; if women, their faces are like men; if human, their teeth are sharp as lions'. These devils are on a mission to torture humankind.

At the **sixth trumpet**, four fallen angels are released at the Euphrates River, for only fallen angels are bound. One thousand years before, the riverbed was dried when a sixth angel in 16:12 poured out his bowl for the kings of the East to cross it on their way to Armageddon. As his armies head for Israel's unwalled villages, they destroy one third of mankind, seen in 20:7-10.

Notice the word "sorceries" in 9:21, also in chapter 18. The Greek is *pharmakeia,* "drugs," or potions, used by sorcerers or drug-dealers, seducing minds to bring them under the powers of the spirit world. These kinds of *pharmakeia* are used in primitive and sophisticated cultures and will be used until the very end, but the people of God must be sober. (1 Thes. 5:6; 1 Pet. 4:7; 5:8)

Watching Jerusalem

Zechariah depicts the Messiah's city as safely inhabited:

> [9] <u>And the LORD shall be king over all the earth</u>: in that day shall there be one LORD and his name one...[11] And men shall dwell in it, and there shall be no more utter destruction; but <u>Jerusalem shall be safely inhabited</u>. (Zec. 14:9, 11) ["Safely inhabited" is a key to its time.]

Meshech and Tubal are areas in eastern and western Turkey. The Black Sea is north; Ukraine and Russia are north of the sea. [Some biblical lands have unknown locations today.] Jerusalem is *safely inhabited* when Gog gathers an army at the sixth trumpet:

> 38 The word of the LORD came to me: [2] "Son of man, set your face toward Gog, of the land of Meshech, the chief prince of Meshech and Tubal, an prophesy against him ... [5] Persia, Cush, and Put are with them, all of them with shield and helmet; [6] Gomer and all his hordes; Beth-Togarmah <u>from the uttermost parts of the north</u> with all his hordes—many peoples are with you.
> ... [8] <u>After many days you will be mustered. In the latter

Insights: Chapter 9

> years you will go against the land that is restored from war, the land whose people were gathered from many peoples upon the mountains of Israel, which had been a continual waste. Its people were brought out from the peoples and <u>now dwell securely, all of them</u>. [9] You will advance, coming on like a storm. You will be like a cloud covering the land, you and all your hordes, and many peoples with you.
> [10] "Thus says the Lord GOD: On that day, thoughts will come into your mind, and you will devise an evil scheme [11] and say, 'I will go up against the land of unwalled villages. <u>I will fall upon the quiet people who dwell securely, all of them dwelling without walls, and having no bars or gates,</u>' [12] to seize spoil and carry off plunder, to turn your hand against the waste places that are now inhabited, and the people who were gathered from the nations, who have acquired livestock and goods, who dwell at the center of the earth. ...
> [14] "Therefore, son of man, prophesy, and say to Gog, Thus says the Lord GOD: On that day when my people Israel are <u>dwelling securely</u>, will you not know it? [15] <u>You will come from your place out of the uttermost parts of the north</u>, you and many peoples with you, all of them riding on horses, a great host, a mighty army. [16] You will come up against my people Israel, like a cloud covering the land. <u>In the latter days I will bring you against my land, that the nations may know me, when through you, O Gog, I vindicate my holiness before their eyes</u>.
> (Ezk. 38:8-12, 14-16 ESV) [There are no burial grounds here.]

The horses must be metaphors of military vehicles that kill a third of mankind by the fire and brimstone out of their "mouths" and the harm in their "tails."

When we compare Ezekiel 38 and 39, there's an element of redundancy because Gog battles Israel both before and after the thousand years. It's normal for the prophecies to be out of order; when they're redundant, they're repeated. Ezekiel 38 describes Gog after the thousand years, as prophesied:

> [7] <u>When the thousand years are over</u>, Satan will be released from his prison [8] and will go out to deceive the nations in the four corners of the earth—Gog and Magog—and to gather them for battle. In number they

are like the sand on the seashore. ⁹ They marched across the breadth of the earth and surrounded the camp of God's people, the city he loves. <u>But fire came down from heaven and devoured them</u>. ¹⁰ And the devil, who deceived them, was thrown into the lake of burning sulfur, <u>where the beast and the false prophet had been thrown</u>. They will be tormented day and night for ever and ever. (Rev. 20:7-10 NIV)

Ezekiel 38 continues to the end of time:

¹⁷ "Thus says the Lord GOD: Are you he of whom I spoke in former days by my servants the prophets of Israel, who in those days prophesied for years that I would bring you against them? ¹⁸ But on that day, <u>the day that Gog shall come against the land of Israel</u>, declares the Lord GOD, my wrath will be roused in my anger. ¹⁹ For in my jealousy and in my blazing wrath I declare, On that day <u>there shall be a great earthquake in the land of Israel</u>. ²⁰ The fish of the sea and the birds of the heavens and the beasts of the field and all creeping things that creep on the ground, and all the people who are on the face of the earth, shall quake at my presence. And the mountains shall be thrown down, and the cliffs shall fall, and every wall shall tumble to the ground. ²¹ I will summon <u>a sword against Gog on all my mountains</u>, declares the Lord GOD. Every man's sword will be against his brother. ²² With pestilence and bloodshed I will enter into judgment with him, and <u>I will rain upon him and his hordes and the many peoples who are with him torrential rains and hailstones, fire and sulfur</u>. ²³ So I will show my greatness and my holiness and make myself known in the eyes of many nations. Then they will know that I am the LORD. (Ezk. 38:17-23 ESV; cf. Rev. 11:13)

The **sixth trumpet** brings the **second woe** with two parts, separated by chapter 10. In 9:18 three plagues, i.e., catastrophes, finish the first part of its woe. The rebellion is identified in 9:20-21. It's also in the second part of the sixth trumpet's woe when two witnesses rise in 11:3. It ends in 11:14: *the second woe is past; behold, the third woe is coming quickly.* In 11:15 **the last trump** is at the end of time. After the Great Judgment Day, the eternal Kingdom comes (in 11:18).

The Revelation of Jesus Christ

CHAPTER 10

10 Then I saw another mighty angel coming down from heaven, surrounded by a cloud, with a rainbow over his head. His face was like the sun, his legs were like fiery pillars, ² and he had a little scroll opened in his hand. He put his right foot on the sea, his left on the land, ³ and he cried out with a loud voice like a roaring lion. When he cried out, the seven thunders spoke with their voices. ⁴ And when the seven thunders spoke, I was about to write. Then I heard a voice from heaven, saying, "Seal up what the seven thunders said, and do not write it down!"

⁵ Then the angel that I had seen standing on the sea and on the land raised his right hand to heaven. ⁶ He swore an oath by the One who lives forever and ever, who created heaven and what is in it, the earth and what is in it, and the sea and what is in it: "There will no longer be an interval of time, ⁷ but in the days of the sound of the seventh angel, when he will blow his trumpet, then God's hidden plan will be completed, as He announced to His servants the prophets."

⁸ Now the voice that I heard from heaven spoke to me again and said, "Go, take the scroll that lies open in the hand of the angel who is standing on the sea and on the land."

⁹ So I went to the angel and asked him to give me the little scroll. He said to me, "Take and eat it; it will be bitter in your stomach, but it will be as sweet as honey in your mouth."

¹⁰ Then I took the little scroll from the angel's hand and ate it. It was as sweet as honey in my mouth, but when I ate it, my stomach became bitter. ¹¹ And I was told, "You must prophesy again about many peoples, nations, languages, and kings." (Revelation 10:1-11 HCSB)

Insights

An angel interrupts the judgments of the vision, holding out a little scroll for John to take it from His hand and to read, swallow, and digest its difficult message. **In the midst of the middle woe,** He prepares the prophet to speak again.

The Revelation

The angel crowned with grace cried out like a lion and seven voices thundered in heaven but their words were sealed. The mysterious plan is complete when all that is perfect arrives. Now we see through dark glasses, but one day, we will see clear-eyed and face-to-face when He judges the living and the dead on the last day. (1 Cor. 13:12; Rev. 11:18)

What about the little scroll John took and ate? Whatever it said, it wasn't easy for John. It likely refers to the words he must deliver in chapter 11, but only John knows the mystery in the message that parted the sixth trumpet's woe. At that time two witnesses send international judgments against the rebels. John is probably one of the witnesses who judges the earth for three-and-a-half biblical years.

When he received the scroll, he ate it to digest it—taking it into his spirit, mulling over it, and receiving its words, which lead us to **the second half of Daniel's seventieth week.** *And he said unto me, Thou must prophesy again about many peoples, and nations, and tongues, and kings. (Rev. 10:11)*

The Revelation of Jesus Christ

CHAPTER 11

11 Then I was given a reed like a measuring rod. And the angel stood, saying, "Rise and measure the temple of God, the altar, and those who worship there. ² But leave out the court which is outside the temple, and do not measure it, for it has been given to the Gentiles. And they will tread the holy city underfoot *for* forty-two months. ³ And I will give *power* to my two witnesses, and they will prophesy one thousand two hundred and sixty days, clothed in sackcloth."

⁴ These are the two olive trees and the two lampstands standing before the God of the earth. ⁵ And if anyone wants to harm them, fire proceeds from their mouth and devours their enemies. And if anyone wants to harm them, he must be killed in this manner. ⁶ These have power to shut heaven, so that no rain falls in the days of their prophecy; and they have power over waters to turn them to blood, and to strike the earth with all plagues, as often as they desire.

⁷ When they finish their testimony, the beast that ascends out of the bottomless pit will make war against them, overcome them, and kill them. ⁸ And their dead bodies *will lie* in the street of the great city which spiritually is called Sodom and Egypt, where also our Lord was crucified. ⁹ Then *those* from the peoples, tribes, tongues, and nations will see their dead bodies three-and-a-half days, and not allow their dead bodies to be put into graves. ¹⁰ And those who dwell on the earth will rejoice over them, make merry, and send gifts to one another, because these two prophets tormented those who dwell on the earth.

¹¹ Now after the three-and-a-half days the breath of life from God entered them, and they stood on their feet, and great fear fell on those who saw them. ¹² And they heard a loud voice from heaven saying to them, "Come up here." And they ascended to heaven in a cloud, and their enemies saw them. ¹³ In the same hour there was a great earthquake, and a tenth of the city fell. In the earthquake seven thousand people were killed, and the rest were afraid and gave glory to the God of

The Revelation

heaven.

¹⁴ The second woe is past. Behold, the third woe is coming quickly.

¹⁵ Then the seventh angel sounded: And there were loud voices in heaven, saying, "The kingdoms of this world have become *the kingdoms* of our Lord and of His Christ, and He shall reign forever and ever!" ¹⁶ And the twenty-four elders who sat before God on their thrones fell on their faces and worshiped God, ¹⁷ saying:

> "We give You thanks, O Lord God Almighty,
> The One who is and who was and who is to come,
> Because You have taken Your great power and reigned.
> ¹⁸ The nations were angry, and Your wrath has come,
> And the time of the dead, that they should be judged,
> And that You should reward Your servants the prophets and the saints,
> And those who fear Your name, small and great,
> And should destroy those who destroy the earth."

¹⁹ Then the temple of God was opened in heaven, and the ark of His covenant was seen in His temple. And there were lightnings, noises, thunderings, an earthquake and great hail. (Revelation 11:1-19 NKJV)

Insights

In 20:1-3 an angel captures the dragon, Apollyon, locks him in the abyss, and chains and seals him till a thousand years pass. Although Messiah reigns, sin still dominates human nature. His worshipers are in the temple, but sinners are on the outside. *The holy city shall they tread underfoot forty and two months. (11:2b)* The rebels in 11:18 stirred God's wrath in chapter 8. In 9 the worldwide revolt continues, and Gog rises to destroy Jerusalem.

9:1-11: An angel falls from heaven with **a key** to unlock the pit and release the devil at the fifth trumpet. The rebels resist the Lord, even in Jerusalem, till **the end at the last trump** in 11:15. After 20:7-10 reveals the wrath of God against Gog and Magog, the dragon's second death sends the deceiver to his interminable end in the lake of fire.

Insights: Chapter 11

11:18 reveals the prophetic revolt after Christ reigns: *The nations were angry* and refused to repent (in 9:20-21), justifying the wrath unleashed against them. A thousand years before, the beast and his prophet were destroyed, and the devil was locked in a pit. After the thousand-year reign of Jesus the King, sinners incite a revolution, and He orders seven angels with trumpets to send His wrath against the insurrectionists. The devil is released from the pit at the fifth trumpet (in 20:2-3). The revolt continues to the last day at the last trump. (1 Cor. 15:51-54)

> 2 Why do the heathen rage, and the people imagine a vain thing? ² The kings of the earth set themselves, and the rulers take counsel together, against the LORD, and against his anointed, *saying*, ³ Let us break their bands asunder and cast away their cords from us. ⁴ <u>He that sitteth in the heavens shall laugh: the LORD shall have them in derision.</u> ⁵ <u>Then shall he speak unto them in his wrath, and vex them in his sore displeasure.</u> ⁶ <u>Yet have I set my king upon my holy hill of Zion.</u> ⁷ I will declare the decree: the LORD hath said unto me, Thou art my Son; this day have I begotten thee. ⁸ Ask of me, and I shall give thee the heathen for thine inheritance, and the uttermost parts of the earth for thy possession. ⁹ <u>Thou shalt break them with a rod of iron; thou shalt dash them in pieces like a potter's vessel.</u> ¹⁰ Be wise now therefore, O ye kings: be instructed, ye judges of the earth. ¹¹ Serve the LORD with fear, and rejoice with trembling. ¹² Kiss the Son, lest he be angry, and ye perish from the way, when his wrath is kindled but a little. <u>Blessed are all they that put their trust in him.</u> (Ps. 2:1-12) [note repeated prophecies]

The events of chapter 11 don't appear till after the thousand years. The seven trumpets begin at the seventh seal in chapter 8. In 9 we see why: it's an attempted coup against Israel's Messiah:

> ²⁰ But the rest of mankind, who were not killed by these plagues, did not repent of the works of their hands, that they should not worship demons, and idols of gold, silver, brass, stone, and wood, which can neither see nor hear nor walk. ²¹ And they did not repent of their murders or their sorceries or their sexual immorality or their thefts. (Rev. 9:20-21 NKJV; cf. Rev. 20:7-15)

The Revelation

The Seventieth Week

During the revolt, two prophets judge the nations for forty-two biblical months, or 1,260 days. It's the last half of Daniel's **seventieth week** (in Dan. 9:27). Saints and sinners are all judged by their works (in 11:18) on **the last day** (in Jn. 6:39-54, p. 239; 1 Cor. 15:24-28, last paragraph, p. 119-20).

Two witnesses are anointed as two olive trees that stand before the Lord (in Zec. 4:14). They are also two candlesticks, shining in the dark; the anointing feeds their flames.

The destroyer who rose out of the earth with his locusts slays the witnesses, but death can't keep them. The breath of God raises them to life and calls them up to heaven. Astonished, the idolaters watch as the armies surround Jerusalem. Their revolt ends when God destroys the destroyers (in 20:9-10).

Chapter 20 retells it: the dragon is locked in the abyss; Jesus rules for a thousand years; the destroyer is loosed; Gog and Magog surround the city; Satan is destroyed, Judgment Day arrives.

The **first half of Daniel's seventieth week** preceded the thousand years. The beast had *authority to continue for forty-two months*, 1,260 days, in Rev. 13:5—not the 1,290 days (in Dan. 12:11). Before the **first half of the seventieth week** ended, its firstfruits led its martyrs as they ascended together with the living who were left to meet the Lord in the air. His wrath fell till He returned to destroy the beast, his prophet, and the armies in Armageddon and to lock the dragon in the abyss.

At the end of a thousand years of peace on earth, rebels rise against the King, and His trumpeters go forth. The **first woe** is at **the fifth trumpet** and Satan is loosed from the pit (in 9:1-2, 11). At **the sixth trumpet,** two witnesses judge the rebels for 1,260 days **in the second part of the sixth trumpet's woe, the latter half of Daniel's seventieth week.** Satan kills the two witnesses, but they rise to life again. An earthquake shakes the city. The *second woe is past (in 11:14).*

Rev. 9:1-2, 11; 11:7 reveal Satan's release from the pit; he rises as the Destroyer. The **last half of the seventieth week** is in the **latter part of the second woe.** As it ends the devil kills the prophets, but they ascend to God. **At the last trump**, he's hurled into the lake of fire (in 20:10), destroyed when **the last judgment** begins at the great white throne (in 20:11; cf. 11:18).

Insights: Chapter 11

²² With pestilence and bloodshed I will enter into judgment with him, and I will rain upon him and his hordes and the many peoples who are with him torrential <u>rains and hailstones, fire and sulfur</u>. (Ezk. 38:22 ESV)

⁷ Now when the thousand years have expired, <u>Satan will be released</u> from his prison ⁸ and will go out to deceive the nations which are in the four corners of the earth, Gog and Magog, <u>to gather them together</u> to battle, whose number *is* as the sand of the sea. ⁹ They went up on the breadth of the earth and surrounded the camp of the saints and the beloved city. <u>And fire came down from God out of heaven and devoured them</u>. (Rev. 20:7-9 NKJV)

Gog and Magog represent the nations of which Gog is chief. At the end their influence covers the earth. Encircling Jerusalem in Ezekiel 38, they are not slain by the sword of His mouth, but by fire, sulfur, and hail from heaven when time ends **on the last day**. There are no burial grounds or eagles to feast on the dead. Things come to a quick conclusion at the end of time.

11:17 is literally, *Thou hast taken thy great power <u>and didst reign (YLT)</u>,* <u>not</u> *have begun to reign.* The devil is released at the fifth trumpet. At the seventh trumpet, both saints and sinners are judged and death is destroyed (in 1 Cor. 15:52, 54). In 20:10-15 the dead are judged after the thousand years; so the trumpets sound after He reigns. [KJV has *hast reigned;* ZGE, *didst reign.*]

The **last trump** hails the **third woe**: fire, hail, and sulfur destroy the armies in Armageddon (in Ezk. 38:22, above). The dragon is destroyed. The Sanctuary in heaven reveals the ark of the covenant. Heaven and earth disappear, and space is gone (in 20:11). Saints and sinners rise before Yeshua on the great white throne (in 11:18). [It sets on a *bema,* its platform.] In judgment one is condemned or justified. The judge decides each case based on his wisdom, the facts, the laws, and perhaps grace.

About Judgment

⁴² And the Lord said, "Who then is the faithful and sensible steward, whom his master will put in charge of his servants, to give them their rations at the proper time? ⁴³ Blessed is that slave whom his master finds so doing when he comes. ⁴⁴ Truly I say to you that he will

put him in charge of all his possessions. ⁴⁵ But if that slave says in his heart, 'My master will be a long time incoming,' and begins to beat the slaves, *both* men and women, and to eat and drink and get drunk; ⁴⁶ the master of that slave will come on a day when he does not expect *him* and at an hour he does not know, and will cut him in pieces, and assign him a place with the unbelievers. ⁴⁷ And that slave who knew his master's will and did not get ready or act in accord with his will, will receive many lashes, ⁴⁸ but the one who did not know *it*, and committed deeds worthy of a flogging, will receive but few. From everyone who has been given much, much will be required; and to whom they entrusted much, of him they will ask all the more.
(Luke 12:42-48 NASB)

¹⁰ For we must all appear before the judgment seat of Christ; that every one may receive the things done in his body, according to that he hath done, <u>whether it be good or bad.</u> ¹¹ <u>Knowing therefore the terror of the Lord, we persuade men</u>; (2 Cor. 5:10-11a; cf. Rev. 20:11-15)

Most Bibles translate the Greek *krisis* as "judgment," but in some versions it is *will not be condemned*. In the *Wycliffe Bible*, it is *cometh not into doom*. In *King James* it is *shall not come into condemnation*. Literally, condemnation is *katakrima*, not *krisis*.

²⁴ Truly, truly, I say to you, whoever hears my word and believes him who sent me has eternal life. He does <u>not come into judgment</u>, but has passed from death to life. (John 5:24 ESV) [This is when He calls the elect to rise.]

We presume *krisis* is adverse judgment, as at times it is. We think of Paul, who wrote, <u>*We must all stand before the judgment seat of Christ*</u>. *¹¹ For it is written, As I live, saith the Lord, every knee shall bow to me, and every tongue shall confess to God. ¹² So then every one of us shall give account of himself to God.* *(Rom. 14:10b-12)* It is true for Paul and his contemporaries and is normative for everyone; but still, *krisis* is correctly "judgment." We should expect to stand before the Judgment Seat. All who hate truth are damned, but whoever practices living in the light is saved (in Jn. 3:19-21). We won't be lost in the shameful nakedness of our sins if we clothe ourselves with His holiness.

Insights: Chapter 11

The Three Resurrections

Jesus introduced two resurrections that escape the judgment, saying, *He that heareth my word and believeth on him that sent me hath everlasting life and* <u>*shall not come into [krisis]; but is passed from death unto life.*</u>

1.) Saying, *the hour* <u>*now*</u> *is,* He foretold His resurrection: the elect who heard His voice and believed in the Father rose after Him. These heroes entered Jerusalem apart from judgment. (Mat. 27:52-53; cf. Heb. 11:1-12:1) Their lives were epics.

2.) He also said, *the hour* <u>*is coming*</u>: *Immediately after* the *tribulation ...* His angels gather the elect who <u>*hear* His voice *and live*</u> (in Mat. 24:29-31; 1 Thes. 4:15-16). *I saw the souls of them that were beheaded .. who had not worshipped the beast ... and they lived and reigned with Christ a thousand years. (See Rev. 20:4b)* They are *passed from death to life* apart from judgment.

3.) Finally He said, <u>*And he has given him power to execute judgment*</u>, *because he is the Son of Man. ... The rest of the dead will hear His voice and rise to be judged* when all confess Jesus Christ is Lord. (Rom. 14:11; cf. Rev. 11:18; 20:5; 1 Pet. 4:5) Listen:

1–2.) ²⁴ Truly, truly, I say to you, whoever hears my word and believes him who sent me has eternal life. <u>He does not come into judgment</u>, but has passed from death to life. ²⁵ Truly, truly, I say to you, <u>an hour is coming, and is now here, when the dead will hear the voice of the Son of God, and those who hear will live.</u> ²⁶ For as the Father has life in himself, so he has granted the Son also to have life in himself. (Jn. 5:24-26 ESV)

3.) ²⁷ And he has given Him <u>authority to execute judgment</u>, because he is the Son of Man. ²⁸ Do not marvel at this, for an hour is coming in which <u>all who are in the tombs will hear his voice</u> ²⁹ and come out, those who have done good to the resurrection of life, and those who have done evil to the resurrection of judgment.
(Jn. 5:27-29 ESV) [Tombs/graves is Grk.: *mnemeion*.]

²² For as in Adam all die, even so in Christ shall all be made alive. ²³ But every man in his own order: Christ the firstfruits; afterward they that are Christ's at his coming. ²⁴ Then *cometh* the end, when he shall have delivered up the kingdom to God, even the Father; when he shall

The Revelation

have put down all rule and authority and power. ²⁵ For he must reign, till he hath put all his enemies under his feet. ²⁶ The last enemy *that* shall be destroyed *is* death. ²⁷ For he hath put all things under his feet." But when he saith all things are put under *him, it is* manifest that he is excepted which did put all things under him. ²⁸ And when all things shall be subdued unto him, then shall the Son also himself be subject unto him that put all things under him, that God may be all in all. (1 Cor. 15:22-28)

There are three resurrections, but only one judgment, which is on the last day at the last trump (in 11:18-19; cf. 20:7-15). Some feared the dead wouldn't rise, but Paul revealed that supernatural laws govern nature as well as the resurrection of the dead:

⁴¹ There is one glory of the sun, and another glory of the moon, and another glory of the stars: for one star differeth from another star in glory. ⁴² So also is the resurrection of the dead. It is sown in corruption; it is raised in incorruption: ⁴³ It is sown in dishonour; it is raised in glory: it is sown in weakness; it is raised in power: ⁴⁴ It is sown a natural body; it is raised a spiritual body. There is a natural body, and there is a spiritual body. (1 Cor. 15:41-44)

Our bodies will be like Jesus' body but will vary in glory as stars do, some outshining others.

¹⁴ Blessed are they that do his commandments, that they may have right to the tree of life, and may enter in through the gates into the city. ¹⁵ For without are dogs, and sorcerers, and whoremongers, and murderers, and idolaters, and whosoever loveth and maketh a lie. ¹⁶ I Jesus have sent mine angel to testify unto you these things in the churches. I am the root and the offspring of David, and the bright and morning star. (Rev. 22:14-16)

¹¹ "He who has an ear, let him hear what the Spirit says to the churches. <u>He who overcomes</u> shall not be hurt by the second death." (Rev. 2:11 NKJV)

Enoch did not come into judgment; neither did Moses nor Elijah. They passed from death to life. The judgments of God are perfect, and His ways are hidden. (See Gen. 5:24; Mat. 17:3)

⁵ <u>He who overcomes</u> shall be clothed in white garments, and I will not blot out his name from the Book of Life, but

Insights: Chapter 11

I will confess his name before My Father and before His angels. ⁶"He who has an ear, let him hear what the Spirit says to the churches." (Rev. 3:5-6 NKJV)

Spirits are waiting under the altar. Paul wrote, *For in this we groan, earnestly desiring to be clothed upon with our house which is from heaven: if so be that being clothed, we shall not be found naked. (2 Cor. 5:2-3)* We wait for new bodies, dwellings that are eternal: *for we also who are in the tabernacle do groan, being burdened, seeing we wish not to unclothe ourselves, but to clothe ourselves, that the mortal may be swallowed up of the life. (2 Cor. 5:4 YLT)* We *clothe ourselves* with righteousness.

> ²⁶ And above the firmament over their heads *was* the likeness of a throne, in appearance like a sapphire stone; on the likeness of the throne *was* a likeness with the appearance of a man high above it. ²⁷ Also from the appearance of His waist and upward I saw, as it were, the color of amber with the appearance of fire all around within it; and from the appearance of His waist and downward I saw, as it were, the appearance of fire with brightness all around. ²⁸ Like the appearance of a rainbow in a cloud on a rainy day, so *was* the appearance of the brightness all around it. This was the appearance of the likeness of the glory of the LORD.
> So when I saw *it*, I fell on my face, and I heard a voice of One speaking. (Ezk. 1:26-28 NKJV)

> ¹⁵ As it is said,
>
> "Today, if you hear his voice,
> do not harden your hearts as in the rebellion."
>
> ¹⁶ For who were those who heard and yet rebelled? Was it not all those who left Egypt led by Moses? ¹⁷ And with whom was he provoked for forty years? <u>Was it not with those who sinned</u>, whose bodies fell in the wilderness? ¹⁸ And to whom did he swear that they would not enter his rest, but to those who were disobedient? ¹⁹ So we see that <u>they were unable to enter because of unbelief</u>. (Heb. 3:15-19 ESV)

Had they believed, they would not have sinned in the desert. By faith we partake in His righteousness as new creatures, living in the divine nature of His Spirit, not after the material nature of

The Revelation

the flesh. He told us if we don't hate our lives, we can't be His disciples. We follow Christ by giving up our selfish wills to do the will of God. He loves us who love Him but chose us long before we were free to choose Him. (Receive Romans 9.)

While reading Romans 6-8, we should believe in the power of the risen Christ who lives to deliver us from our sins. The crux of our faith is in our surrender to the Spirit by faith in His words. *... the just will live by his faith.* (Hab. 2:4b) It's how we live. As we mature we test ourselves and don't look for faults in others.

And above all things have fervent charity among yourselves: for charity shall cover the multitude of sins. (1 Pet. 4:8) Obeying Him we prove we love God, and by His love, we love others.

> [22] Judas (not Iscariot) said to him, ""Lord, how is it that you will manifest yourself to us, and not to the world?" [23] Jesus answered him, "If anyone loves me, he will keep my word, and my Father will love him, and we will come to him and make our home with him. [24] Whoever does not love me does not keep my words. And the word that you hear is not mine but the Father's who sent me. (Jn. 14:22-24 ESV)

> [23] May God himself, the God of peace, sanctify you through and through. May your whole spirit, soul and body be kept blameless at the coming of our Lord Jesus Christ. [24] The one who calls you is faithful and he will do it. (1 Thes. 5:23-24 NIV)

The vast number of saints from ages past are judged **on the last day** at the great white throne.

> [18] The nations were angry, and Your wrath has come,
> And the time of the dead, that they should be judged,
> And that You should reward Your servants the
>   prophets and the saints,
> And those who fear Your name, small and great,
> And should destroy those who destroy the earth."
> (Rev. 11:18 NKJV)

The Last Trump!

At the **last trump**, i.e., the seventh one, Gog the man of Satan, entices the earth by Magog as Babylon had done till her destruction. Christ proves the sin in sinners who refuse to repent. In the best conditions, no one seeks God—not one. (Rom. 3:10-

Insights: Chapter 11

11; Phil. 2:12-16) Fire falls from above, and Satan is cast into a lake of fire on **the last day**:

> **11** Then I saw a great white throne and Him who sat on it, from whose face the earth and the heaven fled away. And there was found no place for them. **12** And I saw the dead, small and great, standing before God, and books were opened. ... (Rev. 20:11-12a NKJV)

In 20:5 *the rest of the dead* rise after the thousand years at the great white throne where Jesus judges humankind. *The rest of the dead,* i.e., all who will have died but are not yet risen—the living and the dead, saints and sinners—are judged **on the last day** in 11:18. We all have our salvation to work out and our own changes to embrace. Some stumble for their purification at the end, but God is faithful to deliver us from evil. (Dan. 12:35)

> **2** Multitudes who sleep in the dust of the earth will awake: some to everlasting life, others to shame and everlasting contempt. (Dan. 12:2 NIV)

Without partiality losses and rewards are given to saints and rejection and wrath to sinners and hypocrites. Its day reveals the choices we've made and the things we've done by faith when we rise to eternal life in degrees of glory. Judgments and rewards, sorrows and joys, regrets and comforts follow our works whether by the flesh or by the Spirit. When Paul said we must all stand before the judgment seat of Christ, he referred to the last trump:

> **50** Now this I say, brethren, that flesh and blood cannot inherit the kingdom of God; nor does corruption inherit incorruption. **51** Behold, I tell you a mystery: We shall not all sleep, but we shall all be changed— **52** in a moment, in the twinkling of an eye, <u>at the last trumpet</u>. For the trumpet will sound, and the dead will be raised incorruptible, and we shall be changed. **53** For this corruptible must put on incorruption, and this mortal *must* put on immortality. **54** So when this corruptible has put on incorruption, and this mortal has put on immortality, <u>then shall be brought to pass the saying that is written: *"Death is swallowed up in victory."*</u> (1 Cor. 15:50-54 NKJV)
>
> **55** "O death, where is your victory?
> O death, where is your sting?"

The Revelation

⁵⁶ The sting of death is sin, and the power of sin is the law. ⁵⁷ But thanks be to God, who gives us the victory through our Lord Jesus Christ. ⁵⁸ Therefore, my beloved brothers, be steadfast, immovable, always abounding in the work of the Lord, knowing that in the Lord your labor is not in vain. (1 Cor. 15:55-58 ESV)

²⁴ The sins of some people are conspicuous, going before them to judgment, but the sins of others appear later. ²⁵ So also good works are conspicuous, and even those that are not cannot remain hidden.
(1 Tim. 5:24-25 ESV)

¹⁷ Even so faith, if it hath not works, is dead, being alone. ... ²⁴ Ye see that by works a man is justified, and not by faith only. (James 2:17, 24; cf. Rom. 8)

¹¹ Then I saw a great white throne and Him who sat upon it, from whose presence earth and heaven fled away, and no place was found for them. ¹² And I saw the dead, the great and the small, standing before the throne, and books were opened; and another book was opened, which is *the book* of life; and the dead were judged from the things which were written in the books, according to their deeds. ¹³ And the sea gave up the dead which were in it, and death and Hades gave up the dead which were in them; and they were judged, every one *of them* according to their deeds. ¹⁴ <u>Then death and Hades were thrown into the lake of fire</u>. This is the second death, the lake of fire. ¹⁵ And if anyone's name was not found written in the book of life, he was thrown into the lake of fire. (Rev. 20:11-15 NASB)

⁴⁴ "Again, the kingdom of heaven is like treasure hidden in a field, which a man found and hid; and for joy over it he goes and sells all that he has and buys that field. (Mat. 13:44 NKJV)

Christ is the man who found the treasure in the field and bought the whole field just for the treasure in it. The world is the field, and we are its treasure. He is patient and kind toward us, and is not willing that any of us should perish, having chosen us for sanctification by faith in the truth before the foundations of the earth:

Insights: Chapter 11

⁹ The Lord is not slack concerning his promise, as some men count slackness; <u>but is longsuffering to us-ward, not willing that any should perish, but that all should come to repentance.</u>   [No believer should perish: Jn. 3:16.]
¹⁰ But <u>the day of the Lord</u> will come as a thief in the night; in which the heavens shall pass away <u>with a great noise</u>, and the elements shall melt with fervent heat, the earth also and the works that are therein shall be burned up.
¹¹ *Seeing* then *that* all these things shall be dissolved, <u>what manner *of persons* ought ye to be in *all* holy conversation and godliness,</u>
¹² Looking for and hasting unto the coming of the day of God, wherein the heavens being on fire shall be dissolved, and the elements shall melt with fervent heat?
¹³ Nevertheless we, according to his promise, look for <u>new heavens and a new earth</u>, wherein dwelleth righteousness.
¹⁴ Wherefore, beloved, seeing that ye look for such things, <u>be diligent that ye may be found of him in peace, without spot, and blameless.</u> (2 Pet. 3:9-14)

The passage by Peter prophesies the end of time at the judgment on the great day of the Lord when the heavens and earth are burned up, making way for new heavens and a new earth. Near the last trump, events rush to the end with no intervals that delay them (in Dan. 10:6). 2 Pet. 3:11-12 refers to the **last day** when the elements melt with fervent heat and disappear. The earth and the heavens dissolve by fire, and there is no place for them—all of space is gone (in Rev. 20:11). After that, Jesus Christ is high up on the judgment throne, and we are very small.

In chapter 11 John measures the temple and its altar but not the courts where rebels rage outside its walls. After Christ's thousand-year reign, in the midst of three woes, **the seventieth week** concludes near the end of **the second woe**.

There's no delay between prophecies anymore. (10:6) After chapter 10, we resume where 9 ended. The second woe continues in 11:3 until it ends at the earthquake that kills seven thousand. *The second woe is past. Behold, the third woe is coming quickly.*

The last trump sounds for the final woe, and twenty-four elders sing praises in heaven. Why on earth would they sing praises in heaven? Yeshua reigned with a rod of iron, the strict

The Revelation

rule of law, and finally His justice is meted out equitably. The wars have been won; it's all over!

They worship the King Yeshua who is seated in Jerusalem, *Saying, We give thee thanks, O Lord God Almighty, which art, and wast, and art to come;* because thou hast taken to thee thy *great power and hast reigned (in Rev. 11:17).*

Many who are first are last, and the last, first. Many who are exalted are diminished, and those who seem the least significant are lifted. Only that which is spiritual remains forever. Holiness exceeds the riches of this world and is more exuberating than carnal minds can imagine. Where there is love, there is life, and where there is life, there is Jesus.

All who trust in this world are disillusioned and disappointed at the end, but faith in the words of God guide us throughout our lives. Life with the Savior speaks volumes of answered prayers and fulfilled hopes, leading to everlasting joy. Faith in false gods leads to destruction. Faith in the Savior proves He is alive from the dead by the life of His Spirit sent to us. By faith in Him alone we are gaining victories over all the allurements of the world, over all its adversity and opposition, even over spiritual battles that rise against us. Outwardly, we're aging, but inwardly, He renews us day by day. We win because He won and reveals Himself in us by His Word and by His Holy Spirit.

Our objective is to value time as men do their finances since how we invest our lives (and our money) matters most. Living by faith, we surrender all to Christ as He gives everything up to the Father. We believe the Father who declared a new covenant, beginning in Genesis when God put enmity between the woman and the serpent, promising her seed would bruise the dragon's head, and leading to Revelation where His eternal Kingdom is revealed.

> Now faith is the substance of things hoped for, the conviction of things not seen. For by it the people of old received their commendation. By faith we understand that the universe was created by the word of God, so that what is seen was not made out of things that are visible. (Heb. 11:1-3 ESV)

The Revelation of Jesus Christ

CHAPTER 12

12 A great sign appeared in heaven: a woman clothed with the sun, and the moon under her feet, and on her head a crown of twelve stars; ²and she was pregnant and she cried out, being in labor and in pain to give birth.

³Then another sign appeared in heaven: and behold, a great red dragon having seven heads and ten horns, and on his heads *were* seven crowns. ⁴And his tail swept away a third of the stars of heaven and hurled them to the earth. And the dragon stood before the woman who was about to give birth, so that when she gave birth he might devour her Child.

⁵And she gave birth to a Son, a male, who is going to rule all the nations with a rod of iron; and her Child was caught up to God and to His throne. ⁶Then the woman fled into the wilderness where she had a place prepared by God, so that there she would be nourished for 1,260 days.

⁷And there was war in heaven, Michael and his angels waging war with the dragon. The dragon and his angels waged war, ⁸and they did not prevail, and there was no longer a place found for them in heaven. ⁹And the great dragon was thrown down, the serpent of old who is called the devil and Satan, who deceives the whole world; he was thrown down to the earth, and his angels were thrown down with him. ¹⁰Then I heard a loud voice in heaven, saying,

"Now the salvation, and the power, and the kingdom of our God and the authority of His Christ have come, for the accuser of our brothers *and sisters* has been thrown down, the one who accuses them before our God day and night. ¹¹And they overcame him because of the blood of the Lamb and because of the word of their testimony, and they did not love their life *even* when faced with death. ¹²For this reason, rejoice, you heavens and you who dwell in them. Woe to the earth and the sea, because the devil has come down to you with great wrath, knowing that he has *only* a short time."

¹³And when the dragon saw that he was thrown down to

The Revelation

the earth, he persecuted the woman who gave birth to the male *Child*. ¹⁴ But the two wings of the great eagle were given to the woman, so that she could fly into the wilderness to her place, where she *was nourished for a time, times, and half a time, away from the presence of the serpent. ¹⁵ And the serpent hurled water like a river out of his mouth after the woman, so that he might cause her to be swept away with the flood. ¹⁶ But the earth helped the woman, and the earth opened its mouth and drank up the river which the dragon had hurled out of his mouth. ¹⁷ So the dragon was enraged with the woman, and went off to make war with the rest of her children, who keep the commandments of God and hold to the testimony of Jesus. (Revelation 12:1-17 NASB)

Insights

Listen to the eloquence of their speech as the stars announce the news of their glorious Creator. *Their line* is lyrical:

19 The heavens declare the glory of God; and the firmament showeth his handiwork.
² Day unto day uttereth speech, and night unto night showeth knowledge.
³ There is no speech nor language, where their voice is not heard.
⁴ Their line has gone out through all the earth, and their words to the end of the world. In them hath he set a tabernacle for the sun,
⁵ Which is as a bridegroom coming out of his chamber, and rejoiceth as a strong man to run a race. (Ps. 19:1-5)

Chapter 12 became the study of *The Star of Bethlehem,* an educational video that reveals the stars of the sky on the night the magi visited the village.[114] "Virgo the virgin" was clothed by the sun with the moon at her feet. By the interpretation of Joseph's dream in Genesis 37, the moon is her spiritual mother, Sarah. A great star slipped through the constellation, representing the birth of Messiah by the king planet Jupiter.

The night the magi saw the star over Bethlehem was history to John as it is to us. The sky revealed more than the past; it was a portal to the future—even for today. (Mic. 5:2) Its universal news is retold by the stars through the ages.

Insights: Chapter 12

And there appeared a great wonder in heaven. (12:1) The night sky surrounded Virgo who labored to deliver a male Child. The Anointed One would rule with a rod of iron but was first taken up to God. The Spirit covered the woman [*clothed with the sun*] who conceived the Word who'd be the Son of God. (Is. 7:14; Lk. 1:35; Jn. 1:14; cf. Gen. 37:9-10) Israel was set apart for Him.

And the moon under her feet showed a daughter of Sarah by her faith though Mary's blessing was greater than hers, but the One who blesses is honored above the one who is blessed. She's compared to Sarah since both had given miraculous births by the promises of God. (Cf. 1 Pet. 3:6; Heb. 7:7) [In chapter 12 the Greek *gune* can be "virgin: but is often "wife" {129x} or "woman" {92x} and is used for its double-meaning. Though the Greek *parthenos* {14x}, or "virgin," is not used, the constellation Virgo reveals a virgin.]

In Is. 7:14 *almah* means "virgin." The woman in chapter 12 must also be a virgin, fulfilling the prophecy. Since its revelation is in the stars, we now know this pertains to the virgin birth by Mary as a descendant of David.

At her birth, Rome was the sixth head, but long before Mary was born, all seven heads had crowns. This means Israel is also in the vision. A remnant was always true to the faith as the *virgin daughter of Israel (in Jer. 31:4; Am. 5:2),* preceding Mary.

Before losing any monarchs, the red dragon pursued Israel to prevent the birth of the promised seed, the Child. When famine covered the land, the sons of Israel went to Egypt for grain but were enslaved for four centuries. Moses freed them, but many perished in unbelief, yet she cried out to give birth and prevailed in her pains; at last a young Jewish girl gave birth to the Savior.

Jupiter and Venus appeared as one star. Astronomers, called "magi," followed its light until it seemed to stop over Bethlehem —on December 25, 2 BC, in the documentary that searched the skies. The magi went to their house at night, bearing three gifts "for the young Child." [Gr: *paidion* is <u>*a young child*</u> from infant to school age.] (See Mat. 2:9; cf. Mt 18:4)

John looked up and saw twelve stars on the head of Virgo: the twelve tribes of Israel blessed the virgin with a garland. (See Rev. 21:9-12) She wore the crown since the days when Rome was foretold. (cf. Rev. 17) 12:5-6 reveals the flight of believing Israel, the woman after the ascension of Jesus Christ to heaven. (12:5)

The Revelation

Thirty-six years later, Jewish believers were in Jerusalem when armies compassed the city. Josephus wrote about the war, attesting that, for an unknown reason, Roman troops turned back to Rome and later returned to Jerusalem. This allowed time for the congregation to cross the Jordan to Pella in 66 AD.[115]

Archeologists recently discovered caves near the town where believers allegedly hid during the siege.[116] (12:16) Wherever it was, they hid for forty-two months, according to the prophecy: *And the woman fled into the wilderness, where she hath <u>a place prepared of God</u>, that they should feed her there <u>a thousand two hundred and threescore days</u>. (Rev. 12:6)*

Jesus had warned the church to flee at Jerusalem's siege. (Lk. 21:21) As He'd foretold, its temple was razed with not a stone on another when God scattered the Jews to all nations. (Lk. 21:20-24)

Josephus cited history to mark time. Though scholars say the Bethlehem star never existed, they also believe Herod died in 3 BC and ruled from 37-3 BC; therefore, they search the sky of 5-7 BC, but the Word corrects the date Herod died. The scholars challenge the inspired writings, but scholars rely on the writings of historians, which are fallible. [Christ was born in 4-3 BC.]

Unless Kepler or the astronomical software is wrong, Jupiter joined Venus in 2 BC, one year after Herod, who wanted to kill the Child, supposedly died. In Larson's research, however, the earliest writings of Josephus attest to Herod's death in 1 BC:

> [10] And I heard a loud voice saying in heaven, Now is come <u>salvation</u>, and <u>strength</u>, and <u>the kingdom</u> of our God, <u>and the power</u> of his Christ: for the accuser of our brethren is cast down, which accused them before our God day and night. (Rev. 12:10)

The Word of God offered **salvation** to the Hebrews since Yeshua gave His life as the sacrificial Lamb of the new covenant for the renewal of their hearts and lives. (Jer. 31:33) By faith in His blood, **slavery to sin is abolished**. We were set free to live in **His strength**. He sent His Spirit to establish His **Kingdom and power** forever. The events above are historically ordered.

Salvation: The Great Awakening was an ongoing work of the Holy Spirit, discovered by Waldo in the 12th century and Wycliffe and Hus in the 14th, respecting the Bible above church dogma. John Wycliffe corrected the Latin Vulgate in his Greek

Insights: Chapter 12

translation; then, translated an English version of the Bible. In the 15th century, the movable type press printed translations for the public, and the good news spread. In the 16th Tyndale, Erasmus, Luther, and Calvin impacted Christian theology. They had seen the truth in part, but the church was just beginning its restoration. In the 17th King James called for an *Authorized Version of the Holy Bible*, mostly Tyndale's translation. In the 18th century, a Great Awakening brought the gospel to the world as missionaries went forth with its wonderful news.[117] Our body was making our way through the darkness by the light we had.

Strength: In the 19th century, the abolition of slavery came as the Holiness Movement stirred the evangelical cause in then non-denominational churches. Finney, Palmer, Booth, Moody, Smith, and Wesley were among many others who led revivals.

The **Kingdom and the power**: In the 20th century, the Welsh and Azusa Street revival reintroduced Pentecost to the church.[118] At the fullness of time, in 1948 Israel became a nation in a day. In 1967 the Jews regained ancient Jerusalem, and the Holy Spirit revisited the nations with the gifts manifested in the early days. Its latter rain was foretold in Joel 2:28-3:2 when He returns the captives to Judah and Jerusalem, which was just occurring.

Satan has stalked the sons of Israel, spewing out accusations like a flood. (12:13-15) The earth swallows up his words since God doesn't renege His promises; His Word never fails; what He says He does. He sent an eagle to return His people to their land:

> [14] But the woman was given two wings of a great eagle, that she might fly into the wilderness <u>to her place</u>, where she is nourished for a time and times and half a time, <u>from the presence of the serpent</u>. (Rev. 12:14 NKJV)

In 70 AD the Jews fled a fruitful land for the wilderness of the nations. Languishing in the absence of her people, her nation became a barren wasteland until Israel was <u>*given two wings of a great eagle that she might fly into the wilderness to her place*</u>. The words, *time, times, and half a time* are not quantified here. The eagle's wings were pulled off a lion's back in Daniel 7 as an independent nation rose to become Israel's great ally, America.

Prophecy can appear, shift, and resettle like the *abomination of desolation* in Daniel 8, 11, and 12. The kings are supernatural,

The Revelation

reappearing centuries later. Unlike Rev. 12:6, in 12:14 she flies *into the wilderness to her place* by the *wings of a great eagle*. She returns to her homeland, a desolated Israel. (ZGE, YLT agree)

Since the Jews' return, she's been unconquerable, frustrating far more powerful enemies who want to eliminate her. The Jews are the main focus in the spiritual war; wittingly, willingly, or not, they were chosen by God to prove His faithfulness:

> ³⁴ And the land that was desolate shall be tilled, instead of being the desolation that it was in the sight of all who passed by. ³⁵ And they will say, 'This land that was desolate has become like the garden of Eden, and the waste and desolate and ruined cities are now fortified and inhabited.' (Ezk. 36:34-35 ESV) ['Have strong defense']

The Night the Stars Fell

From as early as 902, a phenomenon has recurred in the sky. The Leonid showers appeared as tens of thousands of meteors fell toward the earth and lit up the black sky in 1833. The stars poured like rain for three nights.[119] People thought it was the end of the world. A hundred years later, the little horn in Daniel 7:8 rose after ten kings received their kingdoms. (Rev. 17:12)

So-called "falling stars" are signs in the heavens. In John's time, men called all the sky's shining objects "stars." Angels also fall, appearing like stars. In 12:4 stars were angels who followed the dragon and were swept out of heaven. (Cf. Jude) Seven stars in Jesus' right hand were seven angels of seven churches. (1:20)

12:5-6 refers to the congregation that fled to Pella for safety during the siege of Jerusalem by the Romans. In the holocaust, Jews hid in caves again. A remnant escaped Europe's genocide by hiding in homes of sympathetic citizens. Others found forests or hid in holes. Satan sent a flood, but *the land helped* her.

When they saw the star, the magi knew the King was born. Finding the babe in Bethlehem, they returned to the East. No one could have predicted the astronomy of the skies in those days. Its mathematics were discovered in the 17th century when Johannes Kepler wrote the Three Laws of Planetary Motion.[120] Now its software uses his calculations, and we can watch the reruns.

One night nearly two thousand years ago, the stars revealed the birth of a Jewish King, and magi from the East rejoiced. It

Insights: Chapter 12

wasn't a bad omen, but a wonderful sign when again the stars spoke of a different birth. Their signal appeared in the Days of Awe in the seventieth year after the Jews returned to their land.

Revelation displays an ancient sky and alerts us to observe its stars. The constellations reappeared recently as they were in chapter 12, but not exactly the same as at the holy birth. There was an interesting variation.[121]

September 23, 2017, was Tishrei 3, 5778, in Israel; the third day of the seventh month. After Rosh Hashanah, the civil New Year, the sign reappeared during the Days of Awe for the first time in two thousand years. (Lev. 23:23-32) It was clear to Israel and to most of the world. Though we shouldn't look for signs, when God sends them, we must acknowledge them. Revelation 12 reveals the sign that marks the season of His return.

The Savior's birth is related to the rebirth of Jerusalem. In ancient days, the stars had spoken, but how did they know Israel would be pregnant again? Rather than the star of Bethlehem, in 2017, Mercury, Mars, Venus, and Regulus formed a straight line through Leo the lion's feet, His rod of iron! (12: 5)

Mercury and Mars spell imminent war. Regulus and Venus, the kingly star and the virgin, refer to a royal marriage. The first event makes way for the second. The tribulation precedes them.

On May 14, 2018, Jerusalem welcomed the U.S. Embassy when America was the first to recognize Israel's capital after her two thousand year absence. It was the seventieth anniversary of Israel's national day of rebirth and a signal to all the world.[122] (See Ps. 48:1-2; Mat. 5:34-35; Lk. 21:24)

About Words

People who aspire to lead others bear the onus of their words; we all do, but those of us who affect many lives have a greater responsibility. A serpent saw a subtle chance to influence the leaders in WW2. Their conversations have left lasting effects on the world since that time. Now we see they weren't alone, but powerful, invisible forces were present with them.

Words are like seeds planted in hearts; once rooted, they produce fruit. We saw the fruit of a man's speech in Germany when crowds took an oath of allegiance to the dragon that spoke, but *the beast was slain* by a mortal wound and went to perdition.

The Revelation

How many itching ears did the adversary attract before his head was wounded?

The Lamb of God used Russia as a weapon to bruise the serpent's head, Babylon, in the Second World War. He chose America, Great Britain, France, and the Allies to heal it. It's strange that the Allies healed the dragon's head. Who are these beasts?

At the end of the war, the dragon's body was burned, and he was sent to perdition, but the Judge gave the saints the Kingdom. Even so, Satan returns as another beast, *diverse from the first.*

Invisible words are powerful enough to overthrow kings and empires. Words command nations and alter the course of history. The words we speak by faith can change our destiny. A personal conversation can make a difference forever; so can a prayer.

In their meetings, Churchill was slighted by the president's cold shoulder. They'd been advocates of freedom and close friends, but Roosevelt was drawn to Stalin's charisma. Though he was a great leader, Stalin was a destroyer. Churchill believed his friend had chosen their enemy above him.[123] And he had.

F.D.R. died shortly before the war ended, and Vice President Harry Truman took the oath to replace him. Truman's former business partner and close friend was a Jew, and he felt honored to help Israel though it's unlikely the former president would have come to her aid. Churchill and Truman shared a kindred bond by supporting the Jews in their time of need.

After the war Churchill was voted from office but became a great statesman, and America remained an ally to Israel. Truman figured he was "God's Cyrus."[124] He believed he was made president by Providence to help the Jews defend their land as Persia's King Cyrus had done more than five centuries before Christ. Truman wasn't a saintly man, but loved Israel because his Christian parents taught him to respect the people who gave us the Holy Bible.

The story of Truman's legacy is a lesson for us to consider: if we're tempted to idolize or to judge those in authority over us, we'd better beware: self-righteousness is among the worst sins; it's quick to condemn and slow to forgive. Yeshua said, ... *wisdom is justified of her children (in Mat. 11:19).*

The Revelation of Jesus Christ

CHAPTER 13

13 Then I stood on the sand of the sea. And I saw a beast rising up out of the sea, having seven heads and ten horns, and on his horns ten crowns, and on his heads a blasphemous name. ² Now the beast which I saw was like a leopard, his feet were like *the feet of* a bear, and his mouth like the mouth of a lion. The dragon gave him his power, his throne, and great authority. ³ And I saw one of his heads as if it had been mortally wounded, and his deadly wound was healed. And all the world marveled and followed the beast. ⁴ So they worshiped the dragon who gave authority to the beast; and they worshiped the beast, saying, "Who *is* like the beast? Who is able to make war with him?"

⁵ And he was given a mouth speaking great things and blasphemies, and he was given authority to continue for forty-two months. ⁶ Then he opened his mouth in blasphemy against God, to blaspheme His name, His tabernacle, and those who dwell in heaven. ⁷ It was granted to him to make war with the saints and to overcome them. And authority was given him over every tribe, tongue, and nation. ⁸ All who dwell on the earth will worship him, whose names have not been written in the Book of Life of the Lamb slain from the foundation of the world.

⁹ If anyone has an ear, let him hear. ¹⁰ He who leads into captivity shall go into captivity; he who kills with the sword must be killed with the sword. Here is the patience and the faith of the saints.

¹¹ Then I saw another beast coming up out of the earth, and he had two horns like a lamb and spoke like a dragon. ¹² And he exercises all the authority of the first beast in his presence, and causes the earth and those who dwell in it to worship the first beast, whose deadly wound was healed. ¹³ He performs great signs, so that he even makes fire come down from heaven on the earth in the sight of men. ¹⁴ And he deceives those who dwell on the earth by those signs which he was granted to do in the sight of the beast, telling those who dwell on the earth to make an image to the beast who was wounded by the sword and lived. ¹⁵ He was granted

The Revelation

power to give breath to the image of the beast, that the image of the beast should both speak and cause as many as would not worship the image of the beast to be killed. [16] He causes all, both small and great, rich and poor, free and slave, to receive a mark on their right hand or on their foreheads, [17] and that no one may buy or sell except one who has the mark or the name of the beast, or the number of his name.

[18] Here is wisdom. Let him who has understanding calculate the number of the beast, for it is the number of a man: His number *is* 666. (Revelation 13:1-18 NKJV) [In 13:11, Gr.: *ghay* is soil, solid land. In 13:1, 17, Gr.: *onoma*, translated "name," means attributes/qualities as in a title.]

Insights

The apostle stood by the Great Sea on the Isle of Patmos and watched as a beast was rising from the same sea Daniel had seen in Babylon centuries before. (Dan. 7:1-2; p. 21) All of the beasts of Daniel 7 appear in John's vision: *After this I beheld, and lo another, like a leopard ... and dominion was given to it. (From Dan. 7:6) And the beast which I saw was like unto a leopard, and his feet were as the feet of a bear, and his mouth as the mouth of a lion. And to it the dragon gave his power, his throne, and great authority. (Rev. 13:2)* The main Allies in the Second World War were America as a leopard; Great Britain as a lion; and Russia as a bear. In February 1945 the Big Three planned the UN before the war ended when Berlin fell and *the beast was slain (in Dan. 7:11).* In 13:3 his head was healed, and so was its beast.

The keys: *the head of Syria is Damascus, and the head of Damascus is Rezin (in Is. 7:8a).* Heads are kings or thrones—capitals, but all seven kings in chapter 12 had fallen before 13. In 17 the seven heads are capital cities; each had a king, but five had fallen. The order then is chapter 12, then 17; then 13.

Revelation pulls back the curtain; behind it are the invisible beasts. In 20:2 the dragon is Satan who lost WW2 and gave the beast his throne, the head with a deadly wound. His ten kings received crowns again after the war and are on the beast in 13:1. By 1990 their crowns were restored and Berlin *was healed (in 13:3).* Berlin wasn't one of the seven, but Babylon was. She was

Insights: Chapter 13

the throne of the dragon whose altar was behind her walls in Berlin. Ten horns rose with the beast that now has the dragon's throne. Next *another beast* rises that speaks *as a dragon*.

In chapter 12 none of the horns had crowns. The ten horns *received no kingdom as yet* in 17:12; thus, the horns in 17 are still waiting for crowns after chapter 12. All ten have crowns in 13:1, having received them in 1920 for Hitler to rise in Daniel 7. WW2 ended and their crowns were restored in 13:1 when the dragon was healed after giving his throne to the beast. Therefore, the final order is: chapter 12, then 17, Daniel 7, and then 13.

> [12] 'And the ten horns that thou sawest, are ten kings, who a kingdom did not yet receive, but authority as kings the same hour do receive with the beast, [13] these have one mind, and their own power and authority to the beast they shall give over; [14] These with the Lamb shall make war, and the Lamb shall overcome them, ...
> (Rev. 17:12-14a YLT) [The beast here is the dragon/Hitler.]

A religio-political beast rises after the ten kings are restored (in 13:11). The first to rise after them in Daniel was a little horn (in Dan. 7:8), the eighth king of the seven (p. 20). The dragon was *the first beast, whose deadly wound was healed. (13:3, 12; p. 19)*

> [24] And the ten horns out of this kingdom are ten kings that shall arise: and another shall rise after them; and he shall be diverse from the first, and he shall subdue three kings. (Dan. 7:24) [The ten rise again with the beast in 13:1.]

> [12] It exercises all the authority of the first beast in its presence, and makes the earth and its inhabitants worship the first beast, whose mortal wound was healed.
> (Rev. 13:12 ESV) [Gr.: *Enopion*, 'In his presence/before him.']

The red dragon was the scarlet beast whose head was bruised (in Gen. 3:15). His capital was mortally wounded in the war (in 13:3, 12). Mystery Babylon was the capital whose walls hide the Altar of Satan in Berlin. A mystery: she is the throne he gave the beast like a leopard.

Of Beasts and Men

When a man speaks as a beast, he has his mouth and thus his heart; if a beast is in a man, the man becomes the beast. The man in a little horn in Germany was its commander-in-chief, second in authority until Satan ruled through him. (Dan. 7:8, 20; Is. 14:16) [Antiochus was also a little horn and an eighth king in Dan. 8:9.] The one with two horns is *diverse from the first (in Dan. 7:24)*. To gain the world's worship, he controls its false religions (in 13:11).

Ten kings of the Third Reich were restored after WW2 and are on the beast in 13:1. *Another beast* rises after them (in 13:11). *Diverse from the first (in Dan. 7:8)*, *he shall subdue three kings (in 7:24, on p. 137)*. Present with the beast before him, the beast that has *two horns like a lamb* has all his authority by his tenure. He who speaks as a dragon <u>is the dragon</u> who gave his throne to the beast after he lost the war (in 13:2; cf. Dan. 7:11). Superior in the kingdom of darkness, he is in both a religious leader and a king as one of the two horns, and he abases the three.

Two different first beasts are in 13:12. The dragon gave the first beast his throne, but the dragon that gave him his throne was before him: he'd been the terrible beast in Daniel 7:8 and the red dragon in 12:3. Daniel said, *another beast, diverse from the first shall rise* after the ten horns rise again. The dragon is *the first beast whose mortal wound was healed (in 13:12b p. 137)*. The first to rise after the ten horns would rise after them again (in Dan. 7:8, 23-24; cf. Rev. 13:1, 11). Its prophecy is repeated (on pp. 38-40).

Like Daniel, John also saw <u>another beast rising</u> after them (in 13:11; cf. Dan. 7:24). The *beast with two horns* rises after the ten as Hitler had done in 1932, but he's *diverse from the first* that rose after them. Gone to hell and back, now it's a religious beast.

Satan lost the greatest war in history to the Lamb and gave his throne to the next beast, formed by three diverse Allies; the three were an alliance as one beast with ten horns and seven heads that collude with a false prophet and the dragon (in 16:13) as the beast that was healed (in 13:3, 12; see p. 19; cf. Dan. 7:11).

Two false religious leaders are its horns: its prophet and the dragon that rules its religious empire. (see 20:2) The paradigm is Medo-Persia, a ram with two horns (in Dan. 8). The beast was Persian, but its horns were the unseen kings of two kingdoms: Persia and Media, merged as one kingdom, one of the seven.

Rising after the ten the second time, the beast comes out of the earth—out of hell. He *went to perdition* after his body was *given to the burning flame (in 17:11; cf. Is. 14:9-20, Dan. 7:11)*. His two horns are the leaders of his duplicitous politico-religious

Insights: Chapter 13

kingdom. United by its beast, they are like-minded. A man who is the dragon is one; the other is his false prophet. (See 16:13) The dragon was the eighth king out of the seven when he founded Berlin. For his own capital city, he planted his altar.

The next kingdom is the dragon's fourth kingdom, *which shall be diverse from all kingdoms, and shall devour the whole earth, and shall tread it down, and break it in pieces (in Dan. 7:23)*. The first beast (in 13:12b, p. 137) was mortally wounded. Struck and divided by Russia, his throne in Berlin was ruined. When Berlin was healed, so was the dragon's head, Mystery Babylon, which he gave to the beast in 13:2 as its throne.

His throne was his mysterious capital, physically in Berlin. Mystery Babylon was also his throne in Pergamon (in Rev. 2:13), which wasn't a capital city. After it was invaded and razed, he carried Babylon to Rome, using the church to gain the REGN. Then his altar went to Berlin where his throne was destroyed, and the dragon was slain. (We never see the spirit of Babylon except by her characteristics, revealed by her city in chapter 18.)

The dragon gave the beast *great authority*, but <u>not his own authority</u>. (YLT, NIV, KJV, HCSB, NASB, TLV) [Authority rules; power overcomes.] The one with two horns like a lamb rules over the beast, having all his authority and subduing the three kings. [The dragon appears in 16:13 with his prophet and the beast.]

One interpretation has one with two horns like a lamb with authority *on behalf of the beast,* as if representing the beast, but no one represents a king in his presence. *All the authority of the first beast doth it do before it. (YLT)* The beast with two horns takes authority over his victor (in 13:2) as he did by deceit to get the (H)RE. When he's in authority, the beast is his chancellor: "Who is able to make war with [the beast]?" (See 13:4; cf. 19:19)

The world worships the beast, fearing his military power. He leads the armed forces of the world. *And I saw the beast, and the kings of the earth, and their armies, gathered together to make war against him that sat on the horse, and against his army. (Rev. 19:19)* [The Lord returns with an army on white horses.]

The throne of the beast is his government seat. She is anti-Christ, anti-Semitic, anti-Zionist, and anti-God. Creation reveals the truth by the light of God, but the city of the beast exchanges light for darkness.

The Revelation

³ Don't let anyone deceive you in any way. For that day will not come unless the apostasy comes first and the man of lawlessness is revealed, the son of destruction. ⁴ He opposes and exalts himself above every so-called god or object of worship, so that he sits in God's sanctuary, publicizing that he himself is God.

... ⁶ <u>And you know what currently restrains him, so that he will be revealed in his time.</u> ⁷ For the mystery of lawlessness is already at work, but the one now restraining will do so until he is out of the way, ⁸ and then the lawless one will be revealed. The Lord Jesus will destroy him with the breath of His mouth and will bring him to nothing with the brightness of His coming.
(2 Thes. 2:3-4, 6-8 HCSB)

Till he may be out of the way (YLT) doesn't mean the Holy Spirit leaves the world. *The man of lawlessness* is *hindered* by the one who prevents him from rising *until he* [is] *out of the way*. The one who has been *in the way* for centuries is *keeping down (lit., YLT) the man of lawlessness* until he is *out of the way*. This angel is stronger than the beast, or he couldn't stand in the way.

Four entities are in the story of Balaam: a king, a prophet, a beast, and an angel. (See Num. 22:22-32) A donkey carried the evil prophet to prophesy to a king. The angel stood *in the way* of the beast to keep the prophet–for–hire Balaam from appeasing King Balak, Israel's enemy. (Josh. 13:22)

²³ And <u>the ass saw the angel of the LORD standing in the way</u>, and his sword drawn in his hand: and the ass turned <u>out of the way</u>, to turn into the field: and Balaam smote the ass, to turn her <u>into the way</u>. (Num. 22:23)

The angel was *in the way*, so the beast *turned out of the way*. At midnight the church is in apostasy when the one that is *in the way ... is out of the way*. *(2 Thes. 2:7-8)*

Healing Berlin

After WW2 the Allies returned the West German Republic to its people, ostensibly to stabilize post–war Europe. Marxism took China the year the Allies rescued their enemies in 1949.

In '45 Berlin was crushed and the dragon, slain. Healing the city was no easy job. Three of the Allies divvied up Germany: the USSR took East Germany and East Berlin by Marxism. The

Insights: Chapter 13

U.S. and Britain supervised West Berlin in East Germany till the Russian government fell. Soon after the war, its Allies joined the United Nations. Finally, communism ruined the USSR, and Berlin was healed as was the head that was the dragon's throne.

In 1948–49 Russia disconnected East Berlin from railways, highways, and waterways, leaving the people helpless, alienated, and starving—nearly as isolated as the Jews they'd forced into ghettos just a few years before.[126] In August 1961 word spread about a wall, and twenty-four hundred Germans escaped to West Berlin that day.[127] Khrushchev broke the Allies' pact, crushing Berlin whose favorite leader had betrayed Stalin. His communist troops built a wall around East Berlin overnight, imprisoning its people, and the seeds of the cold war between Marxism and the Free World were sown in the furrowed soil of post-war Berlin.

> ³ One of its heads seemed to have a mortal wound, but its mortal wound was healed, and the whole earth marveled as they followed the beast. (Rev. 13:3 ESV)

Day and night America, Britain, France, and their allies airlifted food and supplies for Berlin to survive.[128] *I saw one of its heads as it were wounded to death; and his deadly wound was healed: and all the world wondered after the beast. (13:3)* Now we see why: Germans had adored Hitler, but not much later, in a cold war against Marxism, its Allies rescued East Berlin.

Socialism ruined Russia when the realities of life disproved its Marxist ideals. In June 1987 Russians waited in long lines for bread to eat. In Berlin President Reagan took a few moments to address the premier: "Mr. Gorbachev, tear down this wall!"[129]

In 1989 the Iron Curtain fell. Soon after that Russian soldiers left the city for lack of pay. After two days the wall came down, and the world cheered for a city liberated by nations that had sacrificed their sons for freedom.[130] The post-war Allies supervised West Berlin till 1990 when Russia fell and Berlin was healed as Germany's capital city again.[131]

Reagan and Thatcher opposed communism as others did; but seventy years of Marxist ideologies folded when the system went bankrupt by socialism, and the wall fell with it. The beast in 13 could take its nations' sovereignties overnight like the wall that took Berlin. Liberty is priceless but not without cost; it works for those who value it.

The Revelation

Remembering by turning ahead to 17, a scarlet beast had ten horns that _received_ crowns by a treaty and _received_ them back by treaties. (Rev. 17:12)

The Tail of the Dragon

And his tail drew a third part of the stars of heaven, and did cast them to the earth: ... Woe to inhabiters of the earth and of the sea, for the devil has come down unto you <u>having great wrath, because he knows that he hath but a short time</u>! (Rev. 12:4a, 12b) After Jesus ascended to heaven, the dragon was cast out and swept a third of the stars to earth to serve him.

The dragon was the national symbol on the flag of China from 1615–1911.[132] Its "Heavenly Kingdom" banner displayed the dragon as its king as well, but since the insurrectionist of this world lost the war in heaven, his end is near and he knows it.

A Marxist coup d'état took Russia's provisional government by the Bolshevik Revolution of 1917, resulting in multitudes of deaths, a sign of the dragon's insurrections. At the time Chiang Kai-shek had returned from military training to bolster Sun Yat-sen and overcome the harsh Qing Dynasty in 1911–12, and the flag of the dragon fell as the democratic republic rose. Afterward China joined the Allies in each world war. Chiang led China's democracy from 1928–75, joining the UN in October 1945.[133]

Soon after Sun established her republic, Russian Marxists incited a revolution in northern China by Mao Zedong just ten years after the insurrection in Russia, but the Chinese Civil War paused when Japan invaded Manchuria.[134] Stranger than fiction, the enemies united for World War Two, fighting side-by-side as allies against Japan till their Civil War resumed in late 1945.

Russia and China were closely related, sharing their borders and at times, political philosophies, bringing Gog and Magog to mind. [Gog is head of Magog as an international force that forms an insurrection against Israel's King near the end of time.] From *the uttermost parts of the north,* Gog is Satan's prince who leads Russia with Magog, covering the earth like Babylon.

In 1949 West Berlin rose from its ashes, and the communists won the Chinese Civil War. Chiang fled to Taiwan, a nation-in-exile, recently oppressed by communists.[135] She'd represented Chiang's China till the UN expelled her in 1971 for Communist China to have a permanent seat in its Security Council.[136]

Insights: Chapter 13

History is the mirror of humanity. The authority to govern is a test of character. All who are entrusted with authority should study their faces in its mirror or abuse the trust and face an angry God. *It is a fearful thing to fall into the hands of the living God. (Heb. 10:31)*

Now the feet of the bear may be China's since Russia led the Chinese into Marxist communism under Mao, but all nations are judged on the Great Day of God when everyone is judged by the works done in the body, good or evil. Even so, God gave His Son to save us by grace through faith: ... w*hosoever shall call on the name of the* LORD *shall be delivered. (Joel 2:32; Acts 2:21, 39)*

A Slice of Babylonia

God warns His own people to come out of Babylon. Many of us have lived in her ways. Deceptions are taught in the pulpits, blinding congregations to the Word of God. Believers hear only parts of the truth and have false assumptions. We must study His words diligently to truly believe every one of them since every word of God is life to us. Gainsayers abound, and most of us fall for the words of our teachers, not comparing them to the Bible.

The apostasy is preserved in the words of the early bishops' councils. In Nicaea, they adopted the ancient festival of Rome for the church, calling it "holy," incorporating the resurrection of Jesus Christ with pagan revelry. While rejecting the Bible, they purposely changed the biblical day of Jesus' victory over death:

"... We further proclaim to you the good news of the agreement concerning the holy Easter, that this particular also has through your prayers been rightly settled; so that <u>all our brethren in the East who formerly followed the custom of the Jews are henceforth to celebrate the said most sacred feast of Easter at the same time with the Romans and yourselves and all those who have observed Easter from the beginning</u>." [From the Synodic Letter of the Council of Nicaea, 325 AD.] [137]

Each year Rome held a feast for Ishtar, or Ashterah, goddess of fertility.[138] Her idol had a part in the epic poem, *Gilgamesh,* in Babel. (p. 56-7) They "worshiped" in sexual orgies, fornication, and perversion, parading the streets as if celebrating *Mardi Gras.*

The newly institutionalized church began its fall away from the Word of God, but true believers kept the faith. The rift was set by a presumptuous attitude against the Hebrew Bible, which laid the foundation of the new covenant. Enriched by its wisdom, the apostles referred to it constantly as they wrote, but bishops later cut off the roots of our faith, steering people away from the Bible to the teachings and traditions of men. The religious Jews had done the same and rejected the Savior when he came. Since then instead of celebrating Christ who rose on the Day of Firstfruits as *the firstfruits of the dead,* we lost our way by shunning the history of our faith. Reconsider the Firstfruits and repent for the church as the light of the world and the salt of the earth.

The dragon takes people by guile, inducing them to fear his deceptions. Carnally-minded bishops expected wolves to rescue them from their fears. Constantine perhaps unwittingly enticed them. The longer the apostate church was an institution, the more she perverted the truth. Since her separation from the Hebrew Bible, she has misrepresented Christianity and the Lord Jesus Christ. He told His disciples that false christs and false prophets would come in His name—and they have. (Lk. 21:8)

Another beast rises with two horns like a lamb and speaks as a dragon. Its leaders are intolerant of a personal relationship to God; but if we trust Jesus Christ, we receive Him into our hearts. That's personal, and it's how Bible believers threaten Rome's conflicting dogma and idolatry. Have we realized churches are divided by deceptions? It began in the 4th century by men who led the churches away from the Scriptures. These days we look to teachers who aren't careful to believe the pure Word of God.

Jews turned from the Scriptures long ago by believing their priests are anointed to write for the Talmud like the prophets of God were anointed for the Tenakh, but that's a lie. The Bible is inspired for us to believe every word and divide it correctly. The apostasy resulted in wars and genocides.

Pope Innocent III (1198–1216) began Inquisitions in Rome with four Crusades to eradicate the Jews, rewarding their killers with forgiveness and eternal life.[139] Pope Gregory IX (1227–1241) led Inquisitions against Bible-believing Christians in France, and villages were destroyed. Accused of heresy, the defendants were kept in dungeons till their prosecutors tried them as their judges. Those who survived the torture were burned alive. In six hundred years of Crusades and Inquisitions, multitudes suffered

Insights: Chapter 13

at the apostate church's hands for daring to part from Rome. But Jesus came to save those with ears to hear—not to destroy, not to judge, not to rule as the kings of this world rule. (Mat. 11:29)

After His death and resurrection, many Jews trusted in Him though as He had prophesied, their Jewish leaders crucified Him by the hands of Rome. Like the Jews the bishops didn't trust in Jesus, or they would have believed His words. (Rom. 6:7, 18)

In 1200–1500, Papal bulls [laws] increased against alleged heretics who believed the few scriptures they had rather than their dogma.[140] In 1288 Jews also became their targets.[141]

Had Israel believed, the Kingdom would have come, but it wasn't God's plan. He would save gentiles and humble the Jews. (2 Cor. 10:4-6; Eph. 6:10-20) After the bishops denied the Word, its believers were identified by their faith. (1 Cor. 11:18-19)

The Inquisitions went to Spain in 1481 when Queen Isabella and King Ferdinand asked permission from the Papacy for *auto de fe,* "acts of faith." These were burnings of the "heretics," popular events. As Inquisitors, the Dominicans and Jesuits were the arms of a Department of Inquisition, *sanctum officium,* "the Holy Office." Estimates of the killings are in the millions.[142]

The throne of Mystery Babylon went west in 1945, and the Paris Peace Treaties restored the ten kings' crowns by 1949, but one retained an injury.[143] Sixty million had died with justice undone, yet *Vengeance is mine, I will repay, saith the Lord (in Rom. 12:19; cf. Deut. 32:35).*

Her curse did not prevent the dragon from carrying the spirit of his capital city to her proxies. Human sacrifices were given on her altar in Pergamon; the guilt of sinners filled her coffers in Rome; war projects paid her expenses in Berlin; now wars and taxes support the city the dragon put on the back of the beast:

²⁰ <u>It shall never be inhabited, neither shall it be dwelt in from generation to generation</u>: neither shall the Arabian pitch tent there; neither shall the shepherds make their fold there. (Is. 13:20)

The red dragon was cast to earth in chapter 12. He moved to 17; then to Daniel 7:11, 23; then to the beast to whom he gave his throne (in Rev. 13:2-3). His false prophet works wonders by his devils. He erects *an image to the beast which had the wound by a sword, and did live (in Rev. 13:14b).*

The Revelation

¹³ And I saw three unclean spirits like frogs *come* out of the mouth of the dragon, and out of the mouth of the beast, and out of the mouth of the false prophet.
¹⁴ For they are the spirits of devils, working miracles, *which* go forth unto the kings of the earth and of the whole world, to gather them to the battle of that great day of God Almighty. (Rev. 16:13-14) [Exposed at the 6ᵗʰ bowl.]

Seeing through the darkness, we should prepare for what's coming and always pray for one another. Lying spirits scheme to deceive Christians and Jews as targets. God does miracles, signs, and wonders today, but most teachers deny the true gospel.

John the baptizer had Elijah's Spirit but did no miracles at all (in Jn. 10:41). Like John Elijah does come but to restore what was lost. (Mal. 4:5-6) Either seek the truth or be tricked by a fraud.

The false prophet seems like Elijah (in 13:13; 2 Kg. 1:10) but isn't a prophet at all. He mimics miracles and announces the false messiah, the deceiver, whom Israel initially receives.

⁸ <u>And then the lawless one will be revealed</u>, whom the Lord Jesus will kill with the breath of his mouth and bring to nothing by the appearance of his coming. ⁹ The coming of the lawless one is <u>by the activity of Satan</u> with all power and false signs and wonders,¹⁰ and with all wicked deception for those who are perishing, because they refused to <u>love the truth and so be saved</u>.
(2 Thes. 2:8-10 ESV; cf. Rev. 1:16; 19:15, 21.) ... *whom the Lord Jesus will ... bring to nothing* by *the outshining of the presence of him. (from 2 Thes. 2:8 ZGE)*

If we meet the sword of persecution, let it be with shining faces, knowing Jesus comes for the elect before His wrath falls:

²⁹ "<u>Immediately after the tribulation</u> of those days the sun will be darkened, and the moon will not give its light, and the stars will fall from heaven, and the powers of the heavens will be shaken. ³⁰ Then will <u>appear</u> in heaven the sign of the Son of Man, and then all the tribes of the earth will mourn, and they will see the Son of Man <u>coming on the clouds of heaven</u> with power and great glory. ³¹ And he will send out his angels <u>with a loud trumpet call</u>, and they will gather <u>his elect</u> from the four winds, from one end of heaven to the other.
(Mat. 24:29-31 ESV; cf. 1 Thes. 4:16; Rev. 20:4)

Insights: Chapter 13

The Beast Is a Man

The number of the beast is the number of a man: This means the beast is a man (in 13:18). *He had two horns like a lamb, and he spoke as a dragon (in 13:11b),* identified in a false religion.

The beast has a body like a leopard. In authority over the nations, he's a man with a mouth like a lion. He co-rules with the dragon and false prophet, commanding devils to work "miracles" (revealed in 16:13-14). A bleeding idol? or fire from the sky? Nothing seems too difficult for them when *night cometh, and no man can work (in Jn. 9:4).*

Yeshua said before He returns, Jerusalem receives someone who comes in his own name, though He came in His Father's name. (Jn. 5:43) As He foretold, another like the eighth Seleucid king deceives Jerusalem. *His power hath been mighty, and not by his own power (in Dan. 8:24a).* In ages past Satan entered into eighth kings. In 167 BC he stood in the temple by his idol Zeus; *the abomination of desolation* was the dragon[144] (in Dan. 11:31).

> 23 "In the latter period of their rule,   [I.e., the Greeks' rule]
> When the transgressors have run *their course,*
> A king will arise,   [He appeared as a man.]
> Insolent and skilled in intrigue.
> 24 "His power will be mighty, but not by his *own* power,
> And he will destroy to an extraordinary degree
> And prosper and perform *his will;*
> He will destroy mighty men and the holy people.
> 25 "And through his shrewdness
> He will cause deceit to succeed by his influence;
> And he will magnify *himself* in his heart,
> And he will destroy many while *they are* at ease.
> He will even oppose the Prince of princes,
> But he will be broken without human agency.
> (Dan. 8:23-25 NASB) The invisible kings rule by men.

There are two kingdoms but three entities: the beast and the dragon and a false prophet who endorses them (in 13:1, 11; 16:13).

> 13 It performs great signs, even making fire come down from heaven to earth in front of people, 14 and by the signs that it is allowed to work in the presence of the beast it deceives those who dwell on earth, telling them to make an image for the beast that was wounded by the

The Revelation

sword and yet lived. ¹⁵ And it was allowed to give breath to the image of the beast, so that the image of the beast might even speak and might cause those who would not worship the image of the beast to be slain.
(Rev. 13:13-15 ESV)

Ten kings give their authority and dominion to the one that speaks as a dragon and rises after them. His prophet does great signs as he works beside the beast, proving the collusion of the three: the beast, the dragon, and the false prophet. In Dan. 7:25 he tries to change the times and law. He wears out the saints who are given into his hands [for fewer than forty-two months].

What if the Jews had done everything right? but all who are chosen must be humbled. Forty years before Romans razed the temple to the ground, Yeshua said no stone would be left on another—none is. The living image of the dragon is either a man or a beast and is in the temple in Jerusalem. Its blueprint is finished; its golden cups, utensils, and menorah are already made.[145]

> ¹⁵ "Therefore when you see the 'abomination of desolation,' spoken of by Daniel the prophet, standing in the holy place" (<u>whoever reads, let him understand</u>), ¹⁶ "then <u>let those who are in Judea</u> flee to the mountains. ¹⁷ Let him who is on the housetop not go down to take anything out of his house. ¹⁸ And let him who is in the field not go back to get his clothes. ¹⁹ But woe to those who are pregnant and to those who are nursing babies in those days! ²⁰ And pray that your flight may not be in winter or on the Sabbath. ²¹ For <u>then there will be great tribulation</u>, such as has not been since the beginning of the world until this time, no, <u>nor ever shall be</u>. ²² And unless those days were shortened, no flesh would be saved; but <u>for the elect's sake</u> those days will be shortened. (Mat. 24:15-22 NKJV)

January 10, 1984: President Reagan recognized diplomatic relations with the Vatican and its ambassador, granting the pope an embassy in Washington, D.C.[146] The beast with two horns like a lamb establishes his fourth kingdom by the beast that rose after the war. Finally, the ten horns return to bolster the scarlet beast (in Rev. 17:15-18, p. 188), now with two horns in 13.

On the papal crown, the "tri-regna" represents three "powers of the pope," translated from the Latin: 1) the father of all kings,

Insights: Chapter 13

2) the governor of the world, and 3) the Vicar of Christ.[147] But the only crown Jesus wore was made of thorns. And who is like the King of kings? or like the Lord of lords? No one compares.

The unique Son of God walked sinless among us and shed His blood to die for us to live forever. He entered hell, bearing our guilt for us (in Is. 53:10; 1 Pet. 3:18-20). Then He rose to life and saved us by His grace with faith for each of us. (Eph. 2:8)

As the biological Son of God, Jesus is the only Mediator of man to God—the Bridge from here to heaven. No one equals Him; no name is like His; no one sits in for Him. His life divided time. His gifts are for us who believe without seeing Him, but liars are among us, using Jesus' name while twisting the truth. Their charm is persuasive. (Prov.31:30) Nevertheless, *God hath from the beginning chosen you to salvation through sanctification of the Spirit and belief of the truth. (2 Thes. 2:13b)*

"Dear Benedict, ..."

On October 7, 2010, the man was busily jotting off a letter to the "pontiff," asking to meet him: "Iranian President Mahmud Ahmadinejad has written a letter to Benedict XVI in which he calls for closer collaboration between religions."[148]

The pope visited the Dome of the Rock, saying, "Here the paths of the world's three great monotheistic religions meet, reminding us of what they share in common."[149] However, theirs has no Son. *Let God be true, but every man a liar. (See Rom. 3:4)*

"I am the way, the truth, and the life."– Pius IX; "It is absolutely necessary for the salvation of every creature to be subject to the Roman Pontiff." – Boniface VIII; "No man outside obedience to the pope can ultimately be saved."– Clement VI; "The Pope holds place on earth, not simply of a man, but of the true God." – Innocent I; "I am in all and above all, so that God Himself and I, the Vicar of God, hath one consistory, and I am able to do almost all that God can do. I, being above all ... seem by this reason, to be above all gods."– Nicholas. "Don't go to God for forgiveness of sins. Come to me." – John Paul II.[150]

Pontiff means "bridge," as a mediator between God and man, but the Bible says, *There is one God and one mediator between God and men, the man Christ Jesus. (1 Tim. 2:5) Pope* means

The Revelation

"papa, or abba." He's called, "Holy Father," but Jesus said, *Call no man your father upon the earth: for one is your Father, which is in heaven. (Mat. 23:9)* If we believe what Jesus said, we obey.

Bishops were called "popes" in 324. Eighteen hundred popes were invited to Nicaea. Three hundred eighteen came; the others dismissed the idea.[151] 17% voted to decide the tenets of the faith. Now its apostasy is worse than ever before with lies abounding.

A false church led by the dragon will unite the world's false religions. Its anti-Christ empire will fall in the war between the kingdom of darkness and the Kingdom of light. Its beast offers peace by forced conversions; his disciples are captives.

> [32] He shall seduce with flattery those who violate the covenant, but the people who know their God shall <u>stand firm and take action</u>. [33] And the wise among the people shall make many understand, though for some days they shall stumble by sword and flame, by captivity and plunder. [34] <u>When they stumble, they shall receive a little help</u>. And many shall join themselves to them with flattery, [35] and some of the wise shall stumble, so that they may be <u>refined, purified, and made white</u>, until the time of the end, for it still awaits the appointed time.
> [36] And the king shall do as he wills. He shall exalt himself and magnify himself above every god, and shall speak astonishing things against the God of gods. He shall prosper until the indignation is accomplished; for that which is decreed shall be done. (Dan. 11:32-36 ESV)

The man of lawlessness *opposeth and exalteth himself above all that is called God or that is worshipped; so that he as God sitteth in the temple of God, shewing himself that he is God. (2 Thes. 2:4)* But God sent His only Son, crucified for our sins and risen to life to prove our justification. *Though we, or an angel from heaven, preach any other gospel unto you than that which we have preached unto you, let him be accursed. (Gal. 1:8)*

Known as "Francis," he entered the Blue Mosque in Istanbul to pray with an imam, kiss the Koran, and say the religions are one, and "we all worship the same God."[152] But our faith is in the Son of God who paid our penalty. Prophets foretold His birth centuries before the NT confirmed it. (Is. 7:14; 9:6; 53; Dan. 9:25)

"Vatican Calls for New World Economic Order." The Fox News headline declared radical changes in international banking;

Insights: Chapter 13

a Vatican Pontifical Council for Justice and Peace ..."a world political authority" ... "universal jurisdiction" ... "fair distribution of the world's wealth."[153] He has a knack for numbers:

> [16] He causes all, both small and great, rich and poor, free and slave, to receive a mark on their right hand or on their foreheads, [17] and that no one may buy or sell except one who has the mark or the name of the beast, or the number of his name. [18] Here is wisdom. Let him who has understanding calculate the number of the beast, for it is the number of a man: His number *is* 666. (Rev. 13:16-18 NKJV)

Ahmadinejad gave gifts to win the favor of the Vatican. One gift released fifteen British sailors who'd allegedly entered Iran's sea by 0.5 km. The Easter gift freed them on April 4, 2010.[154]

On January 14, 2017, "Francis" met with Mahmoud Abbas to open a Palestinian embassy in Vatican City—odder yet, they have no capital or nation other than their Arab homelands.[155]

Of the two horns, one is a false prophet, playing Elijah. The other is the dragon. The imposter seems like Elijah, but is a liar. *Whoever denieth the Son, the same hath not the Father: he that acknowledgeth the Son hath the Father also. (1 Jn. 2:23)* If we receive the beast, we deny the Son of God.

The image of the dragon who speaks by a man both moves and speaks. We're familiar with images; they're commonplace. We watch them living and speaking every day. The image of a beast will be in the temple beside another beast. The world bows to images. He is the *first beast, whose deadly wound was healed, diverse* from his figure in Daniel 7. And the beast is a man. The mark is his own; those who refuse it are beheaded.

The Greek word, *onoma,* is not just a name. It refers to the character, authority, rank or title of a man. Its blasphemy is in its claim as the mark of the beast. His *onoma* and his number mark him as the chief adversary of God. It's time to discern the truth of the Word though our eyes can't yet see its manifestation.

In the 18th century, Arabia had its first Saudi kings, imams who bestowed the kingdom to their sons, also imams. At the end of the 19th, a forty-year gap separated its powers. In 1932 modern Saudi Arabia was established as Hitler was rising.[156] In 2015 her seventh king rose. Interrupting the line of successors, he made a

The Revelation

younger son crown prince who took the reins of power, upending the old order.[157] If welcomed by Israel, he's likely to succeed by uniting the East with the West.

Though the consensus of our beliefs seems a reasonable way to unite, we mix leaven into the lump of dough by mingling the words of God with men's ideas that change them. _Study to show thyself thyself approved_ unto God, a workman that needeth _not to be ashamed_, rightly dividing the word of truth. (2 Tim. 2:15)

A national leader used a copy of Pergamon's Altar to display his power, yet people who professed Christianity received him. He gave his amphitheater speech to scores of thousands, posing between the columns at its podium in the blackness of the night, towering over the throngs, and the crowds roared! [158]

> [16] ... *Is* this the man that made the earth to tremble, that did shake kingdoms; [17] that made the world as a wilderness, and destroyed the cities thereof; *that* opened not the house of his prisoners? (Is. 14:16b-17)

Hitler said the world would rotate on the Rome-Berlin Axis; hence, the "Axis powers."[159] The dragon of the (H)REGN ruled the Third Reich. He'd been king of Babel, Rome, and Berlin but gave his throne to the beast as his fourth kingdom.

Is Lucifer a man? If he speaks by a man, he sure looks like a man. Devils debase people and work by men. If devils enter men, they're filled with ice-cold death. Given a mouth, the beast speaks like a man. Liars mingle with others like themselves and deny the truth when it's spoken. (Only Jesus can free a liar.)

> [16] And the ten horns which thou sawest upon the beast, these shall hate the whore, and shall make her desolate and naked, and shall eat her flesh, and burn her with fire. [17] For God hath put in their hearts to fulfil his will, and to agree, and give their kingdom unto the beast, until the words of God shall be fulfilled. (Rev. 17:16-17)

The beast with *two horns like a lamb* has the number of a man because he's in a man. After rising the second time, the ten kings give _their kingdom_ to the dragon, the scarlet beast (in 17:17; cf. 17:13) Satan regains his power through the EU and is stirred to destroy his infamous, mystical city of Babylon, the throne he gave the beast after the war. (We'll meet her in chapter 17.)

Insights: Chapter 13

A king is not recognized as a king unless he has a capital city, because he's less powerful without a government. A king and his kingdom are as strong as his government, housed in his capital city. The two are united in a marriage, or in the case of the dragon, as a man with his harlot in bed with many kings.

The seven heads of the beast are a great mystery. Are they capitals or are they kings? Since Berlin was healed of the deadly wound, and the dragon's throne went to the beast, we can deduce that the heads in 13 are the seven capitals that include Babylon.

Jews were cut off as branches of their own olive tree by their slothful faith. Gentiles were received but were warned not to despise Jews, or we'll be cut off too. We're not accountable for the sins of others, but for our own, which may be by omission or by commission. We're kept by faith, but without works, faith is dead: *he that doeth truth cometh to the light, that his deeds may be manifest, that they are wrought in God. (Jn. 3:21)*

Israel's right to her homeland is denied by those who say they're saved by their free will and can never be lost, no matter what they do. *Gainsaying* fills the church, but the fear of God turns us from sin while those who are presumptuous are warned,

> [20] ... Do not be conceited, but fear; [21] for if God did not spare the natural branches, He will not spare you, either. [22] Behold then the kindness and severity of God; to those who fell, severity, but to you, God's kindness, <u>if you continue in His kindness</u>; otherwise you also will be cut off. [23] And they also, if they do not continue in their unbelief, will be grafted in, for God is able to graft them in again. (Rom. 11:20b-23 NASB)

Two friends, Roosevelt and Churchill, gained an unexpected ally after Hitler betrayed Stalin by invading Russia. Despite his early ties to Hitler and his Marxist ideology, Stalin met with two free-world leaders in late 1943 in Tehran, Persia, to strategize against the Axis powers.[160] In February 1945 the Big Three met again in Yalta, a city in Ukraine's Crimean Peninsula. [Crimea is recently Russia's]. They planned the UN on paper before setting it in stone, hoping for peace on earth with a devil as a friend.[161]

Beasts have a way with men's wills. The beast (in 13:1-3) is like a leopard, rising with dominion from WW2. (Dan. 7:6, 23) Its wartime coalition formed the dragon's fourth empire: like the

The Revelation

leopard but not. Surreptitiously embedded in her bureaucracy, the devouring beast is the key that discloses the present state of our nation (in 13:1; cf. Dan. 7:23). A lion, a bear, and a leopard lose their dominion but continue as nations *for a season and time (in Dan. 7:12).* Beasts and horns are kings of deception.

All who worship the beast, taking the number of his *onoma*, his mark, <u>in the right hand or forehead</u> will be condemned. It's a physical mark made by a tool that breaks the skin with a scratch, etching, or stamp. [Grk.: *charagma*] 666 ... a bio-chip perhaps?

"The world had never before known a godlessness as organized, militarized, and tenaciously malevolent as that practiced by Marxism. Within the philosophical system of Marx and Lenin, and at the heart of their psychology, <u>hatred of God is the principal driving force, more fundamental than all their political and economic pretensions</u>." – Alexander Solzhenitsyn, 1983.[162]

Jerusalem above All

> 14 Behold, the day of the LORD cometh, and thy spoil shall be divided in the midst of thee. ² For I will gather all nations <u>against Jerusalem to battle</u>; and the city shall be taken, and the houses rifled, and the women ravished; and half of the city shall go forth into captivity, and the residue of the people shall not be cut off from the city. ³ <u>Then shall the LORD go forth, and fight against those nations, as when he fought in the day of battle</u>.
> (Zec. 14:1-3) [This refers back to WW2.]

In her darkest hour, God is with Jerusalem, but on account of sin, He scourges those He loves. Still He is on our side and hers and will defeat His enemies and exalt her above the highest mountains—no, He will never abolish His nation Israel.

In chapter 13 the wisdom of the living God is glorified when fallen angels scheme and sinful men make plans until the end of the age. Revelation reveals other prophetic writings of the Bible as well as the words of historians, and both history and prophecy open the mysteries in *The Revelation of Jesus Christ.*

The Revelation of Jesus Christ

CHAPTER 14

14 And I looked, and, lo, a Lamb stood on the mount Sion, and with him an hundred forty and four thousand, having his Father's name written in their foreheads.

² And I heard a voice from heaven, as the voice of many waters, and as the voice of a great thunder: and I heard the voice of harpers harping with their harps:

³ And they sung as it were a new song before the throne, and before the four beasts, and the elders: and no man could learn that song but the hundred and forty and four thousand, which were redeemed from the earth.

⁴ These are they which were not defiled with women; for they are virgins. These are they which follow the Lamb whithersoever he goeth. These were redeemed from among men, being the firstfruits unto God and to the Lamb.

⁵ And in their mouth was found no guile: for they are without fault before the throne of God.

⁶ And I saw another angel fly in the midst of heaven, having the everlasting gospel to preach unto them that dwell on the earth, and to every nation, and kindred, and tongue, and people,

⁷ Saying with a loud voice, Fear God, and give glory to him; for the hour of his judgment is come: and worship him that made heaven, and earth, and the sea, and the fountains of waters.

⁸ And there followed another angel, saying, Babylon is fallen, is fallen, that great city, because she made all nations drink of the wine of the wrath of her fornication.

⁹ And the third angel followed them, saying with a loud voice, If any man worship the beast and his image, and receive his mark in his forehead, or in his hand,

¹⁰ The same shall drink of the wine of the wrath of God, which is poured out without mixture into the cup of his indignation; and he shall be tormented with fire and brimstone in the presence of the holy angels, and in the presence of the Lamb:

¹¹ And the smoke of their torment ascendeth up for ever and ever: and they have no rest day nor night, who worship the beast and his image, and whosoever receiveth the mark of his name.

The Revelation

¹² Here is the patience of the saints: here are they that keep the commandments of God, and the faith of Jesus.
¹³ And I heard a voice from heaven saying unto me, Write, Blessed are the dead which die in the Lord from hence forth: Yea, saith the Spirit, that they may rest from their labours; and their works do follow them.
¹⁴ And I looked, and behold a white cloud, and upon the cloud one sat like unto the Son of man, having on his head a golden crown, and in his hand a sharp sickle.
¹⁵ And another angel came out of the temple, crying with a loud voice to him that sat on the cloud, Thrust in thy sickle, and reap: for the time is come for thee to reap; for the harvest of the earth is ripe.
¹⁶ And he that sat on the cloud thrust in his sickle on the earth; and the earth was reaped.
¹⁷ And another angel came out of the temple which is in heaven, he also having a sharp sickle.
¹⁸ And another angel came out from the altar, which had power over fire; and cried with a loud cry to him that had the sharp sickle, saying, Thrust in thy sharp sickle, and gather the clusters of the vine of the earth; for her grapes are fully ripe.
¹⁹ And the angel thrust in his sickle into the earth, and gathered the vine of the earth, and cast it into the great winepress of the wrath of God.
²⁰ And the winepress was trodden without the city, and blood came out of the winepress, even unto the horse bridles, by the space of a thousand and six hundred furlongs. (Revelation 14:1-20) [1600 fur. = 200 mi./322 km]

Insights

Revelation 13 ends with the identity number of the beast. After the tribulation, Jesus takes up the elect at the sixth seal just before His wrath. Chapter 7 follows the sixth seal with its winds held back for the male virgins to be sealed first. Faultless before the throne, they are the firstfruits who ascend after the beheaded martyrs rise from their graves (in 20:4-5):

> 7   And after these things I saw four angels standing on the four corners of the earth, holding the four winds of the earth, that the wind should not blow on the earth, nor on the sea, nor on any tree. ²And I saw another angel ascending from the east, having the seal of the living God:

Insights: Chapter 14

and he cried with a loud voice to the four angels, to whom it was given to hurt the earth and the sea, ³ Saying, Hurt not the earth, neither the sea, nor the trees, till we have sealed the servants of our God in their foreheads.
(Rev. 7:1-3)

The angel in 14:6 is *another angel* after the one in chapter 7; they connect. The martyrs are tagged in 6:11 at **the fifth seal**. In chapter 7 the virgins are sealed before the winds of **the sixth seal** are loosed to shake the powers of the heavens (in 6:12; 14:14). The sun turns black and the moon, red; the earth shakes, and the Lord appears **at the right hand of glory on a cloud** to raise the elect from their graves. (Mat. 24:29-30) The firstfruits ascend; then its martyrs ascend together with survivors of the tribulation. 7 shows the male virgins sealed before the sixth seal. Chapter 14 reports their presence in heaven, worshiping the Lamb together.

> ⁶ And I saw another angel fly in the midst of heaven, having the everlasting gospel to preach unto them that dwell on the earth, and to every nation, and kindred, and tongue, and people, (Rev. 14:6) [before the tribulation]

Two prophets call the world to repent and to believe in Jesus Christ, warning people of the wrath to come. (14:6-12) The third prophet warns the world of God's wrath against all who take the mark or worship the beast or his image [at the fifth seal].

Jesus rose, *the firstfruits of them that slept,* leading the elect who rose to enter Jerusalem and appeared to many Jews (in Mat. 27:52-3). When He comes seated in glory, the firstfruits of Israel, male virgins like Christ, lead the elect to Him in the air:

> ¹² Now if their fall is riches for the world, and their failure riches for the Gentiles, how much more their fullness! ... ¹⁵ For if their being cast away is the reconciling of the world, what *will* their acceptance *be* but life from the dead? ... ²⁵ For I do not desire, brethren, that you should be ignorant of this mystery, lest you should be wise in your own opinion, that blindness in part has happened to Israel until the fullness of the Gentiles has come in.
> (Rom. 11:12, 15, 25 NKJV)

Yeshua comes for the chosen ones at the first harvest of Sukkot (in 14:13-16). The beheaded martyrs of the great tribulation

The Revelation

rise. Together with the saints who survive, having refused the beast, his image, and his mark, they ascend to meet Jesus in the air (in 14:14). These were mentioned to others who had died bore them and were under the altar at the fifth seal (in 6:11). After His wrath leaves the Sanctuary, they return to earth with Him for the marriage supper of the Lamb (in 19:7-9, 11-16; cf. 20:4-6).

The elect martyrs rise from death. [Gr.: *anistemi*, "stand up"] The firstfruits are last to be sealed but are first to ascend before the martyrs who ascend when its survivors are caught up to meet the Lord in the air together with them. [Gr.: *anabaino*, "go up"] The survivors remain in heaven: *so shall we ever be with the Lord. (1 Thes. 4:14; cf. Rev. 20:4c)*

Chapter 14 has two harvests (in 14:14-20): Jesus sits on His throne on a cloud (in 6:16; cf. 14:14) and gathers His elect (in Mat. 24:31). Others are gathered by the mark for the winepress. (14:19)

After His bowls of wrath in 16, Yeshua returns to Jerusalem with 144.000 male virgins of Israel and martyrs who are called to reign with Him. (14:1; 19:11-16; 20:4-6) ... *them also which sleep in Jesus will God bring with Him. (1 Thes. 4:14)* ... *they lived and reigned with Christ for a thousand years. (Rev. 20:4c)*

Another Abomination

The abuse of the Jews by Antiochus IV in 168-165 BC was foretold four hundred years ahead of time. (Dan. 8:24) Jesus spoke of a vast passage of events before another abomination is in the temple, alluding to its place in Jerusalem. *After that tribulation,* Jesus *[parousia] comes near/appears on a cloud* to gather His elect from all the earth. (1 Thes. 4:15-17; Mk. 13:24-27)

The Roman general Titus destroyed the temple in 70 AD, not as Antiochus "Epiphanes," who demanded worship and set up an idol, desecrating the temple. No Roman general ever demanded worship as Antiochus had done; it would have cost him his life.

Caesar Hadrian set up a statue of Jupiter in a temple built for Venus in Palestina, but that was not the "holy place," which had been leveled. The enormity of the holocaust exceeded the Judean butchery, and the world could have been destroyed in 1945, but the temple was absent, and the Jews were still scattered.

The tribulation is the worst time new covenant saints would ever know, but its days are shortened. The elect who endure to

Insights: Chapter 14

the end, not yielding to the beast or his mark, ascend to Jesus in the air before the first bowl of His wrath (in 14:17-20).

> [12] I saw when the Lamb opened the sixth seal, and there was a great earthquake. The sun became as black as sackcloth made of goat's hair, and the full moon became like blood. [13] The stars of heaven fell to the earth like a fig tree drops unripe figs when shaken by a great wind. [14] The heaven ripped apart like a scroll being rolled up, and every mountain and island was moved from their places.
> [15] Then the kings of the earth and the great men and the military commanders and the rich and the mighty and everyone—slave and free—hid themselves in the caves and among the rocks of the mountains. [16] And they tell the mountains and the rocks, "Fall on us, and hide us from the face of the One seated on the throne and from the wrath of the Lamb. [17] For the great day of their wrath has come, and who is able to stand?"
> (Rev. 6:12-17 TLV)

The Shortcut

The heavens are shaken. Islands and mountains are moved; *immediately after the tribulation,* i.e., the martyrdom of saints in the days of the beast and this mark, the elect rise from the dead and are changed into Christ's likeness. Its trials are harsh before His wrath is poured out. *God hath not appointed us to wrath, but to obtain salvation by our Lord Jesus Christ. (See 1 Thes. 5:9)*

> [16] For the Lord himself shall descend from heaven with a shout, with the voice of the archangel, and with the trump of God: and the dead in Christ shall rise first: [17] Then we which are alive and remain shall be caught up together with them in the clouds, to meet the Lord in the air: and so shall we ever be with the Lord. [18] Wherefore comfort one another with these words.
> (1 Thes. 4:16-18) [Gr.: *anistemi* means "to stand up, get up, or arise." This happens at the first resurrection in 20:4-6.]

> [14] Then the LORD will be seen over them,
> And His arrow will go forth like lightning.
> The Lord GOD will blow the trumpet.
> And go with whirlwinds from the south.
> (Zec. 9:14 NKJV)

The Revelation

Yeshua comes with a shout, with the voice of the archangel, and <u>the trumpet of God</u>. Michael the archangel is the prince of Israel, sent for their ascension. (Dan. 10:21) He also ministers to the saints of Israel on behalf of God. At the **trumpet of God,** His angels catch us up. **This is** not the last trump, which is one of seven at the end. The day and hour are hid, but the season is not. Only fools say they know the day or hour; not even Jesus knew that! But He died on Passover and rose on the Day of Firstfruits. This tells us the feasts are for seasons and signs, but no one can know when Jesus will come; the calendars were changed!

It's time to apply our trials against the nature of our flesh in preparation for the tribulation preceding the first resurrection and its saints' ascension. After His indignation Jesus returns to reign with the elect martyrs and 144,000 virgins. <u>They return</u> riding like lightning on white horses, flashing across the skies:

> ^{26} "Therefore if they say to you, 'Look, He is in the desert!' do not go out; *or* 'Look, *He is* in the inner rooms!' do not believe *it*. ^{27} For as the lightning comes from the east and flashes to the west, so also will the coming of the Son of Man be. ^{28} <u>For wherever the carcass is, there the eagles will be gathered together</u>. (Mat. 24:26-28 NKJV)

After He comes on a cloud to take up the elect, those who are left behind will think He returned though He's with the elect in heaven till the last bowl of wrath has left the Sanctuary in chapters 14–16. They won't correctly divide the Word. Before Yeshua returns with His armies, Babylon is utterly decimated. He returns to destroy the armies in Armageddon, and even eagles eat their flesh, a sign that fulfills the prophecy of His return.

The living who are worthy are caught up before the wrath and may not return but remain in the presence of God: *Then we which are alive and remain shall be caught up together with them in the clouds, to meet the Lord in the air: and so shall we ever be with the Lord. (1 Thes. 4:17)* Not having died, we ascend to heaven; not bowing a knee to the beast, we confess Jesus is Lord and do not suffer the judgment. (See Rev. 2:8b-11)

After we who are elect martyrs rise to life, we ascend to the Lord in the air (Mat. 24:29-31) but return to reign for a thousand years with Jesus, bypassing the judgment. (20:5; 7:13-17; 13:11-18; 14:9-16) Note the distinction between martyrs and survivors.

Insights: Chapter 14

One out of two are short of oil, not filled with the Spirit, not yielded to His will. Half are unprepared for His coming and are left behind. One of two are taken and one of two, left behind.

Certain of teachings that shun God's words, we argue with vain opinions. Our leaders say we can never be perfect. Although people set purity aside, the Word is clear:

> ³ For what the law was powerless to do because it was weakened by the flesh, God did by sending his own Son in the likeness of sinful flesh to be a sin offering. And so he condemned sin in the flesh, ⁴ <u>in order that the righteous requirement of the law might be fully met in us, who do not live according to the flesh but according to the Spirit.</u> (Rom. 8:3-4 NIV)

If our minds are set on this world as sinners are, we won't be ready to meet Him when He comes on a cloud. If our thoughts are set on its foods, pleasures, or possessions, we're living in the nature of the flesh. If we're proud of our positions, discontent, ambitious, or envious of others, we're carnal. (1 Cor. 2:15-3:3)

If we press for the goal of our high calling of God in Christ, He prepares us to meet Him, leaving everything and everyone behind. The Spirit performs the impossible: His righteousness in us raises us out of sin to live by the same Spirit that raised Him to life. *If any man have not the Spirit of Christ, he is none of his. (Rom. 8:9b) For as many as are led by the Spirit of God, they are the sons of God. (Rom. 8:14) He must increase, but I must decrease. (Jn. 3:30)* We live by the Spirit if we die by the cross.

When the sun turns black and the moon, red, and powers in the heavens are shaken, look up! Jesus comes on a cloud. *Every eye sees Him* when we're caught up to meet Jesus at *the great trumpet of God.* It's not a secret. He foretold it ahead of time.

We are saved by grace through faith, not works, but James 2:26 says *faith without works is dead.* In Romans 8 Paul agrees. Jesus knows our works in chapters 2 and 3. (Rev. 21:5-8, 27; 22:14-15) We are His workmanship; our works are not our own.

> ⁶ For to be carnally minded is death, but to be spiritually minded is life and peace. ⁷ Because the carnal mind is enmity against God; for it is not subject to the law of God, nor indeed, can be. ⁸ So then, those who are in the flesh cannot please God. (Rom. 8:6-8 NKJV)

The Revelation

If we live in sin or refuse to forgive, we're in the unbelief of the flesh. If we profess the faith but live for this world, we're left behind. (1Thes. 4:13-18; Lk.21:25-36) The Lord said, *pray that ye may be able to escape*—not the persecution that perfects the saints, but His indignation against the world:

> ³⁴ "Be careful, or your hearts will be weighed down with carousing, drunkenness and the anxieties of life, and that day will close on you suddenly like a trap. ³⁵ For it will come on all those who live on the face of the whole earth. ³⁶ <u>Be always on the watch, and pray</u> that you may be able to escape all that is about to happen, and that you may be able to stand before the Son of Man." (Lk. 21:34-36 NIV; cf. 21:25-36)

Mysterious Messengers

Four angels hold back the winds while others swiftly seal the male virgins of Israel in chapter 7. Before the winds shake the heavens, the word goes out to refuse the mark though it costs our lives (in 14:9-12). The dragon, a prophet, and a beast demand the deaths of their opponents, but saints keep the faith and endure to the end (in 13:5-17). The pending rapture is soon past. Then in the passion of His justice, God sends His wrath:

> ⁷ And will not God bring about justice for his chosen ones, who cry out to him day and night? Will he keep putting them off? ⁸ I tell you, he will see that they get justice <u>and quickly</u>. ... (Lk. 18:7-8a) [the fifth seal]

> ¹³ In Him, you also, after listening to the message of truth, the gospel of your salvation—having also believed, you were <u>sealed in Him with the Holy Spirit</u> of promise, ¹⁴ who is given as a pledge of our inheritance, with a view to <u>the redemption of God's own possession</u>, to the praise of His glory. (Eph. 1:13-14 NASB) [the hope]

> ¹² So then, brothers, we are debtors, not to the flesh, to live according to the flesh. ¹³ For if you live according to the flesh you will die, but if by the Spirit you put to death the deeds of the body, you will live. ¹⁴ For all who are led by the Spirit of God are sons of God. (Rom. 8:12-14 ESV)

The last hour of the age began as the gospel went forth from space with its warnings (in 14:6-7). Then Babylon was declared

Insights: Chapter 14

morally fallen past the point of return (in 14:8). In September 2001 the harlot was a marked woman.

> 1.) ⁶And I saw another angel fly in the midst of heaven, having the everlasting gospel to preach unto them that dwell on the earth, and to every nation, and kindred, and tongue, and people, ⁷<u>Saying with a loud voice</u>, Fear God, and give glory to him; for the hour of his judgment is come: and worship him that made heaven, and earth, and the sea, and the fountains of waters. (Rev. 14:6-7)

At the right time in history, Billy Graham was a herald who obeyed his calling. His brother heard him preach at a young age and said, "He preached loud ... so loud he didn't need a microphone or any amplification. ... You could hear him a quarter mile away!" His mother warned him, "Son, you can't preach so loud. You'll scare people away!" [163] But his stentorian voice would reach the world, mostly by radio and television.

Saints have given their lives to propagate the good news of salvation, hiking from village to village, mountain to mountain, and valley to valley, taking the gospel to sinners and baptizing. Even so, the sign is a strong voice in the signal from heaven.

> 2.) ⁸ And another angel followed, saying, "Babylon is fallen, is fallen, that great city, because she has made all nations drink of the wine of the wrath of her fornication." (Rev. 14:8 NKJV) [She's judged in 16 and 18.]

David Wilkerson was a pastor who warned NYC of its soon coming judgment.[164] His book *The Vision* foresees its destruction by fire. Jonathan Cahn wrote a book based on the city's history. *The Harbinger* reveals its prophetic place in the Scriptures.[165]

> 3.) ⁹And the third angel followed them, saying with a loud voice, If any man worship the beast and his image, and receive his mark in his forehead, or in his hand, ¹⁰ the same shall drink of the wine of the wrath of God, which is poured out without mixture into the cup of his indignation; and he shall be tormented with fire and brimstone in the presence of the holy angels, and in the presence of the Lamb: (Rev. 14:9-10)

A third messenger warns multitudes to reject the beast and his mark, for God will condemn anyone who accepts the number,

The Revelation

or the mark, or who bows before the beast. We must redeem the time, not entertain ourselves with wasteful living. Seeking His Kingdom and His righteousness should be all that's on our minds and in our hearts, knowing the time is short.

By books, discs, and recordings, the messages might remain in the time of wrath to tell those who are left behind, even Israel, "Repent and keep the faith!" Although His fury encircles them and hope seems gone, His Word endures: repent and come out of Babylon forever—pray for Jerusalem—Yeshua will return!

Two Autumn Harvests

Martyrs cry out from under the altar at the fifth seal but are exhorted to be patient. Others must be killed as they were. The firstfruits are sealed before the tribulation ends. **The sixth seal** breaks *after the tribulation* at His coming on a cloud to gather the chosen ones to Himself. (Mat. 24:29-31; 14:14-16)

Stunned by His Presence, men plead for an escape, but as Lot left Sodom, the brimstone fell. Noah's family gathered in an ark; its door shut, and the flood came. Mockers resist miracles but will see Jesus on the throne before His wrath. He opens the **sixth seal** as the tribulation ends to gather believers to Himself.

> [17] Then another angel came out of the temple which is in heaven, he also having a sharp sickle. [18] And another angel came out from the altar, who had power over fire, and he cried with a loud cry to him who had the sharp sickle, saying, "Thrust in your sharp sickle and gather the clusters of the vine of the earth, for her grapes are fully ripe." (Rev. 14:17-18) – the sickle of His wrath

After the elect rise and are caught up, six angels leave the Sanctuary in heaven to pour out the wrath of God from six bowls while the beast musters the nations' armies against the Lamb to fulfill the prophecy: *And the king shall do according to his will; and he shall exalt himself and magnify himself above every god, and shall speak marvelous things against the God of gods, <u>and shall prosper till the indignation be accomplished</u> for that that is determined shall be done. (Dan. 11:36; cf. Is. 66:14b, p. 222)*

At last God recalls Babylon, and the city falls into the sea at the **seventh bowl**. Then Yeshua returns with His armies against the nations in Armageddon, turning it into a graveyard. Angels

Insights: Chapter 14

cast the beast and false prophet into the lake of fire, ending the wrath when the devil is locked in the abyss. At last the Messiah judges the nations with equity.

> [13] "Enter by the narrow gate; for wide is the gate and broad is the way that leads to destruction, and there are many who go in by it. [14] Because narrow is the gate and difficult is the way which leads to life, and there are few who find it. (Mat. 7:13-14 NKJV)

His disciples, apostles, and prophets were killed, living by faith to lay hold of life. They died for their love of His goodness.

> [10] "Do not fear any of those things which you are about to suffer. Indeed, the devil is about to throw some of you into prison, that you may be tested, and you will have tribulation ten days. Be faithful until death, and I will give you the crown of life. (Rev. 2:10 NKJV)

Whether we support His nation or turn against Israel, Christ wins her in the end. Though all nations stand against them, the world can't destroy the Jews. He punished them for His Name's sake but favors them for His promises to the fathers. (Dan. 7:18; cf. Gen. 17:5-6; Rom. 4:16-18)

A Great Tribulation

Since they hate the truth that shines its light on darkness, the world adores the beast. (13:7) When a nation accepts Babylon, Christians suffer for righteousness. If we are weak, God gives us strength according to our faith. Nothing overcomes Christ in us.

False teachers and false prophets draw crowds by miracles and wonders even though miracles and wonders are for today. By delivering only half the gospel, however, teachers have often deceived the elect. Most of us have believed the lies—lies about Israel; lies about practicing sin. But God is not mocked; what we sow we reap. We carry a cross to follow Jesus Christ or don't follow Him at all. He can use anyone for His purposes, even an apostate church, to fulfill His prophecies, which are unavoidable though their time is in the Father's hands.

Leaders have had their own motives from noble to nefarious; men are moved by thoughts and impulses, but God calls us to believe His every word; receive it. At times translators err by interpreting instead of translating; it's warfare for them too.

The Revelation

Satan himself fulfills the words of God while attempting to shut them up. In days like these, the apostles wrote about trials:

> [7] These have come so that your faith—of greater worth than gold, which perishes even though tried by fire—may be proved genuine and may result in praise, glory and honor when Jesus Christ is revealed. [8] Though you have not seen him, you love him; and even though you do not see him now, you believe in him and are filled with an inexpressible and glorious joy, [9] for you are receiving the goal of your faith, the salvation of your souls.
> (1 Pet. 1:7-9 TLV)

> [10] "And I will pour out on the house of David and the inhabitants of Jerusalem a spirit of grace and supplication. They will look on me, the one they have pierced, and they will mourn for him as one mourns for an only child, and grieve bitterly for him as one grieves for a firstborn son. (Zec. 12:10) [The Days of Awe foretell this.]

Mountains move and islands disappear. *Behold, he cometh with clouds; and every eye shall see him, and they also which pierced him: (Rev. 1:7a)* Even from their graves, they'll see Him:

> [16] And they tell the mountains and the rocks, "Fall on us, and hide us from the face of the One seated on the throne and from the wrath of the Lamb. [17] For the great day of their wrath has come, and who is able to stand?"
> (Rev. 6:16-17 TLV) [The sixth seal has seven bowls of wrath.]

Faith proves itself in our most adverse circumstances. When we can't understand, tenacious faith outlasts the tests sent to humble us and turn us from our own ways to do the will of God:

> [19] ... They stoned Paul and dragged him outside the city, thinking he was dead. [20] But after the disciples had gathered around him, he got up and went back into the city. ... [21] ... Then they returned to Lystra, Iconium and Antioch, [22] strengthening the disciples and encouraging them to remain true to the faith. "We must go through many hardships to enter the kingdom of God," they said.
> (Acts 14:19b-20a, 21b-22 NIV)

> [32] And what more shall I say? I do not have time to tell about Gideon, Barak, Samson and Jephthah, about David and Samuel and the prophets, [33] who through faith

Insights: Chapter 14

conquered kingdoms, administered justice, and gained what was promised; who shut the mouths of lions, [34] quenched the fury of the flames, and escaped the edge of the sword; whose weakness was turned to strength; and who became powerful in battle and routed foreign armies. [35] Women received back their dead, raised to life again. There were others who were tortured, refusing to be released so that they might gain an even better resurrection. [36] Some faced jeers and flogging, and even chains and imprisonment. [37] They were put to death by stoning; they were sawed in two; they were killed by the sword. They went about in sheepskins and goatskins, destitute, persecuted and mistreated— [38] the world was not worthy of them. They wandered in deserts and mountains, living in caves and in holes in the ground.
[39] These were all commended for their faith, yet none of them received what had been promised, [40] since God had planned something better for us, so that only together with us would they be made perfect.
(Heb. 11:32-40 NIV), and the *Tree of Life Version* continues,
12 Therefore since we have such a great cloud of witnesses surrounding us, let us also get rid of every weight and entangling sin. Let us run with endurance the race set before us, [2] focusing on *Yeshua*, the initiator and perfecter of faith. For the joy set before Him, He endured the cross, disregarding its shame; and He has taken His seat at the right hand of the throne of God. (Heb. 12:1-2)

We overcome by trusting Jesus. The battle is His; its victory, ours. We're tried by fire, not just by the normal tests of life:

[12] Beloved, think it not strange, concerning the fiery trial which is to try you, as if some strange thing happened unto you: But rejoice, in as much as ye are partakers of Christ's sufferings; that, when his glory shall be revealed, ye may be glad also with exceeding joy. (1 Pet. 4:12-13)

[33] Those who are wise among the people will give understanding to many, yet they will die by sword and flame, and be captured and plundered for a time. [34] When defeated, they will be helped by some, but many others will join them insincerely. [35] Some of the wise will fall so that they may be refined, purified, and cleansed until the time of the end, for it will still come <u>at the appointed time</u>. (Dan. 11: 33-35 HCSB)

The Revelation

His perfect will is done through us when we practice living by faith as Abraham did, entrusting himself to God, believing in His words. It took time; he learned as he lived. We can do this.

> ⁷ He who overcomes shall inherit all things, and I will be his God and he shall be My son. ⁸ But the cowardly, unbelieving, abominable, murderers, sexually immoral, sorcerers, idolaters, and all liars shall have their part in the lake which burns with fire and brimstone, which is the second death." (Rev. 21:7-8 NKJV)

We had done the same things but are saved by grace through faith, yet we've claimed to have turned to Him by our own will.

> ¹⁸ In your seed all the nations of the earth shall be blessed, <u>because you have obeyed My voice</u>."
> (Gen. 22:18 NASB) – Abraham feared and obeyed.

False teachers convince us we are righteous apart from good works, as if faith isn't substantive. Have we risked eternity for a false teaching? The way to life is difficult and narrow.

> ³ Sojourn in this land, and I will be with you and will bless you, for to you and to your offspring I will give all these lands, and I will establish the oath that I swore to Abraham your father. ⁴ I will multiply your offspring as the stars of heaven and will give to your offspring all these lands. And in your offspring all the nations of the earth shall be blessed, ⁵ <u>because Abraham obeyed my voice and kept my charge, my commandments, my statutes, and my laws</u>." (Gen. 26:3-5 ESV)

But he that doeth truth cometh to the light, that his deeds may be made manifest, that they are <u>wrought in God</u>. (Jn. 3:21)

> ¹² Who can understand *his* errors? Cleanse thou me from secret *faults*. ¹³ <u>Keep back thy servant also from presumptuous *sins*</u>; let them not have dominion over me: then shall I be upright, <u>and I shall be innocent from the great transgression</u>. ¹⁴ Let the words of my mouth, and the meditation of my heart, be acceptable in thy sight, O LORD, my strength, and my redeemer. (Ps. 19:12-14)

> ⁷ And shall not God avenge his own elect, which cry day and night unto him, though he bear long with them? ⁸ I tell you that he will avenge them speedily. Nevertheless,

Insights: Chapter 14

when the Son of man cometh, shall he find faith on the earth? (Lk. 18:7-8; cf. Rev. 6:9-10)

In 1917 the Balfour Declaration offered a Jewish state for the persecuted Jews. In June 1967 the Jews took Jerusalem's Old City. December 6, 2017, President Donald J. Trump officially recognized the city as the capital of Israel.[166] The events were each fifty years apart like the Year of Jubilee every fifty years when the people's debts are cancelled, *and ye shall return every man unto his possession, and ye shall return every man unto his family*. *(Lev. 25:10b)*

In 2015 the UN celebrated its 70th anniversary with President Obama opening its morning session.[167] In 2018 the U.S. Embassy moved to Jerusalem on Israel's 70th anniversary.[168] Revelation is the story about a war between two cities: Mystery Babylon and Jerusalem, each with a king.

> [9] The coming of the lawless one is by the activity of Satan with all power and false signs and wonders, [10] and with all wicked deception for those who are perishing, because <u>they refused to love the truth and so be saved</u>. [11] Therefore God sends them a strong delusion, so that they may believe what is false, [12] in order that all may be condemned who did not believe the truth but had pleasure in unrighteousness. (2 Thes. 2:9-12 ESV)

> [16] The LORD also shall roar out of Zion, and utter his voice from Jerusalem; and the heavens and the earth shall shake: but the LORD will be the hope of his people, and the strength of the children of Israel. (Joel 3:16)

When these things begin to come to pass, then look up and lift up your heads; for your redemption draweth nigh. (Lk. 21:28):

> [30] "I will show wonders in the heavens
>   and on the earth,
>   blood and fire and billows of smoke.
> [31] The sun will be turned to darkness
>   and the moon to blood
>   before the <u>coming of the great and dreadful
>   day of the LORD</u>.
> [32] <u>And everyone who calls
>   on the name of the LORD will be saved</u>;
>   for on Mount Zion and in Jerusalem

The Revelation

> there will be deliverance,
>   as the LORD has said,
> among the survivors
>   whom the LORD calls. (Jl. 2:30-32 NIV)

> ² And behold, the glory of the God of Israel was coming from the east. And the sound of his coming was like the sound of many waters, and the earth shone with his glory. ... ⁴ As the glory of the LORD entered the temple by the gate facing east, ⁵ the Spirit lifted me up and brought me into the inner court; and behold, the glory of the LORD filled the temple.

> ⁶ While the man was standing beside me, I heard one speaking to me out of the temple, ⁷ and he said to me, "Son of man, <u>this is the place of my throne</u> and the place of the soles of my feet, where I will dwell in the midst of the people of Israel forever. <u>And the house of Israel shall no more defile my holy name</u>, neither they, nor their kings, by their whoring and by the dead bodies of their kings at their high places, (Ezk. 43:2, 4-7 ESV)

Whoever believes that God only blesses us, or that trouble is only from the devil will reconsider if they hope to love the truth. In the *Revelation of Jesus Christ*, angels pour out His bowls of wrath and later blow their trumpets for His indignation against the earth. The Lamb breaks the seals and sends hurricanes, famines, floods, and pestilence: judgments against the world and He is good. He scourges His own (in Heb. 12:6-11) and He is good. He returns to destroy multitudes and He is good. He reigns by a rod of iron and yet is good for ever and ever. This calls for endurance, obedience, and the faith of Jesus (in 13:10; 14:12) ... *and his name shall be called Wonderful, Counsellor, The mighty God, The everlasting Father, The Prince of Peace. (Is. 9:6b)*

Our destiny isn't based on what we've done for Him, but on what He's done through us. We'll prepare for His coming by loving one another, emptied of ourselves, filled with Christ, and willing to die for His name's sake. We are His servants, or we are not His who sends the trials as well as the blessings:

> ¹³ When I shut up the heavens, so that there is no rain, or command the locust to devour the land, or send pestilence among my people,¹⁴ if my people who are

Insights: Chapter 14

called by my name humble themselves, and pray and seek my face and turn from their wicked ways, then I will hear from heaven and will forgive their sin and heal their land. (2 Chron. 7:13-14 ESV) [Pestilence = fatal epidemics.]

One of the dragon's chief princes rules as Gog *in the uttermost parts of the north.* In respect to Israel, Russia is remotely north of the Black Sea. When hunting for passages with words to connect prophecies, we exclude those that are irrelevant or don't fit. Ezekiel 38 follows the Kingdom, but 37 and 39 precede it:

> **39** "And you, son of man, prophesy against Gog and say, Thus says the Lord GOD: Behold, I am against you, O Gog, chief prince of Meshech and Tubal. ^{2}And I will turn you about and drive you forward, and bring you up <u>from the uttermost parts of the north</u>, and lead you <u>against the mountains of Israel</u>. ^{3}Then I will strike your bow from your left hand, and will make your arrows drop out of your right hand. ^{4}You shall fall on the mountains of Israel, you and all your hordes and the peoples who are with you. <u>I will give you to birds of prey of every sort</u> and to the beasts of the field to be devoured. ^{5}You shall fall in the open field, for I have spoken, declares the Lord GOD. ^{6}I will send fire on Magog and on those who dwell securely in the coastlands, and they shall know that I am the LORD.
>
> ^{7}"<u>And my holy name I will make known in the midst of my people Israel, and I will not let my holy name be profaned anymore</u>. And the nations shall know that I am the LORD, the Holy One in Israel. ^{8}Behold, it is coming and it will be brought about, declares the Lord GOD. That is the day of which I have spoken.
>
> ^{9}"<u>Then those who dwell in the cities of Israel will go out and make fires of the weapons and burn them</u>, shields and bucklers, bow and arrows, clubs and spears; and they will make fires of them for seven years, ^{10} **so** that they will not need to take wood out of the field or cut down any out of the forests, for they will make their fires of the weapons. They will seize the spoil of those who despoiled them, and plunder those who plundered them, declares the Lord GOD.
>
> ^{11}"On that day I will give to Gog a place for burial in Israel, the Valley of the Travelers, east of the sea. It will

block the travelers, <u>for there Gog and all his multitude will be buried</u>. It will be called the Valley of Hamon-gog. ¹² For seven months the house of Israel will be burying them, in order to cleanse the land. ...

¹⁷ "As for you, son of man, thus says the Lord God: <u>Speak to the birds of every sort and to all beasts of the field: 'Assemble and come, gather from all around to the sacrificial feast that I am preparing for you, a great sacrificial feast on the mountains of Israel, and you shall eat flesh and drink blood.</u> ...

²¹ "And I will set my glory among the nations, and all the nations shall see my judgment that I have executed, and my hand that I have laid on them. ²² <u>The house of Israel shall know that I am the L</u>ORD <u>their God, from that day forward.</u> ²³ <u>And the nations shall know that the house of Israel went into captivity for their iniquity, because they dealt so treacherously with me that I hid my face from them and gave them into the hand of their adversaries</u>, and they all fell by the sword.

... ²⁶ <u>They shall forget their shame and all the treachery they have practiced against me, when they dwell securely in their land</u> with none to make them afraid, ²⁷ when I have brought them back from the peoples and gathered them from their enemies' lands, and through them have vindicated my holiness in the sight of many nations.
(Ezk. 39:1-12, 17, 21-23, 26-27 ESV)

The keys that place Ezekiel 39 before Messiah's Kingdom are these: the reason the Jews were scattered (v.7 above); their return to the land; melting weapons for plowshares (also in Is. 2:3-4; Mic. 4:2-3); the burial of the dead; *birds of prey of every sort,* (even eagles). And deaths by the sword of the Lord—the Word of His mouth (in Rev. 19:15, 21). The nations will know God scattered them because of their iniquity, but they will forget their shame when they dwell securely in their land. These are clustered prophecies and are premillennial. There's no need for these after Christ reigns for a thousand years till the end of time.

The Revelation of Jesus Christ

CHAPTER 15

15 Then I saw another great and wonderful sign in heaven: seven angels who have seven plagues—the last ones, for with them God's wrath is finished. ²And I saw something like a sea of glass mixed with fire, and those who had overcome the beast and his image and the number of his name standing by the sea of glass, holding the harps of God. ³And they are singing the song of Moses the servant of God and the song of the Lamb, saying,

> "Great and wonderful are Your deeds,
>   ADONAI *Elohei-Tzva'ot!*   [O LORD God the Almighty!]
> Just and true are Your ways,
>   O King of the nations!
> ⁴ Who shall not fear and glorify Your name, O Lord?
>   For You alone are Holy.
> All the nations shall come and worship before You,
>   for Your righteous acts have been revealed!"

⁵ After these things I looked, and the Temple of the Tent of Witness in heaven was opened. ⁶ Out of the Temple came the seven angels having the seven plagues, dressed in pure bright linen and wearing wide gold sashes around their chests.

⁷ Then one of the four living creatures gave the seven angels seven golden bowls full of the wrath of God, who lives forever and ever. ⁸ And the Temple was filled with smoke from the glory of God and from His power. No one was able to enter the Temple until the seven angels' seven plagues were finished. (Revelation 15:1-8 TLV)

Insights

God ends this age as Yeshua returns after seven angels pour out His bowls of wrath. In 15 the saints who resist the beast and his image appear with harps in heaven. Overcoming pain and fear, we rise above the trials of earth to sing the songs of Moses and the Lamb—Jews and gentiles—filled with the Spirit of the LORD. Our Union answers the prayer of Messiah for the Jewish apostles and their proselytes, united together as one new man, the testimony that shows the world Jesus Christ came from God:

The Revelation

[20] "My prayer is not for them alone. I pray also for those who will believe in me through their message, [21] that all of them <u>may be one</u>, Father, just as you are in me and I am in you. <u>May they also be in us</u> so that the world may believe that you have sent me. [22] I have given them the glory that you gave me, that they may be one as we are one— [23] I in them and you in me—so that they may be <u>brought to complete unity</u>. Then the world will know that you sent me and have loved them even as you have loved me. (Jn. 17:20-23 NIV)

The firstfruits were sealed in 7, which leads to chapters 14 and 15 when martyrs from the tribulation are with their number in heaven before seven angels pour out His wrath. The firstfruits are joined by the chosen victors from the tribulation in 14 and 15. Together they sing praises by the glassy sea while His wrath leaves the Sanctuary. The winepress ends its harvest (in 14:19).

We were sinners when He gave us faith and made us victors in Christ—witnesses of God. He planted His words in us to free us from our sinful nature by a new birth. We were dead but are alive. We were alienated but are family. Yeshua is with us who die daily to sin, freed to live in Him forever. Sanctification is the process leading to life.

What's an Antichrist?

Since the first century, antichrists have appeared. Some deny Yeshua was born in mortal flesh. (Rom. 8:3-4) Others deny He enters our flesh as the Spirit. (1 Jn. 4:2-6; Rom. 8:9-11) *Antichrists* oppose Jesus or are false christs. Only John described them:

[18] Little children, it is the last time: and as ye have heard that antichrist shall come, even now are there many antichrists; whereby we know that it is the last time. [19] <u>They went out from us</u>, <u>but they were not of us</u>: for if they had been of us, they would *no doubt* have continued with us: but *they went out* that they might be made manifest that they were not all of us. (1 Jn. 2:18-19)

[7] For many deceivers are entered into the world, who confess not that Jesus Christ is come in the flesh. This is a deceiver and an antichrist. (2 Jn. 7) [... *who are not confessing Jesus Christ coming in flesh.* (from 2 Jn. 7 YLT)]

Insights: Chapter 15

> ² By this you know the Spirit of God: Every spirit that confesses that <u>Jesus Christ has come in the flesh</u> is of God, ³ and every spirit that does not confess that Jesus Christ has come in the flesh is not of God. And this is the *spirit* of the Antichrist, which you have heard is coming, and is already in the world.
> ⁴ You are of God, little children, and have overcome them, because <u>He who is in you is greater than he who is in the world</u>. (1 Jn. 4:2-4 NKJV) [No paragraphs in Greek]

The Lord is that Spirit. (See 2 Cor. 3:17) Within our bodies of carnal flesh, He lives by the Spirit of the Father who gave Him the victory over its likeness. Now that Jesus is beside the Father; souls who are vicariously in Him abide in His Spirit.

> ²² Who is a liar but he who denies that Jesus is the Christ? He is antichrist who denies the Father and the Son. ²³ Whoever denies the Son does not have the Father either; he who acknowledges the Son has the Father also. (1 Jn. 2:22-23 NKJV)

The hour for the man of lawlessness waits for the fullness of iniquity when the one who is *in the way* moves *out of the way*. Then he rises at the great apostasy when the church no longer cares for the fear of God. He is likely in the news today.

> ¹³ For such are false apostles, deceitful workers, transforming themselves into apostles of Christ. ¹⁴ And no wonder! <u>For Satan himself transforms himself into an angel of light.</u> ¹⁵ Therefore it is no great thing if his ministers transform themselves into ministers of righteousness whose end will be according to their works.
> (2 Cor. 11:13-15 NKJV)

Preachers often tell us what we want to hear; and is that why we listen? Do we seek affirmation for our desires? Jesus never spoke to please others. To the contrary, He often said what they didn't want to hear. They turned away, but He was unconcerned by the loss. He said those His Father had chosen *would hear* — even His hard and narrow words, and we'd remain: *Simon Peter answered him, Lord, to whom shall we go? thou hast the words of eternal life. (Jn. 7:68)*

The voice of the dragon speaks by a man in a living image, maybe as a hologram, sating their desires for a tangible god and offering a false peace while demanding worship. He persuades whoever is of the world, but believers resist him though we may lose our families, our friends, and our lives. (See Lk. 14:26-28)

The spirit of the false prophet was here before we were. He is permitted to give life to the image of the beast so that the image speaks. We watch images in theaters and arenas, churches and concerts, and on computers and televisions, even in 3-D! Accustomed to images, we've been conditioned by them; seeing one in Jerusalem's temple won't shock us. (13:18 cf. Is. 14:12-16)

> [41] "I do not receive honor from men. [42] But I know you, that you do not have the love of God in you. [43] I have come in My Father's name, and you do not receive Me; if another comes in his own name, him you will receive. [44] How can you believe, who receive honor from one another, and do not seek the honor that *comes* from the only God? (Jn. 5:41-44 NKJV) – Yeshua

Devils never warn us but tell us we are good or grace has no limit or God has no wrath or He sees no sin or there *is* no sin, but there's no darkness with God; He sees it all. (Ps. 139:12) Sins defile the new covenant as they did the old. His requisites are unchangeable. His Spirit is not a lawbreaker, but is *Christ in you, the hope of glory. (See Col. 1:27)*

> [22] Then he said to his disciples, "The time is coming when you will long to see one of the days of the Son of Man, but you will not see it. [23] People will tell you, 'There he is!' or 'Here he is!' Do not go running off after them. [24] For the Son of Man in his day will be like the lightning, which flashes and lights up the sky from one end to the other. [25] But first he must suffer many things and be rejected by this generation.
>
> [26] "Just as it was in the days of Noah, so also will it be in the days of the Son of Man. [27] People were eating, drinking, marrying and being given in marriage up to the day Noah entered the ark. Then the flood came and destroyed them all.
>
> [28] "It was the same in the days of Lot. People were eating and drinking, buying and selling, planting and building. [29] But the day Lot left Sodom, fire and sulfur rained down from heaven and destroyed them all.

Insights: Chapter 15

³⁰ "It will be just like this on the day the Son of Man is revealed. ³¹ On that day no one who is on the housetop, with possessions inside, should go down to get them. Likewise, no one in the field should go back for anything. ³² Remember Lot's wife! ³³ Whoever tries to keep their life will lose it, and whoever loses their life will preserve it. ³⁴ I tell you, on that night two people will be in one bed; one will be taken and the other left. ³⁵ Two women will be grinding grain together; one will be taken and the other left. [³⁶ Two men will be in the field; one will be taken and the other left."

³⁷ "Where, Lord?" they asked.

He replied, "Where there is a dead body, there the vultures will gather." (Lk. 17:22-37 NIV)

In Matthew 24 Jesus describes the tribulation; in Luke 17 He details our ascension before the indignation: *It will be as it was in the days of Noah.* Before His wrath destroyed the world, He saved His elect, Noah's family, but killed all life on earth. Half of the virgins are left behind at His coming. Later He returns with His armies to destroy His enemies. (Rev. 16:15, p. 181-82; 19:14, 19; Mat. 25:1-13, p. 101; Dan. 11:36, p. 150; Is. 66:14b, p. 222)

The Word warns us to walk in the Spirit and live by faith or be left behind. (Lk. 17: 32-3) He always regards a remnant of the house of Israel. As watchmen we pray for her protection and care for her children since her prophets and apostles cared for us. We love His chosen people without qualification as He does. He adopts Jews and gentiles as family. (Rom. 9:4; Rom. 11; Eph. 1:5)

The Return

After He comes on a cloud for the elect, His wrath falls till He returns for Jerusalem, leading His armies of martyrs:

²⁷ "For as the lightning comes from the east and flashes to the west, so also will the coming of the Son of Man be. ²⁸ For wherever the carcass is, there the eagles will be gathered together. (Mat. 24:27-28 NKJV)

Tishrei 15th is Yom Teruah, the Day of Trumpets. Its week recalls their return from Egypt to their promised land. Messiah returns to Jerusalem for His Bride and establishes the city as His throne when He rules over all the earth as the Word of God.

The Revelation

At the end of the thousand-year reign, the seventh trumpet calls the living and the dead as *the rest of the dead rise* (in Dan. 7:18; Rev. 20:5). Passover prefigured the sacrificed Lamb of God. Its Day of Firstfruits awaited His resurrection. The feasts signal His prophetic seasons. God set the festivals in order, designating the days that would fulfill the prophecies. It stands to reason.

Suddenly Jesus will come on a cloud to take up the elect to Himself (in 14:14-16; 1 Thes. 4:13-18; Mat. 24:30-31). The catching up will not be secret. Strong men will tremble with fear, hiding their faces from His, certain of imminent wrath. Even the souls of the dead will see Him from their graves. (1:7)

When the bowls of indignation are poured out, the saints who reject the beast and his mark are in heaven. Afterward He returns like lightning, leading armies on white horses to finish His fury when He rescues Jerusalem for His throne (in 19:11-16).

He divides the nations as sheep from goats and sends those on the left to destruction but draws to Himself the sheep on the right. (Mat. 25:32-3) Jesus has no compromised position; we are either for or against Him, and are either for or against His nation and Kingdom Israel.

It's the saga of Jerusalem, the city of the King, where what does not exist is spoken into being. She remains corruptible till He makes her incorruptible, preparing her for an everlasting universe as He prepares us by His Spirit for His eternal Kingdom.

When His terror strikes the earth, Jews worldwide see their Messiah, Yeshua, coming for the elect on a cloud, and every Jewish household that has not believed travails with grief. The LORD is touched with compassion for them. As He promised He pours out the Spirit of grace and supplications for mercy on them and hears their cry for His return. He is the Sovereign of all.

Why do the Jews suffer so much till He hears them? They've suffered by His vengeance for profaning His holy name. God is no respecter of persons, because there is no boasting in heaven. The proud and self-righteous are ruled out. All who love their darkness stay in the darkness forever. Then what should we do? We should turn to the light of His words and give thanks to God for choosing the Jews since out of them we have a Savior!

The nations are bound together after rejoining Babylon. The city is a mystery since she was cursed long ago, yet her spirit

Insights: Chapter 15

corrupts the earth by her sins. She is always attached to a city by which she rules the earth. She is a spiritual parasite, drawing the life out of people. She began as Babel and grew into Babylon till God cursed her city. Its spirit went to Pergamon and dominated empires; Pergamon fell, but she entered the church for another Roman empire until it fell, and her altar went to Berlin. After the Second World War, she entered her final host.

God's indignation continues when at last Babylon the Great is made a heap of ashes. Then out of His mouth goes a sword as the Word of God destroys His enemies in Armageddon. The end of the age comes to us quickly and violently. He commanded us to prepare by His holiness and unending love for one another.

Israel is divided and in peril when she cries out to Yeshua, and her mourning continues as His wrath falls on her enemies. All the world is in disarray and her adversaries are closing in on her while she mourns for her Savior. That's how it is when a mother grieves for her only son. He's all she can think about.

> ² "Behold, I am about to make Jerusalem a cup of staggering to all the surrounding peoples. The siege of Jerusalem will also be against Judah. ³ On that day I will make Jerusalem a heavy stone for all the peoples. All who lift it will surely hurt themselves. <u>And all the nations of the earth will gather against it</u>. ⁴ On that day, declares the LORD, I will strike every horse with panic, and its rider with madness. But for the sake of the house of Judah I will keep my eyes open, when I strike every horse of the peoples with blindness. ⁵ Then the clans of Judah shall say to themselves, 'The inhabitants of Jerusalem have strength through the LORD of hosts, their God.'
>
> ⁶ "On that day I will make the clans of Judah like a blazing pot in the midst of wood, like a flaming torch among sheaves. And they shall devour to the right and to the left all the surrounding peoples, while Jerusalem shall again be inhabited in its place, in Jerusalem.
>
> ⁷ "And the LORD will give salvation to the tents of Judah first, that the glory of the house of David and the glory of the inhabitants of Jerusalem may not surpass that of Judah. ⁸ On that day the LORD will protect the inhabitants of Jerusalem, so that the feeblest among them on that day shall be like David, and the house of David shall

be like God, like the angel of the LORD, going before them. ⁹ And on that day I will seek to destroy all the nations that come against Jerusalem. (Zec. 12:2-9 ESV)

²⁵ "Therefore thus says the Lord GOD: Now I will restore the fortunes of Jacob and have mercy on the whole house of Israel, and I will be jealous for my holy name. ²⁶ They shall forget their shame and all the treachery they have practiced against me, when they dwell securely in their land with none to make them afraid, ²⁷ when I have brought them back from the peoples and gathered them from their enemies' lands, and through them have vindicated my holiness in the sight of many nations. ²⁸ Then they shall know that I am the LORD their God, because I sent them into exile among the nations and then assembled them into their own land. I will leave none of them remaining among the nations anymore. ²⁹ And I will not hide my face anymore from them, when I pour out my Spirit upon the house of Israel, declares the Lord GOD." (Ezk. 39:25-29 ESV)

When Yeshua is enthroned in Jerusalem, the river of life flows from the city to the seas, to the east and the west, purging their waters from death to life again. With a rod of iron, He'll bring peace to the nations, to their towns and to their farmlands worldwide. Then everyone will confess that Jesus Christ is Lord.

Jerusalem will be safely inhabited when He finally dwells in her heart. The earth will be healed, and Israel will be at peace with the world for a thousand years. Lions will rest with calves, and children will play by the dens of serpents. (Is. 11:8) There will be peace on earth when Yeshua returns for His Bride.

It's the testimony of Jesus Christ. A day is like a thousand years in His sight. (2 Pet. 3:8) Jerusalem celebrates the seventh day, and what an occasion it is! She rests in His arms at last!

Chapter 16 details His wrath, shown in 14:7-11 and chapters 17 –20. God pours His indignation by seven angels who leave His Sanctuary carrying its bowls after the first resurrection of the autumn harvest when the elect ascend together to meet the Lord in the air. His fury ends after the destruction of Babylon when H'Meshiach Yeshua returns against His enemies and establishes *Yerushalayim* His throne.

The Revelation of Jesus Christ

CHAPTER 16

16 And I heard a great voice out of the temple saying to the seven angels, Go your ways, and pour out the vials of the wrath of God upon the earth.

2 And the first went, and poured out his vial upon the earth; and there fell a noisome and grievous sore upon the men which had the mark of the beast, and *upon* them which worshipped his image.

3 And the second angel poured out his vial upon the sea; and it became as the blood of a dead *man:* and every living soul died in the sea.

4 And the third angel poured out his vial upon the rivers and fountains of waters; and they became blood.

5 And I heard the angel of the waters say, Thou art righteous, O Lord, which art, and wast, and shalt be, because thou hast judged thus.

6 For they have shed the blood of saints and prophets, and thou hast given them blood to drink; for they are worthy.

7 And I heard another out of the altar say, Even so, Lord God Almighty, true and righteous *are* thy judgments.

8 And the fourth angel poured out his vial upon the sun; and power was given unto him to scorch men with fire.

9 And men were scorched with great heat, and blasphemed the name of God, which hath power over these plagues: and they repented not to give him glory.

10 And the fifth angel poured out his vial upon the seat of the beast; and his kingdom was full of darkness; and they gnawed their tongues for pain

11 And blasphemed the God of heaven because of their pains and their sores, and repented not of their deeds.

12 And the sixth angel poured out his vial upon the great river Euphrates; and the water thereof was dried up, that the way of the kings of the east might be prepared.

13 And I saw three unclean spirits like frogs *come* out of the mouth of the dragon, and out of the mouth of the beast, and out of the mouth of the false prophet.

14 For they are the spirits of devils, working miracles, *which* go forth unto the kings of the earth and of the whole world, to gather them to the battle of that great day of God Almighty.

15 Behold I come as a thief. Blessed is he that watcheth

and keepeth his garments, lest he walk naked, and they see his shame.

¹⁶ And he gathered them together into a place called in the Hebrew tongue Armageddon.

¹⁷ And the seventh angel poured out his vial into the air; and there came a great voice out of the temple of heaven, from the throne, saying, It is done.

¹⁸ And there were voices, and thunders, and lightnings; and there was a great earthquake, such as was not since men were upon the earth, so mighty an earthquake, *and so great*.

¹⁹ And the great city was divided into three parts, and the cities of the nations fell: and great Babylon came in remembrance before God, to give unto her the cup of the wine of the fierceness of his wrath.

²⁰ And every island fled away, and the mountains were not found.

²¹ And there fell upon men a great hail out of heaven, *every stone* about the weight of a talent: and men blasphemed God because of the plague of the hail; for the plague thereof was exceeding great.

(Revelation 16:1-21)

Insights

Verse 2 is a **key**: *And the first went, and poured out his bowl upon the earth; and there fell a noisome and grievous sore upon the men which had the mark of the beast, and upon them which worshipped his image.* Verse 13 is another **key**: *And I saw three unclean spirits like frogs come out of the mouth of the dragon, and out of the mouth of the beast, and out of the mouth of the false prophet.* Its **keys** tell us His **bowls of wrath** follow the ascension of the elect who refuse to bow to the beast or take his mark. (20:4-5; 14:14-20; Mat. 24:29-31; Mk. 13:24-27; Lk. 17:26-37)

There is no mistaking the Lord when we see Him returning in His glory (in 19:11-16). Not even His adversaries will doubt He is the King of kings (in 16:16-21; 19:17-21, Armageddon).

The **first bowl** causes a painful sore with a terrible odor on everyone who has the mark in his hand or forehead. The **second bowl** turns the sea into blood, and every soul in it dies. The **third** makes rivers and springs like blood since they killed the prophets and slaughtered the innocents, even infants and children. Hence, they have only blood to drink (in 16:6).

Insights: Chapter 16

The **fourth** sends the intensity of the sun, scorching their skin as fire burns wood. The **fifth bowl** strikes the throne of the beast, Babylon (in 16:10-11). Darkness covers the kingdom of the three beasts as agonizing plagues infect its people. The dragon had given his throne to the beast (in 13:2). Now its judgment impacts the world but doesn't deter God's enemies.

At the **sixth bowl,** the kings of the East, likely from the land of Japheth's son Magog, east of the Euphrates—cross the dried riverbed to war against the Lamb, anticipating His return. They expect their modern weapons will destroy the coming King.

Like frogs, three evil spirits leap out of the mouths of the dragon, the beast, and the lying prophet (in 16:13; cf. Ex. 7-11). Ironically, the frog-like spirits attract the nations, mustering them to the wide valley Armageddon. Repentance would remit His wrath, but they refuse, so He pours His indignation on them.

> ¹¹ And [they] blasphemed the God of heaven because of their pains and their sores, and repented not of their deeds. (Rev. 16:11)

It's a mystery of iniquity: *no one seeks God; not even one.* (See Rom. 3:11-12; Ps. 14:1-3) He works in us to will and do what pleases Him till we believe by His gift of faith. Then He sets us free to resist or to choose Him. Whether we choose life or death is up to us. (Rom. 9:20) When we surrender all, we're born again.

Though we're taught that we choose a new nature by a free will and are predestined to be saved no matter what we do, the truth is exactly the opposite. This is the great apostasy. We must tear down the strongholds and believe God alone. To those who are left behind, He says, *Behold I come as a thief. Blessed is he that watcheth and keepeth his garments, lest he walk naked, and they see his shame. (16:15b)*

Persuaded by miracles and amazed by wonders, we've been confused by false teachers. The miracles may be from God, but what have the teachers taught? The Holy Spirit works by signs, wonders, and miracles, but convicts men of sin, of righteousness, and of judgment. Few have divided the truth from deceptions.

God alone knows each of us. We can't pander to the flesh and believe in Jesus. Refusing to see the future, we are disarmed by deceptions. (Jer. 5:30-31; 14:14-16) Seeking His righteousness and Kingdom, when trials come we look up to the Savior.

The Revelation

At the **seventh bowl** (in 16:14), the whole earth shakes. God remembers Babylon and destroys her. He sends fire and hail as prophesied (in 16:19; 17:16-17; 18:17-20; 19:1-3). While this befalls the world, Israel mourns for her Son.

All Things Are Possible

Most people agree that it wasn't possible for God to create the universe in six days; that Noah couldn't have saved those animals from a flood in an ark; that Moses could not have freed the Hebrews from slavery; that God could not have parted the Red Sea for them to cross it though the Egyptians drowned; that a great fish never swallowed Jonah; that God never fathered a Son as a mortal; that Jesus couldn't have risen from the dead. Most people didn't believe that the Jews would return to their land or speak their native tongue again, but now they're there, and most people want them destroyed while Jews are turning to Yeshua daily. Soon *all Israel will be saved,* including all who endure to the end, despite what most people think.

> [34] And I will bring you out from the people, and will gather you out of the countries wherein ye are scattered, with a mighty hand, and with a stretched out arm, and with fury poured out. (Ezk. 20:34)

As slaves in Egypt, Hebrews painted the blood of lambs to the doorposts and lintels. In Persia they all prayed for three days without food or water, hoping the king would extend his scepter to Esther, his Jewish wife. When Jerusalem takes the dragon into her temple, God gathers the nations against her until as one man they call out for His Son by name; then Yeshua returns.

> [4] And his feet shall stand that day upon the mount of Olives, which is before Jerusalem on the east, and the mount of Olives shall cleave in the midst thereof toward the east and toward the west, and there shall be a very great valley; and half of the mountain shall remove toward the north, and half of it toward the south. ... [9] <u>And the LORD shall be king over all the earth</u>: in that day shall there be one LORD, and his name one. ... [11] And men shall dwell in it, and there shall be no more utter destruction; but <u>Jerusalem shall be safely inhabited</u>. (Zec. 14:4, 9, 11; cf. Ezk. 38; Rev. 16:18-21)

Insights: Chapter 16

Assembling the Pieces

The One who walked through the storm on the sea was God in Christ. In the day of battle, He bruised the serpent's head and gave the saints the Kingdom. He stands on the Mount of Olives and splits it in two for His people to flee their enemies. In that day the LORD is King over all the earth, and *Jerusalem shall be safely inhabited* for a thousand years till the world's rebels rise, and God's wrath falls on them who hate Him. (Rev. 20:7-10)

Ezekiel 38 and 39 are similar, but each has its time, divided by the Messianic Kingdom. Reading and comparing the words, chapter 39 precedes 38 by a thousand years, splitting Daniel's seventieth week in half with the indignation of the bowls and the trumpets on either side of the Messianic Kingdom.

Here is the order of history: Revelation 12; then 17, which is mostly fulfilled, including the seventh and eighth kings. When its ten kings (in 17:12) received kingdoms after WW1, the dragon rose as a little horn, a king-to-be, the eighth, but *of the seven*.

The terrible scarlet beast was finally slain when Babylon, his throne, fell in Berlin, and he gave it to the next beast. The dragon was *the first beast, whose deadly wound was healed (in 13:2-3, 12)*. After the next beast, he rose as *another, diverse from the first (in Dan. 7:24; cf. Rev. 13:11)*.

In Rev. 2:13 Yeshua cites *where Satan's seat* is and *where Satan dwells* as Pergamon, but it isn't contradictory to say that Babylon was his throne, which he gave the beast in Rev. 13:2 and yet destroys in 17:16-17. The city's spirit is his evil throne, mystical Babylon, which he carried to cities that took her in. Her spirit covered Europe and entered the church before he carried her to 8th century Rome; then to 19th century Berlin.

> 13 "I know thy works, and <u>where thou dwellest</u>, even <u>where Satan's seat</u> *is*. And thou holdest fast my name, and hast not denied my faith, even in those days wherein Antipas *was* my faithful martyr, who was slain among you, <u>where Satan dwelleth</u>. (Rev. 2:13)

Babylon's culture is one of death. She had power over the cities of the Greeks and Persians long before the dragon carried her to Rome. When he carries his throne, he moves the spirit of Babylon to another city for another empire. Wherever his throne

The Revelation

is, its city is taken by Babylon's culture, weakening the people by enticing them to revel in sin through their denial of God. The wealth of the world is in her. Her description is repeated in 18 where we learn more about the cursed city the dragon carried.

Chapter 18 immediately precedes the return of the Lord and Armageddon where He destroys His enemies and casts the beast and false prophet into the lake of fire. The devil is chained in the pit till the thousand years are over.

Following 18, 19 refers to Jesus' return for His Bride. It leads to 20 and the future that culminates in chapters 8 through 11 when the devil is released till his destruction. After the living and the dead are judged, Revelation takes us to eternity.

The way to know Christ is by sacrifice. All we have, everything and everyone, are His. It's time to take up our cross and prepare for the tribulation. We have a window of opportunity to save our nation and our souls if we continue living by faith.

This is the apostasy when a large number of us have believed lies. It's natural to believe deceivers, but we must not be subject to a nature that rejects the truth. The prophets are misled by easy messages out of their own hearts, ensnaring the unstable. (See Jer. 14:13-15; 23:17, 21-22) Truly, the great tribulation is imminent.

The woman riding a scarlet beast is the city of the red dragon (in 17:18). Today the throne of the dragon is the city of the beast that houses all nations as Babylon in chapter 18. The dragon who carried her gave his throne to the beast that now owns her (in 13:2). The spirit of the throne is the mystery of chapter 17.

In 18 she is full of violence, idolatry, sorcery, mind-altering drugs, deceptions, immorality, and the sale of human souls. She could be many big cities since her influence covers the world, but there's much more in the prophecy that pinpoints the site of the dragon's throne. Mystery Babylon's nemesis is Jerusalem. *The city of the great King* is the throne of Messiah Yeshua; thus Satan's city Babylon is the throne he gave the beast:

> [17] <u>At that time they shall call Jerusalem the throne of the</u> LORD; and all the nations shall be gathered unto it, to the name of the LORD, to Jerusalem: neither shall they walk any more in the imagination of their evil heart. (Jer. 3:17)

The Revelation of Jesus Christ

CHAPTER 17

17 And there came one of the seven messengers, who were having the seven vials, and he spake with me, saying to me, `Come, I will shew to thee the judgment of the great whore, who is sitting upon the many waters,
² with whom the kings of the earth did commit whoredom; and made drunk from the wine of her whoredom were those inhabiting the earth;'
³ and he carried me away to a wilderness in the Spirit, and I saw a woman sitting upon a scarlet-coloured beast full of names of evil-speaking, having seven heads and ten horns,
⁴ and the woman was arrayed with purple and scarlet-colour, and gilded with gold, and precious stone, and pearls, having a golden cup in her hand full of abominations and uncleanness of her whoredom,
⁵ and upon her forehead was a name written: `Secret, Babylon the Great, the Mother of the Whores, and the Abominations of the earth.'
⁶ And I saw the woman drunken from the blood of the saints, and from the blood of the witnesses of Jesus, and I did wonder -- having seen her -- with great wonder;
⁷ and the messenger said to me, `Wherefore didst thou wonder? I -- I will tell thee the secret of the woman and of the beast that [is] carrying her, which hath the seven heads and the ten horns.
⁸ `The beast that thou didst see: it was, and it is not; and it is about to come up out of the abyss, and to go away to destruction, and wonder shall those dwelling upon the earth, whose names have not been written upon the scroll of the life from the foundation of the world, beholding the beast that was, and is not, although it is.
⁹ `Here [is] the mind that is having wisdom; the seven heads are seven mountains, upon which the woman doth sit,
¹⁰ and there are seven kings, the five did fall, and the one is, the other did not yet come, and when he may come, it behoveth him to remain a little time;
¹¹ and the beast that was, and is not, he also is eighth, and out of the seven he is, and to destruction he doth go away.
¹² `And the ten horns that thou sawest, are ten kings,

The Revelation

who a kingdom did not yet receive, but authority as kings the same hour do receive with the beast,
¹³ these have one mind, and their own power and authority to the beast they shall give over;
¹⁴ these with the Lamb shall make war, and the Lamb shall overcome them, because Lord of lords he is, and King of kings, and those with him are called, and choice, and stedfast.'
¹⁵ And he saith to me, `The waters that thou didst see, where the whore doth sit, are peoples, and multitudes, and nations, and tongues;'
¹⁶ and the ten horns that thou didst see upon the beast, these shall hate the whore, and shall make her desolate and naked, and shall eat her flesh, and shall burn her in fire,
¹⁷ for God did give into their hearts to do its mind, and to make one mind, and to give their kingdom to the beast till the sayings of God may be complete,
¹⁸ and the woman that thou didst see is the great city that is having reign over the kings of the land.'   [of the earth] (Revelation 17:1-18 YLT) [Gr.: *ghay* is land, region, or earth. The messengers are angels; their vials are the seven bowls.]

Insights

2 The word that Isaiah the son of Amoz saw concerning Judah and Jerusalem.

² It shall come to pass in the latter days
  that the mountain of the house of the LORD
shall be established as the highest of the mountains,
  and shall be lifted up above the hills;
and all the nations shall flow to it,
³ and many peoples shall come, and say:
"Come, let us go up to the mountain of the LORD,
  to the house of the God of Jacob,
that he may teach us his ways
and that we may walk in his paths."
For out of Zion shall go forth the law,
  and the word of the LORD from Jerusalem.
    (Is. 2:1-3 ESV) [Cf. Jer. 51:25-26]

Israel is a little nation. Her size roughly equals the fourth smallest state in America, New Jersey.[169] After Solomon's death

Insights: Chapter 17

she was divided as Judah and Israel; of the two, the smaller was Judah. Isaiah wrote of Jerusalem, the city of the God of Jacob.

> 48 Great is the LORD, and greatly to be praised
> <u>In the city of our God,</u>
> <u>In His holy mountain.</u>
> ² Beautiful in elevation,
> The joy of the whole earth,
> Is Mount Zion on the sides of the north,
> <u>The city of the great King</u>. (Ps. 48:1-2 NKJV)

The psalmist said God will reign from His city, the highest of all mountains (in Is. 2:2). Mt. Zion, King David's Jerusalem, was not the highest mountain; nor is Jerusalem today. What did this mean? Figuratively, heads are mountains as capital cities of empires. The **key** is Isaiah's: *the head of Syria is Damascus, and the head of Damascus is Rezin (in Is. 7:8)*. In other words, heads can be capitals [thrones] or their kings, depending on the context.

The head of Syria is its capital, and the head of the eternal Kingdom is Jerusalem, the highest mountain of all. With heads as mountains in chapter 17, it follows that mountains are capitals of empires, and five of their kings had fallen. In John's time, the king of Rome *is* sixth: *the five did fall, and one is (in 17:10)*.

In 12 the seven heads had crowns as kings over kingdoms, but not the horns. In 17 horns are kings with *no kingdom yet*.

> ⁹ And here *is* the mind which hath wisdom. The seven heads are seven mountains, on which the woman sitteth.
> ¹⁰ And <u>there are seven kings: five are fallen,</u> <u>and one is</u>, and the other is not yet come; and when he cometh, he must continue a short space. (Rev. 17:9-10)

The Seven Mountains

Standing on a hill in the Decapolis ruins, we were informed that a city beneath our feet would soon be excavated. On top of buried piles, we were struck by the stillness. Its once busy streets were silent like the mystery of the mountains and their kings:

1. Egypt:[170] Jacob's sons threw their brother Joseph into a pit; then, pulled him out to sell him as a slave to Egypt. But Pharaoh exalted him at his right hand. A famine struck, and his brothers went there for food. Their sons were enslaved four hundred years till God chose Moses to deliver them. Egypt's capital is Cairo.

The Revelation

2. Assyria:[171] Israel turned to idols, so God sent idolaters, Assyrians, to ravage them. They scattered its ten tribes to the nations though a remnant stayed in Samaria. The Assyrian king sent his people to marry the survivors. The next time Jews were threatened, the Samaritans denied being Jews. The Judeans hated them for denying their race, but today the tribes are making *aliyah* to Israel.[172] Assyria's capital was Nineveh.

3. Babylon:[173] A hundred thirty-five years after Israel fell to Assyria, for Judah's violence, God sent the Babylonian armies to overtake Judah. As it turned out, Babylon took the Jews captive, treating them too harshly, so God cursed the city. Alexander the Great hoped to revive it but died young. Later Saddam Hussein began to restore her, but he and his sons were killed in the Iraq War.[174] Babylon is still uninhabited. Baghdad is Iraq's capital.

> **19** And Babylon, the glory of kingdoms, the beauty of the Chaldees' excellency, shall be as when God overthrew Sodom and Gomorrah. **20** <u>It shall never be inhabited, neither shall it be dwelt in from generation to generation:</u> neither shall the Arabian pitch tent there; neither shall the shepherds make their fold there. (Is. 13:19-20)

4. Medo-Persia: [175] In the 6th century BC, Cyrus II of Persia gained Media, merging it with Persia, joining two kingdoms as one. Their king Belshezzar was killed, and Darius the Mede was made king of Babylon. After him, Cyrus of Persia favored the Jews by the *Edict of Cyrus,* supporting their return by sending materials to rebuild both the temple and Jerusalem. (Ezk. 1:2-4)

Jews who stayed in Persia under Xerxes faced Haman whose scheme to kill them backfired when Haman was hanged on the gallows he'd built for a Jew. Esther, the king's Jewish wife, was the wise heroine of Purim, its feast. In 1935 Persia was renamed Iran.[176] In a coup d'état in 1979, the Ayatollah Khomeini ousted its Shah and ruled over the nation.[177] Tehran is its capital today.

5. Greece: [178] Macedon was a province in northwest Greece, birthplace to Alexander the Great whose father, Phillip II, overcame and unified its city-states. At his death, Alexander fulfilled his father's dream to conquer Persia, merging Babylonian and Greek cultures and advancing the Greek language from Anatolia and Egypt to Persia. He died at thirty-three with no legal heir.[179]

Insights: Chapter 17

Four generals divided Alexander's kingdom. The largest part went to Seleucus Nicator I, from the Mediterranean to India.[180]

Enraged by a defeat in Egypt, its eighth king, Antiochus IV, desecrated the temple in Judea in 167 BC.[181] He set up an image of Zeus, his "god of gods," the *abomination of desolation,* in the temple where he demanded worship. He crucified, mutilated, and slew multitudes of Jews. Afterward, the Maccabees, a family of priests, purified and rededicated the temple. When he returned, they defeated his army.[182] *Hanukkah* marks the occasion.[183] Jesus was in Jerusalem to celebrate its feast (in Jn. 10:22).

Ptolemy's portion was Alexander's Egypt. From Egypt he took Jerusalem, and as a result, Israelites and most of the world learned Greek.[184] Greek became the language of the gospel to the world, and Rome's Latin vanished. Athens is the Grecian capital.

6. Rome: [185] By 30 BC Rome conquered Greece but split in two. Its western side fell twice: in 410 and 476. Babylon had pervaded Rome's empire and affected the church. In 800 her pope formed a new Roman empire. In 962 a pope crowned its first German king as its emperor. Over time the lands became the "Holy Roman Empire of the German Nation," the (H)REGN.

In 1453 Muslims invaded Constantinople, the capital of the Eastern Roman Empire, aka the Byzantine Empire. Renaming its capital "Istanbul," Ottoman Turks converted most but not all of its churches. Its Romanized city was held by the Ottomans for four hundred sixty-four years.[186] She was the second foot of the idol in the king's dream. Ankara is Turkey's capital today.

7. France: [187] December 1804: Napoleon crowned himself First Consul of France.[188] He soon defeated the (H)REGN. By him the seventh king took Rome. Predestined to win, he ruled fewer than ten years but dramatically affected the world. (1804 – 1814) ... *the one is, the other did not yet come, and when he may come, <u>it behoveth him to remain a little time</u>. (Rev. 17:10)* His empire was cut short in 1814–16. Paris is the French capital.

Germany: At Rome's fall, Attila's Huns settled in Germania and Austria. 962–1806: Rome ruled as the (H)REGN. 1871: Berlin became its first capital to regain the empire. 1920: the ten kings received crowns. 1932: of the seven, the eighth king ruled as Hitler till his death in 1945. Berlin was fully restored in 1990.

The Revelation

¹¹ and the beast that was, and is not, *he also is eighth*, and *out of the seven he is*, and to destruction he doth go away. (Rev. 17:11 YLT) [Beasts are the greater kings.]

To Begin with, ...

³ And another sign appeared in heaven: behold, a great, fiery red dragon having seven heads and ten horns, and seven diadems on his heads. (Rev. 12:3 NKJV)

Scarlet is a bright, *fiery red*. The scarlet beast *was* the *fiery red dragon* from chapter 12, known by its **bright red color** and its **keys to history**: seven heads, ten horns, and seven kings.

Mystery Babylon was the dragon's whore whose sensualities she spread, passing them on to the great empires, and they gloried in their shame because of her. Today she seduces the world by her sins, the reasons for the seven bowls of wrath.

The woman isn't a nation, but a city (in 17:18). She rides the scarlet beast that carries her and has power over the kings of the earth. Mystery Babylon ruled seven cities that seduced and destroyed the earth. Proud, godless, carnal—all her ways lead to death, deceit, and ruin. She knows the ways of Satan. Emperors knew her well. Walking her streets, we sense her evil presence.

In 17:10 (p. 187) there are no crowns on the heads or horns. Although the seven empires had seven kings, five had fallen; *and one is* means Rome is sixth at the time of John. *The other is not yet come*—the seventh, the king of France. (1804–1814)

Satan was *about to come up out of the abyss.* First he deceived the church by her desire to escape persecution at any cost. Then he caused Rome's fall and enticed a fearful church to take the city by a hoax as his capital for over a thousand years. The seventh king, Napoleon, briefly ruled and conquered Rome.

After the ascension of Christ, the scarlet beast was banished from heaven. Cast down to earth [ending chapter 12], he was about to come up as John prophesied. That was near the time of the Huns who rose in the late third century. When the dragon came out of the earth, he surely returned to his throne in Pergamon (in 2:13), out of the city's earthquake in 262.[189] Soon after it shook the city, the Huns appeared. Under the spell of Babylon, the Greek and Roman civilizations had famously been Babylonian; thus the dragon already had a place in Rome.

Insights: Chapter 17

The Beast that Was

Pergamon was like Hollywood with Babylon's attractive images, drawing Israel by Baal and the church by pagan idols. [See p. 143, Council Letter] Under Roman emperors, Christians were thrown to lions, crucified, beheaded, burned alive, maimed, and tortured while crowds cheered.[190] But Constantine changed the attitude of the empire toward the church, and she responded by favoring pagans over Jews and her Jewish heritage. In time the bishops changed the church, turning away from the Jews by ignoring their Scriptures, which are foundational to our faith.

Having no capital, the eighth king of the Huns, Attila, forced Rome's fall by chasing other tribes into the city. (pp. 47 –50) In the mid-eighth century, the institutional church was in fear when her popes founded a Roman empire for protection from invading jihadists. (The dragon's fear works as well as any sword.)

An 8th C. pope deceived a king to conquer central Italy for the church under the pretense that Constantine had willed his empire to Rome (but no one knew it … for hundreds of years!) Thus the church called for kings to go to war to gain many lands on her behalf as the first horseman (in 6:2) rode forth to conquer.

Few stopped to think: the Roman Empire didn't belong to Constantine; he was just one of its many emperors. His so-called "Donation" relied on the people's ignorance to succeed; thus the father of lies has kept the church in the dark over the centuries.[191] Deceivers easily fool people who are not armed with the truth.

Since ancient days, the spirit of Babylon has seduced the world. The mother of harlots beguiles her children, keeping them in spiritual darkness. (Prologue, p. 55) She persuades the nations against Israel to their own destruction. She deludes deceivers.

In chapter 1 Daniel was dreaming in Babylon when he saw four beasts rise from the Great Sea. In 17 John was exiled to an island on that sea when he saw the woman on the dragon *in the wilderness,* not in Rome. There she was—drunk *from the blood of saints and from the blood of the witnesses of Jesus (in 17:6)!* John refers to the Jews as saints, set apart for God's glory; their blood was why Babylon was cursed. *The witnesses of Jesus* were new covenant believers, *the people of the saints* (in Dan. 7:27). Most of the saints in Hebrews 11 were Semites, and we are their heirs in Eph. 2:19. The spirit of Babylon is guilty of the blood of

The Revelation

the saints and of the witnesses of Jesus to this day. As heirs with the saints, we are related in the faith, together as one new man.

John saw the scarlet beast carrying her mystery when *it was,* though in John's time, the beast *is not*. The prophecy looks back to when the dragon first carried Babylon, cursed for her cruelty: *It shall never be inhabited, neither shall it be dwelt in from generation to generation. (Is. 13:20a)* A *wilderness*, uninhabited, is no place for a city unless that city was Babylon after her curse, hundreds of years earlier.

In 17:1 the angel began to describe the judgment of Babylon but first revealed the city. Staring at her emptiness, John learned the dragon *is not* the sixth king that ruled Rome's emperors, but was a rogue king. Soon after the scarlet beast rose from the abyss Rome fell. He rose out again but in an unexpected way.

> [9] 'Here [is] the mind that is having wisdom; the seven heads are seven mountains, upon which the woman doth sit, [10] and there are seven kings, the five did fall, and the one is, the other did not yet come, and when he may come, it behoveth him to remain a little time; [11] and the beast that was, and is not, <u>he also is eighth, and out of the seven he is, and to destruction he doth go away</u>.
> (Rev. 17:9-11)

John was filled with the Spirit, and God set him apart on Patmos Isle to see Babylon on a scarlet beast. *The beast that was,* he was told, *is not, and yet is.* This means *the beast that was* had been present, but *is not; and yet is* because he still exists. (17:8)

Chapter 12 ends with the dragon seeking retribution, and he was about to rise out of the sea, the abyss. The one *about to come up* is the scarlet beast that *was and is not* because the fiery red dragon was absent, either losing the war in heaven, or in the depths of the earth with his cohorts (in 12:7-9). Thrown down to earth, he'd rise *from the abyss (in 17:8).*

Upon rising the dragon deceived the church. Jesus warns us of wolves in sheepskin, false believers. Despite His advice, their bishops received a pagan culture from Constantine and claimed another Roman Empire for a thousand years. Their false gospel misled the churches to persecute true believers in Jesus Christ, as well as Jews, His chosen nation. He calls many to repentance but only responds to those given ears to hear.

Insights: Chapter 17

After the seventh king overcame the (H)REGN in 1806, the dragon moved his capital from Rome to Berlin in 1871. The city transported the Altar of Zeus out of Pergamon in 1889.[192] Thus the dragon was obviously involved. By 1930 the wall of Babylon became its entryway.

The Iron Kingdom

After the fifth kingdom, Rome was sixth as the iron of the idol in Daniel 2. The dragon used his unholy Roman Empire of the German Nation with Germanic kings hitched to Rome, the sixth capital city. Paris was seventh; the beast that was *about to come up from the abyss,* the *eighth of the seven (in 17:8, 11),* was the king of Babylon, speaking as a little horn in Berlin.

When popes sought out the brutal German kings as emperors in 962, they conquered central Europa, blanketing hundreds of lands, cities, fiefs, and hamlets, suppressing them and breaking them into little pieces (in Dan. 7:7, 19). The fiery red dragon is the terrible beast in Daniel 7 and the scarlet one in 17, depictions of Satan (in 20:2), carrying his harlot city from place to place.

In the Roman Empire of the German Nation, Rome was the nominal capital of her protectors. Germania shared her capital. The "Holy Roman Empire" was a blasphemous name for it. The French philosopher Voltaire said, "Its agglomeration ... was neither holy, nor Roman, nor an empire."[193] He may not have seen the forces behind it but was keenly aware of its fakery.

In 1806 the seventh king overcame the church empire by Napoleon, forcing Rome's final fall.[194] It is written: *it behoveth him to continue a little time (in 17:10 YLT).* In 1814 and in 1816, he was defeated and exiled twice. The Treaty of Vienna merged his lands to thirty-nine nations to bolster them against invasions.

[The ten horns] ... have one mind, and their own power and authority to the beast they shall give over (in 17:12-13 YLT). At first they had no kingdom but weakened the iron feet of Rome (in Daniel 2). They waited millennia to *receive* crowns; then instantly gave them to **the eighth king**, the dragon in Hitler. All ten had *one mind with him,* appearing on the beast's head (in Dan. 7:20).

In 17:7 the beast *carries* Babylon. [Gr.: *bastazo,* "lift, bear, or carry"] When something is carried it's transported. The spirit of Babel spread when people scattered across the earth with her culture and her false gods, but the dragon himself transported the

The Revelation

evil throne, which he relinquished to the beast that won the world war.

Invisible powers are at war, inciting their nations to envy and bloodlust. At war we do not concede; the enemy is panicked; he has little time. *Fight the good fight of faith, lay hold on eternal life, whereunto thou art also called, and hast professed a good profession before many witnesses. (1 Tim. 6:12; Eph. 6:10-20)*

To regain Europe, the dragon returned as the *eighth of the seven (in 17:11)* out of the (H)REGN into the man who murdered millions. Putting it all together, it's easier to see it now:

> [10] and there are seven kings, the five did fall, and the one is, the other did not yet come, and when he may come, it behoveth him to remain a little time; [11] and the beast that was, and is not, he also is eighth, and out of the seven he is, and to destruction he doth go away. [12] 'And the ten horns that thou sawest, are ten kings, who a kingdom did not yet receive, but authority as kings the same hour do receive with the beast, [13] these have one mind, and their own power and authority to the beast they shall give over; [14] these with the Lamb shall make war, and the Lamb shall overcome them, because Lord of lords he is, and King of kings, and those with him are called, and choice, and stedfast.' (Rev. 17:10-14)

The LORD shall fight for you, and ye shall hold your peace. (Ex. 14:14) Unseen kings empower armies. Ten gave their power and authority to Hitler, at one mind with him in 17:13, leading to Dan. 7:13 where the victorious Lamb approached the throne.

Famous heroes from Hebrews 11 were *the called, chosen, and faithful* warriors, providing the speed, strength, and skills the Allied forces needed to win (in 17:14). The Lamb struck the dragon's head, and the leopard was given dominion (in Dan. 7:6).

> [15] And he saith to me, 'The waters that thou didst see, <u>where the whore doth sit</u>, are peoples, and multitudes, and nations, and tongues;' (Rev. 17:15 YLT)

The head of Berlin was a dragon. Enmity bruised his head, and *the beast was slain (in Dan. 7:11).* Thus the Lamb overcame His enemies, fulfilling the Word: *And I will put <u>enmity</u> between thee and the woman, <u>and between thy seed and her seed</u>; <u>it</u> shall bruise thy head, and thou shalt bruise his heel. (Gen. 3:15)*

Insights: Chapter 17

How did the devil have seed? Before his kings received their kingdoms, out of Mystery Babylon, their minions and they were iron mingling with the seed of men. In Daniel 2 the idol's metals change by their origins, not by rulers. The dragon ruled Babylon; then gained Rome and Germania; and finally, a German Empire.

When Rome and Germania ruled together, its iron had mixed with the seed of men; thus God put enmity between the dragon's seed and the woman's seed when Berlin was crushed, and the beast was slain. He was healed by the next beast rising to whom he relinquished his throne; then, returned for his fourth kingdom, yet the world worshiped the dragon along with the beast.

He *was* the serpent in Eden; he *was* the enemy to Job; he *was* king of Babel; he *was* Haman the Jew-hater, outwitted by Esther. At Jesus' birth, he *was* Herod; in the desert he *was* the tempter; he *was* the voice of Peter, admonishing Jesus for the disciples to hear him; he *was* Judas the betrayer; he is *the beast that was.*

> ⁸ The beast that thou sawest was, and is not; and shall ascend out of the bottomless pit, and go into perdition: and **they that dwell on the earth shall wonder**, whose names were not written in the book of life from the foundation of the world, **when they behold the beast** that was, and is not, and yet is. (Rev. 17:8; cf. Is. 14:16)

Isaiah foresaw him in a vision:

> ⁴ That thou shalt take up this proverb against the king of Babylon, and say, How hath the oppressor ceased! the golden city ceased! ⁵ The LORD hath broken the staff of the wicked, and the scepter of the rulers. ... ¹² How art thou fallen from heaven, O Lucifer, son of the morning! how art thou cut down to the ground, which didst weaken the nations! ¹³ For thou hast said in thine heart, I will ascend into heaven, my throne above the stars of God: I will sit also upon the mount of the congregation, in the sides of the north: ¹⁴ I will ascend above the heights of the clouds; I will be like the most High. ¹⁵ Yet thou shalt be brought down to hell, to the sides of the pit.
> ¹⁶ **They that see thee shall narrowly look upon thee**, *and* consider thee, *saying,* **Is this the man** that made the earth to tremble, that did shake kingdoms; ¹⁷ *That* made the world as a wilderness, and destroyed the cities thereof; *that opened not the house of his prisoners?*

The Revelation

¹⁸All the kings of the nations, even all of them, lie in glory, every one in his own house. ¹⁹ But thou art cast <u>out of thy grave like an abominable branch</u>, and as the raiment of those that are slain, thrust through with a sword, that go down to the stones of the pit; as a carcase <u>trodden under feet</u>. ²⁰ <u>Thou shalt not be joined with them in burial</u>, because thou hast destroyed thy land, *and* slain thy people: the seed of evildoers shall never be renowned. (Is. 14:4-5, 12-20)

Those whose names were not in *the scroll of life* beheld *the beast that was.* In hell they saw *the man that made the world as a wilderness.* His throne was on its bema in Germany, northwest of Israel, <u>to the sides of the north.</u> (Is. 14:13, p. 197) Hitler's body was burned, and its ashes, covered in an unmarked grave. (above)

We envision him through the windows of history as Adolf Hitler, but in hell they saw the man as Lucifer. After the war the dragon gave his harlot, Babylon, to the next beast as his throne (in 13:2). Driven by hatred, the ten kings return to him (in 17:16) before God's bowls of wrath end with Babylon destroyed. (16:19)

¹⁶ and the ten horns that thou didst see upon the beast, these shall hate the whore, and shall make her desolate and naked, and shall eat her flesh, and shall burn her in fire,¹⁷ for God did give into their hearts to do its mind, and to make one mind, and to <u>give their kingdom to the beast</u> till the sayings of God may be complete.
(Rev. 17:16-17 YLT) [This beast is the scarlet dragon of 17.]

The Invisible War

The last verses of 13 precede the sixth seal (in 6:12-17) when the martyrs beheaded for the first resurrection ascend with the elect to the Lord in the air (in Mat. 24:29-31, p. 92). They are in heaven in 14 and 15 before the bowls of wrath are poured out. At the seventh bowl (in 16:16; 17:16-18), Babylon the Great is erased from the earth. Then Yeshua returns to slay the armies gathered in Armageddon whose design is a war against the Lamb.

God entrusted His oracles to the Hebrews, and the dragon has attempted to destroy the sons of the light carriers since then. As a beautiful angel, he'd carried the torch in heaven but fell into pride, envy, and darkness. He loathes the words of the prophets and apostles that enlighten us and expose him as the devil.

Insights: Chapter 17

We can't fathom the value of suffering that prepares us for the height of our calling in Jesus Christ. We are seated with Him at the Father's right hand in heaven. If we only knew … !

When a nation trains its troops, the officers put them through rigorous trials to test their endurance for combat. They develop strength of character, not forgotten in battle. Why volunteer for that? Isn't it for the victory? Now we are promised a seat with God in Christ, but we must die to live for the victory.

The beast is given authority over the world and overcomes the saints, but we who endure and keep the faith till death will win the crown of life. We'll trust in God to keep our souls for the prize set before us as members of God's holy family forever:

> 3 See how great a love the Father has bestowed on us, that we would be called children of God; and *such* we are. For this reason the world does not know us, because it did not know Him. ² Beloved, now we are children of God, and it has not appeared as yet what we will be. We know that when He appears, we will be like Him, because we will see Him just as He is. ³ And everyone who has this hope *fixed* on Him purifies himself, just as He is pure. (1 John 3:1-3 NASB)

Lucifer attracts human nature but opposes righteousness and conscience. His false Elijah fools men by his signs, wonders, and miracles, ordering the world to worship the image of *the first beast that was slain by the sword but lived (cf. Dan. 7:11, 24).* The dragon speaks as a living idol in the temple (in 13:15).

When they return to him, we realize his power was in ten united kings in WW2. He prompts the nations to war by their reunion with him. Though iron mixed with clay, invisible kings have the dragon's mind, and their single-mindedness empowers them as four heads and their four wings empowered the leopard, America, in WW2.

Jerusalem the Prize

In the Second World War, the Arabs fought the British but lost land they'd occupied for centuries; they later lost Jerusalem, which they'd taken. Melchizedek, King of Righteousness, had given Abram bread and wine near the walls of the city that still recalls the blessing.[195] (Ps. 2:6, 48:2; Gen. 14:18-20)

The Revelation

The Scriptures contain an allegory of two cities at war—cities that rule the world, one for evil and one for good. Though small, Jerusalem is ordained to win the war as light overcomes the darkness. Until then the dragon carried his harlot for several thousand years. Today she embraces the world. She controls seven capitals, some of the greatest on earth, whose cultures she formed. Since the days of Babel, she has thrived in her lifestyle. She spreads her idolatries and seduces the nations by sexual sins. The mother of whores, she fills the earth with false religions. She is utterly perverse, killing infants and subjecting children to her sexual obsessions. For these, Babylon the Great is doomed.

Rome is a figure of Babylon with seven hills. An eighth is across the Tiber River, Janiculum Hill, outside ancient Rome's walls like the eighth capital city.[196] But hills are not mountains, and she is the sixth. Her church empire fell short of the Roman Empire in size, but in infamy was its equal. Like Babylon Rome is destined for destruction. Babylon isn't just a city, but a powerful principality, a spiritual stronghold; yet the one with horns like a lamb will attack her by ten kings of one mind (in 17:16-18), and she will plunge into darkness. By then she will have taken the land whose power goes out at the fifth bowl of wrath, leaving everyone in the dark, in the heat, in the blood, and in their sores.

Until his head was healed, the first beast could not return, but in 16:13 at the sixth bowl, all three—the dragon, the beast, and the false prophet, are together till the end of the age.

At the end, earth's topography changes by disasters; Israel is exalted; Jerusalem is the highest mountain. Damascus is ruined; towers are fallen; cities are fields where flocks graze. America is destroyed; mountains are leveled; islands disappear; armies are destroyed; nations are judged, and Jesus Christ reigns. It seems surreal, yet its hour is near because it's in the Book:

> [9] In that day their strong cities will be like the deserted places of the wooded heights and the hilltops, which they deserted because of the children of Israel, and <u>there will be desolation</u>.
>
> [10] <u>For you have forgotten the God of your salvation
>   and have not remembered the Rock of your refuge</u>;
> therefore, though you plant pleasant plants
>   and sow the vine-branch of a stranger

Insights: Chapter 17

¹¹ though you make them grow on the day
  that you plant them,
and make them blossom in the morning
  that you sow,
yet the harvest will flee away
  in a day of grief and incurable pain.

¹² Ah, the thunder of many peoples;
  they thunder like the thundering of the sea!
Ah, the roar of nations;
  they roar like the roaring of mighty waters!
¹³ The nations roar like the roaring of many waters,
  but he will rebuke them, and they will flee far away,
chased like chaff on the mountains before the wind
  and whirling dust before the storm.
¹⁴ At evening time, behold, terror!
Before morning, they are no more!
This is the portion of those who loot us,
  and the lot of those who plunder us. (Is. 17:9-14 ESV)

The Bible names Israel as a people, a nation, or its northern tribes {2,543 x}; Judah, Judea {861 x}; and Jerusalem {814 x}. No other land can claim its history but that of Jacob whom God called Israel. {55 x} (See Gen. 32:28).[197] A war of two kingdoms holds mankind captive: the kingdom of darkness vs the Kingdom of light. The choice is for those given ears to hear:

¹⁴ In righteousness you will be established;
You will be far from oppression, for you will not fear;
And from terror, for it will not come near you.
(Is. 54:14 NASB) [The King of kings to His servants.]

Fear of the enemy has no place in us. If we love God, we serve Him faithfully. It costs our lives, our families, our wealth, but He surpasses them all. We own no one. Time's pain is temporal. We who endure to the end enter the Kingdom of God. We thank and praise Him in all things because *greater is he that is in us than he that is in the world. (1 Jn. 4:4b)*

The night cometh when no man can work (from Jn. 9:4b). What can the righteous do? In fear the world is in lockdown and poverty; the light exposes its darkness. The strong man is bound by his weaknesses: the fear of death and the love of comfort. If we renew our minds, we'll never see things the old way again.

The Revelation

> For a thousand years in your sight are but as yesterday when it is past, or as a watch in the night. (Ps. 90:4 ESV)

Babylon will be destroyed never to rise again. She first appeared in chapter 17 but existed long before the Lord revealed her. In 17 two kings remained, but the heads that were mountains wore no crowns at all. As chapter 17 begins, the fall of the seven kings is foreseen; the eighth is predicted. The time is short; the ten kings are with the beast for just one hour (in 17:12).

All ten gave their power and authority to the dragon (in 17:13), but the Lamb overpowered him and the dragon and its kings lost the world war (in Dan. 7:11; Rev. 17:14). Then the Lamb ascended to heaven for the Victor's crown (in Dan. 7:13).

After seeing the Lamb defeat Hitler, John said, *[15] And he saith to me, 'The waters that thou didst see, where the whore doth sit, are peoples, and multitudes, and nations, and tongues;'* (Rev. 17:15 YLT) He saw the red dragon carrying her after all seven fell. After World War Two, the eighth king was slain, but the whore still covers the nations. Now her end is at hand.

She has slain prophets and saints through the ages and has spoken evil of us who believe in God in the Father, the Son, and the Holy Spirit. As with Israel, a remnant endure great tribulation to the end while a nefarious, lawless imposter reigns. He divides believers from unbelievers for our faith to prove itself true while all who believe the lie are condemned for not loving the truth. (Jn. 3:18-21; 2 Thes. 2:3-12)

At last the Lord Jesus Christ returns to rule from His holy mountain, which is above all other mountains and hills. His law goes forth from Jerusalem to cover the world like waters cover the sea. (See Is. 11:9)

> [11] I say then, Have they stumbled that they should fall? God forbid: but rather through their fall salvation is come unto the Gentiles for to provoke them to jealousy. [12] Now if the fall of them be the riches of the world, and the diminishing of them the riches of the Gentiles; how much more their fullness? (Rom. 11:11-12)

We've located mountains and metaphors, principalities and powers, kingdoms and kings, heads and horns. One thing leads to another till history catches up to us. Now let's find the harlot:

The Revelation of Jesus Christ

CHAPTER 18

18 After these things I saw another angel coming down from heaven, having great authority, and the earth was illumined with his glory. ²And he cried out with a mighty voice, saying, "Fallen, fallen is Babylon the great! She has become a dwelling place of demons and a prison of every unclean spirit, and a prison of every unclean and hateful bird. ³For all the nations have drunk of the wine of the passion of her immorality, and the kings of the earth have committed *acts of* immorality with her, and the merchants of the earth have become rich by the wealth of her sensuality."

⁴I heard another voice from heaven, saying, "Come out of her, my people, so that you will not participate in her sins and receive of her plagues; ⁵for her sins have piled up as high as heaven, and God has remembered her iniquities. ⁶Pay her back even as she has paid, and give back *to her* double according to her deeds; in the cup which she has mixed, mix twice as much for her. ⁷To the degree that she glorified herself and lived sensuously, to the same degree give her torment and mourning; for she says in her heart, 'I SIT *as* A QUEEN AND I AM NOT A WIDOW, and will never see mourning.' ⁸For this reason in one day her plagues will come, pestilence and mourning and famine, and she will be burned up with fire; for the Lord God who judges her is strong.

⁹"And the kings of the earth, who committed *acts of* immorality and lived sensuously with her, will weep and lament over her when they see the smoke of her burning, ¹⁰standing at a distance because of the fear of her torment, saying, 'Woe, woe, the great city, Babylon, the strong city! For in one hour your judgment has come.'

¹¹"And the merchants of the earth weep and mourn over her, because no one buys their cargoes any more— ¹²cargoes of gold and silver and precious stones and pearls and fine linen and purple and silk and scarlet, and every *kind of* citron wood and every article of ivory and every article *made* from very costly wood and bronze and iron and marble, ¹³and cinnamon and spice and incense and perfume and frankincense and wine and olive oil and

The Revelation

fine flour and wheat and cattle and sheep, and *cargoes* of horses and chariots and slaves and human lives. [14] The fruit you long for has gone from you, and all things that were luxurious and splendid have passed away from you and *men* will no longer find them. [15] The merchants of these things, who became rich from her, will stand at a distance because of the fear of her torment, weeping and mourning, [16] saying, 'Woe, woe, the great city, she who was clothed in fine linen and purple and scarlet, and adorned with gold and precious stones and pearls; [17] for in one hour such great wealth has been laid waste!' And every shipmaster and every passenger and sailor, and as many as make their living by the sea, stood at a distance, [18] and were crying out as they saw the smoke of her burning, saying, 'What *city* is like the great city?' [19] And they threw dust on their heads and were crying out, weeping and mourning, saying, 'Woe, woe, the great city, in which all who had ships at sea became rich by her wealth, for in one hour she has been laid waste!' [20] Rejoice over her, O heaven, and you saints and apostles and prophets, because God has pronounced judgment for you against her."

[21] Then a strong angel took up a stone like a great millstone and threw it into the sea, saying, "So will Babylon, the great city, be thrown down with violence, and will not be found any longer. [22] And the sound of harpists and musicians and flute-players and trumpeters will not be heard in you any longer; and no craftsman of any craft will be found in you any longer; and the sound of a mill will not be heard in you any longer; [23] and the light of a lamp will not shine in you any longer; and the voice of the bridegroom and bride will not be heard in you any longer; for your merchants were the great men of the earth, because all the nations were deceived by your sorcery. [24] And in her was found the blood of prophets and of saints and of all who have been slain on the earth." (Revelation 18: 1-24 NASB)

Insights

Mystery Babylon's effects are most evident when the throne of the dragon settles in the kingdom of the beast. Within her realm of influence, alcohol and drugs divide families and destroy

Insights: Chapter 18

lives. Political profiteers exchange cash for human souls, victimizing all races, genders, and ethnicities. Violence and bloodshed, injustice and cruelty are her fruit. She encourages infanticide, genocide, and euthanasia. Bloodthirsty, she disregards a suffering world. God calls us out of her. How were we taken in?

The Great Whore

If we don't come out of Babylon, we'll be guilty of her sins: of her mind-altering drugs [*pharmakeia*]; of sorcery, witchcraft, greed, drunkenness, false witness, immorality, thievery, idolatry, covetousness, human trafficking, the blood of innocents, and the deaths of saints and prophets. They divide His nation. Jerusalem had fallen into the same sins by Baal worship and was judged:

> [21] How is the faithful city become an harlot! it was full of judgment; righteousness lodged in it; but now murderers. [22] Thy silver is become dross, thy wine mixed with water. [23] Thy princes are rebellious, and companions of thieves: everyone loveth gifts and followeth after rewards: They judge not the fatherless, neither doth the cause of the widow come unto them. (Is 1:21-23)

Thankfully, our merciful God doesn't leave it there; instead, after purging her, He restored Israel's judges *as at the first, and her counselors, as at the beginning: afterward* she would be *called the city of righteousness, the faithful city. Zion* would be *redeemed with judgment, and her converts with righteousness.* (from Is. 1:26-27)

> [4] I heard another voice from heaven, saying, "Come out of her, my people, so that you will not participate in her sins and receive of her plagues; [5] for her sins have piled up as high as heaven, and God has remembered her iniquities. (Rev. 18:4-5; cf. 16:19-20)

At the seventh bowl of wrath, God remembers Babylon (in 16:19). In chapter 18 she is a prosperous city on the seacoast and purchases the world's products but is thoroughly depraved. Her land is the greatest consumer of them all, buying nearly 30% of the world's merchandise.[198] The nations rely on her prosperity.

Ancient Babylon lay inland like Rome, but this metropolis is neither of them. She's lascivious, violent, idolatrous, spreading her sins across the world; lifting her sensualities and deceptions to the heavens, yet she's a cultural center of the fine arts: *And the sound of harpists and musicians and flute-players and trumpeters will not be heard in you any longer; and no craftsman of any craft will be found in you any longer; and the sound of a mill will not be heard in you any longer.* (18:22)

As it was in Noah's day, those who crossed the waters to take the faith of God to the New World gave what they received to those who followed. Babel's divided languages confused and separated her people. Today's churches have departed from the Scriptures and are divided and confused when faced with the truth. It's as though we speak a different language than God, but the love of the truth keeps its believers in the end.

America's taxpayers support the UN as the leopard undergirding the nations of the earth, bolstering terrorist states that profit in their sins while her consumers buy the world's *cinnamon and spice and incense and perfume and frankincense and wine and olive oil and fine flour and wheat and cattle and sheep, and cargoes of horses and chariots <u>and slaves and human lives</u>! (Rev. 18:13)* [automobiles, etc.] Even some who profess the faith want the United Nations to rule the world, but we'll be deceived by our ignorance if we don't love the truth, and if we don't invest the time to search it out, then we don't love the truth.

When the man of lawlessness is exposed, there's no way to stop him or to prevent his evil plans. He will lead the nations to fulfill the prophecy of the God he hates, and the world will adore him. God calls us to repent and believe His Son. Most hypocrites will deny their sins while those who refuse to worship the beast or take his mark will inherit everlasting life.

On September 11, 2001, scriptures rushed to my mind as I watched the stunning news on TV.[199] The prophecies struck this writer like electric jolts: images of billowing smoke filled the air from the first tower when suddenly, a second plane burst into her sister skyscraper, and thousands of souls were lost in minutes. People were covered in ash as their cries resounded to heaven. *Babylon is fallen, is fallen, that great city, because she made all nations drink of the wine of the wrath of her fornication! (from Rev. 14:8)* The alarm sounded to awaken America. At sunset we knew our land would never be the same.

Insights: Chapter 18

Merchant ships watch as her distant smoke rises. On her last day, Babylon is razed from the face of the earth. Her merchants cry out on that terrible day—not for the souls who perish in her destruction, but greed and lust, materialism and perversions—her own great sins—have overtaken them by her seductions:

> [17] for in one hour <u>such great wealth has been laid waste</u>!' And every shipmaster and every passenger and sailor, and as many as make their living by the sea, stood at a distance, [18] and were crying out as they saw the smoke of her burning, saying, 'What *city* is like the great city?' [19] And they threw dust on their heads and were crying out, weeping and mourning, saying, 'Woe, woe, the great city, in which all who had ships at sea became rich by her wealth, for in one hour she has been laid waste!' (Rev. 18:17-19 NASB)

On August 2, 2012, the president wrote on a final beam of the One World Trade Center: "We remember. We rebuild. We come back stronger." [200] What did he mean? I wasn't sure.

Retrospect and Foresight

We suffer His righteous judgments in unbelief as hurricanes, floods, tornadoes, volcanoes, infestations, droughts, plagues, and earthquakes—catastrophic events, things that had never occurred before, strike the earth. We watch the experts, removed from the stories till their realities strike our own homes. At the pummeling hand of judgment, we don't know what hit us. We find fault in sinners who have no fear of God, but the church herself doesn't fear Him. We say we believe but dare to curse our leaders whom God has chosen to bless or judge our land. How can we be silent at a time like this? the virgins are sleeping:

> 25 Then shall the kingdom of heaven be likened unto ten virgins, which took their lamps, and went forth to meet the bridegroom. [2] And five of them were wise, and five were foolish. [3] They that were foolish took their lamps, and took no oil with them: [4] But the wise took oil in their vessels with their lamps. (Mat. 25:1-4)

God prefers love to hatred but exercises both. Are His words too difficult for politics? If He *scourges every son He receives,*

The Revelation

what becomes of the sinner? (Heb. 12:6) Did we realize we were creating another gospel and another Jesus, even another god who would never raise His hand? We reason it should be easy for people to believe in the Savior, but He never said that. He said it's not easy. We must take up the cross and die to follow Him.

The church has been living like the world, but that's a deadly deception. He called us to repent and die to this world to believe in Him. We have turned people to the faith who have no idea about keeping it through the trials that are ahead. It would be better not to have heard the gospel than to turn away from it as many have already done. This was why Jesus spoke in parables. (Jn. 12:39-46; Heb. 6:4-12; 10:26-36; 2 Pet. 2:20-22)

As Israel served Baal, have we returned to the idols we once served? Loving this world and its stuff as though we belong to it, we waste our lives with fun and games and don't redeem our time for eternity. We stand with those who give up their children to the fire believing they're in the arms of Jesus. (See 1 Cor. 7:14)

The pervasiveness of Babylon threatens our schools from kindergarten to college with perversions as "sex education" that targets their minds; yet we wonder why so many are deceived.

America's soul has been divorced from God—immoral and reprobate. We should be repenting for a nation and a church that have fallen away from the Creator. The Bible warns us against sodomy [perversions, even in heterosexual marriages]; fornication [sex apart from marriage], and sexual immorality [lasciviousness]. Deceivers would have us believe that a fib is no worse than sexual sin or murder, but that's a lie. God will expose everything when the secrets of our hearts and minds are judged. (Gal. 5:19-26; Rev. 20:11-15; 21:4-8; 1 Cor. 6:9-11)

> [2] For if the word spoken through angels proved steadfast, and every transgression and disobedience received a just reward, [3] how shall we escape if we neglect so great a salvation, which at the first began to be spoken by the Lord, and was confirmed to us by those who heard *Him,* [4] God also bearing witness both with signs and wonders, with various miracles, and gifts of the Holy Spirit, according to His own will? (Heb. 2:2-4 NKJV)

The scripture tells us that Christ went before us, leading the way, crowned with glory and honor after tasting death for us all.

Insights: Chapter 18

God made our Captain perfect by sanctification through suffering to bring many sons to glory, sanctified in Him. Therefore He isn't ashamed to call us family. If we share His sufferings, we'll also share His comfort. (Rom. 8:18; 2 Cor. 1:5-7; Phil. 3:10-11; 1Pet. 4:12-19)

The Mother of Harlots

Consider the immigrants, entering New York Harbor out of all nations and languages, hoping for freedom and a future:

> [15] And he saith to me, 'The waters that thou didst see, where the whore doth sit, are peoples, and multitudes, and nations, and tongues;' ... [18] and the woman that thou didst see is the great city that is having reign over the kings of the land.' (Rev. 17:15, 18 YLT) [Mystery Babylon]

America's first capital, the home of the Constitution, is New York City. International laws are being made in the chamber of the UN even now.[201] Eight hundred languages are spoken in the streets of the most linguistically diverse metropolis on earth.[202]

> [15] Shout against her round about: she hath given her hand, her foundations have fallen, her walls are thrown down: for it is the vengeance of the LORD. Take vengeance upon her; as she hath done, do unto her. (Jer. 50:14-15)

Her foundations are crumbling. Her infrastructure is frail. Will they sustain the city's weight when the rocks beneath her quake?[203] What happened to her foundations and the walls that once protected her? The LORD will destroy the harlot Babylon for her seductions and for the blood on her hands.

Manhattan is known as New York City, one of the foremost seaports with one of the largest natural harbors on the earth. She is the city of the prophecy: [204] ... *Alas, alas that great city, wherein were made rich all that had ships in the sea by reason of her costliness! for in one hour is she made desolate. (Rev. 18:19)*

The city of the nations is an island of many hills, seated with many ambassadors in a tower. She seduces the kings of the earth where Israel's adversaries are aligned against the nation that warmly welcomes them. One World Trade Center is the sign of her defiance, towering over the city from Ground Zero.[205] It's the highest structure New York City has ever seen.

The Revelation

The "Empire State" confirms her place in history.[206] In 2016 NYC welcomed a replica of the Arch of Bel [Baal] in Central Park.[207] At the end, she is the capital of the beast's empire.

> [6] I saw the woman, drunk with the blood of the saints and with the blood of the martyrs of Jesus. And when I saw her, I marveled with great amazement. (Rev. 17:6 NKJV)

The wine of the wrath of her fornication and *the abundance of her delicacies* fill the pockets of her profiteers. *A habitation of devils, a hold of every foul spirit,* she broadcasts her sins, filling the world with fornication, murdering the infants to sell the body parts, shamelessly celebrating their deaths. She's Satan's whore.

> [9] "Woe to him who strives with him who formed him,
>   a pot among earthen pots!
> Does the clay say to him who forms it, "What are you making?'
>   Or 'Your work has no handles'?
> [10] Woe to him who says to a father, 'What are you begetting?' or to a woman,
>   "With what are you in labor?'" (Is. 45:9-10 ESV)

America was founded by the Biblical principles of imperfect men aiming for a more perfect union. Throughout her history she was governed with respect for God even through the years when human slavery filled the world. The church challenged its darkness with her light. William Wilberforce and John Newton lived to see slavery abolished in England.[208] In the 19th century the Holiness Movement decried slavery till it was abolished by the Christian president Abraham Lincoln. In the 20th century, Martin Luther King opened American eyes to her injustices.

Hard times implanted the fear of God in us till we esteemed His wisdom and goodness. Like Israel, Americans were unable to keep His laws apart from a relationship with God. When the Bible was taken out of daily life, her children rebelled against our Creator. The depth of her sins is great; therefore, we repent.

> [8] They were *as* fed horses in the morning: every one neighed after his neighbor's wife. [9] Shall I not visit for these *things?* saith the LORD: and shall not my soul be avenged on such a nation as this? ...

Insights: Chapter 18

> [12] They have belied the LORD, and said, *It is* not he; neither shall evil come upon us; neither shall we see sword nor famine: [13] And the prophets shall become wind, and the word *is not* in them: thus shall it be done unto them. (Jer. 5:8-9, 12-13)

> [13] If I shut up heaven that there be no rain, or if I command the locusts to devour the land, or if I send pestilence among my people; [14] If my people, which are called by my name, shall humble themselves, and pray, and seek my face, and turn from their wicked ways; then will I hear from heaven, and will forgive their sin, and will heal their land. (2 Chron. 7:13-14)

We must look to ourselves as the first to change, confessing our sins to Jesus who forgives and cleanses us of evil. We prove our love for the truth of His Word, shunning the lies that deny it.

> [3] O LORD, *are* not thine eyes upon the truth? thou hast stricken them, but they have not grieved; thou hast consumed them, *but* they have refused to receive correction: they have made their faces harder than a rock; they have refused to return. [4] Therefore I said, Surely these *are* poor; they are foolish: for they know not the way of the LORD, *nor* the judgment of their God. [5] I will get me unto the great men, and will speak unto them; for they have known the way of the LORD, *and* the judgment of their God: but these have altogether broken the yoke, *and* burst the bonds. (Jer. 5:3-5)

> 3 Yes, <u>in those days and at that time</u>,
>   when I restore the fortunes of Judah and Jerusalem,
> [2] <u>I will gather all the nations</u>
>   and take them to the Valley of Jehoshaphat.
>   <u>I will enter into judgment with them there</u>
>   <u>My inheritance Israel</u>.
>   The nations have scattered the Israelites
>   in foreign countries
>   and <u>divided up My land</u>.
> [3] They cast lots for My people;
>   they bartered a boy for a prostitute
>   and sold a girl for wine to drink. (Joel 3:1-3 HCSB)

The city that was once a beacon of hope is condemned, and few of us recall America as she used to be. Much of her blood was spilt for liberty, but what's left at the end? an idol, crushed to dust and strewn to the wind, lost to oblivion. God calls to us, "Come out of her!" yet Babylon fills the world with her sins. We dare not walk her highway to hell. If we haven't shared her sins, God would not have commanded us to come out of her.

NYC and the UN have been marked for destruction, but America is ours to redeem since there's not just one government, but two in the land. Satan is a thief and a deceiver who comes to steal, kill, and destroy; that tells us who has the microphone. As servants of God, we speak the good news of salvation with its warnings and prayers for people to return to their Creator.

Will He vomit out her church? (3:14-22; 21:24) Will we turn to our Maker or race to our extinction? We are His servants in a momentous hour. Let's not be deceived: the truth should unite us. *Can two walk together except they be agreed? (Am. 3:3)*

Our nation has been losing her sovereignty to the dominion of the New World Order, introduced by President George H.W. Bush in 1989.[209] "A thousand points of light," he said, "with law and order under one world government."—chilling words for those of us who knew even a little about prophecy.

With one hundred ninety-three member states, the UN holds virtually every nation, ostensibly for peace on earth, but most of them are at war today.[210] And most are set to destroy Israel.

How did it happen? For the first time in nearly two hundred years, the nation's Supreme Court removed the Bible and prayer out of schools, and the church felt helpless when she should have prayed. As a result, our nation began her descent. Living day by day, we didn't realize how quickly she was falling.

Her sins are abominable, but in the past, revivals have ended injustices when her national conscience responded by righteous reforms. It takes a lot of prayer to rebuild a nation.

> **21** Then a strong angel took up a stone like a great millstone and threw it into the sea, saying, "So will Babylon, the great city, be thrown down with violence, and will not be found any longer. (Rev. 18:21 NASB)

We were small when we first heard Jesus loved us, and His love touched our hearts. *Out of the mouths of babes ... thou hast perfected praise. (Mt. 21:16; Ps. 8:2) Whosoever shall offend one of these little ones that believes in me, it is better for him that a*

Insights: Chapter 18

millstone were hanged about his neck and he were cast into the sea. (Mk. 9:42)

In 1973 the U.S. Supreme Court broke the Ten Commandments by legalizing the act of abortion.[211] God warned us: it is better to have a great stone hanging from one's neck and to be cast into the ocean than to offend or to make one of these little ones sin. He knew about the immoral, unnatural, and satanic sins that would rise against the children. Babylon's spirit has spread from her shores to the world. Now her judgment is imminent.

The great liar rose from the abyss, seeking to destroy the hope of the gospel. When Babylon is decimated, heaven breaks into song like the righteous do when the wicked are gone:

> [10] The righteous shall rejoice when he seeth the vengeance: he shall wash his feet in the blood of the wicked. [11] That a man shall say, Verily *there is* a reward for the righteous: Verily he is a God that judgeth in the earth. (Ps. 58:10-11)

> [10] Then I heard a loud voice in heaven saying, "Now have come the salvation and the power and the kingdom of our God and the authority of His Anointed One, for the accuser of our brothers and sisters—the one who accuses them before our God day and night—has been thrown out. [11] They overcame him by the blood of the Lamb and by the word of their testimony, and they did not love their lives even in the face of death.
> (Rev. 12:10-11 TLV)

With the arrival of the duplicitous kings of chapter 13, the prostitute's city moves. Just before the Lord returns, in 17:16 the ten kings grow to hate the harlot city and give their power to the dragon to make her desolate and naked; to eat her flesh, and burn her with fire. Her judgment comes at the seventh bowl with the greatest earthquake of all:

> [16] And he gathered them together into a place called in the Hebrew tongue Armageddon.
> [17] <u>And the seventh angel poured out his vial into the air</u>; and there came a great voice out of the temple of heaven from the throne, saying, It is done. [18] And there were voices, and thunders, and lightnings; and there was a great earthquake, such as was not since men were upon

the earth, so mighty an earthquake, *and* so great. ¹⁹ And the great city was divided into three parts, and the cities of the nations fell: and <u>great Babylon came in remembrance before God</u>, to give unto her the cup of the wine of the fierceness of his wrath.²⁰ And every island fled away, and the mountains were not found.
²¹ And there fell upon men a great hail out of heaven, *every stone* about the weight of a talent: and men blasphemed God because of the plague of the hail; for the plague thereof was exceeding great. (Rev. 16:16-21)

At the seventh bowl (in 16:18), God recalls Babylon while ending His wrath (in 18:21). The Almighty crushes her like chaff —threshed and blown away by the wind. (Dan. 2:35). The earth trembles as Babylon plummets like an enormous millstone fallen into the sea. Repercussions of her judgments are felt around the world: tsunamis overcome the nations' cities and islands are swallowed up. The nefarious spirit Mystery Babylon is removed from the earth as the nations bow at Yeshua's feet.

Nothing can save the great harlot, but we may save a nation that has fallen for her evil ways. It wasn't by might, by power, by inheritance, or by our own will, but by His Spirit, God in Yeshua alone saved us. Solely by His grace, He set us free forever—free to make choices that affect our destinies. The way to success is the life led by His words in thankfulness.

We who believe in the One who rose to life from death never lose hope, but repent and pray for America's salvation. At the end, the nations are judged, lost or saved forever. We don't live by what we see, but receive what we don't see by faith.

Lucifer was a bright light in heaven, but now he's the prince of darkness on earth. He is the archenemy of God's light-bearers because the Word of God exposes and condemns him. This is why the beast, the dragon, and the false prophet are determined to destroy every vestige of faith in Israel's God. They fear their own destruction.

The beast devours the world, and when he does, we're his main targets. The body of Christ suffers all kinds of trials, but since we don't live for a material world, our greatest days are ahead. As Jesus said, when all these signs begin, look up because our redemption is near; so we look up to our victorious King!

The Revelation of Jesus Christ

CHAPTER 19

19 And after these things I heard a great voice of much people in heaven, saying, Alleluia; Salvation, and glory, and honour, and power, unto the Lord our God:
² For true and righteous are his judgments: for he hath judged the great whore, which did corrupt the earth with her fornication, and hath avenged the blood of his servants at her hand.
³ And again they said, Alleluia And her smoke rose up for ever and ever.
⁴ And the four and twenty elders and the four beasts fell down and worshipped God that sat on the throne, saying, Amen; Alleluia.
⁵ And a voice came out of the throne, saying, Praise our God, all ye his servants, and ye that fear him, both small and great.
⁶ And I heard as it were the voice of a great multitude, and as the voice of many waters, and as the voice of mighty thunderings, saying, Alleluia: for the Lord God omnipotent reigneth.
⁷ Let us be glad and rejoice, and give honour to him: for the marriage of the Lamb is come, and his wife hath made herself ready.
⁸ And to her was granted that she should be arrayed in fine linen, clean and white: for the fine linen is the righteousness of saints.
⁹ And he saith unto me, Write, Blessed are they which are called unto the marriage supper of the Lamb. And he saith unto me, These are the true sayings of God.
¹⁰ And I fell at his feet to worship him. And he said unto me, See thou do it not: I am thy fellowservant, and of thy brethren that have the testimony of Jesus: worship God: for the testimony of Jesus is the spirit of prophecy.
¹¹ And I saw heaven opened, and behold a white horse; and he that sat upon him was called Faithful and True, and in righteousness he doth judge and make war.
¹² His eyes were as a flame of fire, and on his head were many crowns; and he had a name written, that no man knew, but he himself.
¹³ And he was clothed with a vesture dipped in blood: and his name is called The Word of God.
¹⁴ And the armies which were in heaven followed him upon

The Revelation

white horses, clothed in fine linen, white and clean.
¹⁵ And out of his mouth goeth a sharp sword, that with it he should smite the nations: and he shall rule them with a rod of iron: and he treadeth the winepress of the fierceness and wrath of Almighty God.
¹⁶ And he hath on his vesture and on his thigh a name written, KING OF KINGS, AND LORD OF LORDS.
¹⁷ And I saw an angel standing in the sun; and he cried with a loud voice, saying to all the fowls that fly in the midst of heaven, Come and gather yourselves together unto the supper of the great God;
¹⁸ That ye may eat the flesh of kings, and the flesh of captains, and the flesh of mighty men, and the flesh of horses, and of them that sit on them, and the flesh of all men, both free and bond, both small and great.
¹⁹ And I saw the beast, and the kings of the earth, and their armies, gathered together to make war against him that sat on the horse, and against his army.
²⁰ And the beast was taken, and with him the false prophet that wrought miracles before him, with which he deceived them that had received the mark of the beast, and them that worshipped his image. These both were cast alive into a lake of fire burning with brimstone.
²¹ And the remnant were slain with the sword of him that sat upon the horse, which sword proceeded out of his mouth: and all the fowls were filled with their flesh.
(Revelation 19:1-21)

Insights

¹⁰ At that time many will turn away from the faith and will betray and hate each other, ¹¹ and many false prophets will appear, and deceive many people. ¹² Because of the increase of wickedness, the love of most will grow cold, ¹³ but the one who stands firm to the end will be saved.
(Mat. 24:10-13 NIV)

A worldwide religio-political empire is at hand. Martyrs cry out from *under the altar* until they're clothed with white linen. They wait for their brothers and sisters to be killed as they were until justice prevails against their murderers.

The face of the earth changes before Jesus comes on a cloud with a shout for the first resurrection. We prepare by confessing our sins, forgiving, and loving others; released, we're free at last.

Insights: Chapter 19

Nazis crammed Jews into ghettos; then tightly packed them in cattle cars and transported them to work camps. They shaved their heads and tattooed their arms with numbers, stealing their identities. Guards physically and psychologically abused the captives. They beat them, worked them, and starved them to death. Forced to stack the dead in mass graves, those too weak to work went to death camps for gas showers. Their enemies made Jews carry their brothers' bodies to ovens and shovel out their ashes. Now the day of reckoning is at hand.

> [24] Jesus told them another parable: "The kingdom of heaven is like a man who sowed good seed in his field. [25] But while everyone was sleeping, his enemy came and sowed weeds among the wheat, and went away. [26] When the wheat sprouted and formed heads, then the weeds also appeared.
> [27] "The owner's servants came to him and said, 'Sir, didn't you sow good seed in your field? Where then did the weeds come from?'
> [28] "'An enemy did this,' he replied.
> "The servants asked him, "Do you want us to go and pull them up?'
> [29] "'No,' he answered, 'because while you are pulling the weeds, you may root up the wheat with them. [30] Let both grow together until the harvest. At that time I will tell the harvesters: <u>First collect the weeds</u> and tie them in bundles to be burned; <u>then gather the wheat</u> and bring it into my barn." (Mat. 13:24-30 NIV)

The story refers to false brethren. Its prophetic irony reminds us of the marks the saints will reject. Contrary to the marks the Nazis forced on Jews, the wicked will be marked. The weeds are those among us who will bow to the beast. Gathered together by a mark, they are bound to be burned, but the elect will be saved.

At midnight in Tel Aviv, music and laughter fell silent. The dance ended at the roar of warplanes. Their hands held weapons, and their arms bared tattoos, reminding them of their cause. The fight for life goes on till the end.

When the fourth kingdom turns its laws against us who are true to Jesus Christ, the persecution we've seen from a distance will be at our doors. It may seem that He's late in coming, but His plans for us include our victory over the fear of death.

The Revelation

After the tribulation Christ appears in the sky *with a great sound of a trumpet (in Mat. 24:31; 1 Thes. 4:16-17)*, and martyrs beheaded for resisting the beast rise from the graves transformed. Together with them, the saints who survive ascend, transfigured. His trumpet is terrifying! Its blast alerts the angels who catch us up just as others pour out His wrath to the earth.

> [25] "And there will be signs in the sun, in the moon, and in the stars; and on the earth distress of nations, with perplexity, the sea and the waves roaring; [26] men's hearts failing them from fear and the expectation of those things which are coming on the earth, for the powers of the heavens will be shaken. [27] Then they will see the Son of Man coming in a cloud with power and great glory. [28] Now when these things begin to happen, look up and lift up your heads, because your redemption draws near." (Lk. 21:25-28 NKJV) – Yeshua

> [31] And he shall send his angels with a great sound of a trumpet, and they shall gather together his elect from the four winds, from one end of heaven to the other.
> (Mat. 24:31)

His apostles wrote to believers about His *coming on a cloud.* [Gr.: *ĕrchŏmai*, coming/appearing] John wrote of the elect who rise at the first resurrection. (Rev. 20:4) Paul gave other details:

> [17] Then we which are alive *and* remain shall be caught up together with them in the clouds, to meet the Lord in the air: And so shall we ever be with the Lord. [18] Wherefore comfort one another with these words.
> (1 Thes. 4:17-18)

A woman when she is in travail hath sorrow, because her hour is come, but as soon as she delivereth the child, she remembereth no more the anguish, for joy that a man is born into the world. (Jn. 16:21) The Lord spoke the parable to comfort His friends before his death. The story also applies at the end when trials are past and pain is forgotten for joy that the work is done:

> [9] After these things I looked, and behold, a great multitude which no one could number, of all nations, tribes, peoples, and tongues, standing before the throne and before the Lamb, clothed with white robes, with palm branches in their hands, [10] and crying out with a

Insights: Chapter 19

loud voice, saying, "Salvation *belongs* to our God who sits on the throne, and to the Lamb!" ...
¹³ Then one of the elders answered, saying to me, "Who are these arrayed in white robes, and where did they come from?"
¹⁴ And I said to him, "Sir, you know."
So he said to me, "These are the ones who come out of the great tribulation, and washed their robes and made them white in the blood of the Lamb. ¹⁵ Therefore they are before the throne of God, and serve Him day and night in His temple. And He who sits on the throne will dwell among them. (Rev. 7:9-10, 13-15 NKJV)

⁵ "He who overcomes shall be clothed in white garments, and I will not blot out his name from the Book of Life; but I will confess his name before My Father and before His angels. ⁶ He who has an ear, let him hear what the Spirit says to the churches.'" (Rev. 3:5-6 NKJV)

Ezekiel's Revelation

A political upheaval comes at the end when ten horns [kings] rejoin the dragon to assault the city. At last (in 16:17-21), Babylon is annihilated. Then Yeshua strikes the nations in Armageddon:

39 "And you, son of man, prophesy against Gog and say, Thus says the Lord GOD: Behold, I am against you, O Gog, chief prince of Meshech and Tubal. ² And I will turn you about and drive you forward, and bring you up from the uttermost parts of the north, and lead you against the mountains of Israel. ³ Then I will strike your bow from your left hand, and will make your arrows drop out of your right hand. ⁴ You shall fall on the mountains of Israel, you and all your hordes and the peoples who are with you. I will give you to birds of prey of every sort and to the beasts of the field to be devoured. ⁵ You shall fall in the open field, for I have spoken, declares the Lord GOD. ⁶ I will send fire on Magog and on those who dwell securely in the coastlands, and they shall know that I am the LORD.

⁷ "And my holy name I will make known in the midst of my people Israel, and I will not let my holy name be profaned anymore. And the nations shall know that I am the LORD, the Holy One in Israel. ⁸ Behold, it is com-

The Revelation

ing and it will be brought about, declares the Lord GOD. That is the day of which I have spoken.

⁹ "Then those who dwell in the cities of Israel will go out and <u>make fires of the weapons and burn them</u>, shields and bucklers, bow and arrows, clubs and spears; and they will make fires of them for seven years, ...

¹¹ "On that day I will give to Gog a place for burial in Israel, <u>the Valley of the Travelers, east of the sea</u>. It will block the travelers, for there Gog and all his multitude will be buried. It will be called the Valley of Hamon-gog. ¹² <u>For seven months the house of Israel will be burying them, in order to cleanse the land</u>. ¹³ All the people of the land will bury them, and it will bring them renown on the day that I show my glory, declares the Lord GOD. ¹⁴ They will set apart men to travel through the land regularly and bury those travelers remaining on the face of the land, so as to cleanse it. At the end of seven months they will make their search ...

¹⁷ "As for you, son of man, thus says the Lord GOD: <u>Speak to the birds of every sort and to all beasts of the field: 'Assemble and come, gather from all around to the sacrificial feast that I am preparing for you, a great sacrificial feast on the mountains of Israel, and you shall eat flesh and drink blood</u>. ...

²¹ "And I will set my glory among the nations, and all the nations shall see my judgment that I have executed, and my hand that I have laid on them. ²² <u>The house of Israel shall know that I am the LORD their God, from that day forward</u>. ²³ <u>And the nations shall know that the house of Israel went into captivity for their iniquity, because they dealt so treacherously with me that I hid my face from them and gave them into the hand of their adversaries, and they all fell by the sword</u>. ²⁴ I dealt with them according to their uncleanness and their transgressions, and hid my face from them.

²⁵ "Therefore thus says the Lord GOD: <u>Now I will restore the fortunes of Jacob and have mercy on the whole house of Israel, and I will be jealous for my holy name</u>. ²⁶ <u>They shall forget their shame and all the treachery they have practiced against me, when they dwell securely in their land with none to make them afraid</u>, ²⁷ when I

Insights: Chapter 19

have brought them back from the peoples and gathered them from their enemies' lands, and through them have vindicated my holiness in the sight of many nations.
²⁸ <u>Then they shall know that I am the LORD their God, because I sent them into exile among the nations and then assembled them into their own land.</u> I will leave none of them remaining among the nations anymore.
²⁹ <u>And I will not hide my face anymore from them, when I pour out my Spirit upon the house of Israel, declares the Lord GOD.</u>" (Ezk. 39:1-9, 11-14, 17, 21-29 ESV)

The chief Prince of Satan is Gog, from the uttermost parts of the north [Heb.: *sar is an* official, prince, ruler, et al]. He leads Russia and rules Magog as Satan did Babylon. After Russia, he led China into Marxist communism. He also leads Meshech and Tubal on the south side of the Black Sea, Turkey today.

The Marxist feet of Russia mobilize the beast in chapter 13. His armies meet east of the Great Sea in Armageddon, called *Hamon-Gog*—their burial ground. ["multitudes of Gog"; cf. 16:16]

² "Behold, I am about to make Jerusalem a cup of staggering to all the surrounding peoples. <u>The siege of Jerusalem will also be against Judah.</u> ³ On that day I will make Jerusalem a heavy stone for all the peoples. All who lift it will surely hurt themselves. <u>And all the nations of the earth will gather against it.</u>
⁴ On that day, declares the LORD, I will strike every horse with panic, and its rider with madness. But <u>for the sake of the house of Judah I will keep my eyes open</u>, when I strike every horse of the peoples with blindness. ⁵ Then the clans of Judah shall say to themselves, 'The inhabitants of Jerusalem have strength through the LORD of hosts, their God.'
⁶ "On that day I will make <u>the clans of Judah</u> like a blazing pot in the midst of wood, like a flaming torch among sheaves. And they shall devour to the right and to the left all the surrounding peoples, <u>while Jerusalem shall again be inhabited in its place, in Jerusalem.</u>
⁷ "And the LORD will give salvation to the tents of Judah first, that the glory of the house of David and the glory of the inhabitants of Jerusalem may not surpass that of Judah. ⁸ On that day the LORD will protect the inhabitants of Jerusalem, so that the feeblest among them on that

The Revelation

day shall be like David, and the house of David shall be like God, like the angel of the LORD, going before them. <u>⁹And on that day I will seek to destroy all the nations that come against Jerusalem.</u> (Zec. 12:2-9 ESV)

The nations gather to war after the **sixth bowl,** and a voice from heaven speaks: "It is done!" (16:17), signaling His return. An earthquake splits *the great city in three.* An angel reveals the method by which God deftly carries out His plan to annihilate Babylon forever. When He recalls Babylon the Great and pours out His wrath on her, islands and mountains disappear. (16:19-21)

The Day of the Lord

¹⁰ "Rejoice with Jerusalem,
And be glad with her, all you who love her;
Rejoice for joy with her, all you who mourn for her;
¹¹ That you may feed and be satisfied
With the consolation of her bosom,
That you may drink deeply and be delighted
With the abundance of her glory."
¹² For thus says the LORD: "Behold, I will extend peace to her like a river,
And the glory of the Gentiles like a flowing stream.
Then you shall feed;
On *her* sides shall you be carried,
And be dandled on *her* knees.
¹³ As one whom his mother comforts,
So I will comfort you;
And you shall be comforted in Jerusalem."
¹⁴ When you see *this,* your heart shall rejoice,
And your bones shall flourish like grass;
<u>The hand of the LORD shall be known to His servants,</u>
<u>And *His* indignation to His enemies.</u>
¹⁵ <u>For behold, the LORD will come with fire</u>
<u>And with His chariots, like a whirlwind,</u>
<u>To render His anger with fury,</u>
<u>And His rebuke with flames of fire.</u>
¹⁶ <u>For by fire and by His sword</u>   [from His mouth?]
The LORD will judge all flesh;
And the slain of the LORD shall be many.   Rev 19:1
(Is. 66:10-16 NKJV)

² For you yourselves know full well that the day of the Lord will come just like a thief in the night. ³ While they

Insights: Chapter 19

are saying, "Peace and safety!" then destruction will come upon them suddenly like labor pains upon a woman with child, and they will not escape. [4] But you, brethren, are not in the darkness, that the day would overtake you like a thief; [5] for you are all sons of light and sons of day. We are not of night nor of darkness; [6] so then let us not sleep as others do, but let us be alert and sober.
(1 Thes. 5:2-6 NASB)

Like lightning Jesus returns and destroys the nations that are His enemies. The beast and his prophet are cast into the fire.

[27] For as the lightning cometh out of the east, and shineth even unto the west; so shall also the coming of the Son of man be. [28] For wheresoever the carcass is, there will the eagles be gathered together.
(Mat. 24:27-28; cf. Rev. 19:17-21)

He rides ahead, shining with His armies, yes, all of them on white horses! Then Jesus establishes Jerusalem as His throne.

[21] <u>Whoever has my commandments and keeps them, he it is who loves me.</u> And he who loves me will be loved by my Father, and I will love him and manifest myself to him." (Jn. 14:21 ESV)

The Savior really *did* wash away our sins, but disobedience is the fruit of unbelief while the substance of faith is evidenced by the works of His Holy Spirit:

[28] Do not be afraid of those who kill the body but cannot kill the soul. Rather, be afraid of the One who can destroy both soul and body in hell. [29] Are not two sparrows sold for a penny? Yet not one of them will fall to the ground outside your Father's care. [30] And even the very hairs of your head are all numbered. [31] So don't be afraid; you are worth more than many sparrows.
(Mat. 10:28-31 NIV) [His warning precedes His assurance.]

[7] That the trial of your faith, being much more precious than of gold that perisheth, might be found unto praise and glory and honour at the appearing of Jesus Christ: [8] whom having not seen, ye love; in whom, though now ye see him not, yet believing, ye rejoice with joy unspeakable and full of glory: [9] receiving the end of your faith, even the salvation of your souls. (1 Pet. 1:7-9)

The Revelation

¹⁴ How narrow is the gate and difficult the way that leads to life, and those who find it are few." (Mat. 7:14 TLV)

We appeal to all who hear His words: Repent and believe on Jesus Christ who forgives our sin when we call on His name. Be baptized, immersed in His death to sin, raised to newness of life:

Do not be overcome by evil, but overcome evil with good. (Rom. 12:21 TLV)

³ For God has done what the law, weakened by the flesh, could not do. By sending his own Son in the likeness of sinful flesh and for sin, he condemned sin in the flesh, ⁴ in order that the righteous requirement of the law might be fulfilled in us, who walk not according to the flesh, but according to the Spirit. (Rom. 8:3-4 ESV)

Her 5-Minute Misstep

Until 1962 every child in public school knew the five-minute period that began our day by acknowledging the Judeo-Christian God. No one objected. It never started an inflammatory debate among us about our diverse faiths. We understood the principle of tolerance, and we knew its definition too.

The first book in the public schools was the Holy Bible. The nation's founders established our government on its principles, as throughout the world, nations are founded by the faith of their fathers. Our nation did not impose a state religion or imprison men for their faith though our founders never intended to deny God or to separate governance from Providence.

In 1962–1963 the Supreme Court voided two hundred years of our founding standards when they removed the Holy Bible and prayer from public schools.[212] The decline in education and in student conduct correlated with the loss of the few minutes begun by the Pledge of Allegiance to the flag as to "one nation under God, indivisible, with liberty and justice for all," a motto and goal of our country. We read from Psalms or Proverbs; then said a Judeo-Christian prayer: *Our Father, which art in heaven, hallowed be thy name. Thy kingdom come; thy will be done on earth as it is in heaven. Give us this day our daily bread, and forgive us our trespasses as we forgive those who trespass against us. And lead us not into temptation, but deliver us from*

Insights: Chapter 19

evil. For thine is the kingdom, and the power, and the glory for ever. Amen. (Mat. 6:9-13) We've sinned, but God's gracious.

He will not heal the harlot city, but He may heal our land if, in the fear of God, we humble ourselves in prayer, seek His face, and turn from our many wicked ways. By grace He'll hear us, forgive our sins, and restore our nation in our sincere repentance. (2 Chron. 7:13-14)

The Dragon's Pride

God uses His enemies to judge the earth and to purify the saints; as He did for Israel, He'll do for us. He tests our hearts to prove His wisdom, righteousness, and power to men, angels, and all living things while working everything for the good of those who love and obey Him. (See Is. 54: 11-17; Rom. 8:28; cf. Jn. 14:15, 21)

Before the Lord comes on a cloud, His nemesis returns. The dragon, cloaked in a religious façade, leads people into the pit by their faith in his false promises. For the sake of all who love the truth, though he hides in the dark, the Lord will expose him when the time comes.

Never before have we seen so many icons and false teachers, gathering audiences by their own desires. They easily find eager ears that love the promises but spurn the warnings. Even so, our obedience qualifies us for the promises by shunning sin in the fear of God:

> [3] For the time will come when they will not endure sound doctrine; but after their own lusts shall they heap to themselves teachers, having itching ears; [4] And they shall turn away *their* ears from the truth, and shall be turned unto fables. (2 Tim. 4:3-4)

Satan deceives those who read the Bible but live far from its truth. He gives breath to a living image in Jerusalem as the world breathlessly adores him. Afterward the Lord destroys him by His holy breath, the Sword of His Word in all His shining brightness!

> [9] The coming of the lawless one will be in accordance with how Satan works. He will use all sorts of displays of power through signs and wonders that serve the lie, [10] and all the ways that wickedness deceives those who are perishing. They perish because they refused to love the truth and so be saved. [11] For this reason God sends them a powerful delusion so that they will believe the lie

The Revelation

¹² and so that all will be condemned who have not believed the truth but have delighted in wickedness. (2 Thes. 2:9-12 NIV)

¹⁹ And this is the judgment: the light has come into the world, and people loved the darkness rather than the light because their works were evil. (John 3:19 ESV)

¹³ And I saw three unclean spirits like frogs *come* out of the mouth of the dragon, and out of the mouth of the beast, and out of the mouth of the false prophet. ¹⁴ For <u>they are the spirits of devils, working miracles</u>, *which* go forth unto the kings of the earth and of the whole world, to gather them to the battle of that great day of God Almighty. (Rev. 16:13-14)

Shortly before Armageddon, at the sixth bowl of wrath, the beast, the dragon, and his prophet speak as three men. (16:12-16) Together with one mind, the dragon and his ten kings eat her flesh and burn Babylon with fire. (17:16-18) These three lead the world: the beast who is skilled at war and the king over the false faith beside his prophet as a beast with two horns like a lamb.

¹⁵ Therefore when you see the ABOMINATION OF DESOLATION which was spoke of through Daniel the prophet, standing in the holy place (let the reader understand), ¹⁶ then those who are in Judea must flee to the mountains. (Mat. 24:15-16 NASB)

¹³ It performs great signs, even making fire come down from heaven to earth in front of people, ¹⁴ and by the signs that it is allowed to work in the presence of the beast it deceives those who dwell on earth, telling them to make an image for the beast that was wounded by the sword and yet lived. ... ¹⁸ This calls for wisdom: let the one who has understanding calculate the number of the beast, for it is the number of a man, and his number is 666. (Rev. 13:13-14, 18 ESV)

The beast with two ostensibly small horns will test our faith with the beast before him. Two men lead the religious kingdom along with the beast, but one of them reigns over the nations of Babylon. [He was also in a small horn that rose after the ten.]

3 Remind them to be subject to rulers and authorities, to obey, to be ready for every good work, ² to speak evil of

Insights: Chapter 19

> no one, to be peaceable, gentle, showing all humility to all men. ³ For we ourselves were also once foolish, disobedient, deceived, serving various lusts and pleasures, living in malice and envy, hateful, and hating one another. ⁴ But when the kindness and the love of God our Savior toward man appeared, ⁵ not by works of righteousness which we have done, but according to His mercy He saved us, through the washing of regeneration and renewing of the Holy Spirit, ⁶ whom He poured out on us abundantly through Jesus Christ our Savior, ⁷ that having been justified by His grace we should become heirs according to the hope of eternal life.
> (Ti. 3:1-7 NKJV)

The new covenant is not an addendum to Moses' regulations but reminds us that the Ten Commandments lay a foundation for righteousness. We can't walk in love and break them. Even so, God gave a new covenant, not under law, but by grace. It isn't contradictory to the gospel to say there are times when the right thing to do is contrary to the authority over us. For example, the disciples were reprimanded by their rulers, but it didn't stop them from sharing the gospel, because Yeshua is superior to the rulers of this age, and He commanded us to take the gospel to all with ears to hear:

> ¹⁸ So they called them and charged them not to speak at all in the name of Jesus. ¹⁹ But Peter and John answered them, "Whether it is right in the sight of God to listen to you rather than to God, you must judge, ²⁰ for we cannot but speak of what we have seen and heard."
> (Acts 4:18-20 ESV)

We trust in Jesus Christ and are set apart by the Spirit whose moral laws never change. He empowers us to obey His words as we keep them in our hearts. Jesus said whoever breaks the least commandment is least in the Kingdom, and He raised the bar, saying we keep them from our hearts. (Mat. 5:19; Jas. 2; Rom. 13:8-10) However, patching the old with a new one tears the old and renders the new ineffective. (Jer. 31:31-34; Mat. 9:16-17)

We must decide between two covenants and stand with our Savior Yeshua. His blood is irreplaceable. There's no other way to salvation. The gospel itself is simple, but if we entrust our lives to Him and live by our faith, we follow Him as we walk in the steps of His Spirit. Any requirements outside of the apostles' words would insult the Spirit of grace by whom we are sealed:

> ³¹ Behold, the days come, saith the LORD, that I will make a new covenant with the house of Israel, and with the house of Judah: ³² <u>Not according to the covenant that I made with their fathers in the day that I took them by the hand to bring them out of the land of Egypt; which my covenant they brake, although I was an husband unto them, saith the LORD</u>: ³³ But this shall be the covenant that I will make with the house of Israel; After those days, saith the LORD, I will put my law in their inward parts, and write it in their hearts; and will be their God, and they shall be my people. ³⁴ And they shall teach no more every man his neighbour, and every man his brother, saying, Know the LORD: for they shall all know me, from the least of them unto the greatest of them, saith the LORD: for <u>I will forgive their iniquity, and I will remember their sin no more</u>. (Jer. 31:31-34)

The eternal Word came as mortal flesh and lived among us. The Author of prophecy, Jesus Christ, came to save, heal, teach, and lead us into everlasting life. He came as the Word from the heart of God, and as a Father teaches his children, He opens His words to us by His Holy Spirit.

The first resurrection of His martyrs is represented by Rosh Hashanah, the Feast of Trumpets, when a great trumpet outdoes them all. The firstfruits lead the entourage who are caught up together to meet Him in the air.

We remain to redeem anyone who hears His words, repents, and follows Him: *For the promise is unto you, and to your children, and to all that are afar off, even as many as the Lord our God shall call. (Acts 2:39)* His body on earth, we're called to know the Truth and shine a Light darkness cannot comprehend.

When the trumpet of God blasts, strong men will cry out and tremble. Our own legs will give way, but Yeshua sends angels to catch us up to Him. After His wrath He returns with the elect to Jerusalem and establishes the throne of His Kingdom to reign over all the earth. At the end of a thousand years, *the rest of the dead* rise on the last day at the last trump for the Last Judgment. (20:4-5; cf. 11:18; Jn. 6:39-54)

The Revelation of Jesus Christ

CHAPTER 20

20 Then I saw an angel coming down from heaven, having the key to the bottomless pit and a great chain in his hand. ² He laid hold of the dragon, that serpent of old, who is *the* Devil and Satan, and bound him for a thousand years; ³ and he cast him into the bottomless pit, and shut him up, and set a seal on him, so that he should deceive the nations no more till the thousand years were finished. But after these things he must be released for a little while.

⁴ And I saw thrones, and they sat on them, and judgment was committed to them. Then *I saw* the souls of those who had been beheaded for their witness to Jesus and for the word of God, who had not worshiped the beast or his image, and had not received *his* mark on their foreheads or on their hands. And they lived and reigned with Christ for a thousand years. ⁵ But the rest of the dead did not live again until the thousand years were finished. This *is* the first resurrection. ⁶ Blessed and holy *is* he who has part in the first resurrection. Over such the second death has no power, but they shall be priests of God and of Christ, and shall reign with Him a thousand years.

⁷ Now when the thousand years have expired, Satan will be released from his prison ⁸ and will go out to deceive the nations which are in the four corners of the earth, Gog and Magog, to gather them together to battle, whose number *is* as the sand of the sea. ⁹ They went up on the breadth of the earth and surrounded the camp of the saints and the beloved city. And fire came down from God out of heaven and devoured them. ¹⁰ The devil, who deceived them, was cast into the lake of fire and brimstone where the beast and the false prophet *are*. And they will be tormented day and night forever and ever.

¹¹ Then I saw a great white throne and Him who sat on it, from whose face the earth and the heaven fled away. And there was found no place for them. ¹² And I saw the dead, small and great, standing before God, and books were opened. And another book was opened, which is *the Book* of Life. And the dead were judged according to their works, by the things which were written in the books.

The Revelation

¹³ The sea gave up the dead who were in it, and Death and Hades delivered up the dead who were in them. And they were judged, each one according to his works. ¹⁴ Then Death and Hades were cast into the lake of fire. This is the second death. ¹⁵ And anyone not found written in the Book of Life was cast into the lake of fire.
(Revelation 20:1-15 NKJV)

Insights

The original scrolls had no chapters, or 20:1-3 would have ended chapter 19. Verse 4 would have begun chapter 20 with its thrones for the elect judges from heaven. Its twenty-four elders are sitting on thrones in 4:4, worshiping the Lamb in 5:8. The elders worship the Father in chapters 4, 5, 11, and 19; they worship Yeshua in 5:11-14. They worship before and after thousand years. He said His twelve apostles would be judges in His Kingdom. (Mat. 19:28; Lk. 22:30) They're among those in 20:4. The four *living creatures* also praise the Lamb in chapter 5:

⁹ And they sang a new song, saying,

"Worthy are you to take the scroll
    and to open its seals,
for you were slain, and by your blood you ransomed
    people for God
from every tribe and language and people and
    nation,
¹⁰ and you have made them a kingdom and priests to
    our God,
and they shall reign on the earth." (Rev. 5:9-10 ESV)

During the 19th century's Industrial Revolution, John Nelson Darby believed an idea that attracted millions of Christians but weakened our resolve to face death for Christ.[213] It was only an idea, but it might be why Jesus asked, *When the Son of man cometh, shall he find faith on the earth?* (Lk. 18:8b)

Shortly before Darwin, Darby introduced the hypothesis of a pretribulation rapture. Was Darwin's proof in the random chance of the mathematical laws of science? Where was Darby's proof? Still we look to teachers who are often deceived by their own assumptions. After repeatedly listening to false ideas, we're deaf to the truth while wondering why we can't understand the words of nature's God. And if we can't, we presume no one else can.

Insights: Chapter 20

The Bible tells us God created male and female. Was it by evolution, selective mutation, random chance, or by design? But evolution can't be explained by common sense, so atheists deny the self-evident truth of the creation of male and female. We're upset that creation is denied, but have we believed *immediately after the tribulation,* the Lord comes on a cloud for the elect? or have we believed our own desires and not His words?

Paul wrote the living do not ascend before the dead rise. *The first resurrection* of the church in 20:4-5 is of the beheaded who resisted the beast. None of the living ascend before the dead rise from their graves. Jesus comes enthroned on a cloud right *after the tribulation.* (cf. Rev. 6:16; Mat. 24:30; 1 Thes. 4:17)

Most of us are confused about which saints are raised from death and which of the living ascend with them. False teachings have fooled and blinded the church to what the Bible says. We think we can be casual about what we believe, but we can't. By study, prayer, and meekness, we receive the Word as it truly is.

Without a verse to substantiate a "pretribulation rapture," our false hope cannot prepare us to meet Christ *after the tribulation.* Shunning the words of God by our own desires, we gainsay by serpentine paths, insisting a rapture takes us up without facing martyrdom. Churches worldwide are fooled by that teaching, even though their families and friends have died in Christ for the faith. Martyrs who resist the beast are caught up together with the elect when most of the saints are still sleeping:

> [35] "Be dressed ready for service and keep your lamps burning, [36] like servants waiting for their master to return from a wedding banquet, so that when he comes and knocks they can immediately open the door for him. [37] It will be good for those servants whose master finds them watching when he comes. Truly I tell you, he will dress himself to serve, will have them recline at the table and will come and wait on them. [38] It will be good for those servants whose master finds them ready, even if he comes in the middle of the night or toward daybreak. [39] But understand this: If the owner of the house had known at what hour the thief was coming, he would not have let his house be broken into. [40] You also must be ready, because the Son of Man will come at an hour when you do not expect him." (Lk. 12:35-40 NIV)

The Revelation

The First Resurrection

When will He come for us? Christ the firstfruits rose with believers in the promise of a new covenant. He revealed Himself to them who searched for God and believed His words. The elect of the ancient world yearned to see their Messiah's birth and are the witnesses who surround us today.

> [22] For as in Adam all die, even so in Christ shall all be made alive. [23] But every man in his own order: Christ the firstfruits; afterward they that *are* Christ's at His coming. [24] Then cometh the end, when He shall have delivered up the kingdom to God, even the Father; when He shall have put down all rule and all authority and power.
> (1 Cor. 15:22-24) ["Coming" is Gr.: *parousia,* or "nearness."]

When Yeshua rose as the firstfruits of the dead, many saints who'd died before Him appeared in Jerusalem. But just those who heard His voice rose with Christ at His resurrection:

> [25] "Most assuredly, I say to you, that the hour is coming, and now is, when the dead will hear the voice of the Son of God; and those who hear will live. (John 5:25 NKJV)

> [52] And the graves were opened; and many bodies of the saints which slept arose, [53] And came out of the graves after his resurrection, and went into the holy city, and appeared unto many. (Mat. 27:52-53)

The hour ... now is ... (see Jn. 5:25) This reveals His own resurrection in which the elect heard His voice and rose after Jesus did as saints who turned to God by His laws. In appealing to His mercies and receiving His grace, they lived by faith in the Scriptures, and God gave them new hearts. (Jer. 31:33; Hab. 2:4)

The hour is coming refers to the first resurrection after Christ arose as firstfruits to God. Out of the tribulation, its martyrs are chosen to rise to life, having resisted the beast and his mark.

With no scriptural witness, most churches believe the whole church is caught up before the tribulation though no one ascends before the first resurrection. *The first resurrection* after Christ is of the martyrs, beheaded for denying the beast and his image, not receiving his mark or worshiping him. The living cannot ascend to the Lord in the air before the dead rise to life. (1 Thes. 4:15)

Insights: Chapter 20

According to the Bible, Jesus raises *the rest of the dead* after the thousand years, not until then. (Rev 20:4-5) If we believe the Word is true to the gospel, all other doctrines fade in its light:

> [28] "Do not marvel at this; for the hour is coming in which all who are in the graves will hear His voice [29] and come forth—those who have done good, to the resurrection of life, and those who have done evil, to the resurrection of condemnation. (Jn. 5:28-29 NKJV)

> [22] For as in Adam all die, even so in Christ shall all be made alive. ... [26] The last enemy to be destroyed is death. (1 Cor. 15:22, 26)

Before the living are caught up, <u>the dead in Christ will rise first</u>. At *the first resurrection* of new testament believers, martyrs are the first to <u>rise from their graves</u> and are caught up together with the survivors. (1 Thes. 4:16-17) Few teachers explain the resurrections, but we've read their words many times. If we believe men but not God, we'll be the gainsayers—spurning His words as we read them. Faith in the Word destroys the carnal nature and exposes false teachings. If we prefer vanity, the Word will shine its light on our hearts until we repent and believe.

Two resurrections of believers remain. His Kingdom is in the midst of them. We should rejoice in our sanctification by the knowledge of the truth that leads to redemption. Longsuffering for us, He waits for us to believe His words, but few of us have done that, *and few there be that find it. (from Mat. 7:14)*

As Jesus led the dead out of their tombs, the firstfruits of Israel lead the ascension of believers after the first resurrection. *Blessed and holy is he that hath part in the first resurrection: on such the second death hath no power, but they shall be priests of God and of Christ, and shall reign with him a thousand years. (Rev. 20:6)* Yeshua comes on a cloud to take up only the elect:

> [13] And I heard a voice from heaven saying unto me, Write, Blessed are the dead <u>which die in the Lord from hence forth</u>: Yea, saith the Spirit, that they may rest from their labours; and their works do follow them. [14] And I looked, and behold a white cloud, and <u>upon the cloud one sat</u> like unto the Son of man, having on his head a golden crown, and in his hand a sharp sickle. (Rev. 14:13-14)

The Revelation

At the sixth seal, the great trumpet of God sounds, and Jesus comes *on/in the clouds (in Mat. 24:29; Mk. 13:26)*. His appearance alarms the world. He is seated on a throne. After rising from the dead, Yeshua walked through walls, cooked fish, ate with His disciples, and finally ascended into a cloud until, on a cloud, He comes for the elect. (Mat. 24:29-31; Rev. 6:12-17; Thes. 4:16-18)

> ⁹And when he had spoken these things, while they beheld, he was taken up; and a cloud received him out of their sight. ¹⁰And while they looked stedfastly toward heaven as he went up, behold, two men stood by them in white apparel; ¹¹Which also said, Ye men of Galilee, why stand ye gazing up into heaven? <u>this same Jesus</u>, which is taken up from you into heaven, shall so come in like manner <u>as ye have seen him go into heaven</u>.
> (Acts 1:9-11) S*hall so come,* [Gr.: *ĕrchŏmai*], has a variety of applications. This means He comes/appears on a cloud.

The crown of life rewards martyrdom, but Jesus comes for us with terrible signs at His appearing as He told us in advance:

> ¹²I saw when the Lamb opened <u>the sixth seal</u>, and there was a great earthquake. The sun became as black as sackcloth made of goat's hair, and the full moon became like blood. ¹³The stars of heaven fell to the earth like a fig tree drops unripe figs when shaken by a great wind. ¹⁴The heaven ripped apart like a scroll being rolled up, and every mountain and island was moved from their places.
> ¹⁵Then the kings of the earth and the great men and the military commanders and the rich and the mighty and <u>everyone</u>—slave and free—hid themselves in the caves and among the rocks of the mountains. ¹⁶And they tell the mountains and the rocks, "Fall on us, and hide us from the face of the One seated on the throne and from <u>the wrath of the Lamb</u>. ¹⁷For the great day of their wrath has come, and who is able to stand?" (Rev. 6:12-17 TLV)

> ⁴ ... And I saw the souls of those who had been beheaded because of their testimony for Jesus and because of the word of God. They had not worshiped the beast or his image and had not received his mark on their foreheads or their hands. They came to life and reigned with Christ a thousand years. (Rev.20:4b NIV)

Insights: Chapter 20

Thy Kingdom Come

> ⁷ Behold, he is coming with the clouds, and every eye will see **him**, <u>even those who pierced him</u>, and <u>all tribes</u> of the earth will wail on account of him. Even so. Amen. (Rev. 1:7 ESV)

> ²⁸ "Do not marvel at this, for an hour is coming when all who are in the tombs will hear His voice (Jn. 5:28 ESV) [Gr.: *mnēmĕiŏn,* "monuments, tombs, or graves"]

Before the thousand years, during His wrath, Israel is envied by the world. Esau envied Jacob; his brothers envied Joseph, but all the world envied Israel. Yeshua descends on the Mount of Olives and splits it in two as an escape for the city. The great city divides in three by the great earthquake that shakes the world.

When Jesus returns He comes with armies to slay Israel's enemies. Mountains fall, cities crumble, and the earth reels. The beast and his prophet are cast into the lake of fire when the Lamb destroys their armies in Armageddon. (2:16; 19:15, 21) All kinds of birds of prey eat their dead, even eagles. (See Ezk. 39; Zec. 14.)

A mighty angel descends with a key and imprisons Satan in the pit till the thousand years end. (Cf. 9:1,11) With a rod of iron, Yeshua rules His Kingdom to bring peace to the earth and to all who trust and obey Him. God came in His Son to save us from sin, and He returns to destroy Satan's kingdom.

> ²⁶ And if Satan has risen up against himself and is divided, he cannot stand, but is coming to an end. ²⁷ But no one can enter a strong man's house and plunder his goods, unless he first binds the strong man. Then indeed he may plunder his house. (Mk. 3:26-27 ESV)

Jesus revealed the wars of the kingdoms to John after taking and unsealing its scroll to disclose it from beginning to end. At the end of time, *the heavens shall pass away with a <u>great noise</u>, and the elements shall melt with fervent heat. ... (from 2 Pet. 3:10)* John describes Yeshua as the One *from whose face the earth and the heavens fled away; and there was found no place for them. (from Rev. 20:11)* At first *empty space and darkness was upon the face of the deep.* Studying it, physicists unwittingly discovered its end: *Rolled up like a scroll (in Is. 34:4)* without any space left, the universe disappears with a big bang!

The Revelation

¹⁰ He also says,

"In the beginning, O Lord, you laid
  the foundations of the earth
 and the heavens are the work of your hands.
¹¹ They will perish, but you remain;
  they will all wear out like a garment.
¹² You will roll them up like a robe;
  like a garment they will be changed.
But you remain the same, and your years never end."
(Heb. 1:10-12a ESV)

But the day of the Lord will come like a thief, and then the heavens will pass away like a roar, and the heavenly bodies will be burned up and dissolved, and the earth and the works that are done on it will be exposed. (2 Pet. 3:10 ESV) – This happens at the end of time.

Then I saw a great white throne and him who was seated on it. From his presence earth and sky fled away, <u>and no place was found for them</u>. (Rev. 20:11 ESV) Space is gone.

The Destroyer's Last Hour

As the thousand years begin Babylon is absent. Armageddon is a grave, and the earth is changed. After Messiah reigns, at the sixth trump, four fallen angels, bound in the Euphrates, are freed as an army of two hundred million kill a third of mankind. (9:16)

In 11:18 *the nations were angry, and thy wrath is come. (Cf. 20:7-10; Ps. 2:1-3)* Ezekiel 38 sees Israel **living in peace and safety in villages without walls**—not so of their nation until the Millennial Kingdom of Yeshua (seen in Zec. 14:11 and Ezk. 39:26). At last Gog leads her enemies against Jerusalem. Fire and hail destroy them, not the sword of His mouth (in 19:15, 21; 20:7-10).

⁹ <u>And the LORD shall be king over all the earth</u>: in that day shall there be one LORD, and his name one. ... ¹¹ And men shall dwell in it, and there shall be no more utter destruction; but <u>Jerusalem shall be safely inhabited</u>. (Zech. 14:9, 11)

38 The word of the LORD came to me: ² "Son of man, set your face toward Gog, of the land of Magog, the chief prince of Meshech and Tubal, and prophesy against him ³ and say, Thus says the Lord GOD: Behold, I am against

Insights: Chapter 20

you, O Gog, chief prince of Meshech and Tubal. [4] And I will turn you about and put hooks into your jaws, and I will bring you out, and all your army, horses and horsemen, all of them clothed in full armor, a great host, all of them with buckler and shield, wielding swords. [5] Persia, Cush, and Put are with them, all of them with shield and helmet; [6] Gomer and all his hordes; Beth-togarmah from the uttermost parts of the north with all his hordes—many peoples are with you. ...

[10] "Thus says the Lord GOD: On that day, thoughts will come into your mind, and you will devise an evil scheme [11] and say, '<u>I will go up against a land of unwalled villages. I will fall upon the quiet people who dwell securely, all of them dwelling without walls and having no bars or gates</u>' ...

[14] "Therefore, son of man, prophesy, and say to Gog: Thus says the Lord GOD: On that day, when my people Israel are <u>dwelling securely</u>, will you not know it? [15] You will come from your place out of <u>the uttermost parts of the north</u>, you and many peoples with you, all of them riding on horses, a great host, a mighty army. [16] You will come up against my people Israel like a cloud covering the land. ...

[17] "Thus says the Lord GOD: Are you he of whom I spoke in former days by my servants the prophets of Israel, who in those days prophesied for years that I would bring you against them? [18] But on that day, the day that Gog shall come against the land of Israel, declares the Lord GOD, my wrath will be roused in my anger. [19] For in my jealousy and in my blazing wrath I declare, <u>On that day there shall be a great earthquake in the land of Israel</u>. [20] The fish of the sea and the birds of the heavens and the beasts of the field and all creeping things that creep on the ground, and all the people who are on the face of the earth, shall quake at my presence. <u>And the mountains shall be thrown down, and the cliffs shall fall, and every wall shall tumble to the ground</u>. [21] <u>I will summon a sword against Gog on all my mountains, declares the Lord GOD. Every man's sword will be against his brother</u>. [22] With pestilence and bloodshed I will enter into judgment with him, and I will rain upon him and his hordes and the many peoples who are with him <u>torrential rains and hailstones</u>, <u>fire and sulfur</u>. [23] So I will show

The Revelation

my greatness and my holiness and make myself known in the eyes of many nations. Then they will know that I am the LORD. (Ezk. 38:1-6, 10-11, 14-16a, 17-23 ESV)

In 20:19 *there was a great earthquake in the land of Israel,* seen at the second half of the **sixth trumpet** in 11:13 after the witnesses ascend to God at the end of **the seventieth week.** The last judgment (v. 22, p. 237) is **at the last trumpet** (in 11:15-18). **On the last day,** the dragon is cast into a lake of fire, the second death, where the beast and his false prophet are (in 20:10). The living and the dead rise before His throne for **the last judgment.**

> [8] "But the cowardly, unbelieving, abominable, murderers, sexually immoral, sorcerers, idolaters, and all liars shall have their part in the lake which burns with fire and brimstone, which is the second death."
> (Rev. 21:8 NKJV; cf. 20:15)

After the thousand years, the dragon is released at the fifth trumpet till the rest of the dead rise—saints and sinners—**at the last trumpet on the last day.** (See Rev. 11:15-18; Jn. 5:28-29)

> [7] Now <u>when the thousand years have expired</u>, Satan will be released from his prison [8] and will go out to deceive the nations which are in the four corners of the earth, <u>Gog and Magog</u>, to gather them together to battle, whose number *is* as the sand of the sea. [9] They went up on the breadth of the earth and surrounded the camp of the saints and the beloved city. <u>And fire came down from God out of heaven</u> and devoured them.
> (Rev. 20:7-9 NKJV) [Gog is a man led by Satan.]

> [2] <u>And many of those who sleep in the dust of the earth shall awake, some to everlasting life, and some to shame and everlasting contempt</u>. (Dan. 12:2 ESV)

After the tribulation the elect are caught up to Yeshua, but many more rise on the last day than at any other time. *[28]... <u>all that are in the graves</u> shall hear his voice [29] and shall come forth; they that have done good, unto the resurrection of life; and they that have done evil, unto the resurrection of damnation. (from Jn. 5:28b-29)* [adverse judgment] Some of the last shall be first.

The elect were chosen as the first resurrection of the martyrs two millennia after Jesus rose as *the firstfruits of them that slept.*

Insights: Chapter 20

The beheaded who rejected the beast and its mark rise to life at the first resurrection. They ascend together with the living to meet the Lord in the air. These are the wedding guests, waiting for the marriage to begin while His wrath is poured out on the earth. After His wrath leaves the temple, the martyrs return to earth with Messiah for His Bride. They reign a thousand years until the seventh seal's trumpets sound (in chapters 8, 9, and 11).

> [39] This is the will of the Father who sent me, that of all He has given Me, I should lose nothing, but should raise it up <u>at the last day</u>. [40] And this is the will of Him who sent Me, that everyone who sees the Son and believes in Him may have everlasting life; and I will raise him up at <u>the last day</u>. ...
> [44] No one can come to Me unless the Father who sent Me draws him; and I will raise him up <u>at the last day</u>. ...
> [54] Whoever eats My flesh and drinks My blood has eternal life, and <u>I will raise him up at the last day</u>.
> (Jn. 6:39-40, 44, 54 NKJV) [His metaphors are spiritual.]

> [11] For no one can lay any other foundation than what is already laid—which is *Yeshua* the Messiah. [12] Now if anyone builds on the foundation with gold, silver, precious stones, wood, hay, straw, [13] each one's work will become clear. For the Day will show it, because it is to be revealed by fire; and the fire itself will test each one's work—what sort it is. [14] If anyone's work built on the foundation survives, he will receive a reward. [15] If anyone's work is burned up, he will suffer loss—he himself will be saved, but as through fire. (1 Cor. 3:11-15 TLV)

The general will of God for us is that we press on for the high calling of God in Christ Jesus until we rise **on the last day** at **the last trump** when He divides the wheat from the tares and the good catch from the bad. (Mat. 13:24-30; 47-50) He judges and rewards us by the good or evil works we've done. All who are blotted out of the Book of Life are cast into the fire.

> [15] And **the seventh angel sounded**; and there were great voices in heaven, saying, The kingdoms of this world are become the kingdoms of our Lord, and of his Christ; and he shall reign for ever and ever. [16] And the four and twenty elders, which sat before God on their

seats, fell upon their faces, and worshipped God, ¹⁷ Saying, We give thee thanks, O LORD God Almighty, which art, and wast, and art to come; because thou hast taken to thee thy great power, and hast reigned. ¹⁸ And the nations were angry, and thy wrath is come, <u>and the time of the dead, that they should be judged, and that thou shouldest give reward unto thy servants the prophets, and to the saints, and them that fear thy name, small and great; and shouldest destroy them which destroy the earth</u>. (Rev. 11:15-18)

Heaven and earth flee from His Presence. There's no place for them; space is gone. All that remains is spiritual when saints and sinners stand before the Judge of all.

Jesus is the Judge on the great white throne when the living and the dead rise before Him. Those whose names are not blotted from the Book of Life have everlasting life, but hypocrites are sent to the lake of fire where the worm never dies.

The Great White Throne

Some men's sins are open beforehand, going before to judgment; and some men they follow after. Likewise also the good works of some are manifest beforehand; and they that are otherwise cannot be hid. (1 Tim. 5:24-25) The degrees of justice in the Scriptures prove God judges fairly in righteousness, according to a person's works, whether good or evil; yet our righteousness is like filthy rags to God. This is why we walk in the Spirit by faith, not in the strength of our flesh. If we discern between the two, He works through us and credits it to us because we live by faith.

When the time for the dead to rise comes, the great white throne is raised high on a *bema,* a platform, for **the judgment seat of Christ** at the **last woe, the last trumpet.** Both saints and sinners stand before Jesus who judges impartially with wisdom:

> ⁹ Therefore <u>we make it our aim</u>, whether present or absent, <u>to be well pleasing to Him</u>. ¹⁰ For we must all appear before the judgment seat of Christ, that each one may receive the things *done* in the body, according to what he has done, whether good or bad. ¹¹ Knowing, therefore the terror of the Lord, we persuade men; but we are well known to God, and I also trust are well known in your consciences. (2 Cor. 5:9-11 NKJV)

Insights: Chapter 20

It's not for us to judge outsiders, but to be unblemished by the world. The door to our heart is unlocked, ready to open for our Savior at any time.

> ¹⁵ Do not love the world or the things in the world. If anyone loves the world, the love of the Father is not in him. ¹⁶ For all that is in the world—the desires of the flesh and the desires of the eyes and pride of life—is not from the Father but is from the world. ¹⁷And the world is passing away along with its desires, but whoever does the will of God abides forever. (1 Jn. 2:15-17 ESV)

Struck by the appearance of a holy messenger, Daniel said, *... and there hath been no power left in me, and my honour hath been turned in me to corruption, yea, I have not retained power. (from Dan. 10:8 YLT)* The angel later said, *at the completion of the scattering of the power of the holy people, finished are all these. (from Dan. 12:7 YLT)* And so it is **on the last day.**

At the first trump, the beast and prophet are ancient history. At the last trump, the red dragon joins them in the lake of fire.

> ¹³ The sea gave up the dead who were in it, and Death and Hades delivered up the dead who were in them. And they were judged, each one according to his works. ¹⁴ Then Death and Hades were cast into the lake of fire. This is the second death. ¹⁵ And anyone not found written in the Book of Life was cast into the lake of fire.
> (Rev. 20:13-15)

> ²⁵ For he must reign till he hath put all enemies under his feet. ²⁶ The last enemy that shall be destroyed is death.
> (1 Cor. 15:25-26) – at the last trump on the last day.

So when this corruptible shall have put on incorruption, and this mortal shall have put on immortality, then shall be brought to pass the saying that is written, Death is swallowed up in victory. (1 Cor. 15:54) – at the last trumpet on the last day.

In *The Revelation of Jesus Christ,* He opens His testimony as the Spirit of prophecy. The one speaking to John was a man like himself whom he nearly worshiped. He described himself: *I am thy fellow servant and of thy brethren that have the testimony of Jesus: worship God: for the testimony of Jesus is the spirit of prophecy. (Rev. 19:10)*

The Revelation

His Revelation discloses the prophecies and proves the one true God is in His Son whose testimony is true. He is the Prophet greater than Moses to whom God said,

> [18] I will raise up for them a prophet like you from among their brothers. And I will put my words in his mouth, and he shall speak to them all that I command him. [19] And whoever will not listen to my words that he shall speak in my name, I myself will require it of him.
> (Deut. 18:18-19 ESV)

That which Is Perfect

After three messengers lead the way; after Elijah repairs the path; after a beast, a false prophet, and the dragon appear; after the saints resist the beast and his mark; after the beast overcomes the saints; after the great tribulation; after the virgins are sealed; after Yeshua calls the martyrs from their graves; after the **great trumpet of God;** after the firstfruits lead the way; after the elect and the martyrs ascend; after the bowls leave the Sanctuary; after the great earthquake; after the city is divided; after the dragon's kings level Babylon; after the merchants wail; after the slaughter of Gog's hordes in Armageddon; after the false prophet and beast are cast into the lake of fire; after an angel chains Satan and locks him in the abyss; after the nations are judged; after the earth is healed; after the thousand-year reign of Messiah from Jerusalem; after the great rebellion; after the first four trumpets; after Satan's release from the pit; after the seventieth week ends; after the two witnesses ascend to heaven; after the **last trumpet** on the last day; after Gog and Magog are consumed; after the devil is destroyed forever; after heaven and earth flee the Presence of the Lord; after the rest of the dead rise and are judged; after the saints are rewarded; after hypocrites and sinners are cast into the lake of fire; after Death and the Grave are added to it—then New Jerusalem descends from heaven, and all things are under Jesus' feet, then He offers His Kingdom to the Father, and Perfection is come at last. Prophecy sweeps through history like a second-hand, right on time:

> [10] For we know in part, and we prophesy in part. But when that which is perfect is come, then that which is in part shall be done away. (1 Cor. 13:10)

The Revelation of Jesus Christ

CHAPTER 21

21 Now I saw a new heaven and a new earth, for the first heaven and the first earth had passed away. Also there was no more sea. ² Then I, John, saw the holy city, New Jerusalem, coming down out of heaven from God, prepared as a bride adorned for her husband. ³ And I heard a loud voice from heaven saying, "Behold, the tabernacle of God *is* with men, and He will dwell with them, and they shall be His people. God Himself will be with them *and be* their God. ⁴ And God will wipe away every tear from their eyes; there shall be no more death, nor sorrow, nor crying. There shall be no more pain, for the former things have passed away."

⁵ Then He who sat on the throne said, "Behold, I make all things new." And He said to me, "Write, for these words are true and faithful."

⁶ And He said to me, "It is done! I am the Alpha and the Omega, the Beginning and the End. I will give of the fountain of the water of life freely to him who thirsts. ⁷ He who overcomes shall inherit all things, and I will be his God and he shall be My son. ⁸ But the cowardly, unbelieving, abominable, murderers, sexually immoral, sorcerers, idolaters, and all liars shall have their part in the lake which burns with fire and brimstone, which is the second death."

⁹ Then one of the seven angels who had the seven bowls filled with the seven last plagues came to me and talked with me, saying, "Come, I will show you the bride, the Lamb's wife." ¹⁰ And he carried me away in the Spirit to a great and high mountain, and showed me the great city, the holy Jerusalem, descending out of heaven from God, ¹¹ having the glory of God. Her light *was* like a most precious stone, like a jasper stone, clear as crystal.
¹² Also she had a great and high wall with twelve gates, and twelve angels at the gates, and names written on them, which are *the names* of the twelve tribes of the children of Israel: ¹³ three gates on the east, three gates on the north, three gates on the south, and three gates on the west.

The Revelation

[14] Now the wall of the city had twelve foundations, and on them were the names of the twelve apostles of the Lamb. [15] And he who talked with me had a gold reed to measure the city, its gates, and its wall. [16] The city is laid out as a square; its length is as great as its breadth. And he measured the city with the reed: twelve thousand furlongs. Its length, breadth, and height are equal. [17] Then he measured its wall: one hundred *and* forty-four cubits, *according* to the measure of a man, that is, of an angel.
[18] The construction of its wall was *of* jasper; and the city *was* pure gold, like clear glass. [19] The foundations of the wall of the city *were* adorned with all kinds of precious stones: the first foundation *was* jasper, the second sapphire, the third chalcedony, the fourth emerald, [20] the fifth sardonyx, the sixth sardius, the seventh chrysolite, the eighth beryl, the ninth topaz, the tenth chrysoprase, the eleventh jacinth, and the twelfth amethyst. [21] The twelve gates *were* twelve pearls: each individual gate was of one pearl. And the street of the city *was* pure gold, like transparent glass.

[22] But I saw no temple in it, for the Lord God Almighty and the Lamb are its temple. [23] The city had no need of the sun or of the moon to shine in it, for the glory of God illuminated it. The Lamb *is* its light. [24] And the nations of those who are saved shall walk in its light, and the kings of the earth bring their glory and honor into it. [25] Its gates shall not be shut at all by day (there shall be no night there). [26] And they shall bring the glory and the honor of the nations into it. [27] But there shall by no means enter it anything that defiles, or causes an abomination or a lie, but only those who are written in the Lamb's Book of Life. (Rev. 21:1-27 NKJV) [12,000 furlongs = 1,500 mi.; 144 cubits = 0.5 mi.]

Insights

She who rejected Him receives Him at last, and He calls her Beloved. She has prepared her heart for Him. At the end New Jerusalem descends from heaven as the Bride He foreknew from the beginning. He saw her as the mother of every believer, and considering her history, we've known her well. (Gal. 4:26) She too is, in a sense, born again. Jerusalem below is in bondage but above is free just as we are set free to be One with God forever.

Insights: Chapter 21

> ⁷ Let us rejoice and exult
>   and give him the glory,
> for the marriage of the Lamb has come,
>   and his Bride has made herself ready;
> ⁸ it was granted her to clothe herself
>   with fine linen, bright and pure"—
>
> for the fine linen is the righteous deeds of the saints.
> (Rev. 19:7-8 ESV)

After heaven and earth pass away, all that remains is new. The Old City is gone; New Jerusalem has come. A new earth and new heavens appear where God and the Lamb are her Temple, and the Lamb is her constant Light on the Eternal Day.

The prophecies encourage us to advance and not retreat, to press in and not fall back, to persevere and not give up. It's enough to know cowards and unbelievers must face the worst truth of all when their sins and transgressions banish them to the place where there is no death. Its worm never dies. There is no way out for hypocrites who profess the faith but live in sin. They must go where their guilt eats away at them forever. (Mk. 9:43-48) It's not that we've never sinned, but we must repent each time sin catches us. Otherwise there's no escape at the judgment.

On the other side, no regrets come to mind. No devils plague us there. Our sins were washed away, and everything is new. We live in the light of His truth and love. We were judged and faced our losses, but our victories are our rewards. Our flesh is like His because His was like ours, and when we see Him, we shall be like Him, clothed in righteous works of faith, not forgetting those who brought us the light of truth; rather, we join them who did.

Her twelve gates are named by twelve tribes of Israel, and the foundations of her walls are twelve great stones on which are inscribed the names of the twelve Jewish apostles who pioneered the faith. He puts her jewels in proper places with purposes for each one. Together we function as the family of God. In New Jerusalem, the prophecies are done and time is past. Everything is spiritual where its metaphors become our new realities.

> ² "The kingdom of heaven may be compared to a king who gave a wedding feast for his son. ³ And he sent out his slaves to call those who had been invited to the wedding feast, and they were unwilling to come. ⁴ Again

The Revelation

he sent out other slaves saying, 'Tell those who have been invited, "Behold, I have prepared my dinner; my oxen and my fattened livestock are *all* butchered and everything is ready; come to the wedding feast."' [5] But they paid no attention and went their way, one to his own farm, another to his business, [6] and the rest seized his slaves and mistreated them and killed them. [7] <u>But the king was enraged, and he sent his armies and destroyed those murderers and set their city on fire.</u> [8] Then he said to his slaves, 'The wedding is ready, but those who were invited were not worthy. [9] Go therefore to the main highways, and as many as you find *there*, invite to the wedding feast.' [10] <u>Those slaves went out into the streets and gathered together all they found, both evil and good; and the wedding hall was filled with dinner guests.</u>

[11] "But when the king came in to look over the dinner guests, he saw a man there who was not dressed in wedding clothes, [12] and he said to him, 'Friend, how did you come in here without wedding clothes?' And the man was speechless. [13] Then the king said to the servants, 'Bind him hand and foot, and throw him into the outer darkness; in that place there will be weeping and gnashing of teeth.' [14] For many are called, but few *are* chosen." (Mat. 22:2-14 NASB) [Lit.: The wedding hall, or chamber, is full of guests. Only the worthy are chosen.]

His disciples invited many Jews who rejected the invitation. They beat and killed them. So God sent the Roman army to kill and scatter them, destroying the temple and burning the city.

God gives it to the teachers to learn from Him. By faith in His Spirit as our Rabbi, we can do the same. Jews who accepted the teachings and traditions of rabbis who learned from other rabbis denied what they refused to believe. Many of our teachers do the same, but He glorifies Himself in us though we have no degrees, but His Spirit is our Teacher.

My people are destroyed for lack of knowledge. (from Hos. 4:6) His words hold true today.

[9] And he saith unto me, Write, Blessed are they which are called unto the marriage supper of the Lamb. And he saith unto me, These are the true sayings of God. (Rev. 19:9)

Insights: Chapter 21

The seventh angel leaves the temple with the last bowl of wrath, and the guests gather for the marriage supper to begin. Who are the guests, and where is the Bride? We are the guests, and His Bride is Jerusalem. (1 Pet. 2:5; Gal. 4:26) Does it test our love for her?

One of the guests wasn't prepared for the celebration of the Lamb's marriage to His Bride but was dressed in street clothes. Jesus teaches the proprieties of heaven; we must honor the Bride because He loves her as she is.

Jerusalem illustrates a supernatural law: the corruptible is first; then the incorruptible. (See 1 Cor. 15) Our body is mortal before it's spiritual, dying to live. Jerusalem is also corruptible and passes away till she descends from heaven to a new earth as His unblemished Bride. But first He makes her His own just as she is. He only desires her to receive Him with all her heart.

> ^{25} Of old hast thou laid the foundation of the earth: and the heavens are the work of thy hands. ^{26} They shall perish, but thou shalt endure: yea, all of them shall wax old like a garment; as a vesture shalt thou change them, and they shall be changed. (Ps. 102:25-26)

The submissive Bride is revealed by her loving Groom. The wedding guests gather in the finest attire. Sealed by the Spirit, our lamps are burning, and our vessels are full.

> **62** <u>For Zion's sake I will not keep silent</u>,
>   <u>and for Jerusalem's sake I will not be quiet</u>,
> until her righteousness goes forth as brightness,
>   and her salvation as a burning torch.   [her $y^e shu^c wâh$]
> ^{2} The nations shall see your righteousness,
>   and all the kings your glory,
> and you shall be called by a new name
>   that the mouth of the LORD will give.
> ^{3} You shall be a crown of beauty in the hand of the LORD,
>   and a royal diadem in the hand of your God.
> ^{4} <u>You shall no more be termed Forsaken</u>,
>   <u>and your land shall no more be termed Desolate</u>,
> <u>but you shall be called My Delight Is in Her</u>,
>   <u>and your land Married</u>;
> for the LORD delights in you,
>   <u>and your land shall be married</u>.

The Revelation

⁵ For as a young man marries a young woman,
　　so shall your sons marry you,
　<u>and as the bridegroom rejoices over the bride,</u>
　　<u>so shall your God rejoice over you.</u>

⁶ On your walls, O Jerusalem,
　　I have set watchmen;
　all the day and all the night
　　they shall never be silent.
　You who put the LORD in remembrance,
　　take no rest,
⁷ and give him no rest
　　until he establishes Jerusalem
　　and makes it a praise in the earth.
⁸ The LORD has sworn by his right hand
　　and by his mighty arm:
　"I will not again give your grain
　　to be food for your enemies,
　and foreigners shall not drink your wine
　　for which you have labored;
⁹ but those who garner it shall eat it
　　and praise the LORD,
　and those who gather it shall drink it
　　in the courts of my sanctuary."

¹⁰ Go through, go through the gates;
　　prepare the way for the people;
　build up, build up the highway;
　　clear it of stones;
　lift up a signal over the peoples.
¹¹ Behold, the LORD has proclaimed
　　to the end of the earth:
　Say to the daughter of Zion,
　　"Behold, your salvation comes;　　[your *yeshua*]
　　behold, his reward is with him,
　　and his recompense before him."
¹² And they shall be called The Holy People,
　　The Redeemed of the LORD;
　and you shall be called Sought Out,
　　<u>A City Not Forsaken</u>. (Is. 62:1-12 ESV)

　　The marriage of the Lamb is His Union with His Bride, and Jerusalem is *prepared ... for her husband. (21:2)* She has beauty for her ashes, oil for her grief, and joy to replace her heavy heart.

Insights: Chapter 21

His stunning Beauty, His Beloved, receives her King when He returns for her at the end of this age. Israel returned to the land, and as He was finishing invitations for the wedding guests, His chosen people regained Jerusalem.

> [4] And they shall rebuild the old ruins,   [their return]
> They shall raise up the former desolations,
> And they shall repair the ruined cities,
> <u>The desolations of many generations.</u> ...
> [7] Instead of your shame *you shall have* double *honor,*
> And *instead of* confusion <u>they shall rejoice in their portion.</u>
> <u>Therefore in their land they shall possess double;</u>
> <u>Everlasting joy shall be theirs.</u> ...
> [10] I will greatly rejoice in the LORD,
> My soul shall be joyful in my God;
> For He has clothed me with the garments of salvation,
> He has covered me with the robe of righteousness,
> <u>As a bridegroom decks *himself* with ornaments,</u>
> <u>And as a bride adorns *herself* with her jewels.</u>
> (Is. 61:4, 7, 10 NKJV) [Jerusalem's response]

> [7] Let us be glad and rejoice, and give honour to him: for the marriage of the Lamb is come, and his wife hath made herself ready. [8] And to her was granted that she should be arrayed in fine linen, clean and white: for the fine linen is the righteousness of saints. (Rev. 19:7-8)

His Bride begins to make herself ready. Her Savior arrives unexpectedly. She hasn't known He was the One and mourns as He passes her by. She anxiously waits for her Bridegroom till He returns. Then sheltered in His tabernacle, shielded from wrath, she rejoices as a mother with children. The curtain is stretched; the cords are lengthened; the stakes are strong. Their wedding banquet lasts a thousand years. It's the Feast of Sukkot.

> [14] I will be found by you, declares the LORD, and I will restore your fortunes and gather you from all the nations and all the places where I have driven you, declares the LORD, and I will bring you back to the place from which I sent you into exile. (Jer. 29:14 ESV)

Lucifer was king of a harlot spread over the nations when he abandoned her to the next beast. Yeshua enters Jerusalem, and though she'd played the harlot, Hosea proved God is faithful to

The Revelation

her, wooing her with His selfless love. Jerusalem is His, and He is hers when Yeshua returns to rescue His Bride:

> [8] On that day living water will flow out from Jerusalem, half of it east to the Dead Sea and half of it west to the Mediterranean Sea, in summer and in winter. [9] The LORD will be King over the whole earth. On that day there will be one LORD, and his name the only name.
> (Zec. 14:8-9 NIV)

In All the World

On Christmas Day 1969, an American evangelist took up a large cross, carrying the gospel on foot to every nation. Often in dangerous places, across deserts, through swamps, and over mountains, Arthur Blessitt returned forty years later from around the globe, the prophetic sign of the end of the age: [214] *And this gospel of the kingdom shall be preached in all the world for a witness to all nations; and <u>then shall the end come</u>. (Mat. 24:14)*

When we can't believe its difficult words because they don't fit into what we've learned, then what we believe keeps us from believing God and turns us away from the truth. When its words contradict what we think we know, then we must tear down the strongholds in order to believe the Bible. We believe His words alone because we know His perfect love casts out the fear. It's spiritual warfare, ours to win by faith, prayer, and perseverance.

When has a religion ever created a government that was not fascist or brutish, but guaranteed liberty and rights to all men and valiantly fought to fulfill them? The Bible was the republic's foundation in 1787, declaring the free exercise of religion without establishing a state church. Somehow we left our foundation.

Babel influenced Israel; she affected the church too, yet God saves His nation and His people and never breaks His Word. When the Hebrews refused to repent, He destroyed all but a remnant. If we refuse, He'll do the same to us. He loves us who love and obey Him—not by our own strength, but by His Spirit.

At the right time, our Savior will reign from Jerusalem over all the earth and all nations will go up to the city to worship the King. If we repent and pray and seek Him, we may be there too.

> [24] "'For I will take you out of the nations; I will gather you from all the countries and bring you back into your own land. (Ezk. 36:24 NIV)

Insights: Chapter 21

He didn't say she wouldn't be tested or refined, but Israel *shall endure forever.* The church glibly reacts, "That's us!" In a way, it's true. We're grafted into her olive tree; nevertheless, she was given a kingdom after the dragon nearly destroyed her in a holocaust. History proved the prophecy. His anger against Israel wouldn't last forever. He assuaged her grief when He delivered her out of the belly of the beast. Then on May 14, 2018, the American Embassy opened in Jerusalem.[215]

A National Debt

God does not forget His Jews, His inheritance. Of all mankind He entrusted them with His oracles. He kept His promises for ages and came as the seed of David. The nations heard He is God from the Jews. We owe them the grace He gave us.

> [7] Wherefore (as the Holy Ghost saith, To day if ye will hear his voice, [8] Harden not your hearts, as in the provocation, in the day of temptation in the wilderness: [9] When your fathers tempted me, proved me, and saw my works forty years. [10] Wherefore I was grieved with that generation, and said, They do always err in their heart; and they have not known my ways. [11] So I sware in my wrath, They shall not enter into my rest.
> [12] Take heed, brethren, <u>lest there be in any of you</u> an evil heart of unbelief, in <u>departing</u> from the living God. [13] But exhort one another daily, while it is called To day; lest any of you be hardened through the deceitfulness of sin. (Heb. 3:7-13) [The Hebrew writer is addressing believers.]

> [28] Concerning the gospel *they are* enemies for your sake, but concerning the election *they are* beloved for the sake of the fathers. [29] For the gifts and the calling of God are irrevocable. (Rom. 11:28-29 NKJV) Re: the Jews

Gabriel assured Daniel the Kingdom would come, but first it needed the Jews in their homeland. WW2 ended with grace after vengeance was spent, and they were free to go. (Cf. Rom. 11:22)

> [6] For <u>a Child</u> hath been born to us, <u>A Son</u> hath been given to us, And the princely power is on his shoulder, And <u>He doth call his name</u> Wonderful Counselor, Mighty God, Father of Eternity, Prince of Peace. (Is. 9:6 YLT)

The Revelation

The Holy Spirit is our Counselor and the Father, the Ancient of Days, but here He calls His Son, "the Counselor, Father of Eternity, and Mighty God." We are baptized in the name of the Father, Son, and Holy Spirit because God is One Spirit in His Son by the Father. Only one name is higher than all, and by that One we are saved. Yeshua/Jesus is His name, and His name is called the Word of God. The Word is "Salvation."

The Child who was born to them, the Son who was given, defeated sin, hell, and death for the Jews and the nations, yet He made His name famous among the gentiles by His Son.

Jesus Christ is the name that saves our whole spirit, soul, and body, offering salvation from hell, even for gentiles, yet it's used as a curse. Peter told his fellow Jews, *Neither is there salvation in any other: for there is none other name under heaven given among men whereby we must be saved. (Acts 4:12)*

> ¹⁰ "And I will pour out on the house of David and the inhabitants of Jerusalem a spirit of grace and supplication. They will look on me, the one they have pierced, and they will mourn for him as one mourns for an only child, and grieve bitterly for him as one grieves for a firstborn son. (Zec. 12:10) [David was king over an undivided Israel.]

> ²⁴ I will take you from the nations and gather you from all the countries and bring you into your own land. ²⁵ I will sprinkle clean water on you, and you shall be clean from all your uncleannesses, and from all your idols I will cleanse you. ²⁶ And I will give you a new heart, and a new spirit I will put within you. And I will remove the heart of stone from your flesh and give you a heart of flesh. ²⁷ And I will put my Spirit within you, and cause you to walk in my statutes and be careful to obey my rules. ²⁸ You shall dwell in the land that I gave to your fathers, and you shall be my people, and I will be your God. (Ezk. 36:24-28 ESV)

Why did God allow a holocaust? History is replete with His severity against them for their unbelief, warning us all:

> ²³ And the nations shall know that the house of Israel went into captivity for their iniquity, because they dealt so treacherously with me that I hid my face from them and gave them into the hand of their adversaries, and they all fell by the sword. (Ezk. 39:23 ESV)

Insights: Chapter 21

Forty years after the resurrection and ascension of Jesus Christ, the Jews lost their nation and their temple. God tracked them down like a hunter after game for almost two thousand years, but just as gentiles are blinded to His Revelation, the Jews can't see what He hides from them until He unveils it them. That is the glorious mystery of the Holy Bible. It takes the Holy Spirit to disclose its words. They are nonsense to the unbeliever:

> [22] For these be the days of vengeance, that all things which are written may be fulfilled. [23] But woe unto them that are with child, and to them that give suck, in those days! for there will be great distress in the land, and wrath upon this people. [24] And they shall fall by the edge of the sword, and shall be led away captive, into all nations: and Jerusalem shall be trodden down of the Gentiles, until the times of the Gentiles be fulfilled.
> (Luke 21:22-24) – Yeshua

In Jeremiah 51 Babylon was cursed for her animosity against the Jews. The vengeance of God ended, but their killers cannot justify their evil works. Grace is apart from its recipient's deeds. It comes from the heart of its benefactor. Thus God graciously gave the Jews the Kingdom but judicially sent the beast to hell:

> [11] "I watched then because of the sound of the pompous words which the horn was speaking; I watched till the beast was slain, and its body destroyed and given to the burning flame. (Dan. 7:11 NKJV)

The grace God granted the Jews was in His faithfulness to Abraham, Isaac, and Jacob. Whoever opposes Israel opposes God who proves Himself in their Bible as a light to the nations. Now Jews are finding a personal Savior in Yeshua their Messiah.

Many Jews are oblivious to God on a daily basis though He continues extending His grace. As tribes make aliyah, Israel and Judah are uniting at last. [See Ezk. 37:15-28] But till they receive Him, their trials continue:

> [7] Your country is desolate, your cities are burned with fire: your land, strangers devour it in your presence, and it is desolate, as overthrown by strangers. ... [9] Except the LORD of hosts had left unto us a very small remnant, we should have been as Sodom, we should have been like unto Gomorrah. (Is. 1:7, 9)

The Revelation

⁹ ... When your judgments come upon the earth,
the people of the world learn righteousness.
(Is. 26:9b NIV)

There is no question that God chastens, even scourges, His own. We know about suffering, or we don't belong to Him. He may bring us to the brink of death, even through its veil, only to sanctify us to keep us. Enduring all kinds of trials, our holiness is in Christ by faith in His power, and He works mightily in us. (See Heb. 12) We can save our nation by laying down our lives for her through the power that works within us by faith.

> ¹² For we wrestle not against flesh and blood, but against principalities, against powers, against the rulers of the darkness of this world, against spiritual wickedness in high places. ¹³ Wherefore take unto you the whole armour of God, that ye may be able to withstand in the evil day, and having done all, to stand. (Eph. 6:12-13)

Let's not let love grow cold. He commands us to love others as ourselves and to love God more than anyone else regardless of the times. We're to do our best to be at peace with everyone, a challenge in today's vitriolic and often violent culture, but He has given us His Holy Spirit, intending to love them through us.

His tapestry of words is interwoven through both testaments. The Witness that the Word is One, their Artisan, is the Author:

> ⁴⁴ Then he said to them, "These are my words that I spoke to you while I was still with you, that everything written about me in the Law of Moses and the Prophets and the Psalms must be fulfilled." ⁴⁵ Then he opened their minds to understand the Scriptures, ⁴⁶ and said to them, "Thus it is written, that the Christ should suffer and on the third day rise from the dead, ⁴⁷ and that repentance for the forgiveness of sins should be proclaimed in his name to all nations, beginning in Jerusalem. (Lk. 24:44-47 ESV)

> ⁴ Who hath ascended up into heaven, or descended? who hath gathered the wind in his fists? who hath bound the waters in a garment? who hath established all the ends of the earth? What is his name, and what is his son's name, if thou canst tell? (Prov. 30:4)

The Revelation of Jesus Christ

CHAPTER 22

22 Then the angel showed me the river of the water of life, as clear as crystal, flowing from the throne of God and of the Lamb ² down the middle of the great street of the city. On each side of the river stood the tree of life, bearing twelve crops of fruit, yielding its fruit every month. And the leaves of the tree are for the healing of the nations. ³ No longer will there be any curse. The throne of God and of the Lamb will be in the city, and his servants will serve him. ⁴ They will see his face, and his name will be on their foreheads. ⁵ There will be no more night. They will not need the light of a lamp or the light of the sun, for the Lord God will give them light. And they will reign for ever and ever.

⁶ The angel said to me, "These words are trustworthy and true. The Lord, the God who inspires the prophets, sent his angel to show his servants the things that must soon take place."

⁷ "Look, I am coming soon! Blessed is the one who keeps the words of the prophecy written in this scroll."

⁸ I, John, am the one who heard and saw these things. And when I had heard and seen them, I fell down to worship at the feet of the angel who had been showing them to me. ⁹ But he said to me, "Don't do that! I am a fellow servant with you and with your fellow prophets and with all who keep the words of this scroll. Worship God!"

¹⁰ Then he told me, "Do not seal up the words of the prophecy of this scroll, because the time is near. ¹¹ Let the one who does wrong continue to do wrong; let the vile person continue to be vile; let the one who does right continue to do right; and let the holy person continue to be holy."

¹² "Look, I am coming soon! My reward is with me, and I will give to each person according to what they have done. ¹³ I am the Alpha and the Omega, the First and the Last, the Beginning and the End.

¹⁴ "Blessed are those who wash their robes, that they may have the right to the tree of life and may go through

The Revelation

the gates into the city. ¹⁵ Outside are the dogs, those who practice magic arts, the sexually immoral, the murderers, the idolaters and everyone who loves and practices falsehood.

¹⁶ "I, Jesus, have sent my angel to give you this testimony for the churches. I am the Root and the Offspring of David, and the bright Morning Star."

¹⁷ The Spirit and the bride say, "Come!" And let the one who hears say, "Come!" Let the one who is thirsty come; and let the one who wishes take the free gift of the water of life.

¹⁸ I warn everyone who hears the words of the prophecy of this scroll: If anyone adds anything to them, God will add to that person the plagues described in this scroll. ¹⁹ And if anyone takes words away from this scroll of prophecy, God will take away from that person any share in the tree of life and in the Holy City, which are described in this scroll.

²⁰ He who testifies to these things says, "Yes, I am coming soon."

Amen. Come, Lord Jesus.

²¹ The grace of the Lord Jesus be with God's people. Amen. (Revelation 22:1-21 NIV)

Insights

³ Blessed is the one who reads aloud the words of this prophecy, and blessed are those who hear it and take to heart what is written in it, because the time is near.
(Rev. 1:3 NIV)

Jesus knew the hardships we would face as we *work out* our *salvation with fear and trembling. (See Phil. 2:12)* He knows the warfare ahead of us and is always with us who love Him and keep His words to the end. He loved us as sinners and gave us new birth to make us holy as He is holy. He gave us His Spirit to empower us so that we can do great feats by faith in His name.

In our love for the truth, we secure our salvation, living by faith in Jesus Christ who removed our curse. God prepares us by our faith in the truth. A blessing is on us who read and hear *The*

Insights: Chapter 22

Revelation of Jesus Christ. Its words open our minds to understanding at the end of the age. As that happens, we realize the end is just the beginning when our pain turns to joy and time, to eternity.

The Mystery in the Midst

Yeshua is in the heart of the Word as the Seed in the bosom of God. He's the Word in the Spirit who spoke in the midst of the fiery bush as the Angel of God. He is in the middle of the Father, Son, and Spirit, in the midst of the seven churches. When two or three are in prayer, He's in the middle of us there. In the midst of the years, He recalled mercy. (Hab. 3:2) He was the Word in the woman's seed, carried in the midst of the virgin. He lived between two covenants and died between two Passover meals on a wooden cross between two thieves. He's the middle of three Seder matzos, the *afikoman,* buried in its linens.[216] He descended to the middle of the earth and rose in the midst of the first day as the Firstfruits in the middle of Passover week. Jesus walked amid two men on their way to Emmaus. He appears in the midst of a cloud and comes for half the virgins at midnight. He rules between two resurrections and between two judgments, amid seven plagues and seven trumpets in the middle of Daniel's seventieth week; between the sabbaths of Succoth; amid twenty-four thrones and four living creatures in the middle of the fire in the midst of the throne of God as the voice that calls out from amid the creatures and dwells in our midst forever.

> 1 In the beginning was the Word, and the Word was with God, and the Word was God. ²The same was in the beginning with God. ³All things were made by him; and without him was not any thing made that was made. ⁴In him was life; and <u>the life was the light of men</u>. ⁵And the light shineth in darkness; and the darkness comprehended it not.
> ⁶There was a man sent from God, whose name was John. ⁷The same came for a witness, to bear witness of the Light, that all men through him might believe. ⁸He was not that Light, but was sent to bear witness of that Light. ⁹<u>That was the true Light, which lighteth every man that cometh into the world</u>. ¹⁰He was in the world, and the world was made by him, and the world knew him not.

The Revelation

¹¹ He came unto his own, and his own received him not. ¹² But as many as received him, <u>to them gave he power to become the sons of God</u>, even to them that believe on his name: ¹³ Which were born, not of blood, nor of the will of the flesh, <u>nor of the will of man, but of God</u>. ¹⁴ And the Word was made flesh, and dwelt among us, (and we beheld his glory, the glory as of the only begotten of the Father,) full of grace and truth. (Jn. 1:1-14) [Gr.: *exousia*, "power or right to become."]

All nature contains similes of spiritual truths for us to see the ways of God. The creation describes its spiritual counterparts, prompting the Savior to parables and metaphors. As Jesus taught the people, God gave His Son knowledge, understanding, and wisdom. Inside each metaphor is its spiritual reason. His insights compared them to heaven, unveiling it to us by what's around us.

²⁴ Then said Jesus unto his disciples, If anyone will come after me, let him deny himself, and take up his cross, and follow me. ²⁵ For whosoever will save his life shall lose it: and whosoever will lose his life for my sake shall find it. ²⁶ For what is a man profited, if he shall gain the whole world, and lose his own soul? or what shall a man give in exchange for his soul? ²⁷ For the Son of man shall come in the glory of his Father with his angels; and then he shall reward every man according to his works. (Mat. 16:24-27)

In 1948 Jews were rejoicing in their freedom when Egypt struck at midnight. Instantly a desperate war for the soul of their nation began when their half-brothers sprang on them like a trap! The Jews weren't ready. Are we? We're enthralled by a revival and enchanted by a rapture, but to suffer and die for our faith, we lack preparedness. (Hos. 4:6; Mat. 22:1-13; Lk. 12:35-40)

We are in His Son at the right hand of the Father—how high a calling! Angels fell into darkness for envy of the gift He freely gives us. He'll appear and raise us from the dust or catch us up—in Him, not even death can destroy us who endure to the end.

> 4 And it will come about in the last days
> That the mountain of the house of the LORD
> Will be established as the chief of the mountains.
> It will be raised above the hills,
> And the peoples will stream to it. ...

Insights: Chapter 22

> ³ And He will judge between many peoples
> <u>And render decisions for mighty, distant nations</u>.
> Then they will hammer their swords into plowshares
> And their spears into pruning hooks;
> Nation will not lift up sword against nation,
> And never again will they train for war.
> ⁴ Each of them will sit under his vine
> And under his fig tree,
> With no one to make *them* afraid,
> For the mouth of the LORD of hosts has spoken.
> (Micah 4:1, 3-4 NASB)

The Jews returned to the land joyfully, but after a holocaust. On their way to its wilderness, the British intercepted them and sent them to internment camps in Cyprus till Britain dropped the mandate in May 1948.[217] Jews learned their lesson well: nothing is treasured that isn't worth the cost it takes to keep it.

> 46 God is our refuge and strength,
>   a very present help in trouble.
> ² Therefore we will not fear though the earth gives way,
>   though the mountains be moved
>   into the heart of the sea,
> ³ though its waters roar and foam,
>   though the mountains tremble at its swelling. Selah
> ⁴ There is a river whose streams make glad the city of God,
>   the holy habitation of the Most High.
> ⁵ God is in the midst of her; she shall not be moved;
>   God will help her when morning dawns.
> ⁶ The nations rage, the kingdoms totter;
>   he utters his voice, the earth melts.
> ⁷ The LORD of hosts is with us;
>   the God of Jacob is our fortress. Selah
> (Psalm 46:1-7 ESV)

Yeshua spoke in parables for His followers to hear, see, and learn what He kept from others. Often not even the disciples could understand the Lord. They were puzzled by the spiritual way He perceived the world. He ascended to send us His Spirit and teach us the foundations of our faith as witnesses of Christ Himself because God is Spirit, and He has given His Spirit to us.

> ²⁸ And it shall come to pass, that like as I have watched over them to pluck up, and to break down, and to throw

The Revelation

down, and to destroy, and to afflict; so will I watch over them, to build, and to plant, saith the LORD. ...
³⁴ And they shall teach no more every man his neighbour, and every man his brother, saying, Know the LORD: for they shall all know me, from the least of them unto the greatest of them, saith the LORD: for I will forgive their iniquity, and I will remember their sin no more. (Jer. 31:28, 34)

What Time Is It?

Although He sends us like sheep among wolves, we contain something far beyond anything the world can imagine. Darkness reigns over the earth. We are the only light they'll ever see. Our significance is in our service to others as we follow Christ. We are here as the light of the world; we are the flavor of life as the salt of the earth, sanctified and made holy by faith, standing for righteousness against ungodliness. We who live for Christ have had the right to vote for the values of our faith, but the nation is fallen; therefore, we confess our sin to God, trusting His promise to cleanse us. Then we get up and go on; that takes faith too.

God called Abram out of Chaldea into an unknown land and increased his fortune as he went. He provided for the Hebrews in the wilderness by Moses and fed Elijah by ravens at a brook. He slew a giant with a stone from a shepherd boy's sling and the Midianites by Gideon's three hundred. With a few small fish and some bread, God in Christ fed five thousand men. *In everything with prayer and supplication <u>with thanksgiving</u>, let your requests be made known unto God. (Phil. 4:6)*

Yeshua has risen and ascended into heaven to send us His Holy Spirit so we can live the lives we were born to live. We've all sinned and offended one another, but by God's grace for us, we can forgive the offenses of others. (Jas. 3:2) Let's do it.

Jesus said when we see the start of these things, redemption is imminent: the perplexity of nations, signs in the earth and signs in the seas and the skies. Jews have returned to the land, and Jerusalem is their capital.

The Middle East is at war, and so is the world. Israel resists the One who loves her while Yeshua waits for her to see Him. *This generation will not pass, till all these things be fulfilled. (Mat. 24:34)* No one knows the exact day or hour, but the signs and the seasons indicate that we are living at the end of the age.

Insights: Chapter 22

³² Now learn a parable of the fig tree; when his branch is yet tender, and putteth forth leaves, ye know that summer *is* nigh: ³³ so likewise ye, when ye shall see all these things, know that it is near, *even* at the doors. ³⁴ Verily I say unto you, <u>this generation shall not pass, till all these things be fulfilled</u>. ³⁵ Heaven and earth shall pass away, but my words shall not pass away. (Mat. 24:32-35) Yeshua

³⁵ Thus says the LORD,
   Who gives the sun for light by day
    And the fixed order of the moon and stars
      for light by night,
   Who stirs up the sea so that its waves roar;
   The LORD of hosts is His name:
³⁶ "If this fixed order departs
   From before Me," declares the LORD,
   "Then the offspring of Israel also will cease
   From being a nation before Me forever."
³⁷ Thus says the LORD,
   "If the heavens above can be measured
   And the fountains of the earth searched out below,
   Then I will also cast off all the offspring of Israel
   For all that they have done," declares the LORD.
   (Jer. 31:35-37 NASB)

He speaks and we fall at His feet as though dead. He comes on a cloud, and Purity penetrates the air. The earth trembles with cataclysms. The great trumpet of God sounds and angels catch us up. Then He comforts us by His Word, resting His Sword on us like a Scepter.

¹² He said therefore, A certain nobleman went into a far country to receive for himself a kingdom, and to return.
¹³ And he called his ten servants, and delivered them ten pounds, and said unto them, Occupy till I come.
(Lk. 19:12-13)

UNVEILED!

The Child ...

The CHILD

The LORD came to Solomon in a dream, saying, "Ask what I shall give you." The idea of ruling a kingdom overwhelmed the new king who requested an understanding heart and the ability to discern good from evil. His desires pleased God who promised his request. He woke and Solomon offered acceptable sacrifices to God on an altar in Gibeon; then, held a feast for his servants:

[16] Then two prostitutes came to the king and stood before him. [17] The one woman said, "Oh, my lord, this woman and I live in the same house, and I gave birth to a child while she was in the house. [18] Then on the third day after I gave birth, this woman also gave birth. And we were alone. There was no one else with us in the house; only we two were in the house. [19] And this woman's son died in the night, because she lay on him. [20] And she arose at midnight and took my son from beside me, while your servant slept, and laid him at her breast, and laid her dead son at my breast. [21] When I rose in the morning to nurse my child, behold, he was dead. But when I looked at him closely in the morning, behold, he was not the child that I had borne." [22] But the other woman said, "No, the living child is mine, and the dead child is yours." The first said, "No, the dead child is yours, and the living child is mine." Thus they spoke before the king.

[23] Then the king said, "The one says, 'This is my son that is alive, and your son is dead'; and the other says, 'No; but your son is dead, and my son is the living one.' [24] And the king said, "Bring me a sword." So a sword was brought before the king. [25] And the king said, "Divide the living child in two, and give half to the one and half to the other." [26] Then the woman whose son was alive said to the king, because her heart yearned for her son, "Oh, my lord, give her the living child, and by no means put him to death." But the other said, "He shall be neither mine nor yours; divide him." [27] Then the king answered and said, "Give the living child to the first woman, and by no means put him to death; she is his mother." [28] And all Israel heard of the judgment that the king had rendered, and they stood in awe of the king, because they perceived that the wisdom of God was in him to do justice. (1 Kg. 3:16-28 ESV)

The Child

Though not an allegory, there's a message hidden in the true story of the two women. Theirs is an ancient argument between envy and ownership that applies to Abraham's sons by different mothers, Hagar and Sarah, whose progeny are Arabs and Jews.

Ishmael was born of a servant in the natural way, but Isaac, of an aged and barren wife's faith and an old man's trust in the promise of God. This courtroom case was included in the Bible to lend insight to an age-old mystery: envy is kindred to hatred.

Both women in Solomon's court were harlots and each had birthed a child. One mother lay on hers, suffocating him as they slept. After her own child's death, she coveted her friend's baby. Though caring nothing for him, she envied the other woman's motherhood. They brought the living child before Solomon.

Ishmaelites and Israelites, present-day Arabs and Jews, live side by side as neighbors. Both had known harlotry though they had each been given lands to keep and nourish.

Since their return to their homeland, the Jews have cultivated its fields, and the desert sands that had lain waste for millennia now thrive with life and greenery because they have faithfully cared for their land. Their half-brothers beside them have lived with similar soil but haven't tilled, cultivated, or seeded it, so the ground remains a vastly barren and fruitless desert.

Israel is the living child. Jerusalem is his heart. The one who gave him life nurtures and protects him as a true mother would. Her neighbors want the land divided because, over the centuries, their envy turned to hatred. If they could acquire the land, they would destroy it, but in Solomon's court, the matter is plain to see: the true mother's child lives.

No one can thwart the promises of God or prevent His words from fulfillment. Though they hate their neighbors, they cannot annihilate the remnant of His chosen people, because the God of Israel is faithful to His Word as the only true God.

Solomon's gift of wisdom was made famous by his solution to the conflict. As the king judged the case between the women, soon the Son of David will be enthroned in Jerusalem as King and Judge to declare the promises and to administer justice on behalf of the true mother on the Day of the Lord when the case goes to Court.

UNVEILED!

Isaiah 18

¹ Ah, land of whirring wings
   that is beyond the rivers of Cush,   [west of Egypt/Africa]
² which sends ambassadors by the sea,
   in vessels of papyrus on the waters! [w/ satchels of papers]
  Go, you swift messengers,   [or angels]
   to a nation tall and smooth,   [drawn out and independent/
   to a people feared near and far,   obstinate]
   a nation mighty and conquering,
    whose land the rivers divide.   [cleave]
³ All you inhabitants of the world,
   you who dwell on the earth,
   when a signal is raised on the mountains, look!
   When a trumpet is blown, hear!
⁴ For thus the LORD said to me:
   "I will quietly look from my dwelling
   like clear heat in sunshine,
   like a cloud of dew in the heat of harvest."
⁵ For <u>before the harvest</u>, when the blossom is over,
   and the flower becomes a ripening grape,
   he cuts off the shoots with pruning hooks,
   and the spreading branches he lops off and clears away.
⁶ They shall all of them be left
   to the birds of prey of the mountains
   and to the beasts of the earth.
   And the birds of prey will summer on them,
   and all the beasts of the earth will winter on them.
⁷ At that time tribute will be brought to the LORD of hosts
   from a people tall and smooth,   [drawn out & independent/
   from a people feared near and far,   obstinate]
   a nation mighty and conquering,
   whose land the rivers divide,   [cleave]
   <u>to Mount Zion, the place of the name
   of the LORD of hosts</u>. (Is. 18:1-7 ESV)

The location of Cush is contested by historians, but biblical Cush was in Africa. Some Bibles call it Ethiopia, a Greek name. Its land was south of Egypt in southern Nubia, now Ethiopia.[228] However, in Isaiah's day the Cushites had conquered Egypt.[229] This is why Cushites came *out of Egypt.* (2 Chr. 12:3 YLT) They would have been there after Egypt regained her land. *Beyond the rivers of Cush* indicates a nation distant from Isaiah, certainly west of Egypt—maybe west of Africa. Anything beyond Cush was distant from the prophet; therefore the land is west, beyond

UNVEILED!

Cush. The nation was unnamed because it was unknown, but its wings are whirring, clattering, spinning, and noisy, unlike birds. [Heb: $ts^olatsal$, "clattering, whirring, buzzing."] It's a picture of wings that contain noisy engines. An American invention in 1903, the airplane came just in time for two world wars.[230]

What about boats of reed carrying ambassadors across the sea? Imagine wooden ships in the middle of the Atlantic Ocean, and we can see why they were compared to vessels of papyrus, or bulrushes. Would we take a trip on a wooden ship miles above the ocean floor? They often died in storms at sea, swallowed by its perilous waves.

One version has, *sending by sea ambassadors, even with implements of reed on the face of the waters. (YLT)* At her inception, Benjamin Franklin was the first American diplomat, taking excursions to England and France with documents and treaties.[231] Europe's diplomats did the same in return.

The nation is "drawn out" [Heb.: *mâshak*], "obstinate, or independent" [Heb.: *mowrat*]. The eagle's wings were *pulled off* the lion's back (in Dan. 7:4). [Aram.: *m'rat*, "pull off"] Drawn out of other nations, her people were obstinate and independent. [The words' double-meanings are intentional.]

Determined to strike out on their own, pioneers explored the land and crossed it to discover its extent. Pressing westward, they plowed its fields; risked their lives; settled its wilderness; and built towns, farms, and ranches. Marking state borders, the populace increased and built highways, railroads, and bridges.

Her people are *feared near and far, mighty and conquering;* she is the leopard, given dominion. (Dan. 7:6) Her *messengers* (Rev. 14:6-9) speak *to the earth and to every nation,* sending out *signals* as the whole world watches and listens. (18: 3, p. 267)

Isaiah saw a mighty nation *whose land the rivers divide.* This undoubtedly pinpoints the nation by her geography, including her many rivers. Some versions have, *whose land the rivers [or floods] have spoiled,* which is incorrect. The Hebrew word *baza* means "cleave, split along natural lines, or divide." *Rivers that divide the land* reveal her location. (18:2) Forty-four of her states have rivers as borders.[232] Together the words describe America, not Britain, Russia, South Africa, or any other land on the earth. Twelve states were *meted out,* surveyed with straight lines.[233]

Isaiah 18

In verse 4 God is Sovereign, intensely but quietly watching. He is in control, unmovable, impassable. *Like a clear heat upon herbs, and like a cloud of dew in the heat of harvest (KJV). A clear heat* is intense, one that can burn the herbs, but *a cloud of dew* refreshes both harvest and harvesters. The way God deals with her is a warning to the world.

In verse 5 at the fullness of time, there is a great slaughter. Multitudes of bodies are left to the scavenging birds and beasts. Her judgment comes <u>before the harvest</u> as her fruit is ripening. In Revelation 15 the first harvest is the first resurrection, and the next yields His wrath, but this is before the harvest. [Heb.: *gamal* is translated *unripe (in YLT);* but is "ripen" in several versions and in (ZGE); *the flower becomes a ripening grape (in ESV).*] This nation nearly reaches her fullness.

Isaiah 18 refers to a powerful nation, unknown in his time; not in her youth, but *when the blossom is over, and her flower becomes a ripening grape (in 18:5).* After that, the symbolism is about a great slaughter, the judgment of God. Israel is a nation, Zion, when this land is broken, humbled, and finally healed.

The importance of America's place as the sister land to Israel can't be overstated. The two have had close ties, and God will not forget her, but like Israel, her sins have separated her from Him. The blood of innocents is on her hands. Before He saves the nation from total destruction, He cuts off her spreading branches, her strength. His pruning hooks reach her high places. The result of her judgment proves His intention to humble her by correcting her course and to save her from utter destruction.

Terrible times have come and gone, and millions of souls have been lost. The bodies had lain in our own fields in earlier years; then in Europe, Africa, Asia, and the ME, but this is when Israel is a nation. Its imagery shows a land out of destruction like life out of death when at last she offers a gift to God in Zion.

The judgment is severe but ends with an offering to God in Jerusalem *from a nation, feared near and far, mighty and conquering, whose land its rivers divide.* She brings a tribute—a gift, an act, or repayment, given in gratitude for a blessing or act of favor—to the LORD on Mount Zion, Jerusalem. ... *for out of Zion shall go forth the law, and the word of the LORD from Jerusalem. (Isaiah 2:3c)*

UNVEILED!

The LORD is *like a cloud of dew in the heat of harvest* to His people. (From 18:4) After the trials, her faith is rewarded, and her survivors humbly rise up with a gift of thanks to God, perhaps for life itself and for a redeemed nation too.

America has been weakened by atheism, immorality, and a drug culture. For decades, millions of children have been losing their future and their hope. Denying her faith under spells that deceive her, America is losing liberty, even foundational natural rights endowed by her Creator.

The church must act as salt and light to preserve civilization. Jesus never compromised His righteousness with the culture that ultimately killed Him; we must never let go of His goodness.

The Word of God is a Sword that divides us. He didn't come to bring peace to this world, but to convict it because the world is evil. He doesn't unite us but by personal radical transformation —the new birth. Though we're divided from this world, we're united together in Him if His Word abides in us and we remain in Him. Our country depends on our return to the Holy Bible and to prayers that embrace our nation's biblical foundations.

No country is separate from its founders' faith. Governments are formed by what their founders believe—it's always been that way. This is a dark world, and we've fallen by blindness to our own sins though we easily spot ours in others.

America matters to God; she's been a sister to Israel since 1947. However, she has fallen by the removal of the Holy Bible from her culture, and we must pray to save the nation God chose for us to inhabit. We must follow Christ in meekness, yielded to do His will if we hope to inherit the new earth. Prayer makes a difference because God hears every word.

> [10] that I may know Him and the power of His resurrection and the fellowship of His sufferings, being conformed to His death; [11] in order that I may attain to the resurrection from the dead. ... (Phil. 3:8, 10-11 NASB)

> [14] I press on toward the goal for the prize of the upward call of God in Christ Jesus. [15] Let us therefore, as many as are perfect, have this attitude; and if in anything you have a different attitude, God will reveal that also to you; (Phil. 3:14-15 NASB) ["Perfect" here is defined as "mature and of full age, made complete" by the exercise of godliness.]

The Order of Events

The Summaries

In Revelation the chapters and their mysteries are mostly out of order and full of metaphors, hidden until the end of the age. Chapter 1 introduces the Messiah as the Sacrifice Lamb Yeshua. His messages to the congregations are in chapters 2 and 3. These things were spoken for anyone who has an ear to hear.

Chapter 4 has four living creatures in heaven, also in 5 when the Lamb is chosen to open the scroll. Chapter 6 describes each of the six seals. After the sixth seal, 7 shows 144,000 male virgin Israelites in heaven who are also there in 14:3 and in 15:7 before the bowls of wrath begin, which end in chapter 16.

Chapters 8, 9, 10, and 11 happen after the thousand years. 12 is a vision of heaven, introducing the dragon from ages past. The fiery red dragon is cast to earth. 17:1-11 is next; then Daniel 7 and WW2 lead to Revelation 13, exposing the collusion of the beasts whose lives are prolonged till they lose their dominion.

Together they formed the UN, and a more sinister union.[218] The leopard has dominion and is the beast's body with the dragon's throne in 13:2. Three beasts in unison, the beast with seven heads and ten horns is an embedded international government. The dragon has two horns like a lamb and rises from the ground, *diverse from the first beast, whose mortal wound was healed;* yet he was the first beast. His prophet orders the mark, the number, and the title of the beast, and the beast with a mark is the dragon. 13 leads us to 17:12-18 when his ten kings return to the scarlet beast to destroy his former city Mystery Babylon.

Some chapters are synchronous with their mates. In 13 the beast gets the dragon's throne, which is his city. Afterward the beast with horns like a lamb rises as a false religious leader and his prophet with the mark of the beast. These bring us to 6:9-17; then chapters 14 –15, all of 16, 17:12-18 to chapter 18; then 19 through 20:1-6. Chapters 6, 7, 12, 13, 14, 15, 16, 17, 18, 19, and 20:1-3 are pre-millennial, but out of order. 20:4-6 is during the thousand years. Chapters 8 –11 are post–millennial with details in 20:7-15. 21 –22 are from the end of this world to eternity.

The end of Babylon in 18 was foreseen in Dan. 2. Rev. 20 is an overview of the Kingdom to the end of time, leading to the new heavens, the new earth, and New Jerusalem in 21 and 22.

UNVEILED!

Let's Track the Beasts

In Revelation 12 a fiery red dragon had seven heads with crowns and ten horns with none. In 17 the same beast had seven heads and seven kings; five had fallen; the sixth was Rome's. Its horns, with no kings in 12, were kings with no kingdom yet in 17. Soon after Napoleon conquered the REGN, he was defeated as the seventh king.

As WW1 ended, Britain overcame the Ottoman Empire and dominated the Middle East. In Versailles Brits set the borders for Iraq, Israel, Trans-Jordan, Syria, and Lebanon by 1922. They established twelve new nations in Europe as well.

In Daniel 7:7 the horns of the dragon rose out of the REGN. With the old order gone, the ten kings were granted kingdoms by the Treaty of Versailles in 1920–1922.[219]

Hitler claimed the German-speaking lands in Europe. Three kings fell before him, but all ten gave up their crowns (in Rev. 17:11-13). Seven heads and ten horns are on the beast that gained the dragon's throne (in Rev. 13:1-2). Its *horns have crowns,* not its heads, which lost great empires to wars. The beast has a mouth, so he speaks by a man who continues forty-two months, the first half of Daniel's seventieth week. (Rev. 13:5; Dan. 9:24-26)

Chapter 13 has three beasts: the dragon with a deadly wound handed his throne to the beast. After the head of the dragon was healed by the beast, he rose from perdition as a beast with lamb's horns. At the end, these beasts rule the nations. The leaders use false wonders and lies to win the world. (2 Thes. 2)

The two-horned beast is the union of false religions, merged in a beast speaking as a dragon. It is the duplicitous kingdom of the dragon who speaks with a false prophet looking like a lamb.

The horns of the terrible beast of Daniel are ten kings that return to the scarlet beast, now the EU. From the beast of 13, they give their kingdom to the dragon in 17:17. Babylon ruled the kings of the earth as his spiritual capital with the scarlet beast in 17, but now the beast in 13 carries the dragon's throne.

The dragon carried Babylon to Rome and into her church; then to Berlin where he destroyed the Jews but was slain when his head was bruised. The smith fans coals into flames to shape an instrument for his work, but no weapon formed against God's servants prospers. (See Is. 54:16-17) Despite the fires we rise.

The Order of Events

After his body was slain, his deadly wound was healed, and the dragon came out of the earth as a beast with two small horns. The wars in Europe and the Pacific proved Dan. 7:6: the leopard was given dominion, but since his alliance with the lion and the bear in 1945, the leopard changed. Roosevelt was influenced by Stalin and Churchill. Their close ties are revealed by the beast in 13. Their governments make the beasts different, but now an international government rises from the deep to devour the earth.

Out of Babylon the Great, a liar rises as a blaspheming ruler who overcomes the saints. After he arrives *the first beast whose deadly wound was healed* rises with the number of a man. *(13:12; 2 Thes. 2)* The dragon, the beast, and the false prophet attempt to steal worship from God, and this is their final ploy of the ages.

Their two kingdoms unite, and they speak together as leaders with false miracles who entice men by promising unity. But the Son of God died for our sins and was raised from the dead to justify our forgiveness. If we repent and confess Him as our Lord and Savior, enduring to the end, we'll be saved.

Coming soon: the truth is marginalized, repudiated, mocked. Believers are prohibited from buying or selling and are put to death for disputing the heresy. The dragon exalts himself in his living image, revered in Jerusalem's temple. The Jews accept the placement of his image beside the beast, and Jerusalem is given into his hands. When the devil demands worship, the world falls on its face before him.

Delivering the Messages

A messenger flying in the midst of heaven speaks the gospel with a loud voice by television, satellite, and radio air waves. Another condemns Babylon's sins, and a third boldly warns men to refuse the mark of the beast or suffer everlasting wrath.

A false religious leader orders the number, mark, and title of the dragon who makes its takers his slaves. As his image in the temple, he demands the world's worship or death by beheading. Thus the enemies of God are identified by the mark of the beast, but His servants are sealed by His Spirit. Believers endure until death in our final battle against the nature of our flesh.

The mark of the beast identifies who goes to the lake of fire, but angels are poised to gather the elect to Jesus, holding back the four winds. As the tribulation ends, 12,000 from each tribe of

UNVEILED!

Israel are sealed as the firstfruits, the first to rise in the ascension after the first resurrection when the four winds have been loosed and the sixth seal, undone. *The sun shall be turned into darkness, and the moon into blood, before that great and notable day of the Lord come: And <u>it shall come to pass</u>, that whosoever shall call on the name of the Lord shall be saved. (Acts 2:20-21)*

The trumpet blasts as everyone trembles in terror; sinners are horrified by His impending wrath; Jesus comes on a cloud with a shout, raising the beheaded from their graves. The firstfruits are taken up, leading the elect to meet Jesus in the air. Then seven angels carry the bowls of plagues for those marked by the beast.

> [42] Watch therefore: for ye know not what hour your Lord doth come. [43] But know this, that if the goodman of the house had known in what watch the thief would come, he would have watched, and would not have suffered his house to be broken up. [44] Therefore be ye also ready: for in such an hour as ye think not the Son of man cometh. (Mat. 24:42-44) –Our eyes close in death and open to see Him.

> 18 And he spoke a parable to them to this end, that <u>men ought always to pray, and not to faint</u>; [2] saying, There was in a city a judge, which feared not God, neither regarded man: [3] And there was a widow in that city; and she came unto him, saying, Avenge me of mine adversary. [4] And he would not for a while: but afterward he said within himself, Though I fear not God, nor regard man; [5] yet because this widow troubleth me, I will avenge her, lest by her continual coming she weary me. [6] And the Lord said, Hear what the unjust judge saith. [7] And shall not God avenge his own elect, which cry day and night unto him, though he bear long with them? [8] I tell you that he will avenge them speedily. Nevertheless when the Son of man cometh, shall he find faith on the earth? (Luke 18:1-8)

When Israel sees Him, she mourns for Him as a mother for her only son. She is given the Spirit of grace and supplications:

> [25] I do not want you to be ignorant of this mystery, brothers and sisters, so that you may not be conceited: Israel has experienced a hardening in part until the full number of the Gentiles has come in, [26] and in this way all Israel will be saved. As it is written:

The Order of Events

"The deliverer will come from Zion;
  he will turn godlessness away from Jacob.
 ²⁷ And this is my covenant with them
  when I take away their sins." (Rom. 11:25-27 NIV)

As His wrath is poured out on the earth, the elect worship the Father and Son in heaven. Those on earth who are left behind, especially Israel, mourn for the Son they never knew. She has faith in His name and awaits His return. (Song of Songs) <u>The faithful endure by faith that leads to their purification</u>, even the whole house of Israel.

Voices, thunders, lightnings, and the greatest earthquake of all shake the whole world. At the last plague, Babylon the Great is utterly destroyed. Her city is *thrown down with violence*, and her *smoke rises forever. (Rev. 18)* Cities crumble as mountains and islands disappear because the Day of the LORD has come.

The invitations were sent, and the hall is filled with wedding guests. After the last bowl of wrath leaves the Sanctuary, the marriage of the Lamb is announced in heaven where angels and saints celebrate the destruction of Babylon. Then Yeshua flashes across the sky with the elect on white horses to rescue Jerusalem.

Blessed are they that are called unto the marriage supper of the Lamb. (Rev. 19:9) He rides with vengeance against the armies of the nations that wait for war in Armageddon. There the Lamb destroys them by the sharp sword of His Word. The birds and beasts consume the flesh of His enemies in the great supper of God, and Yeshua hurls the beast and prophet into the lake of fire.

Finally, an angel chains, locks, and seals the dragon in the pit for a thousand years as the Son of David, Messiah, reigns in Zion. Martyrs beheaded for resisting the beast and his mark are chosen to join the elders and living creatures as priests and kings.

Yeshua enters Jerusalem, riding a white horse with His army after Him. (Rev. 15:5-8) The elect virgins, undefiled men from the twelve tribes, worship Him in the temple, never leaving His Presence. Israel is saved when Messiah Yeshua establishes His throne as Jerusalem and reigns over the earth. (Lk. 12:36; cf. Rev. 19:1-9) The nations are judged. (Mat. 25:31-40; Rev. 20:4)

Justice, mercy, and truth prevail in His Kingdom as heaven and earth sing. Weapons are made into plows to till the earth. Men farm their fields to feed their families. (Is. 2:1-4; Mic. 4:1-4)

UNVEILED!

After the thousand years, a worldwide rebellion rises, and the Lord opens the seventh seal. Seven angels sequentially sound their trumpets till the last judgment. After the first four trumpets, three woes begin at the fifth trump in 9:1 where *Apollyon,* "the destroyer," is loosed out of the bottomless pit, tormenting men for five months with stinging locusts that don't kill them.

At the second woe, the sixth trumpet sends two hundred million troops to destroy one-third of humanity. Gentiles occupy the outer courts of the temple and trample the city underfoot for 1,260 days. It's the second half of the seventieth week. The Lord empowers two witnesses for three-and-a-half years until the destroyer kills the prophets. The world rejoices three-and-a-half days, but the prophets rise to ascend as men watch in awe.

The whole earth is shaken; a tenth of Jerusalem falls, and seven thousand are killed as the judgment against their rebellion ends at the second woe to the glory of God. (Rev. 11:14)

Satan rules Gog of Magog, gathering his armies from all nations. Rebels encircle Jerusalem and the camp of the saints, but fire and brimstone destroy them. The third woe comes as the second ends at **the last trump** when Satan is cast into the lake of fire, and the living and the dead are judged (in 11:18).

Only Yeshua is worthy to reign as King of kings and Lord of lords, and all heaven rejoices. He is the Judge of all men—the Alpha and Omega, seated on the great white throne. At the sight of Him, heaven and earth disappear with a great noise. (2 Pet. 3:10; Rev. 20: 11) The rest of the dead from ages past fall down before Him at His high and lofty judgment throne.

At the great white throne, the judgment seat of Christ (in Rev. 11:18), the saints rise to face the Judge as books are opened with the Book of Life. Rewards and judgments are given for our works, whether good or bad. Hypocrites and sinners go into the fire where their agony never ends; its worm never dies.

In 20:7-15 whoever is not in the Book of Life is hurled into the lake of fire forever. Then death and hell are cast into its fire, and death is destroyed, and the souls in the fire are never-ending.

At last new heavens and a new earth descend from heaven's God. New Jerusalem arrives as His Bride. Though many nations, tribes, and peoples, we are one as the Son is one with the Father. After enduring trials to the end, we worship the one true God!

The Order of Events

Between the Lines

The scarlet beast moves with his government seat, and his city plays the harlot with the nations' kings. Before the thousand years, ten kings return to give their kingdom to the dragon in 17:16-17. As it ends, the feet of the king's idol, East and West, are crushed by Israel's Stone in Daniel 2.

The beast, the dragon, and his prophet will persecute the saints who reject the beast and his mark. They order beheadings of the saints. Jesus assured us, *Immediately after that tribulation,* He comes on a cloud to take us up to Himself. Martyrs and survivors who resist the beast are with Jesus when His wrath goes out in 14:17-15:1. In 15:2-4, they worship Him in heaven. Then comes 15:5 till 16 ends with His bowls of wrath. In chapter 17, Mystery Babylon is described, but from 17:15 to the end of 18 she falls forever. In 19:11-21, the Lord returns to conquer His enemies. (Zec. 14; Ezk. 39) Ezekiel 39 precedes the kingdom, whereas 38 is fulfilled after the thousand years (in 20:7-10).

Twice the ten horns have one mind with the dragon: in 17:13 and in 17:17. First the unseen kings join the dragon in WW2. Before the Kingdom comes, they rejoin his two-horned beast.

On September 11, 2001, the mysterious harlot was a marked woman. In chapter 16 at the fifth bowl the beast and his kingdom are judged. It's a worldwide empire of a leopard with the mouth of a lion and feet of a bear in Mystery Babylon.

Before the leopard was given dominion in WW2, the U.S. joined Britain and Russia to overcome a common enemy, but the union evolved into a plan for the world. Marxism fell in Russia but China had received it while at war. The union of the beasts was allegedly for "peace on earth." By the authority of an orator, the dominion of a leopard, and the power of a bear's feet, a very different beast rises. Power transfers and insurrections destine their nations to fall, but they adore the beast that kills the saints.

The time is at hand when the world will take the mark of the beast. Reprobate in hedonist lusts, they assent to their deaths. In Ezekiel 39 and Revelation 19, the Lord returns to destroy the armies by His penetrating Sword, the Word of God. Birds and beasts cleanse the land of its dead. Eagles feast on corpses to fulfill prophecy. For seven months men bury their remains, and their graves fill the valley of Megiddo for a thousand years.

UNVEILED!

Right after the tribulation, His bowls of wrath follow the first resurrection and the rapture. At the fifth bowl in 16:10-11, the land is full of darkness. They gnaw their tongues in pain, blaspheming God for His judgments, His righteous acts, but they refuse to repent. A sixth angel pours out wrath from his bowl on the Euphrates, which dries up for the kings of the East—perhaps all of them—China, Iran, Afghanistan, Iraq, Jordan, India, with Russia and Turkey, joining others in Armageddon to war against the Lamb. Yeshua warns us ahead of time. All who believe are exhorted to holiness:

> [15] Behold, I come as a thief. Blessed is he that watcheth, and keepeth his garments, lest he walk naked, and they see his shame. (Rev. 16:15)

In 16:16 Christ is about to destroy the armies of the nations gathered to Armageddon. When the seventh angel comes with the last bowl, God remembers Babylon in 16:19 to give her the cup of the wine of His fury, and the seventh bowl empties of His indignation, shaking mountains and islands at Yeshua's return.

His millennial reign is confirmed in Rev. 20:2-7, described in the prophets and in Psalms. [Ezk. 39:21-29; Is. 2:1-4; 62; 65:8-25; Zec. 14:8-11, 16-21; Ps. 2]

Seven Trumpeters

In Revelation 8, 9, and 11, seven trumpeters announce the judgments after Yeshua reigns for a thousand years. At the fifth trumpet in chapter 9, the dragon is released from the pit. At the sixth, two witnesses judge the rebellion. At the last trump in 11, we stand at the great white throne till the past is gone forever.

> [18] Who is a God like you,
>   who pardons sin and forgives the transgression
>   of the remnant of his inheritance?
> You do not stay angry forever
>   but delight to show mercy.
> [19] You will again have compassion on us;
>   you will tread our sins underfoot
>   and hurl all our iniquities into the depths of the sea.
> [20] You will be faithful to Jacob,
>   and show love to Abraham,
>   as you pledged on oath to our ancestors
>   in days long ago. (Mic. 7:18-20 NIV)

The Order of Events

The Kingdom (in 22:10) reveals the inconceivable: All these years, Yeshua has left the Revelation unsealed! Speaking silently with thoughts as words, He reveals the prophecies, and we hear Him in our native tongues. With thoughts as words, Jews from all nations heard one hundred twenty disciples speak in heavenly tongues on Pentecost, and they understood them. Given the gift of interpretation, each man heard them in his own language. But others scoffed because it wasn't given to them (in Acts 2:1-13).

There is a correlation between the angels who pour out seven bowls of wrath before the thousand years and those who sound seven trumpets after the Millennial Kingdom of Yeshua who rules the Eternal Kingdom forever:

Bowls	Assignments	Trumpets
1	Earth	1
2	Sea	2
3	Rivers & Springs	3
4	Sun	4
5	Domains of the Beasts	5
6	Euphrates River	6
7	Final Judgments	7

We who have received His gift are set free to choose life or death. We're given the power to become children of God, *that everyone who is believing in Him may not perish, but may have life age-during* [everlasting] *(Jn. 3:16 YLT) ... But as many as did receive him, to them gave he authority to become sons of God—to those believing on his name. (Jn. 1:12 YLT)*

He wants us who want Him, proving it by yielding to His Spirit and obeying His words. Constantly seeking Him for more of His righteousness, we call others to repentance and faith.

Those who have never been changed by His grace and His love must find it strange that we who've had sordid pasts would openly share our lives. But we glorify God for the transformation we've experienced by faith in Jesus Christ. Not till then did we know for sure that He's alive today.

We can't receive the grace of the gospel until we recognize our desperate need of forgiveness. Then with thankful hearts, we love Him more than life itself because He first loved us.

UNVEILED!

This is the basic order: chapter 12, then most of 17; next Daniel 7, which leads to chapter 13; then 14, 15, and 16 until Babylon is destroyed at the seventh bowl, which coincides with 17:15-18; then chapter 18 and 19:1-10. Babylon is destroyed; Jesus returns from heaven to defeat the armies in Armageddon in 19:11-21; then 20:1-6 leads to His thousand-year Kingdom.

Immediately after the tribulation of chapter 13, the catching up of the elect (in Mat. 24:29; 1 Thes. 4:15-18) follows the first resurrection in 20:4-5. The bowls of wrath in chapter 16 are poured out after the catching up. Afterward, in Rev. 19:11-21, the Lord returns to destroy the armies of Gog in Armageddon. Then He establishes Jerusalem as the highest mountain of all.

After a thousand years of peace on earth, there is a rebellion, and the trumpets of chapters 8, 9, and 11 are heard; then 20:7-8 releases the devil at the fifth trumpet in 9:1-11. In 20:9-10 the dragon is destroyed in the lake of fire as the last trump sounds for the last resurrection at the great white throne judgment in 20:11-15 and 11:15-18.

The seventh trumpet is the last trump when we are made incorruptible and stand at the Judgment Seat of Christ, the great white judgment throne of Rev. 20:11-15 and 11:15-18. Before the judgment, heaven and earth flee at the Presence of the Lord, and we stand before Him by His mercy.

After the judgment, a new heaven and a new earth appear as New Jerusalem descends out of heaven from God, and the Son offers up the Kingdom to the Father from whom all things have come; then the Kingdom continues forever.

The Apocalypse is a jigsaw puzzle; its picture is for the church to see by its revelations. History and the Scriptures work together to clarify the Revelation of Jesus Christ as it shines its light on them.

EPILOGUE

The full solar eclipse that crossed our nation from southeast to northwest on August 21, 2017, divided the country in half.[220] It was not only a spectacular sight, but a true omen. An eclipse isn't the rarest phenomenon, and it will cross America again in 2024, but it is not cause for celebration. Biblically, it is not a good sign, but a bad one. When the sun's light becomes dark, its sign warns the nation whose light has turned to darkness.

Immediately after the eclipse, Hurricane Harvey slammed the southern coast of America and put Houston underwater. Irma hit Florida. Maria nearly destroyed Puerto Rico,[221] and wildfires raged against the West as tornadoes and floods pummeled the central states.[222] Has God been judging the nation? Certainly.

An economic crash in the U.S. would reverberate worldwide, and the world knows it. A crisis like that is useful for globalists to declare an international emergency. With the United Nations in charge, anti-Zionism would gain momentum, and fascism would be empowered. We might wonder if American politicians are positioning themselves as elite rulers of the world.

The heavens have shown their signs for millennia, but let's recognize our short-sightedness and the weakness of our nature. Mortality has a way of distorting the truth, but the truth is not short-lived. Long ago God set signs in the heavens that recur to send warnings to sinners to repent and believe. Though our time runs out, His doesn't.

The Signs of God

> [25] And <u>there shall be signs</u> in the sun, and in the moon, and in the stars; and upon the earth distress of nations, with perplexity; the sea and the waves roaring; [26] Men's hearts failing them for fear and for looking after those things which are coming on the earth: for the powers of heaven shall be shaken. (Luke 21:25-26)

The series of four blood moons divided by a solar eclipse testified to Jerusalem on the Jewish feast days of a Shmitah year [an agricultural sabbath]. No such events had appeared during a Shmitah year in over two thousand years.[223] In Revelation 12 a sign appeared that returned on September 23, 2017. The following events headlined the news in 2015 from Yom Kippur till the last of the four blood moons, which was a super blood moon over Jerusalem: September 22, the Pope Francis landed at Andrews Air Base at 4 p.m. The next day, Yom Kippur, he met with President Obama at the White House. On the 24th he spoke to Congress. On the 25th he spoke at the UN in NYC. The 26th he was in Philadelphia; the 27th he held Mass on the Benjamin Franklin Parkway before boarding his return flight to Rome at 8 p.m.[224] [New York, Philadelphia, and Washington, D.C. have all been national capitals.] September 28, 2017, President Barack Hussein Obama was the first speaker at the 70th Session of the UN General Assembly.[225] That night the super blood moon, the fourth in the series, appeared in Jerusalem's sky.

The signs were profound, but the church was asleep. We should be slow to trust in men but quick to trust in God who puts people in authority to bless or to judge a nation. Blood moons are rarely over Jerusalem during her feasts, but the super blood moon was ominous.

The religious councils that voted against the Jewish Bible in the 4th century led the churches into apostasy by their unbelief. Had they not professed faith in Jesus Christ, they would not have been apostates. Apostates do not rise outside of the church.

At a Fatima celebration in St. Peter's Square, Francis said, "[Mary] takes us with the hand of a mother to the embrace of the Father, to the Father of mercy." [226] Consecrating the world to Mary, he faced an idol to offer a prayer. Is there any question about idolatry in the church? Roman Catholicism is not the mother of believers; neither is Mary a mediator. The mother of believers is named in the New Testament: *Jerusalem which is above is free, which is the mother of us all. (Gal. 4:26)*

> [18] The children gather wood, and the fathers kindle the fire, and the women knead their dough, to make cakes to the queen of heaven, and to pour out drink offerings unto other gods, that they may provoke me to anger. [19] Do they provoke me to anger? saith the LORD: Do they not provoke themselves to the confusion of their own faces? [20] Therefore thus saith the LORD GOD; Behold, my anger and my fury shall be poured out upon this place, upon man and upon beast, and upon the trees of the field, and upon the fruit of the ground; and it shall burn and shall not be quenched. (Jer. 7:18-20) [Also see Jer. chapter 44]

EPILOGUE

> ⁵ For *there is* one God, and one mediator between God and men, *the* man Christ Jesus; ⁶ Who gave himself a ransom for all, to be testified in due time. (1 Tim. 2:5-6)

A wonderful sign appeared after sunset December 21, 2020: the planets Jupiter and Saturn aligned for the first time in 800 years, creating the appearance of a great star. Something very special is about to happen. We should be looking up.

The apostles' writings came from the Tenakh, the Hebrew Testament, which reveals Messiah and lays the foundation of the Christian-Messianic faith. *The just shall live by his faith* was first written by Habakkuk. (2:4) A new covenant was disclosed by its Jewish apostles, eyewitnesses to mysteries and miracles foretold by its prophets before them. Jesus Christ endorsed the words that churches often refute today. He fulfilled prophecy, confirmed the commandments, and taught the Tenakh, opening a new covenant from writings the bishops despised, ignorant of its rich contents.

Whoever doesn't love the truth will believe Satan's lies. If we have the Holy Spirit and the mind of Christ, why do we nearly all disagree? and why haven't we known the truth?

> ¹¹ How is it you don't understand that I was not talking to you about bread? But be on your guard against the yeast of the Pharisees and Sadducees." ¹² Then they understood that he was not telling them to guard against the yeast used in bread, but against the teaching of the Pharisees and Sadducees. (Mat. 16:11-12 NIV)

The falling away, or apostasy, is the rejection of the truth. Its false teachings have had strongholds in our hearts and minds. Paul wept knowing people would enter the church to introduce heresies. By smooth words, they'd persuade believers to dismiss the Bible; but prophets and apostles wrote to deliver the truth of God for us to be one new man, united by their inspired words.

> 2 But there were also false prophets among the people, even as there will be false teachers <u>among you</u>, who will secretly bring in destructive heresies, even denying the Lord who bought them, *and* bring on themselves swift destruction. ² And <u>many will follow</u> their destructive ways, because of whom the way of truth will be blasphemed. ³ By covetousness they will exploit you with deceptive

words; for a long time their judgment has not been idle, and their destruction does not slumber. (2 Pet. 2:1-3 NKJV)

False teachings are pleasant, so we eagerly receive them, but they are not true to its Revelation or to the new covenant. How vital it is to believe the Bible's apostles and prophets!

> ⁸ But though we, or an angel from heaven, preach any other gospel unto you than that which we have preached unto you, let him be accursed. ⁹ As we said before, so say I now again, If any *man* preach any other gospel unto you than that ye have received, let him be accursed. (Gal. 1:8-9)

His Son's good works and His resurrection proved God true and faithful. Had Jesus not overcome death, His eyewitnesses would not have suffered torture and death for the gospel of His resurrection. The testimony of their blood validates their words.

Multitudes are deceived, dying for the devils' lies, but those who are eyewitnesses of fulfilled prophecies, even of His death, resurrection, and ascension, died for the truth they couldn't deny. Persecution will serve us well, refining and proving us whose faith endures.

He makes us holy as He is holy—that's the truth. We are not immune to sin, but will answer to God who has given us His Spirit to be holy. It takes a spiritual person to have His mind:

> ¹⁵ But <u>he that is spiritual</u> judgeth all things, yet he himself is judged of no man. ¹⁶ For who hath known the mind of the Lord, that he may instruct him? But we have the mind of Christ. 3 And I, brethren, could not speak unto you as unto spiritual, but <u>as unto carnal</u>, even as unto babes in Christ. (1 Cor. 2:15-3:1)

Winning the War

John wrote that we who receive Him are given the right to become children of God by faith in His name, *born, not of blood, nor of the will of the flesh, nor of the will of man, but of God. (See Jn. 1:12-13)* We must renew our minds by tearing down the errors we've believed; they put our souls at risk. We presume our popular ideas are acceptable, but they are not. If we believe the truth, why do we alter His words, wrestling and twisting them to fit our own doctrines and traditions? Is it our unbelief?

EPILOGUE

If we are tested to the limit, the fear of God encourages us: *No temptation hath taken you but such as is common to man: but God is faithful, who will not suffer you to be tempted above that ye are able; but will with the temptation also make a way to escape, that ye may be able to bear it. (1 Cor. 10:13)*

Children who believe their fathers are examples of humility to us. *In the fear of the LORD is strong confidence: and His children shall have a place of refuge. (Prov. 14:26)* Have we become children yet, or have we learned too much from others? His Spirit urges us to offer our bodies as living sacrifices:

> 12 Therefore I urge you, brethren, by the mercies of God, to <u>present your bodies a living and holy sacrifice</u>, acceptable to God, *which is* your spiritual service of worship. ² And do not be conformed to this world, but be transformed by the renewing of your mind, so that you may prove what the will of God is, that which is good and acceptable and perfect. (Rom. 12:1-2 NASB)

As children of the Kingdom, we live in opposition to the sin nature into which we were first born. Infants in malice, we were once sophisticated but are more than we once were. However, he calls us to maturity in understanding. (See 1 Cor. 14:20) Now we live by the power of a higher nature, believing God will put us where He wants us when He wants us there:

> ⁴³ Ye have heard that it hath been said, Thou shalt love thy neighbor, and hate thine enemy. ⁴⁴ But I say unto you, Love your enemies, bless them that curse you, do good to those that hate you, and pray for them which despitefully use you, and persecute you; ⁴⁵ That ye may be the children of your Father which is in heaven: for he maketh his sun to rise on the evil and on the good, and sendeth rain on the just and on the unjust. ... ⁴⁸ Be ye therefore <u>perfect as your Father which is in heaven is perfect</u>. (Mat. 5:43-45, 48)

Jesus sent the Holy Spirit for us to live by faith in His Word, not turning from it by unwarily going along with evil. This is the way the warfare works: though our flesh strives against the Holy Spirit and the Word of God, by the Spirit and the Word, we overcome the carnal nature. Jesus asked the Father to send His Spirit to us who believe and obey. (Jn. 14:15-16) He empowers each of

UNVEILED!

us to win the battles. His Spirit is in the Word as its life, and His Word is in the Spirit speaking to us as God who is One.

He's calling us back to our first love since we slipped away. It's not too late to fervently love our Savior as when we were newborns and every word of the Bible was meaningful to us. His words corrected our ways till we looked to teachers for what He had not shown us. And the walls went up. But its Author teaches us who have *ears to hear* and *eyes to see:*

> [19] And this is the condemnation, that light is come into the world, and <u>men loved darkness rather than light</u>, because their deeds were evil. [20] For every one that doeth evil hateth the light, neither cometh to the light, lest his deeds should be reproved. [21] But he that doeth truth cometh to the light, that his deeds may be made manifest, that they are wrought in God. (John 3:19-21)

From the beginning, God chose us to be saved through the sanctification of the Spirit and faith in the truth. Before faith in Jesus Christ set us free, we were bound to sin. The apostles urge us to believe the teachings and traditions <u>their words</u> pass on to us. (2 Thes. 2:13-15) If anyone distorts the gospel of Christ, he is under a curse.

The Word is rich with mysteries for us. Its secrets are in the verses we've questioned. Our questions go unanswered because the answers are hidden in the mysteries. Then let's not shipwreck our faith by a lack of knowledge, but believe the truth and love and win the prize.

On Anti-Semitism

In Paul's letter to the congregation in Rome, he taught that not all Israel is the Israel of the promise and then explained,

> [9] For <u>this is the word of promise</u>, at this time shall I come, and Sarah shall have a son. [10] And not only this; but when Rebecca also had conceived by one, even by our father Isaac; [11] (For the children being not yet born, neither having done any good or evil, that the purpose of God according to election might stand, not of works, but of him that calleth;) [12] It was said unto her, The elder shall serve the younger. [13] As it is written, Jacob have I loved, but Esau have I hated. [14] What shall we say then? Is there unrighteousness with God? God forbid. [15] For

EPILOGUE

> he saith to Moses, I will have mercy on whom I will have mercy, and I will have compassion on whom I will have compassion. [16] <u>So then it is not of him that willeth, nor of him that runneth, but of God that sheweth mercy.</u>
> (Rom. 9:9-16; cf. Mal. 1:2-5)

We don't really *see* the scriptures' words until we believe them; then we understand them. Our faith is dying when we rely on others for explanations. A few are good, but many are mistaken. Some are deceptive, but we only receive what we're willing to believe. Are we willing to believe the difficult parts?

The Bible's words are often like grains of sand in an oyster's shell, irritating our flesh. If we take them into our hearts, mulling over them and not shrinking back, we receive them by faith until we understand, and then out comes the truth like a pearl!

Now we have a free will, and now the choice is ours: will we live by the Spirit or die by the flesh? That's the other half of the gospel in Romans chapter 8. We should be aware of the spiritual forces of darkness that work against the Kingdom of God. Anti–Semitism is on the rise in Europe, nearly as it was in Germany during the war. It's increased on college campuses worldwide.[227]

> [20] And when ye shall see Jerusalem compassed with armies, then know that the desolation thereof is nigh. ...
> [22] <u>For these be the days of vengeance,</u> that all things which are written may be fulfilled. ...
> [24] And they shall fall by the edge of the sword, and shall be led away captive into all nations: and Jerusalem shall be trodden down by the Gentiles, <u>until the times of the Gentiles be fulfilled.</u> (Lk. 21:20, 22, 24)

What if His vengeance against the Jews made a way for His grace to us? Jesus implied it was so. A provocative discourse in Romans leads Paul to a decision about the sovereignty of God:

> [30] For as ye in times past have not believed God, yet have now obtained mercy through their unbelief: [31] Even so have these also now not believed, that through your mercy they also may obtain mercy. [32] For God hath concluded them all in unbelief, that he might have mercy upon all. [33] O the depth of the riches both of the wisdom and knowledge of God! how unsearchable are his judgments, and his ways past finding out! [34] For who hath

UNVEILED!

known the mind of the Lord? or who hath been his counsellor? [35] Or who hath first given to him, and it shall be recompensed unto him again? [36] For of him, and through him, and to him, are all things: to whom be glory for ever. Amen. (Rom. 11:30-36)

Anti-Zionism rejects God by its war against His Kingdom. Anti–Semitism judges Israel as His choice. Watch their enemies rage—multitudes live in rubble and misery, eating bitterness as though it were sweet.

The Seventieth Week

Dan. 9:24-27 predicts seventy weeks; each represents seven years. From the Edict of Cyrus until Jerusalem was rebuilt, seven weeks passed—forty-nine years. Messiah was cut off for others and Rome ruined the temple after sixty-two more sevens passed. Now sixty-nine sevens have passed. Where is the last week?

Christ reigns in its midst. Its halves are *forty-two months* and *1,260 days,* or three-and-a-half Biblical years. <u>Unto the end of the war</u> desolations are determined *(from Dan. 9:26)* alludes to a war between the forces of good and evil.

> [24] Seventy weeks are determined upon thy people and upon thy holy city, to finish the transgression, and to make an end of sins, and to make reconciliation for iniquity, and to bring in everlasting righteousness, and to seal up the vision and prophecy, and to anoint the most Holy. [25] Know therefore and understand, that from the going forth of the commandment to restore and to build Jerusalem unto the Messiah the Prince shall be seven weeks, and threescore and two weeks: the street shall be built again, and the wall, even in troublous times. [26] And after threescore and two weeks shall Messiah be cut off, but not for himself: and <u>the people of the prince that shall come shall destroy the city and the sanctuary; and the end thereof shall be with a flood, and unto the end of the war desolations are determined</u>. [27] And he shall confirm the covenant with many for one week: and <u>in the midst of the week</u> he shall cause the sacrifice and the oblation to cease, and <u>for the overspreading of abominations he shall make it desolate</u>, even until the consummation, and that determined shall be poured upon the desolate. (Dan. 9:24-27; also YLT, CWSOT)

EPILOGUE

Gabriel foretold the days of the Romans who'd destroy the city and the sanctuary. They're the people of the prince that shall come, indicating the illegitimate one. Six thousand years have passed since the beginning of this great war, but *with the Lord, ... a thousand years [is] as one day. (See 2 Pet. 3:8)*

At the end history repeats itself. The ruler that shall come shall make a covenant with the Jews and sit beside an image in the temple, a portent of their desolation. He breaks his end of the deal in the middle of the prophetic week. No mention is made of the end of that week until after the thousand years:

> ^{27} And he shall make a strong covenant with many for one week, and for half of the week he shall put an end to sacrifice and offering. And on the wing of abominations shall come one who makes desolate, until the decreed end is poured out on the desolator." (Dan 9:27 ESV)

The interlinear agrees (ZGE), but another literal translation reads, *he is making desolate, even till the consummation, and that which is determined is poured on the desolate one.' (from Dan 9:27 YLT; KJV agrees.)* It may be an error in a manuscript.

The consummation is at the end of the age at Jesus' return. Is it prophetic irony that the desolator becomes the *desolate one?* [Ar.: *shâmâm* is "stupefied"] Then the victimizer is astonished. The scripture implies, "To look on God is to look on Him":

> ^{10} "And I will pour out on the house of David and the inhabitants of Jerusalem a spirit of grace and pleas for mercy, so that, <u>when they look on me</u>, <u>on him</u> whom they have pierced, they shall mourn for him, as one mourns for an only child, and weep bitterly over him, as one weeps over a firstborn. (Zec. 12:10 ESV) [Literal]

> 13 "On that day there shall be a fountain opened for the house of David and the inhabitants of Jerusalem, to cleanse them from sin and uncleanness. (Zec.13:1 ESV)

Antiochus was a little horn out of four horns on the goat that ruled Greece. He was comparable to the little horn after the ten in Daniel 7. He is not the same man, of course, but the dragon was in each man at different times in history as the eighth king, the scarlet beast in 17, revealed on page 19.

UNVEILED!

> [23] 'And in the latter end of their kingdom, about the perfecting of the transgressors, stand up doth a king, <u>fierce of face, and understanding hidden things</u>; [24] and his power hath been mighty, and <u>not by his own power</u>; and wonderful things he destroyeth, and he hath prospered, and wrought, and destroyed mighty ones, and the people of the Holy Ones. (Daniel 8:23-24 YLT)

God judges nations bent on destruction but uses destroyers like a rod of discipline or like a whip to scourge His own. Many were destroyed in the wilderness because their refusal to enter the land revealed their unbelief. If we continue in sin without repentance, He'll destroy us too. We were not born again to sin but to lead holy lives, the vision without which many perish.

It's unwise to make excuses or cover-ups for the judgments of a holy God against evil. He who reigns on high does as He pleases because He is Sovereign. If we credit ourselves for our faith, we'll despise the Jews for unbelief, but there's no boasting in heaven. Even kings who exceed His intentions are judged:

> [5] O the Assyrian, the rod of my anger,
>   in whose hand is the club of my wrath!
> [6] I send him against a godless nation,
>   I dispatch him against a people who anger me,
> to seize loot and snatch plunder,
>   and to trample them down like mud in the streets.
> [7] <u>But this is not what he intends</u>,
>   <u>this is not what he has in mind</u>;
> <u>his purpose is to destroy</u>,
>   to put an end to many nations ...
>
> [12] When the LORD has finished all his work against Mount Zion and Jerusalem, he will say, "I will punish the king of Assyria for the willful pride of his heart and the haughty look in his eyes. ... (Is. 10:5-7,12 NIV)
>
> [15] <u>Does the ax raise itself above him who swings it</u>,
>   or the saw boast itself against him who uses it?
> As if a rod were to wield him who lifts it up,
>   or a club brandish him who is not wood!
> [16] Therefore, the Lord, the LORD Almighty,
>   will send a wasting disease upon his sturdy warriors;
>   under his pomp a fire will be kindled

EPILOGUE

> like a blazing flame.
> ¹⁷ The Light of Israel will become a fire,
> their Holy One a flame;
> In a single day it will burn and consume
> his thorns and his briers. (Is. 10:15-17 NIV)

If we study the Bible, we find God has a reason for everything He does, including His judgments against the world. It pains Him to see His own children in disobedience because the Father knows our rebellion will lead to our destruction. He warns us to walk on the path that leads to life since His righteousness requires His impartiality when He judges us with all humankind on the last day. Revelation is like the cross: we don't want to face it, but it ends with the resurrection and everlasting life.

God came against His chosen people when they turned from Him to their riches, to the works of their hands, to pride and arrogance, to sexual sins, and to idolatry. When violence was in the streets and sexual immoralities filled their land, He judged them. When they sacrificed their children to fire, He destroyed them. We're on the cusp of His coming. The world will never be the same. Have we believed God or the teachings of men? Who is on the Lord's side?

> ³ Many peoples will come and say,
> "Come, let us go up to the mountain of the LORD,
> To the temple of the God of Jacob.
> He will teach us his ways,
> so that we may walk in his paths."
> The law will go out from Zion,
> the word of the LORD from Jerusalem.
> ⁴ He will judge between the nations
> and will settle disputes for many peoples.
> They will beat their swords into plowshares
> and their spears into pruning hooks.
> Nation will not take up sword against nation,
> nor will they train for war anymore.
> ⁵ Come, descendants of Jacob,
> let us walk in the light of the LORD.
> (Is. 2:3-5 NIV)

APPENDIX to Chapter 13

O, Jerusalem!

In Luke's gospel Yeshua spoke at the temple in Jerusalem when they asked Him about its destruction. He described what must first occur and then said, *Before all these things,* citing the city's destruction in 70 AD and giving the reason for it as well:

> [20] "When you see Jerusalem being surrounded by armies, you will know that its desolation is near. [21] Then let those who are in Judea flee to the mountains, let those in the city get out, and let those in the country not enter the city. [22] For <u>this is the time of punishment</u> in fulfillment of all that has been written. [23] How dreadful it will be in those days for pregnant women and nursing mothers! There will be great distress in the land and wrath against this people. [24] They will fall by the sword and will be taken as prisoners to all the nations. Jerusalem will be trampled on by the Gentiles <u>until the times of the Gentiles are fulfilled</u>. (Lk. 21:20-24 NIV)

The passage by Luke refers to Jerusalem at the destruction of its temple till after their punishment when the Jews repossess Jerusalem. Then there are signs in the earth, the sea, and the sky, more frequent and more unusual than we've known in a lifetime.

Mark and Matthew relayed Yeshua's words, but the venue and audience changed. On the Mount of Olives, four disciples took Him aside and asked about the end of the age. Above the Kidron Valley, they observed the temple:

> [3] And <u>as he sat upon the mount of Olives</u> over against the temple, Peter and James and John and Andrew <u>asked him privately</u>, [4] Tell us, when shall these things be? and <u>what shall be the sign when all these things shall be fulfilled</u>? [5] And Jesus answering them began to say, Take heed lest any man deceive you: [6] For many shall come in my name, saying, I am Christ; and shall deceive many. ...
> [14] But when ye shall see the <u>abomination of desolation</u>, spoken of by Daniel the prophet, standing where it ought not, (<u>let him that readeth understand</u>,) then let them that be <u>in Judaea</u> flee to the mountains: [15] And let him that is on the housetop not go down into the house, neither enter therein, to take any thing out of his house: [16] And

let him that is in the field not turn back again for to take up his garment. [17] But woe to them that are with child, and to them that give suck in those days! [18] And pray ye that your flight be not in the winter. [19] For in those days shall be affliction, such as was not from the beginning of the creation which God created unto this time, <u>neither shall be</u>. [20] And except that the Lord had shortened those days, no flesh should be saved: but for the elect's sake, whom he hath chosen, he hath shortened the days.
[21] And then if any man shall say to you, Lo, here is Christ; or, lo, he is there; believe him not: [22] For false Christs and false prophets shall rise, and shall shew signs and wonders, to seduce, if *it were* possible, even the elect. [23] But take ye heed: behold, I have foretold you <u>all things</u>. [24] But in those days, <u>after that tribulation</u>, the sun shall be darkened, and the moon shall not give her light, [25] And the stars of heaven shall fall, and <u>the powers that are in heaven shall be shaken</u>. [26] And then shall they see the Son of man, coming in the clouds with great power and glory. [27] And then shall he send his angels, and shall gather together <u>his elect</u> from the four winds, from the uttermost part of the earth to the uttermost part of heaven. (Mk. 13:3-6, 14-27)

Gabriel prophesied to Daniel four hundred years before the image of Zeus was set in the temple beside Antiochus. He and his so-called 'god of gods' prepared a great slaughter in Judea. This was prophesied by Christ to reoccur close to His return.

The apostles hadn't written for their generation, but for us to understand. In Daniel 8 and 10 –12, the prophet heard Gabriel describe the scene: An image in the temple led to the desolation of Jerusalem by a king in 167 BC. In chapter 13 a similar event is on its way.

Of Times and Seasons

Israel's civil calendar has 29 or 30-day months. To make up for the lack in her 354-day lunar year, she adds a month in the spring every 3 –4 years, the month of Adar I. Then Passover and the Day of Firstfruits are in Adar II for the season of its harvest.

The rule applied to Israel's Biblical year with its twelve 30-day months. In one of its three years, the extra month was added,

APPENDIX to Chapter 13

making the total number of days 1,290. Its three years and six months qualify as a time, times, and half a time with one year as a leap year: *And from the time that the daily sacrifice is taken away, and the abomination that makes desolate is set up, there shall be a thousand two hundred and ninety days. (Dan. 12:11)*

In 167 BC Antiochus IV *Epiphanes ["god manifest"]* desecrated the temple by an image and a pig on the altar, demanding worship as God. He crucified and tortured hundreds of thousands of Jews for three-and-a-half years, apparently including a leap year.

The Maccabees were a Jewish family of priests who rededicated the temple to God. When Antiochus returned, in their zeal, the family defeated his army. During the Feast of Dedication in Jerusalem in John 10:22, Jesus was in the temple colonnade.

Yeshua predicted another abomination in the temple near His return and cited Daniel, saying, *Except those days should be shortened, there should no flesh be saved, but for the elect's sake, those days <u>shall be shortened</u>. (Mat. 24:22b)* Its beast rules for forty-two months (in 13:5; cf. Dan. 7:23-28). The tribulation is shortened for the living saints who reject the beast and his mark.

> [25] And he shall speak great words against the most High, and shall wear out the saints of the most High, and think to change times and laws: and they shall be given into his hand until a time and times and the dividing of time. (Dan. 7:25)

The martyrs of *the first resurrection* and the elect who are still alive are named in a book. *The rest of the dead,* saints and sinners, awake on the last day when the Book of Life is opened (in 11:18; cf. Dan. 12:2):

> 12 "At that time shall arise Michael, the great prince who has charge of your people. <u>And there shall be a time of trouble, such as never has been since there was a nation till that time. But at that time your people shall be delivered, everyone whose name shall be found written in the book.</u> [2] <u>And many of those who sleep in the dust of the earth shall awake, some to everlasting life, and some to shame and everlasting contempt</u>. (Dan. 12:1-2 ESV)

We believe the words of His eyewitnesses who saw Him ascend from the holy mount [Hermon] into the clouds when He

UNVEILED!

was received in glory. He comes for us in the same way:

> ⁹And when he had said these things, as they were looking on, he was lifted up, and a cloud took him out of their sight. ¹⁰And while they were gazing into heaven as he went, behold, two men stood by them in white robes, ¹¹and said, "Men of Galilee, why do you stand looking into heaven? <u>This Jesus, who was taken up from you into heaven, will come in the same way as you saw him go into heaven</u>." (Acts 1:9-11 ESV)

Americans have lived like kings, but our luxuries have done us no favors if we've trusted in them. We're about to be tested like silver or gold refined by fire. Will we be strong in the Spirit and endure tribulation, not giving up the faith, or will we cling to this world's pleasures? Our goals direct us, so let's look up, fear God, and serve well. Love is primary. Obedience is at the heart of faith. (2 Cor. 3:18)

The End of an Age

As it became clear to Nebuchadnezzar, God appoints kings and leaders for His divine purposes. We must pray for them and for our nation's repentance if we want to see America saved. By our neglect, the land is facing dangerous days.

Mark writes about the signs of the Lord that precede His coming. A vast period of time passes between the days of Mark and when an abomination is in the temple. *After that tribulation,* He comes on a cloud for the elect to meet Him in the air. (Mat. 24:29-31, p. 92) He returns *as lightning* at the last bowl, *flashing from the east to the west.* Prior to His return, there are antichrists who come in His name and lead men astray, acquiring admirers.

Even now leaders are idolized who are misleading many of us who profess the faith. We must not use our words carelessly. Christ is able to do for us what we cannot do for ourselves, and that means righteousness to us who abide in Him.

If our faith is true, we are found in Him; if we keep His words, we remain in Him; if we crucify our old nature, we overcome sin; if we yield to Christ, His Spirit fills us. If we are filled with ourselves, we leave no room for Him; if we judge other people's motives, we expose our own sins; if we contradict or wrestle with His words, we are believing false doctrines and resisting the truth.

APPENDIX to Chapter 13

> [2] Consider it all joy, my brethren, when you encounter various trials, [3] knowing that the testing of your faith produces endurance. [4] And let endurance have its perfect work, so that you may be perfect and complete, lacking in nothing. (Jacob [James] 1:2-4 TLV)

> 4 Therefore, since Christ suffered for us in the flesh, <u>arm yourselves also with the same mind</u>, for he who has suffered in the flesh has ceased from sin, [2] that he no longer should live the rest of *his* time in the flesh for the lusts of men, but for the will of God. ...
> [7] But the end of all things is at hand; therefore be serious and watchful in your prayers. [8] And above all things have fervent love for one another, for *"love will cover a multitude of sins."* (1 Pet. 4:1-2, 7-8 NKJV)

After we receive Jesus Christ as our Savior and Lord, we can do things our way or implore Him to take control of our lives, putting to death our sinful self–will by faith in Him. (Rom. 12:1-2) If we think we aren't worthy of grace, we lack wisdom; no one is. If we're living in sin, we're in unbelief.

> [8] He has shown you, O man, what is good;
> And what does the LORD require of you
> But to do justly,
> To love mercy,
> And to walk humbly with your God? (Mic. 6:8 NKJV)

So wake up, sleeper! Rise from the dead, and Jesus Christ will shine in you! (from Eph. 5:14)

> [20] At that day, you will know that I *am* in My Father, and you in Me, and I in you. [21] He who has My commandments and keeps them, it is he who loves Me. And He who loves Me will be loved by My Father, and I will love him and manifest Myself to him." (Jn. 14:20-21 NKJV)

UNVEILED!

The Scriptural Order

The vision of the heavens, a prophecy for all ages – chapter 12
    A woman garbed w/ sun & moon at her feet/crown of 12 stars
    The dragon and 7 heads with crowns but 10 horns with none
    Her Child ascends & the dragon is cast out forever
The introduction of Jesus Christ, the Alpha & Omega – chapter 1
Jesus gives John messages for the 7 assemblies – chapters 2-3
The four living beasts & 24 elders worship the Father – 4
The Lamb takes the scroll from the Father's right hand – 5:7
    He opens its first six seals:
Six of seven seals – chapter 6
    1st Seal, the apostate church goes forth to conquer – 6:1-2
    2nd Seal, wars and violence – 6:3-4
    3rd Seal, famine and rationing – 6:5-6
    4th Seal, increase in wars, violence, plagues – 6:7-8
Mystery Babylon and the scarlet beast that was, is not; yet is – 17
    The scarlet beast was about to come up. 17:8
    7 heads & 7 kings and 10 kings without kingdoms 17:3, 9-14
The beast with 10 horns is slain, Dan. 7:11; 17:12-14
The dragon gives his throne to another – Rev. 13:2; 17:8, 14:8-11
    The Alliance of the beasts from Daniel – Rev. 13:1
Three Messengers – 14:6-11; Is. 18:2-6
The beast & the two-horned lamb – chapter 13
    A beast w/ 7 heads & 10 horns rises – 13:1-10
        The dragon's fourth kingdom rises – Dan. 7:23-24a
    Another rises, diverse from the first – 13:11; Dan.7:23b-25
5th Seal, <u>the Great Tribulation</u> – 6:9-11; 13:5-18
    (1st half of Daniel's "70th week." See Dan. 9:24-26)
    Elect male Virgins of Israel are sealed, 7:1-8; 14:1-5
6th Seal – 6:12-17; chapter 18-19:3
    <u>1st harvest</u> – <u>1st Resurrection at the Trumpet of God</u>, 20:4-6;
        14:17-20; Mat. 24:4-31; Mk. 13:5-27; Lk. 17:26-36;
        21:24-36; 1 Thes. 4:13-18
    Saints in Heaven, His wrath leaves the temple, 14-15
    <u>2nd harvest</u> – <u>the Indignation of God</u>, 14:17-20
        7 bowls of wrath – Rev. 16
            1st bowl – Rev.16:2 Sores on all with the mark
            2nd bowl – Rev.16:3 Seawater turns to blood
            3rd bowl – Rev.16:4-7 Rivers & waters turn to blood
            4th bowl – Rev.16:8-9 Sun scorches them like fire
            5th bowl – 16:10-11, Babylon's kingdom is judged.
            6th bowl – Euphrates dried – 16:12
                The dragon, beast, & prophet, 16:13-14
                Promise to return / warning to repent, 16:15
            7th bowl – 16:17-21

UNVEILED!

      Earthquake, city is divided in three parts. 16:17-19
      Jerusalem, ravished – Zech. 14:1-2
      Mystery Babylon, destroyed – 16:19-20; 17:15-18; Ch. 18
      Rejoicing in heaven at Babylon's destruction – 19:1-6
      The Marriage of the Lamb is announced in heaven – 19:7-9
Christ Returns – 19:11-16, Zec. 14:3-8
      The LORD splits the Mount of Olives – Zec. 14:4; Rev. 6:12
      Jerusalem's survivors, rescued – Zec. 12:9-10; 19:7-10, et al
      Destroys Gog's armies in Armageddon – 16:16; 19:11-21; Ezk. 39
      Casts beast and false prophet into lake of fire – 19:20
      Locks the Dragon, Satan, in the abyss – 20:1-3
Jerusalem receives her Savior – Rev.19:7-9; Is. 62:1-12
Messianic Kingdom, Jesus reigns for 1,000 years – Dan. 7:26-28
      Rev. 20:3-6; Zec. 14:9-11, 16-21; Ezk. 37:24-28; Is. 65:19-25
      Peace by His rod of iron – 2:27; 12:5, 19:15; Ps. 2:9
      Final rebellion – 9:20-21; 20:7-9; Ps. 2
7th Seal is opened; world's rebellion is judged – chapters 8, 9, 11
      First 4 trumpets – 1) hail, fire, blood burn trees & grass
      2) a mountain falls to the sea, destroying life 3) fallen star, bitter rivers and springs 4) a third of sun, moon, stars darken
      5th Trumpet, 1st woe: Apollyon-Satan released – 9:1-12; 20:7
      6th Trumpet, 2nd woe: Part 1
          One-third of humankind are killed – 9:13-21
          John's small scroll amid the 2nd woe – 10
      2nd woe: Part 2
          2 witnesses – 11 (2nd half of the 70th week)
          One-tenth Jerusalem is judged – 11:13
          Gog's Armies around Jerusalem – 11:15, 18; 20:7-9: Ezk. 38
7th Trumpet, 3rd woe: Judgment Day– 11:15-19; Dan. 12:1-2
      Armies of Gog are destroyed – 20:7-9, Ezk. 38
      Satan thrown into the lake of fire – 20:10
      Great white throne – 11:18; 20:11; Rom. 14:10-12; 2 Cor. 5:10
      Heaven and earth pass away – 21:1
      Last resurrection – 20:12; 1 Cor. 15:50-53
      Saints, sinners, and hypocrites judged – 11:18; 20:11-15
      Death & Hell are destroyed – 20:14: 1 Cor. 15:54-58
      Sinners are thrown into the lake of fire – 20:15
New Heavens and a New Earth – chapter 21:1-8
New Jerusalem His Holy Bride from Heaven – chapter 21
Alpha & Omega – chapters 21:6; 22:13
The Place called Heaven – chapter 22:1-5

UNVEILED!

UNVEILED!

The Writer

My Conversion to Christianity

During a nervous breakdown in my senior year of college in 1969, I repented of sin and received Jesus Christ as my personal Savior. My fascination with the occult had led me to take devils into my body. They turned me into a vain, boastful, audacious liar. When I received Jesus, He changed my heart, and my old ways left me. He had paid my penalty, and He set me free.

He was my first Truth. Jesus is the only biological Son of God, a worthy Mediator to the only true God. He'd taken our sin and guilt, catapulting me into righteousness I'd never known. This new life was all I'd need for the battles that lay ahead of me, and they were severe.

For three years I was a terrified soul with a mind shattered by the devils I'd renounced. Reality became my jigsaw puzzle. Like Job, I often cried out, "I'm not that important. Why are You targeting me?" but the Victor proved He was on my side. When I learned to fear God more than the dragon, I asked Him to apply my trials against the nature of my flesh. No matter what, I trusted in Jesus, looking to Him to fight for me and thanking Him for the victories before they came. It wasn't easy, but I found the pieces and assembled the puzzle as He led me until my mind returned.

He has never ceased to amaze me. He is my courage. I overcome with every page I write. We're tested by the trials that conform us to His likeness. If we keep on believing, we defeat the same devils Jesus overcame, but we must never give up.

[26] For consider your calling, brethren, that there were not many wise according to the flesh, not many mighty, not many noble; [27] but God has chosen the foolish things of the world to shame the wise, and God has chosen the weak things of the world to shame the things which are strong, [28] and the base things of the world and the despised God has chosen, the things that are not, so that He may nullify the things that are, [29] so that no man may boast before God. [30] But by His doing you are in Christ Jesus, who became to us wisdom from God, and righteousness, and sanctification, and redemption, [31] so that, just as it is written, "LET HIM WHO BOASTS, BOAST IN THE LORD." (1 Cor. 1:26-31 NASB)

UNVEILED!

The Mantle

In 1974 I stood in the balcony of Kathryn Kuhlman's First Presbyterian Church of Pittsburgh. There she was just below us when I heard a deep, rumbling, clear, and resonant voice that spoke words I could not possibly have known. He told me she didn't have long to live. Then He said, "I am giving you her mantle." I resisted it until moments later, Kathryn said the Lord told her she didn't have long to live and she'd prayed God would give someone else her mantle. Instantly the Spirit covered me like a heavy blanket, and I fell into my seat face-down until the service ended. When I sat up she was gone.

On the ride home, I told Mike, my best friend who would become my husband. We prayed and returned to Philadelphia where I told my pastor Larry Albanese. He said, "If it's God, He will do it." So I waited. Forty years after my new birth, I wondered if God remembered me, but the day came when He commissioned me to write what He'd teach me.

In 1970 I surrendered my life, offering my body as a living sacrifice for Him to take control. At times I stumbled, tripped, and fell, but I got back up and went on. Having given up my life, I couldn't possibly miss His plan. (See Rom. 12:1-2)

I never met Miss Kuhlman; she never knew what happened that day. I never told her. I was sure if she knew my past, she wouldn't believe me. She said something else that surprised me: she wished she had known the Holy Spirit better than she had.

Why hadn't God used me as He'd used her? John was given Elijah's mantle and baptized, calling men to repent and declaring the Lord's arrival but did no miracles. My work is unlike hers. Mike knew God had a reason for it, so I share its honor with him.

The Commission

Months after the Pittsburgh meeting, God opened a door—radio broadcasting. Beginning at a 50kw AM/FM combination, simulcast in Philadelphia from nine till noon every Sunday, Mike and I co-hosted a contemporary Christian music program called "Man Alive!" Ministering to our listeners as a team, we spread the gospel across America, syndicated on over fifty radio stations as a public service. We carried the studio equipment in our car and set it up in motels. After six years, we leased and operated

The Writer

XERF, Mexico's border blaster, covering about half the world with contemporary Christian music on secular radio. We didn't know Kathryn had hoped to expand her radio ministry.

Together we worked in broadcasting for the length of our marriage, whether on the air, filing FCC applications, or building radio stations, microphone to antenna. In 1995 Mike's dream to be a station owner was fulfilled, but late in 1996, he contracted brain cancer. In 1998 the man who taught me love passed on to sleep in Jesus, but his love never left me; it's always in my heart as the love of Christ. You see, *love never ends. (1 Cor. 13:8a ESV)* Love keeps passing on from those who receive it.

One morning in the fall of 2003, I woke out of sleep to the stunning words: "Write a book!" I had only written commercials for radio, but I began writing *A Thorn in My Flesh* and disclosed my life as I typed its stories, including my sufferings with clarity of recall. I was giving away a book that was self-deprecating. When it saved men in prison, I saw the rewards of my pain as it spread hope and even averted suicide. I was in awe when they rejoiced, having believed in Christ by reading its five hundred verses, which didn't return void. (See Is. 55:11)

The Anointing

In 2007 I felt pregnant with the Spirit, nearly bursting to express something, but I didn't know what it was. I was so full, it was nearly painful. I prayed for direction but still didn't understand what God wanted me to do. Years before He'd shown me He would open Revelation to me, but I was terrified by the idea.

After uncanny events, an odd name came to mind: Reinhard Bonnke. A mere glint of hope would prompt me to obey. That's why I sent him an email about my dilemma. The next day he sent me a personal invitation for a face-to-face meeting in Florida. I threw the materials together and paid the price by faith. In three weeks I was in Orlando, hoping for the solution.

The first day lasted twelve hours: twenty-two of us were standing for early worship when the evangelist took the seat in front of mine, and a great anointing fell on me. No one knew what God had done. I kept it close to my heart. I couldn't talk or write about it for a few years. I was sure the experience had a reason but couldn't imagine what its purpose would be.

UNVEILED!

The next day, I asked the evangelist, "What am I supposed to do with all this power?" He dropped the mike. Then he replied in his normally terse manner. "Press in," he said.

As a pragmatist I thought, "I paid all that money and flew a thousand miles to hear *two words?!*" I was hoping for some direction, but God answered me with His power. I'd work in concert together with His Spirit, and yes, I would "press in."

For several years I was speechless about the outpouring, awestruck. I recalled a request I'd made thirty-five years before; I'd asked for a "double portion" of His Spirit because in my weakness, I was desperate for His strength. "I want it all!" I cried out. "Lord, give me a double portion!" That's how it was.

He didn't give it to me when I asked for it, but He gave me a mantle in 1974 and now this! I still didn't know what to do, but I'd know when its time came. At thirty, I said, "Lord, I won't be credible till I'm sixty." In 2008 He doubled the portion soon after I turned sixty. Sometimes I prophesy unwittingly.

In early January 2010, rising from sleep, the Word of the Lord silently came to me: "Haven't I taught you the truth?" For years He'd been disclosing it to me. "Yes, Lord, You have," I said aloud. He continued, "But the church is divided by deceptions." So that was the answer! It's as Jesus said, "My sheep know My voice, and they follow me."

At the time, I didn't know the details of the commission, but with those words, He planted a seed in my heart to write *The Union*. The one who creates confusion and deception has divided us, but how did that happen, and when did it begin? I did the research, which ended with the deletion of several chapters that were just too dry to read. Living in the truth is what counts.

A few months later, a dream became a vision when a speaker turned to face me, telling me to deliver the message. I sat up with a fire burning in my heart and blurted, "What message?" Many more questions led me to write since the fire in 2010.

All these years, I've been writing what God has revealed. I didn't know what to expect or when He'd be finished. I only knew He'd complete what He'd begun. My writings are evidence of a faith that has gained victories by the Bible's powerful, life-giving words from not just one, but two testaments—both sides of the same report by the same Author.

The Writer

Looking back to 1969, I was aimless, unhappy, and confused when God drew me to His Son. Devils had filled me with their fears, their lies, and their confusion till I couldn't organize my thoughts enough to hold a pencil in my hand. Then God gave me the victory over my enemies and taught me His words to write books about them.

Scholars haven't understood these things because God hides them from the wise to reveal them to fools—or shall I say, His less admired ones? We who see ourselves as fools search for His wisdom, and He lets us see as He sees. He renews our minds if we reject men's opinions to believe Him instead of them.

At first I was angry when I realized the words of the apostles were unlike what I'd been taught by many teachers with theological degrees. In time the Spirit showed me the lies were sown by the deceiver, the adversary of us all, with or without degrees. He even dulls the bright ones. When we do things as the world does, we're bound to miss the words of God. If we think we can't be taken in by lies, we probably already are, but God can empower weak ones like me.

The idea of believing God without considering the various teachings and opinions of scholars was new to me after so many years, but my Rabboni patiently taught me secrets He had hidden for centuries. He is the God of Enoch, Moses, Elijah, and David —people like us. As we grow we do His will till it becomes ours.

> [18] Let no man deceive himself. If any man among you thinks that he is wise in this age, he must become foolish, so that he may become wise. [19] For the wisdom of this world is foolishness before God. For it is written, *"HE IS* THE ONE WHO CATCHES THE WISE IN THEIR CRAFTINESS"; [20] and again, "THE LORD KNOWS THE REASONINGS of the wise, THAT THEY ARE USELESS."
> (1 Cor. 3:18-20 NASB)

Many people are intellectually superior to me, and I don't challenge that; it doesn't matter. The Lord called me to find the truth of His words and to write a book, a trilogy as it turned out. I had no idea how to begin or where it would end. I learned a little and then more. At times, I struggled with His words till the strongholds fell and I believed. The Holy Spirit was more than a

UNVEILED!

Helper to me; He was the Revelator. I wasn't alone. He corrected my mistakes and helped me edit and revise the text for others to understand it. These were more His books than mine.

> [17] To him who overcometh will I give to eat of the hidden manna, and will give him a white stone, and in the stone a new name written, ... (from Rev. 10:17)
>
> [19] For it is written,
>
> "I will destroy the wisdom of the wise,
>   and the discernment of the discerning I will thwart."
> (1 Cor. 1:19 ESV; cf. Is. 29:14)

Had God not lifted the veil, I'd still be reading in the dark. He told me to write and deliver the message. I listened, prayed, and read; meditated, perceived, and wrote. When He called me to do this, I didn't shrink back, but *pressed in* by faith, thanks to a terse word from an evangelist. I'm an apprentice of the Spirit as Jesus' student and disciple. Had I not searched out the truth, He would not have opened it to me. My only credentials are the words He has given me. I've spoken on radio and preached in prisons, nursing homes, homeless shelters, mental health clinics, at prison seminars, and more, but for the past several years, I've been writing by the Holy Spirit. May He vindicate me.

The more He reveals, the more He convicts, and the closer He draws us to Him. Learning is more than just knowing stuff; it's about satisfying our hunger to grow into His likeness. The closer we are to Jesus, the more like Him we become till His gift is made perfect and complete in us as He finishes the work He began in us. (See 2 Pet. 1:1-11) The reason we search the Bible is the goal of our calling, to know Jesus Christ in Spirit and truth.

> [22] No, much rather, those members of the body which seem to be weaker are necessary. [23] And those members of the body which we think to be less honorable, on these we bestow greater honor; and our unpresentable parts have greater modesty, [24] but our presentable parts have no need. But God composed the body having given greater honor to that part which lacks it, [25] that there should be no schism in the body, but that the members should have the same care for one another.
> (1 Cor. 12:22-25 NKJV)

The Writer

(Ken Cobean Photography)

Mike and Joan

… love is strong as death (from Ecc. 8:6).

Website: https://JoanHRichardson.com

Contact for speaking: Joan@FaithOnEarth.org
Other books by this writer:

A Thorn In My Flesh
The Rewards of Persevering Faith
through Life's Toughest Times

The Union
Get Ready to Meet the King!
God Calls His Church
to Truth, Faith, and Holiness

Mysteries of the Ancient Word
Unlocked Treasures, Hidden for the End of Days

UNVEILED!

End Notes

a. Jews for Jesus, "Yeshua: The Jewish Word for Salvation," www.jewsforjesus.org/publications/newsletter/newsletter-dec-1987 December 1987 Newsletter (5748:3)
b. "2424.Iésous," biblehub.com/greek/2424.htm
c. "What Language Did Jesus and the Apostles Speak?" https://askdrbrown.org/library/what-language-did-jesus-and-apostles-speak
   G. Scott Gleaves, "Did Jesus Speak Greek?" www.bibleinterp.com/articles/2015/09/gle398009.shtml
d. www.kingjamesbibleonline.org/1611-Luke-Chapter-1/
e. Richard Cavendish, "The End of the Holy Roman Empire," www.HistoryToday.com/richard-cavendish/end-holy-roman-empire
f. "Donation of Pippin," https://www.britannica.com/event/Donation-of-Pippin
g. "List of Holy Roman Emperors," www.holyromanempireassociation
h. "History of the Holy Roman Empire," http://www.historyworld.net/wrldhis/PlainTextHistories.asp?historyid=aa35
i. Richard Cavendish, "The End of the Holy Roman Empire," www.HistoryToday.com/richard-cavendish/end-holy-roman-empire
j. "Treaty of Versailles," www.history.com/topics/world-war-i/treaty-of-versailles
k. "The Nazi Rise to Power," https://www.ushmm.org/wlc/en/article.php?ModuleId=10008206
l. "Otto von Bismarck," history.com/topics/germany/otto-von-Bismarck (December 6, 2009; updated June 7, 2019)
   "Blood and Iron (speech)," https://en.wikipedia.com/wiki/Blood_and_Iron_%28speech%29, (April 20, 2018)
m. Michael Ray, "Why was Nazi Germany Called the Third Reich?" https://www.britannica.com/story/why-was-nazi-germany-called-the-third reich
01. www.biblegateway.com   Search: Great+Sea
02. www.middle-life-and-times.info/medieval-kings/richard-the-lionheart-biography.htm
03. Cit: C. N. Trueman, "Royal Coat of Arms," https://www.historylearningsite.co.uk/medieval-england/royal-coats-of-arms/
    Mandy Barrow, "Project Britain British Life and Culture," ProjectBritain.com/motto.html
04. www.biographyonline.net/politicians/uk/benjamin-disraeli.html

UNVEILED!

05. David Cody, "Queen Victoria," http://www.victorianweb.org/victorian/history/victoria/1.html
06. John Darwin, "Britain the Commonwealth and the End of the Empire,"www.bbc.co.uk/history/british/modern/end_of_empire_overview_01.shtml
    Jan Erik Mustad, "The Dismantling of the Empire," ndla.no/en/node/98538?fag=71082
07. www.jewishvirtuallibrary.org/ the-balfour-declaration-table-of-contents
    "Conflicting Arab and Jewish Responses to the Balfour Declaration," www.ijs.org.au/The-Balfour-Declaration/default.aspx
08. "The Palestine Mandate of the League of Nations," www.mideastweb.org/mandate.html
    The Hope: The Rebirth of Israel, https://www.youtube.com/watch?v=FDhy5uWPVDM&t=279s
09. "TransJordan," www.britishempire.co.uk/maproom/transjordan.htm
    "Is it true that Britain created Israel?" www.israeladvocacy.net/knowledge/the-truth-of-how-israel-was-created/Britain-created-israel/
10. "Neville Chamberlain," www.biography.com/people/neville-chamberlain-9243721
    "Arthur Neville Chamberlain," http://www.bbc.co.uk/history/historic_figures/chamberlain_arthur_neville.shtml
    "Munich Pact Signed." www.history.com/this-day-in-history/munich-pact-signed
11. "Invasion of Poland, Fall 1939," https://www.ushmm.org/wic/en/article.php?ModuleId=10005070
12. "McDonald White Paper of 1939,"www.palestinefacts.org/pf_mandate_whitepaper_1939.php
13. "Winston Churchill," www.WinstonChurchill.org
14. "Lend-Lease Act (1941)," https://www.ourdocuments.gov/doc.php?flash=true&doc=71
15. "1917 February Revolution Begins in Russia," www.history.com/this-day-in-history/february-revolution-begins-in-russia
16. "Provisional Committee," https://www.marxists.org/glossary/orgs/p/r.htm
17. "Union of Soviet Socialist Republics," https://www.britannica.com/place/Soviet-Union
18. "1848 Marx Publishes Manifesto," www.history.com/this-day-in-history/marx-publishes-manifesto   (Continued)

End Notes

"The Communist Manifesto,"
www.wikipedia.org/wiki/The_Communist_Manifesto
19. "Russian Revolution," http://www.history.com/topics/russian-revolution
"Vladimir Lenin," www.biography.com/people/vladimir-lenin-9379007
20. "Trotsky's Role in the 1917 Russian Revolution," www.trotsky.net/russian_revolution.html
21. "Joseph Stalin," www.biography.com/people/joseph-stalin-9491723
22. Joshua J. Mark, "The Huns," www.ancient.eu/Huns/Germanic-tribes (12/14/2004)
"Barbarian Huns," www.historyfiles.co.uk/FeaturesEurope/BarbarianHuns.htm
23. "Donation of Pippin," https://www.britannica.com/event/Donation-of-Pippin
24. "Leo III," http://www.catholic.org/saints/saint.php?saint_id=1003
"The Historical Charlemagne," http://www.spanport.ucla.edu/santiago/histchrl.html
25. Piero Scaruffi, "A Timeline of the Holy Roman Empire," https://scaruffi.com/politics/holy.html (© Piero Scaruffi, 1999)
26. "John XII Pope," https://www.britannica.com/biography/John-XII
27. "History of the Holy Roman Empire," http://www.historyworld.net/wrldhis/PlainTextHistories.asp?historyid=aa35
"List of Holy Roman Emperors," www.holyromanempireassociation.com/list-of-holy-roman-emperors.html
28. John Foxe, *Foxe's Book of Martyrs*.
29. "Napoleon's Coronation as Emperor of the French," www.georgianindex.net/Napoleon/coronation/coronation.htm
Richard Cavendish, "The End of the Holy Roman Empire," www.HistoryToday.com/richard-cavendish/end-holy-roman-empire
30. "Congress of Vienna," www.encyclopedia.com/history/modern-europe/treaties-and-alliances/congress-vienna
31. "Issues Relevant to U.S. Foreign Diplomacy: Unification of German States," Office of the Historian, Foreign Service Interests, United States Department of State https://history.state.gov/countries/german-unification

(Continued)

UNVEILED!

"Otto von Bismarck," history.com/topics/germany/otto-von-Bismarck (December 6, 2009; updated June 7, 2019)
32. "Tehran Conference World War II," www.britannica.com/event/Tehran-Conference
"The Tehran Conference, 1943." https://history.state.gov/milestones/1937-1945/tehran-conf
33. "Hitler on Trial for Treason," historyplace.com/worldwar2
34. Sarah Yeomans, "Ancient Pergamon," http://www.biblicalarchaeology.org/daily/biblical-sites-places/biblical-archaeology-sites/Pergamon-2/, (December 2016)
35. Lily Rothman, "Who Started the Reichstag Fire?" time.com/3717003/reichstag-fire-1933, (Feb. 27, 2015)
36. "The Nazi Rise to Power," https://www.ushmm.org/wlc/en/article.php?ModuleId=10008206
"Hitler Becomes Führer," www.historyplace.com/worldwar2/holocaust/h-becomes.htm
37. "Adolf Hitler," http://www.biography.com/people/adolf-hitler-9340144#synopsis
"Adolf Hitler Biography," www.secondworldwar.co.uk/index.php/biography-of-adolf-hitler
"The Rise of Nazism in Germany,"https://www.htav.asn.au/documents/item/2487
38. "The Oath to Adolf Hitler," Rudolf Hess, research.calvin.edu/german-propaganda-archive/hess1.htm
39. "Holy Roman Empire" Europe, 1450-1789, Encyclopedia of the Early Modern World, © 2004 The Gale Group Inc. http://www.encyclopedia.com/history/modern-europe/german-history/holy-roman-empire
40. "German Referendum, 1934," (Last edited October 10, 2017) https://wikipedia.org/wiki/German_referendum,_1934
41. "Hitler in Vienna after the Takeover ... ," www.youtube.com/watch?v=ndP7fzbz9rY
42. "The Triumph of Hitler, Nazis Take Czechoslovakia," (2001) https://www.historyplace.com/worldwar2/triumph/tr-czech.htm
43. "The Importance of the Rhineland," www.bbc.co.uk/bitesize/higher/history/roadwar/rhine/revision/1/
44. Gordon Robertson, *Seat of Satan*, Prod. CBN www.tinyurl.com/ndj66rs
45. David Klinghoffer, "Is There a Connection between Hitler and Darwin?" www.Discovery.org/a/4749, (April 18, 2008)
46. "Pact of Steel," www.britannica.com/event/Pact-of-Steel

End Notes

47. "Three-Power Pact between Germany, Italy, and Japan, Signed at Berlin September 27, 1940," http://avalon.law.yale.edu/wwii/triparti.asp
48. Ibid.
49. "Dimensions: A Journal of Holocaust Studies," Victoria J. Barnett, "The Role of the Churches: Compliance and Confrontation," http://archive.adl.org/braun/dim_14_1_role_church.html#.WKFI01UrLtQ
50. "Full Official Record: What the Mufti Said to Hitler," timesofisrael.com/full-official-record-what-the-mufti-said-to-hitler/ (October 21, 2015)
51. Eric W. Gritsch, "Was Luther Anti-Semitic?" (from Martin Luther: The Later Years, 1993), www.christiantiytoday.com/history/issues/issue-39/was-luther-anti-semitic
52. Laurence Reese, "Hitler's Invasion of Russia in World War Two," www.bbc.co.uk/historyHistory/worldwars/wwtwo/Hitler_russia_invasion_01.shtml, (Updated March 30, 2011)
53. "The Nuremberg Laws: Background and Overview," https:/www.jewishvirtuallibrary.org/background-and-overview-of-the-nuremberg-laws
54. *The Roosevelts An Intimate History*, PBS. Ken Burns.
55. "48. The Great Depression." www.ushistory.org/us/48.asp www.pbs.org/wgbh/americanexperience/features/general-article
56. "General Article: The Great Depression," http://www.pbs.org/wgbh/americanexperience/features/general-article/dustbowl-great-depression/
57. "Why Did Japan Attack Pearl Harbor?" www.pearlharbor.org "A Date which Will Live in Infamy," www.historymatters.gmu.edu/d/5166
58. https://visitpearlharbor.org/faqs/how-many-people-died-at-pearl-harbor-during-the-attack/
59. "America Declares War on Japan–President Roosevelt Speech," https://www.youtube.com/watch?v=1K8gYGg0dkE
60. "On this Day: US Now at War with Germany," www.nytimes.com/learning/general/onthisday/big/1211.html#article
61. "World War 2 Timeline," historyplace.com/worldwar2/timeline
62. "January 6, 1942 Franklin D. Roosevelt State of the Union Address," https://www.c-span.org/video/?152565-1/franklin-d-roosevelt-state-union-address

UNVEILED!

63. Ray Pittman, "Face of Battle," www.pbs.org/thewar/at_war_battle_training.htm
64. Jeroline Green, "War Production," www.pbs.org/thewar/at_home_war_production.htm
65. www.usa.gov   Search: Executive Order 90669
66. "Hitler's bodyguard who said he knew nothing of holocaust dies," (09-2013) www.usatoday.com/story/news/world/2013/09/06/hitler-bodyguard/2775459
67. "Bombing of Hiroshima and Nagasaki," HISTORY. https://www.history.com/topics/world-war-ii/bombing-of-hiroshima-and-nagasaki, (December 20, 2018)
68. "Japanese Sign Final Surrender," https://www.youtube.com/watch?v=vcnH_kFzXc (August 6, 2007)
69. "V-E Day is celebrated in America and Britain," https://www.history.com/this-day-in-history/victory-in-europe (Last updated: May 6, 2020)

    "Stutthof," https://encyclopedia.ushmm.org/content/en/article/stutthof
70. "Killing Operations Begin at Chelmno," https://.ushmm.org/learn/timeline-of-events/1939-1941/killing-operations-begin-at-chelmno
71. "The Constitution of the United States: A Transcription," Archives.gov/founding-docs/constitution-transcript
72. One for Israel Ministries, https:www.IMetMessiah.com
73. "The Yalta Conference, 1945," https://history.state.gov/milestones/1937-1945/yalta-conf

    "Charter of the United Nations," un.org/en/charter-united-nations/
    Nimoy, Leonard. *The Miracle of Israel.* DVD. Directed by Lynette Lewis. Phoenix, AZ: The Miracle of Israel Foundation, 2013.
    "Charter of the United Nations and Statute of the International Court of Justice," https://treaties.un.org/doc/Publication/CTC/uncharter.pdf p. 15, (San Fransisco, 1945)
74. "UN General Assembly Resolution 181," http://www.mfa.gov.il/mfa/foreignpolicy/peace/guide/pages/un%20general%20assembly%20resolution%20181.aspx
75. "UN Vote 1947," https://www.youtube.com/watch?v+Xzxod60_Vbs
76. "Today in Zionist History: The San Remo Conference," https://unitedwithisrael.org/today-in-history-the-san-remo-conference, (April 25, 2014)
77. "Declaring the State of Israel," www.newsweek.com/declaring-state-israel-may-14-1948-332152, (May 2015)

End Notes

78. "The Arab-Israeli War of 1948," https://history.state.gov/milestones/1945-1952/arab-israeli-war
79. "The Six-Day War," www.sixdaywar.org/content/ReunificationJerusalem.asp
80. "Territorial Evolution of the British Empire," https://www.youtube.com/ results?search_query=territorial+evolution+of+the+british+empire (1:17)
    "Commonwealth association of states," https://www.britannica.com/topic/Commonwealth-association-of-states (July 20, 1998; update August 11, 2020)
81. "Fall of the Soviet Union," http://www.history.com/topics/cold-war/fall-of-soviet-union
    "The Reagan Years," http://www.ushistory.org/us/59e.asp
82. "Alger Hiss," https://www.fbi.gov/history/famous-cases/alger-hiss
83. Donald L. Wasson, "Hellenistic Warfare," *Ancient History Encyclopedia.* https://www.ancient.eu/Hellenistic_Warfare/ (modified August 22, 2016)
    Joshua J. Mark, "Western Roman Empire," https://www.ancient.eu/Western_Roman_Empire/ (December 1, 2011)
    "Map of the Successor kingdoms." https://www.ancient.eu/image/581/map-of-the-successor-kingdoms-c-303-bce/
84. Collin Hansen, "The Vanishing Act of the Church in Turkey," www.christianitytoday.com/history/2008/august/vanishing-act-of-church-in-turkey.html (August 2008)
    "Byzantine Empire," https://www.history.com/topics/ancient-middle-east/byzantine-empire (Last updated August 20, 2019)
85. Amanda Briney, "Istanbul Was Once Constantinople," http://geography.about.com/od/specificplacesofinterest/a/istanbul.htm (July 2016)
86. "Constantinople," eyewitnesstohistory.com/constantinople.htm
87. Ibid.
    Judith Herrin, "The Fall of Constantinople," www.historytoday.com/judith-herrin/fall-constantinople (July 2003)
    "1453 The Conquest," www.theottomans.org/English/campaigns_army/1453-the-conquest.asp (2002)
88. "John XII Pope," https://www.britannica.com/biography/John-XII
    Peter H. Wilson, "Holy Roman Empire," *International Encyclopedia of the Social Sciences Encyclopedia.com* (July 19, 2017) http://encyclopedia.com/history/modern-europe/german-history/holy-roman-empire
89. Walter Williams, "Socialism's Death Count," https://www.wnd.com/2012/08/socialisms-death-count/ (August 7, 2012)

90. Marx, Karl, and Friedrich Engels. *The Communist Manifesto.* (2019)
91. "Barbarian Europe, The Origins of the Huns," [a perspective] www.historyfiles.co.uk/FeaturesEurope/BarbarianHuns.htm
92. "Odoacer King of Italy," https://www.britannica.com/biography/Odoacer (Last update March 11, 2021)
93. Joshua Mark, "Attila the Hun," https://ancient.eu/Attila_the_Hun (March 18, 2018)
    "Hunnic Empire," www.newworldencyclopedia.org/entry/Hunnic_Empire
94. "Treaty of Versailles," www.history.com/topics/world-war-i/treaty-of-versailles
95. Flavius Josephus, *The Antiquities of the Jews*, Book 1; 4; 2.
96. Mark Isaak, "Flood Stories from Around the World," www.talkorigins.org/faqs/flood-myths.html, (September 2, 2012)
97. "Nebo" and "Nebuchadnezzar," *The New International Dictionary of the Bible,* p. 695-696. (1987)
98. Flavius Josephus, *The Antiquities of the Jews*, Book 1; 4; 2; 118
99. "Zerubbabel," *New International Dictionary of the Bible,* 1086.
100. Theophilus G. Pinches, "The Religion of the Babylonians and Assyrians" Web dissertation.
101. "The Epic of Gilgamesh Summary & Study Guide," www.bookrags.com/studyguide-epicgilgamesh/#gsc.tab=0
102. "Beelzebub," www.biblestudytools.com/dictionary/beelzebub
103. "Comprehensive Bible Helps," *The Topical Reference Bible,* Babel, Babylon, p. 1015 (1985)
104. "Ancient Jewish History: Hellenism," www.jewishvirtuallibrary.org/jsource/History/hellenism.html
    Flavious Josephus, *Antiquities of the Jews.* Book 12; 5; 1, 5.
105. Ernest I. Martin, *The People that History Forgot,* "The Seleucid Capital Moved West to Antioch," www.askelm.com/people/peo017.htm
    R. Russell, "Ancient Babylonia – History of Babylonia," www.bible-history.com/babylonia/BabyloniaHistory_of_Babylonia.com
106. "Zeus," https://www.greekmythology.com/Zeus/zeus.html
107. Flavious Josephus, *Antiquities of the Jews.* Book 12; 3; 3-4.
108. Flavious Josephus, *Antiquities of the Jews.* Book 12; 6-7.
    Rabbi Paul Steinberg, "Antiochus the Madman." from *Celebrating the Jewish Year: The Winter Holiday,* https://www.myjewishlearning.com /article/Antiochus-the-madman/   (2007)

End Notes

109. "Asia," *New International Dictionary of the Bible,* p. 102.
110. "Why Does God Hate the Practices of the Nicolaitans?" www.biblestudy.org/basicart/why-does-god-hate-practices-of-the-nicolaitans.html
 "Nicolaism," https://en.wikipedia.org/wiki/Nicolaism
111. David Pawson, *Romans 9,10, 11 Israel's Past, Present & Future* DVD. www.icejusa.org
112. "The Seleucid Capital Moved West to Antioch," www.askelm.com/people/peo017.htm
113. "Who Is Antipas?," www.antipas.net/whois.htm
114. Rick Larson, *The Star of Bethlehem,* DVD. Stephen Vidano. Mpowerpictires (2009)
 "Herod's Death, Jesus' Birth, and a Lunar Eclipse," https://www.biblicalarcheology.org/daily/people-cultures-in-the-bible/jesus-historical-jesus/herods-death-jesus-birth-and-a-lunar-eclipse/ (To the editor, 03/02/2017)
115. Flavius Jesphus, *The Wars of the Jews,* Book 2, chap. 19-20
116. "Excavating Ancient Pella, Jordan, Archeology investigates the Christians' escape to Pella," Biblical Archeology. (December 13, 2017) https://www.biblicalarcheology.org/daily/biblical-sites-places/biblical-archeology-sites/excavating-ancient-pella-jordan/
117. "Church History Timeline," www.churchhistorytimeline.com
118. Ibid.
119. "Brief history of the Leonid shower," https://leonid.arc.nasa.gov/history.html
120. "Kepler's Laws." www.hyperphysics.phy-astr.gsu.edu/hbase/Kepler.html
121. "More Ominous Biblical Signs in the Sky," www.wnd.com/2017/09/92317-more-ominous-biblical-signs-in-the-sky/
122. "President Donald J. Trump Keeps His Promise to Open U.S. Embassy in Jerusalem, Israel," whitehouse.gov/briefings-statements/president-donald-j-trump-keeps-promise-open-u-s-embassy-jerusalem-israel (Issued: May 14, 2018.)
123. Randy Dotinga, "'Roosevelt and Stalin' details the surprisingly warm relationship of an unlikely duo," *Christian Science Monitor,* March 5, 2015. http://csmonitor.com/Books/Book-Reviews/2015/0305/Roosevelt-and-Stalin-details-the-surprisingly-warm-relationship-of-an-unlikely-duo
124. *The Hope: The Rebirth of Israel.* DVD. Dir. Erin Zimmerman. Prod. CBN.

125. "The Berlin Crisis and the Construction of the BerlinWall," www.bbc.co.uk/history/places/berlinwall
126. Ibid.
127. "Berlin Wall," https://history.com/topics/cold-war/berlin-wall "1961: Berliners wake to divided city," news.bbc.uk/onthisday/hi/dates/stories/august/13/newsid_3054000/3054060.stm
128. "The Berlin Airlift," www.coldwar.org/articles/40s/berlin_airlift.asp
129. Ronald Reagan, "Berlin Wall Speech – President Reagan's Address at the Brandenburg Gate," https://www.youtube.com/watch?v=5MDFX-dNtsM
130. Jonathan Bowen, "The Fall of the Berlin Wall – Clearing the Way for the Uniting of Europe," www.biblemagazine.com/home/view_art.php?id_pag=224
131. "The reunification of Germany," wwww.britannica.com/place/Germany/the-reunification-of-Germany
132. "List if Chinese Flags," https://en.wikipedia.org/wiki/List_of_Chinese_flags, (April 20, 2020 @15:17 UTC)
133. "Chiang Kai-shek," ehistory.osu.edu/biographies/chiang-kai-shek The Ohio State University Department of History.
    Klaus Muhlhahn, "China," https://encyclopedia.1914-1918-online.net/article/china (Updated January 11, 2016)
134. "Assignment: China – The Chinese Civil War," https://china.usc.edu/assignment-china-chinese-civil-war (September 1, 2012)
135. "Chinese Civil War 1927-1949," https://www.britannica.com/event/Chinese-Civil-War
136. Han Cheung, "The day China joined the UN. UN Resolution 2758, passed in 1971, still carries ramifications for Taiwan today," Taipei Times. (October 18, 2015)
137. www.ccel.org/ccel/schaff/mpnf214.vii.ix.html Search > Syndodic Letter of Nicaean Council in 325
138. "Ashtoreth," New International Dictionary of the Bible, 100-101.
139. Arthur Maricle, Ph.D., "A Study in Absolute Catholic Power, www.mtc.org/inquis.html
140. Arthur Maricle, Ph.D., "A Study in Absolute Catholic Power, www.mtc.org/inquis.html
141. Christian-Jewish Relations: The Inquisition," https://www.jewishvirtuallibrary.org/the-inquisition (1998-2020)
142. "Christian-Jewish Relations: The Inquisition," https://www.jewishvirtuallibrary.org/the-inquisition (1998-2020)
143. "Overview Paris Peace Treaties," www.oxfordreference.com/view/10.1093/oi/authority.20110803100306594

(Continued)

End Notes

"Photos: Victory in Europe Day-May 8, 1945," https://www.denverpost.com/2018/05/07/photos-victory-in-europe-day-may-8-1945/

144. Cockerham, Larry, "Antiochus IV Epiphanes: The Antichrist of the Old Testament," prophecyforum.com/bible-prophecy/Antiochus-iv-epiphanes-antichrist-old-testament/ (February 7, 2008)

145. Amanda Casanova, "Plans Underway for Construction of Third Temple in Jerusalem," christianheadlines.com/blog/plans-underway-for-construction-of-third-temple-in-jerusalem.html (May 30, 2017)

   Ben Sales, "Laying the Groundwork for a Third Temple in Jerusalem," timesofisrael.com/laying-the-groundwork-for-a-third-temple-in-jerusalem/ (July 16, 2013)

146. "A Guide to the United States' History of Recognition, Diplomatic, Consular Relations, by Country, since 1776: Holy See," www.history.state.gov/countries/holy-see

147. Search: Papal Crown, Holy See Press Office, "Tiara," https://www.catholic.com/encyclopedia/vicar-of-christ Updated March 4, 2001.

148. Edward Penin, "Mahmoud Ahmadinejad Seeks Pope's Favor," www.newsmax.com/EdwardPenin/MahmoudAhmadinejadPopevatican/2010/10/07/id/372888/

149. Michele Chabin, Luigi Sandri, "Pope Visits Jerusalem's Western Wall, Dome of the Rock," http://www.beliefnet.co/columnists/news/2009/05/pope-visits-jerusalems-western.php

150. *Tares among the Wheat*: *The Untold History of the Bible;* Dir. Christian J. Pinto; Docudrama; DVD; 2012

151. Armenian Prelacy of the Eastern United States, https://www.facebook.com/search/str/Total+number+of+bishops+invited+to+Nicaea%3F/keywords_search (September 1, 2018. 10:29 a.m.)

152. "Pope Francis prays alongside Grand Mufti in Istanbul's Blue Mosque," www.theguardian.com/world/2014/nov/29/pope-francis-turkey-pray-blue-mosque-islam-cooperation

   Natalie Diblasio, William M. Welch, "Pope visits iconic religious sites in Istanbul," http://www.usatoday.com/story/news/world/2014/11/29/pope-visits-istanbul/19655421/

153. "Vatican Calls for New World Economic Order," https://www.*Fox News*.com, October 24, 2011.

154. Jeff Israely, "Iran's Secret Weapon: the Pope," content.time.com/time/world/article/0,8599,1687445,00.html

155. "New Embassy, a Sign of Pope's Love for Palestine, Abbas Says," catholicphilly.com/2017/01/news/world-news/new-embassy-a-sign-of-popes-love-for-palestine-president-abbas-says/
156. "About Saudi Arabia," https://www.saudiembassy.net/history
157. David Malsin, "How Saudi Crown Prince Mohammed Bin Salman Is Upending the Old Order," http://time.com/5068500/how-saudi-crown-prince-mohammed-bin-salman-upending-old-orde/ Time Magazine. (December 25, 2017)
158. Gordon Robertson, *Seat of Satan,* Prod. CBN www.tinyurl.com/ndj66rs
159. "Axis powers," https://www.britannica.com/topic/Axis-Powers (Revised and updated: September 22, 2006)
160. "The Tehran Conference, 1943." https://history.state.gov/milestones/1937-1945/tehran-conf
161. "The Yalta Conference, 1945," https://history.state.gov/milestones/1937-1945/yalta-conf
162. Alexander Solzhenitsyn, "Godlessness: the First Step to the Gulag," Templeton Prize Lecture, May 10, 1983. London. www.orthochristian.com/47643.html. (July 18, 2011)
163. *Billy Graham – God's Ambassador – Part I,* https://www.youtube.com/watch?v=QZ7fTGe4bY4
164. "Times Square Church," tsc.nyc/media_center.php?pg=sermons&spg=davidwilkerson
165. Cahn, Jonathan, *The Harbinger.* (2012)
166. Felicia Schwartz, "Trump Says U.S. Recognizes Jerusalem as Israel's Capital," *Wall Street Journal.* (December 6, 2017) https://www.wsj.com/article/trump-says-u-s-recognizes-Jerusalem-as-israels-capital-1512584043
167. "United States of America H.E. Mr. Barack Obama, President," https://gadebate.un.org/en/70/united-states-america
168. Amir Tibon and Noa Landau, "U.S. Embassy Move to Jerusalem: Everything You Need to Know" (May 14, 2018) "Everything You Need to Know about the U.S. Embassy in Jerusalem," https://www.haaretz.com/Israel-news/.premium-everything-you-need-to-know-about-the-u-s-embassy-in-jerusalem-1.6062554
169. "Israel," history.com/topics/middle-east/history-of-israel (May 14, 2019)
"New Jersey," en.wikipedia.org/wiki/New_Jersey
170. "Egypt," *New International Dictionary of the Bible,* p. 293.
171. "Northern kingdom Falls to Assyria," www.biblestudytools.com/commentaries/revelation/related-topics/northern-kingdom-falls-to-Assyria.html, 17.3.1

End Notes

172. "Coming Home to Israel," https://jewishvoice.org   search: aliyah
173. "The Jewish Temples: The Babylonian Exile (597-538 BCE),"
     www.jewishvirtuallibrary.org/jsource/History/Exile.html
     Joshua J. Mark, "Babylon." Ancient History Encyclopedia.
     (Last mod. April 28, 2011), www.ancient.eu/babylon/
174. Pete Hegseth, "How Iraq Was Won and Lost,"
     https://www.prageru.cpm/how-iraq-was-won-and-lost
     (August 14, 2017)
175. John F. Walvoord, "The Medes and the Persians,"
     https://bible.org/seriespage/chapter-vi-medes-and-persians
     Paul S. Crosby, "Heathen Astrologer or Hebrew
     Prophet?" www.letgodbetrue.com/bible/prophecy/
     cyrus-decree-to-rebuild.php, (May, 2013)
176. "Iran Profile – timeline," https://www.bbc.com/news/world-middle-east-14542438, (June 4, 2008)
177. "Ayatollah Ruholla Komeni," https://www.biography.com/people/ayatollah-ruholla-khomeini-13680544
178. "Macedon," https://history.com/topics/ancient-rome/macedonia (February 13, 2018)
179. Joshua J. Mark, "Alexander the Great," *Ancient History Encyclopedia,* www.ancient.eu/Alexander_the_Great (November 14, 2013)
180. Donald L. Wasson, "Seleucus I Nicator,"
     https://www.ancient.eu/seleucos_I/ (May 29, 2012)
     Robert Werner, "Ptolemy I Soter," https://www.britannica.com/biography/Ptolemy-I-Soter
181. Hans Volmann, "Antiochus IV Epiphanes,"
     www.britannica.com/bioography/Antiochus-IV-Epiphanes, (March 13, 2003)
182. Flavious Josephus, *Antiquities of the Jews.* Book 12, 6-7.
     "The Maccabees/Hasmoneans: History & Overview,"
     www.jewishvirtuallibrary.org/history-and-overview-of-the-maccabeees
183. "The Story of Chanukah," www.chabad.org/holidays/chanukah/article_cdo/aid/102978/jewish/The-Story-of-Chanukah.htm
184. "Ancient Jewish History: Hellenism,"
     www.jewishvirtuallibrary.org/jsource/History/hellenism.html
     Ernest I. Martin, *The People that History Forgot,* "The Seleucid Capital Moved West to Antioch," Chapter 15 www.askelm.com/people/peo017.htm
185. "Roman Empire," https://www.britannica.com/place/Roman-Empire
186. "1453 The Conquest," www.theottomans.org/Engli199/campaigns_army/1453-the-conquest.asp, (2002)

UNVEILED!

187. Gabriel Fournier, Jean F.P. Blondel, et al, "France," https://www.britannica.com/place/France, (June 4, 2018)
188. Dr. John Rikard, "Napoleonic Wars (1799-1815)," www.historyofwar.org/articles/wars_napoleonic.html
189. "Flag of Bergama," crwflags.com/FOTW/FLAGS/tr-35-be.html [The earthquake in Pergamon was in 262 AD.]
190. John Foxe, *Foxe's Book of Martyrs.* pp. 3-60. (2001)
191. "How the Lateran Treaty made the Catholic Church into a State," https://www.concordatwatch.eu/topic-841.843
    "Medieval Sourcebook: The Donation of Constantine (c. 750-800)," © Paul Halsell. (January 1996) [Updated 11/23/96]
192. Joel Richardson, "19 Feb Berlin's Pergamum Museum Closes for Five Years," https://joelstrumpet.com/berlins-pergamum- museum-closes-for-five-years/
193. goodreads.com/quotes/63497-this-agglomeration-which-was-called-and-which-still-calls-itself   search: Voltaire quote
194. Dugdale-Pointon, "Napoleonic Wars (1799-1815)," www.historyofwar.org/articles/wars_napoleonic.html (November 16, 2000)
195. "Melchizedek, Melchisedek" *The New International Dictionary of the Bible,* p. 639
196. "Janiculum," www.wikipedia.org/wiki/Janiculum
    "Janiculum Genicolo," www.aviewoncities.com/rome/Janiculum.htm
197. *The New Strong's Expanded Exhaustive Concordance of the Bible.* (2010) ["Israel, Jerusalem, Judah/Judea"]
198. "The 25 Largest Consumers' Markets ... and the Outlook for 2015," www.internationalbusinessguide.org/25-largest-consumers-markets-outlook-2015/
    "World's Largest Market," https://www.selectusa.gov/largest-market (2016)
199. "9/11 Attacks," www.history.com/topics/9-11-attacks
200. Josh Earnest, "Beam Signed by President Obama Installed at One World Trade Center," https://obamaawhitehouse.archives.gov/blog/2012/08/02/beam-signed-president-obama-installed-world-trade-center (August 2, 2012)
201. "Ask HISTORY: What was the first capital of the United States?" https://www.history.com/topics/us-states/washington-dc/videos/ask-history-first-us-capital
202. Mark Turin, "The World's Most Linguistically Diverse Location? New York City," www.popanth.com/article/the-worlds-most-linguistically-diverse-location-new-york-city (August 9, 2013)

End Notes

203. Adam Foreman, "Caution Ahead: Overdue Investments for New York's Aging Infrastructure," www.nycfuture.org/research/publications/caution-ahead (March 2014)
     Rebecca Fishbein, "Report: NYC Infrastructure Is Crumbling," www.gothamist.com/2014/03/12/nyc_infrastructure_rip.php
204. "New York Harbor," https://en.wikipedia.org/wiki/New_York_Harbor
205. "World Trade Center," www.wtc.com
     "One World Trade Center." www.onewtc.com
206. "Empire State," www.wikipedia.org   search: Empire State
207. "Jonathan Cahn Points to Harbinger of Baal…in New York," www.wnd.com/2016/09/jonathan-cahn-points-to-harbinger-of-baal-in-new-york
208. Gruffudd, Ioan, Ciaran Hinds, Albert Finney. *Amazing Grace.* DVD. Directed by Michael Apted. (2007) www.foxhome.com
209. "George H.W. Bush, 1989," www.youtube.com/watch?v=txukr5zgHnw
210. "Member States," www.un.org/en/member-states/index.html
     Adam Withnall, "These are the only 11 countries in the world that are actually free from conflict," *The Independent.* https://www.independent.co.uk/news/world/politics/world-peace-these-are-the-only-11-countries-in-the-world-that-are-actually-free-from-conflict-9669623.html (August 14, 2014)
211. Diane Rufino, "Abortion: Why the Supreme Court got it WRONG in Roe v. Wade (1973)," firstfreedomdaily.com/abortion-why-the-supreme-court-got-in-wrong-in-roe-v-wade-1973/ (February 24, 2019)
212. Penny Starr, "Education Expert: Removing Bible, Prayer in Public Schools Has Caused Decline," https://www.cnsnews.com/news/article/penny-starr/education-expert-removing-bible-prayer-public-schools-has-caused-decline (August 15, 2014)
213. *Left behind or Led Astray?* Disc 1. Prod. Good Fight Ministries. www.GoodFightMinistries.com
     Dr. Thomas Ice, "John Nelson Darby and the Rapture," www.pre-trib.org/articles/view/john-nelson-darby-and-the-rapture
214. "Arthur Blessitt," www.Blessitt.com

UNVEILED!

215. Amir Tibon and Noa Landau, "U.S. Embassy Move to Jerusalem: Everything You Need to Know" (May 14, 2018) https://www.haaretz.com/Israel-news/.premium-everything-you-need-to-know-about-the-u-s-embassy-in-jerusalem-1.6062554
216. "Why Do We Hide the Afikoman?" https://www.chabad.org/holidays/Passover/pesach-cdo/aid/1910434/jewish/Why-Do-We-Hide-the-Afikoman.htm
217. Bergman, Ingrid. *A Woman Called Golda*. DVD. Directed by Alan Gibson, Harvey Bennett, Paramount Television, 1982.
    Robertson, Gordon. *The Hope : The Rebirth of Israel*. DVD. Directed by Erin Zimmerman. Virginia Beach: CBN, 2015.
218. "The Yalta Conference, 1945," https://history.state.gov/milestones/1937-1945/yalta-conf
219. "Treaty of Versailles," www.history.com/topics/world-war-i/treaty-of-versailles
220. Xavier Jubier, "Maps of the Path of Totality," www.eclipse2017.org/2017/maps.htm
    Emily DeMarco, "Here are the paths of the next total solar eclipses," https://www.sciencenews.org/article/future-total-solar-eclipses. (August 18, 2017)
221. Doyle Rice, "Not your imagination: This hurricane season has been much worse than usual," www.usatoday.com/story/weather/2017/10/05/not-your-imagination-hurricane-season-has-been-much-worse-than-usual/736649001/
222. Seth Berenstein with Monika Mathur, "Nature's gone crazy: winds, fire. Floods, and quakes plague North America," www.denverpost.com/2017/09/08/earthquakes-floods-hurricanes-wildfires-north-america/ (September 8, 2017)
223. Jonathan Bernis and Mark Biltz, "The Jewish Voice," https://www.youtube.com/watch?v=FHgK0zQfuVY
224. "Official Final Schedule of Pope Francis U.S. Visit, 2015," www.popefrancisvisit.com/official-final-schedule-of-pope-francis-u-s-visit-2015/
225. "United States of America H.E. Mr. Barack Obama, President," https://gadebate.un.org/en/70/united-states-america
226. www.visitportugal.com search: Sanctuary of Fatima
    Edward Pentin, "Pope Francis Consecrating the World to Mary," www.NCRegister.com > Edward Pentin. (October 15, 2013)
227. "Antisemitism on rise across Europe 'in worst times since the Nazis,'" https://www.thguardian.com/society/2014/aug/07/antisemitism-rise-europe-worst-since-nazis (August 7, 2014)

(Continued)

End Notes

Josh Levs, "'Unprecedented global study finds 1 in 4 adults ant-Semitic,'" www.cnn.com/2014/05/14/world/anti-semitism-global-survey (May 14, 2014)

228. "Nubia Ancient Region, Africa," https://www.britannica.com/place/Nubia
229. Abarimpublications.com/Meaning/Cush
"Cush," www.Biblestudytools.com/dictionary/Cush
"The History of Ancient Nubia," https://oi.uchicago.edu/museum-exhibits/history-ancient-nubia
230. "1903 – The First Flight," https://www.nps.gov/wrbr/historyculture/thefirstflight.htm, Wright Bothers National Memorial, North Carolina.
231. "Benjamin Franklin: First American Diplomat, 1776-1785," https://history.state.gov/milestones/1776-1783/b-franklin
232. "List of river borders of U.S. States," https://en.wikipedia.org/wiki/List_of_river_borders_of_U.S._states (September 5, 2017)
233. "U.S. River Borders Quiz Stats – By pschmeidt," https://www.sporcle.com/games/pschmiedt/state-river-borders/results

The writer does not endorse the belief systems of the resources listed above and advises caution in studying prophetic sites.

Some of the online sites might be obsolete, but many others are available besides these, which were accessed 02/12/2017 or later. Paperback books are recommended since they can't be erased, altered, or denied access.

References

A Complete Guide to Heraldry; Skyhorse Publishing Inc.: New York, 2007.

Code of Canon Law, New English Translation. Latin-English Edition, Canon Law Society of America: Washington, D.C., 1983.

The Complete Word Study Dictionary New Testament, Revised Edition. AMG Publishers: Chattanooga. TN, 1993.

The Complete Word Study Old Testament, King James Version. AMG Publishers: Chattanooga. TN, 1994.

Cruden's Concordance of the Bible. Dugan Publishers Inc.: Gordonsville, TN, 1985.

Holman Book of Biblical Charts, Maps, and Reconstructions, Broadman & Holman Publishers: Nashville, TN., 1993.

The Hebrew-English Interlinear ESV Old Testament: Biblica Hebraica: Stuttgartensia and English Standard Version. Crossway: Wheaton, Ill., 2014.

The New International Dictionary of the Bible. Zondervan Publishing House: Grand Rapids, MI, 1987.

The New Oxford American Dictionary. Oxford University Press: New York, 2001.

The New Strong's Expanded Exhaustive Concordance of the Bible. Thomas Nelson Publishers: Nashville, TN, 2010.

The Topical Reference Bible, Dugan Publishers, Inc.: Gordonsville, TN, 1987.

The Works of Josephus New Updated Edition, Hendrickson Publishers, Inc., Peabody, MA, 1987.

Young's Literal Translation of the Holy Bible, Revised Edition. Baker Books: Grand Rapids, MI, 1995.

The Zondervan Parallel New Testament in Greek and English. Zondervan Corporation: Grand Rapids, MI, 2010.

Bibliography

The Constitution of the United States of America with the Declaration of Independence; Castle Books: New York, NY, 2014.

Foxe, John. *Foxe's Book of Martyrs: Updated to the 21st Century;* Bridge-Logos: Orlando, FL, 2001.

Gritsch, Eric W. "Was Luther Anti-Semitic?" *Christianity Today*; issue 39, "Martin Luther: The Later Years," 1993.

Marx, Karl, and Friedrich Engels. *The Communist Manifesto;* Arcturus Publishing Limited: London, UK, 2019.

Robinson, James. *Readings in European History, Vol. 1,* Ginn & Co.: Boston & New York, 1904.

Sadler, Robert, and Marie Chapian. *The Emancipation of Robert Sadler,* Bethany Fellowship, Inc., Minneapolis, MN, 1975.

Sparks, Jack N. *The Apostolic Fathers*, Light and Life Publishing Co.: Minneapolis, 1978.

UNVEILED!

Recommended Videos *

Abeles, Ben, Demisa Augustinova, Martin Bandzak. *Nicky's Family.* IMDb. Directed by Matej Minac. Amazon Video, 2011.

Aldrin, Buzz, Andrew Alozie, et al. *When the World Breaks.* IMBd. Directed by Hans Fjellestad. Vision Films, 2010.

Alon, Mina, Richard J. Carson, and Eddie Cohen. *Above and Beyond: The Birth of the Israeli Air Force.* DVD. Directed by Roberta Grosssman. New York City: International Film Circuit, 2014.

Bell, Joshua, Itzhak Perlman, and Zubin Mehta. *Orchestra of Exiles.* DVD. Directed by Josh Aronson. Toronto: Aronson Film Associates, 2012.

Benigni, Roberto. *Life Is Beautiful.* IMDb. Directed by Roberto Benigni. Santa Monica, CA: Miramax, 1997.

Bennett, David M., Dr. Mark Patterson, et al. *Left Behind or Led Astray.* DVD. Directed by Joseph M. Schimmel. Worldwide, www.GoodFightMinistries.org, 2015.

Bergman, Ingrid. *A Woman Called Golda.* DVD. Directed by Alan Gibson, Harvey Bennett, Paramount Television, 1982.

Blessitt, Arthur. *The Cross.* DVD. Directed by Matt Crouch. Nashville: Thomas Nelson, 2009.

Brown, David, Hudson, Henry, et al. *Tares among the Wheat* DVD. Directed by Christian J. Pinto. www.Adullum Films.com, 2012.

Bullock, Sandra, Michael Douglas, Leonard Nimoy, *The Prime Ministers: The Pioneers.* Documentary. Directed by Richard Trank. Moriah Films, 2013.

Butterfield, Asa, and Jack Scanlon. *The Boy in the Striped Pajamas.* IMDb. Directed by Mark Herman. Web, 2008.

Chamberlain, Richard. *Wallenberg A Hero's Story.* DVD. Directed by Lamont Johnson. Burbank, CA: NBC Entertainment, 1985.

Coyote, Peter, Paul Giamatti, Edward Herrmann, et al. *The Roosevelts: An Intimate History.* DVD. Directed by Ken Burns. Arlington, VA: PBS, 2007.

David, Keith, Adam Arkin, and Bobby Cannavale. *The War.* DVD. Directed by Ken Burns. Arlington, VA: PBS, 2007.

Enyart, Bob, "Scientists Baffled-New Discoveries-Darwinian Evolution-Crumbling-Scientists Abandon Theory," CBC Media. https://www.youtube.com/watch?v=WdqYPjA9VxA (July 5, 2016)

Eshcol, Levi, Gamal Abdel Nasser. *Six Days in June.* DVD. Directed by Ilan Ziv. Los Angeles: Seventh Art Releasing, 2007.

Finney, Albert, Vanessa Redgrave, Jim Boadbent. *The Gathering Storm.* Directed by Richard Loncraine. New York City: HBO Entertainment, 2002.

Freeman, Morgan, Abba Eban, *The Long Way Home.* IMDb. Written and directed by Mark Jonathan Harris. Moriah Films, 1997.

Goodman, Henry, *To Life: How Young Israeli Volunteers Are Changing the World.* DVD. Directed by Erin Zimmerman. CBN Documentaries, 2018.

Gruffudd, Ioan, Ciaran Hinds, Albert Finney. *Amazing Grace.* DVD. Directed by Michael Apted. A Sunflower Production by Ingenious Film Partners, 2007.

Ham, Ken, *Darwinian Evolution and Racism,* www.YouTube.com. University of California Television (UCTV) April 24, 2008.

Harris, Julie, and Jeannette Clift. *The Hiding Place.* DVD. Directed by James F. Collier. Charlotte, NC: World Wide Pictures, 1975.

Heston, Charlton, and Yul Brinner. *The Ten Commandments.* DVD. Directed by Cecil B. DeMille. Los Angeles: Paramount, 1956.

Keillor, Garrison. *The Danish Solution: The Rescue of the Jews in Denmark.* IMDb. Directed by Karen Cantor, and Camilla Kjaerulff. Copenhagen: Miracle Film Distribution, 2003.

Kingsley, Ben. *Winston Churchill: Walking with Destiny.* DVD. Directed by Richard Trank. UAE: Front Row Filmed Entertainment, 2010.

Kor, Eva Mozes. *Forgiving Dr. Mengele.* IMDb. Directed by Bob Hercules and Cheri Pugh. NYC: First Run Features, 2006.

Larson, Rick. *The Star of Bethlehem.* DVD. Directed by Stephen Vidano. mpowerpictures.com, 2009.

Recommended Videos *

Netanyahu, Yonathan. *Follow Me: the Yoni Netanyahu Story.* DVD. Directed by J. Gruber, A.D. Pinchot. New York City: Crystal City Entertainment, 2011.

Newman, Paul, Eva Marie Saint, and Sal Mineo. *Exodus.* IMDb. Directed by Otto Preminger. Los Angeles: United Artists, 1960.

Nimoy, Leonard. *The Miracle of Israel.* DVD. Directed by Lynette Lewis. Phoenix, AZ: The Miracle of Israel Foundation, 2013.

Offner, Tomer, and Michael Greenspan. *Against All Odds: Israel Survives.* DVD. Directed by Tom Ivy. TBN, 2005.

Olivier, Laurence. *The World at War.* DVD. Directed by Hugh Raggett. London: BBC, 1973.

Pawson, David. *Romans 9, 10, 11 Israel's Past, Present & Future.* DVD. Hosted by World Outreach Church, Murfreesboro, TN

Rees, Roger. *God's Outlaw: William Tyndale.* DVD. Directed by Tony Tew. Laguna Hills, CA: Synergy Entertainment, 1986.

Robertson, Gordon. *The Hope : The Rebirth of Israel.* DVD. Directed by Erin Zimmerman. Virginia Beach: CBN, 2015.

Robertson, Gordon. *Whose Land Is It? Jewish and Arab Claims to Israel.* DVD. Virginia Beach: CBN.com, 2016.

Rosselini, Isabella. *My Italian Secret.* IMDb. Directed by Oren Jacoby. New York: Storyville Films, 2015.

Savage, John, and Willie Nelson. *Coming Out of the Ice.* Web. Directed by Warris Hussein. EMI Films, TV Movie 1982. https://www.imdb.com/title/tt0083749/

Shea, John, and Eli Wallach. *The Impossible Spy.* IMDb. Directed by Jim Goddard. Boston: The National Center for Jewish Film, 1987.

Sommer-Herz, Aliza, Zdenka Fantlova, and Anita Lasker-Wallfisch. *The Lady in Number Six: Music Saved My Life.* IMDb. Directed by Malcolm Clarke. Worldwide, 2013.

* Some videos may include violence, death, nudity, or language inappropriate for young viewers.